Northrop Frye and Others

Contents

Introduction

This collection of essays considers Northrop Frye's criticism in relation to a group of mostly lesser-known figures in the history of Western culture who influenced his thinking in various ways but about whom he never wrote anything extensive. The impetus for the book actually goes back to my editing of Frye's *Late Notebooks*, when I ran across the rather astonishing proclamation that Henry Reynolds was "the greatest critic before Johnson" (CW 5: 236). I had studied and taught the history and theory of literary criticism, but I could not recall ever having encountered the name Henry Reynolds either in the histories of criticism or in the anthologies of critical texts. There was, I discovered, a passing reference to *Mythomystes* in *Fearful Symmetry*, but if I had ever known about that, I had forgotten it. In any event, with the Collected Works of Frye now in print—twenty-nine volumes plus the Index—it became possible to track down all of the references to Reynolds in Frye's published as well as his previously unpublished writing. If, I surmised, we were to have before us everything Frye wrote about Reynolds, then perhaps we could begin to understand the attraction Reynolds held for him. The references to Reynolds turned out to be rather meagre (eleven, only six of which were substantive), but they were sufficient for me to draw several conclusions about Frye's interest in Reynolds. So the question that motivated this essay was why Frye would lavish such a superlative upon an obscure seventeenth-century writer about whom we know almost nothing. I obviously had to read Reynolds's *Mythomystes*. The resulting essay gives a fairly detailed account of that book, and it shows how Reynolds and Frye are linked by their joint interest in allegory, poetic etymology, and something quite akin to Longinian *ekstasis*.

I then began to contemplate doing a series of essays that I called "Frye and X," "X" standing for other figures I had come to recognize as important in his thinking—including such writers as Giordano Bruno, Joachim of Floris, Robert Burton, Søren Kierkegaard, Frances Yates—but about whom he had had not written separate books or essays, as he had done in the case of Blake, Shakespeare, More, Milton, Dickinson, Keats, Shelley, Butler, Eliot, Joyce, Yeats, Stevens, the Bible, and Spengler, among others. "X" eventually came to represent a space occupied by twelve writers. Twelve is more or less arbitrary, though perhaps there is some symbolic significance in that number, and we do have it on the authority of Frye that twelve is a sacred number (CW 13: 258). No significance should be attached to the order of the essays, which is simply chronological, though the two classical writers, Aristotle and Longinus, perhaps deserve to be in the lead-off position because of the extent of their influence. Too, their complementary critical positions form a dialectic, the oppositions of which Frye never attempts to resolve, which is what he typically does when confronted with dialectical pairs.

If there were to be a second volume of additional figures whom Frye admired for one reason or another but about whom he wrote nothing sustained, it might well include another dozen or so: Jacob Boehme, François Rabelais, Madame Blavatsky, Martin Buber, Jane Ellen Harrison, Mircea Eliade, John Stuart Mill, Thomas Carlyle, Oscar Wilde, Alfred North Whitehead, G. F. W. Hegel, Niccolò Machiavelli, and the Mahayana Sutras (Avatamsaka, Lankavatara).[1]

The essay on Reynolds is, like the other essays, discrete and so intended to stand alone. But as just suggested, it is linked to the Longinus essay, and all of the essays are connected by one or another key topics that emerge from the expositions of each of the twelve chapters. The theory of the coincidence of opposites, for example, which we first meet in Bruno, recurs in the study of both Lewis Carroll's Alice books and Stéphane Mallarmé. We encounter the spatial projection of ascent and descent along the *axis mundi* in the chapters on Carroll, Mallarmé, Colin Still, Longinus, Joachim of Floris, Kierkegaard, and Yates. The schematic or diagrammatic representation of thought meets us in the chapters on Aristotle, Joachim of Floris, Burton, Yates, and Still. The Hegelian process known as *Aufhebung* is central to the chapter on Kierkegaard, but the process also enters the discussions of Aristotle, Longinus, and Bruno. *Ekstasis*, a key term in Longinus's poetics, recurs in the essay on Reynolds. "Concern," a key term in the existentialist project, is examined at some length in the chapter on Kierkegaard, but then it reappears in the chapter on Paul Tillich. Discussions of "interpenetration," another key term in Frye's poetics, find their way into the essays on Aristotle, Longinus, Joachim of Floris, Kierkegaard, and Mallarmé. The movement from oracle to wit, a central though somewhat enigmatic narrative movement in Frye's mind, is examined in the chapter on Mallarmé but gets picked up in the chapters on Still and Bruno as well. The sources of Frye's interest in esoterica are extensive, but two of them—Reynolds and Yates—are treated here. Frye's eight-book project, which he referred to as his ogdoad, is explained most fully in the chapter on Still, but it appears also in the essays on Aristotle, Joachim, Burton, Tillich, and Yates. Frye's so-called HEAP scheme, one of the diagrammatic or spatial projections of his literary cosmos, gets outlined in the essay on Yates, but it gets glanced at in the chapter on Joachim as well. Such repetitions form a kind of network, connecting the themes of one essay to another and often to still others. I refer quite often to Frye's disposition to discover links between things, and this analogical habit of mind enables him to spin the web of connections. One of the clearest examples of the analogical habit of mind is in the essay on Lewis Carroll: fully a third of the entries in the chrestomathy at the end of that essay are based on the simile, Frye's continually likening of a phrase or idea in the Alice books to something else. In any event, the ideas, themes, and critical principles in any given essay are interconnected to those in other essays.

One of the central arguments that emerges from the discrete essays derives from the study of Aristotle and Longinus. In the essay on Longinus I contend that if we step back from the total body of Frye's work, we can see how the Aristotelian and Longinian complementary approaches play out in his own career. The first phase, in which the *Anatomy* looms large, is schematic, analytical, systematic, and, like the first chapters of Aristotle's *Poetics*, given to formal taxonomy. The *Anatomy* focuses on the conventions of the aesthetic product as an object. But once Frye turned his attention to an expanded study of the Bible, the features associated with Longinian *ekstasis* became the focus of his attention. This change or development is most fully elaborated in the chapter on Longinus, but it becomes a part of the argument as well in the chapters on Reynolds, Kierkegaard, Carroll, Mallarmé, and Tillich.

A corollary to this argument, as already suggested, is that privileging Longinus over Aristotle is atypical of Frye's ordinary procedure when confronted with a dialectic of opposites. His usual inclination is to resolve the opposition by showing how the conflicting forces interpenetrate with each other or, as is most often the case, how the resolution comes about by following the principles of what Hegel calls *Aufhebung*. The German verb *aufheben* has a triple meaning: "to lift or raise," "to abolish or cancel," and "to keep or preserve." Frye is a *both/and* rather than an *either/or* thinker. Things lifted to another level do not cancel their connection to the previous level. The application of *Aufhebung* is present everywhere in Frye's late work—books and essays written in the 1980s but especially in *Words with Power* and *The Double Vision*. But the Aristotle/Longinus opposition is, so far as I can tell, never subjected to the *Aufhebung* dialectic. Frye always favoured the notions of synthesis, identity, and unity as opposed to the idea of difference. But Aristotle and Longinus afford not a unified vision of the critical enterprise but complementary approaches.

In the essay on Aristotle, I indicate that over the years Frye greatly expands Aristotle's structural or formal understanding of *anagnorisis* (recognition) to the point where it becomes expressive of religious meanings. *Anagnorisis* comes to stand for anagogic experience, epiphany, and revelation, terms related not to literary structure but to religious vision.

Reflecting on the multiple masks he wears, Frye writes: "In the course of a day, even a day spent in pure solitude, I should go through a bigger dramatic repertoire than any commedia dell'arte. Pedants, buffoons, comedians, debaters, politicians, hermits, saints, sages, middling-sensual men, suburban bourgeoisie all dispute within me, & everything I do & say is the calculus of probabilities resulting from their competition within me" (CW 8: 201). But when we move beyond roles played to critical principles defended, I think it is not overly reductive to contend that there is not one Northrop Frye but two. There is the Northrop Frye of *Anatomy of Criticism*, the book that made his international reputation and the book that in the late 1970s was the most frequently cited book in the arts and humanities written by someone born in the twentieth century. This is Frye the system builder and taxonomist, the schematic organizer of literary conventions, the classifier of modes, symbols, myths, and genres. This is Frye the "terminological buccaneer," as he called himself—the one who provided a whole generation of critics and other readers with a new vocabulary for talking about literature and a synthetic view of the whole of literature. This is Frye the formal or objective theorist. He said he wanted to create a poetics for the modern century, and he did, becoming the modern century's Aristotle. This is the Frye that captured my imagination when I picked up the *Anatomy* in 1964 and realized that its author, who had had eight years of formal schooling before enrolling in Victoria College at Toronto, was a genius. Then there is Frye the Longinian.

In the 1950s, as I say, Frye privileged the Aristotelian over the Longinian approach: the aesthetic view took precedence over the enthusiasm of *ekstasis*, as the feelings generated when we are transported are not subject to critical scrutiny. But as Frye continued to reflect on the complementary critical approaches, he leaned more and more in the Longinian direction. There is a clear connection, then, between affirming the priority of the Longinian approach and the decidedly religious motifs that emerge in the enormously creative decade of the 1980s when kerygma comes to centre stage in Frye's writing. Kerygma gets most fully explored in the chapter on Longinus, but its centrality as a term in Frye's religio-poetics is underlined by the fact that it enters into the discussions of Joachim, Reynolds, Kierkegaard, Mallarmé, and Tillich.

The present essays take advantage of both Frye's published work and the extensive body of writing Frye did that was not intended for publication but which is now part of the *Collected Works of Northrop Frye*. In terms of quantity, the latter is approximately 46 percent of the total (close to five million words). The previously unpublished material appeared in print over an eleven-year period—from 1996 to 2007. It is this material that has caused some revisionary thinking about Frye, the first example of which, coming from a 1994 seminar in Australia, was *Rereading Frye: The Published and Unpublished Works* (1999). The notebooks, diaries, and unpublished papers, student essays, and correspondence, which now account for thirteen of the twenty-nine volumes of the *Collected Works*, reveal features of Frye's thinking not previously known. It seems likely that as this material comes to be assimilated by those interested in Frye's achievement, new dimensions of his thought will be revealed. Much of what I write about in the present essays draws on the previously unpublished material, especially the notebooks, and much of what I say could not have been said with only Frye's published books and articles in front of me. For the essays on Aristotle and Longinus, the class notes from the 1950s taken by one of Frye's students provide a previously untapped source for exploring Frye's ideas.

The degree to which recent scholarship on Frye has taken advantage of the expanded Frye canon has so far not been very encouraging. The chief thing to be observed in this regard is the fact that so little attention has thus far been directed to the notebooks and the other previously unpublished work. Since *Rereading Frye* was published (1999), the five collections of essays that have appeared—*Frye and the Word* (Donaldson), *Northrop Frye: New Directions from Old* (Rampton), *Visiones para una poetica: en el cincuentenario de "Anatomy of Criticism" de Northrop Frye* (Galván), *Northrop Frye and the Afterlife of the Word* (Kee), and *Northrop Frye 100: A Danubian Perspective* (Tóth *et al.*)—have shown only limited interest in the new material. More recently, a special issue of the *University of Toronto Quarterly*, "The Future of Northrop Frye: Centennial Perspectives" (81, no. 1 [2012]: 1–186) provided an opportunity for those interested in Frye to take advantage of the previously unpublished material. The editors' introduction to this special issue rehearses the debates surrounding *Anatomy of Criticism*, and then moves on to express the hope that the essays in the special issue will reveal "what a critic of today will find challenging, provocative, fruitful, and productive in the rich record of a critic at work." The editors hasten to observe that this rich record includes the previously unpublished writing which, with the launching of the *Collected Works* of Frye, a sixteen-year project, began to become available in 1996. The new material more than doubled the Frye canon, the *Collected Works* having brought to light almost ten thousand pages of previously unpublished writing, constituting a large percentage of the total Frye canon. We are encouraged to think that the contributors to the special issue will take advantage of this new material. But except for Michael Dolzani, and to a lesser extent Ian Balfour, Travis DeCook, and Yves Saint-Cyr, the contributors are practically silent about anything Frye wrote, especially the holograph texts, during the last decade and a half of his life. The final volumes of the *Collected Works* came off the presses only in 2012, and no one can be expected to have read the 4,700,000 words that constitute the thirteen volumes of the previously unpublished material. But even the published work of the late Frye, beginning with *The Great Code* and continuing through *Words with Power*, *Myth and Metaphor*, *The Eternal Act of Creation*, and *The Double Vision*, gets only the scantiest attention. Toward the end of their introduction, the editors of the special issue do remind us that Frye's career is rounded off with his two books on the Bible, but the contributors remain largely silent about the great burst of activity in Frye's final years. The present collection of twelve essays depends in large measure on that half of the canon that was previously unpublished. As I have suggested, this material is ripe for developing more complex and revisionary views of Frye.

Frye is an expansive, subtle, complicated, and challenging thinker. There have been fifty-four books devoted entirely to his criticism, and he figures importantly in well over 1500 essays and hundreds of dissertations. Much, however, remains to be discovered and explained and evaluated. We have hardly begun to explore the riches contained in the thousands upon thousands of annotations in the books of Frye's personal library. But the greatest sources for new discoveries and revisionary understanding will continue to be primarily the notebooks and to a lesser extent the diaries, student essays, correspondence, and previously unpublished articles. In *Northrop Frye: Religious Visionary and Architect of the Spiritual World* (2004), I used these materials extensively, and I do so again in the present collection, ten years later, with the hope that these twelve essays will spur others to follow similar lines of inquiry into that half of the Frye canon which remains largely unknown.

As I rely on the notebooks quite extensively, there is perhaps some merit in bringing together some of the things I have written elsewhere about their manner and matter.[2] This will permit us to see, among other things, that notebook writing for Frye was a Longinian process rather than an Aristotelian product. It will also lead into a consideration of the religious thrust that becomes the *telos* of Frye's late work.

Among Frye's papers at the Victoria University Library in Toronto are seventy-seven holograph notebooks in various shapes and sizes (the longest is 253 pages), which he kept from the late 1930s, when he was a student at Oxford, until only a few months before his death in 1991. Although portions of some notebooks are drafts of Frye's various books, essays, reviews, and lectures, most of the material consists of neatly organized and syntactically complete paragraphs separated by blank lines. The entries are not the polished prose of Frye's published work, but they do reveal a genuine concern for the rhetorical unit that can stand alone. The holograph notebooks contain approximately 800,000 words, excluding the drafts. In the 1970s Frye began typing some of his notes. The experiment was not altogether successful in his mind (he even wrote of wanting to destroy his typed notes for *The Great Code* [CW 5: 173]), but a large percentage of these notes is practically identical in form and scope to the holograph material. The typescripts, which have become known in Frye's Collected Works as "Notes" to distinguish them from the holograph "Notebooks," constitute another 350,000 words. All but one of the notebooks have now been published: a recently discovered notebook has just been published in *Northrop Frye's Uncollected Prose* (U of Toronto P, 2015). Altogether, the Notebooks and Notes form a substantial body of work—well over a million words.[3]

While Frye's notebooks do contain material that will be of considerable interest to his biographers, their form is altogether different from the diaries he kept in the 1940s and 1950s, and their intent is neither to record his personal life nor to explore his own psyche. The notebooks are first and foremost the workshop out of which Frye created his books. After *Anatomy of Criticism*, he produced books at the rate of about one per year, giving the impression perhaps that writing for him was a facile enterprise. But while the shorter books that emerged from his lectures were often written quickly, the process was anything but that for his four major books. *Fearful Symmetry* (1947) and the *Anatomy* (1957) were each more than ten years in the making; *The Great Code* (1982) was begun more than a decade before it appeared; and *Words with Power* (1990), as Frye notes in the introduction to *The Great Code*, was "in active preparation" in the early 1980s (CW 19: 5). The notebooks record this deliberate and often labyrinthine process, and the process did not always issue in the product Frye had envisioned, his inability to complete the major book that was to follow *Fearful Symmetry* and *Anatomy of Criticism*—the "third book," he calls it—being the most obvious example of this. At times the workshop function seems to fade away almost completely, for the notebooks contain entries on scores of topics that have no obvious connection to the project at hand. An entry will be triggered by a detective story Frye is reading, a newspaper article, a lecture or sermon he has to prepare, a Latin quotation, a glance at the books on his shelves, a quotation he remembers, a letter received, a memory from a trip, and occasional personal reflections—thoughts about his own status as a critic, about the difficulties of writing, about the bankruptcy of contemporary criticism, and the like.

Writing for Frye, of whatever form, was, if not an obsession, as indispensable a part of his life as eating and sleeping. He wrote because he could do no other, and the process was not always liberating. "I know from experience," he writes, "and I've read the statement often enough, that if one could turn off the incessant chatter in one's psyche one would be well on the way to freedom. In all my life I've never known an instant of real silence" (CW 5: 448). Several times he expresses a deep desire for the apophatic and contemplative life, or at least for certain moments when he could "turn off the chatter in [his] mind, which is making more noise than a punk rock band ('drunken monkey,' the Hindus call it) and relax into the divine knowledge of us which is one of the things meant by a cloud of unknowing" (CW 5: 161). In one of his notebooks, written in the mid-1940s, Frye ruefully wonders "what it would really be like to get one's mind completely clear of the swirl of mental currents. It would be like walking across the Red Sea to the Promised Land, with walls of water standing up on each side" (CW 13: 71). The fact that Frye was never really able to turn off the "drunken monkey" is what accounts for both the sheer mass of material in the notebooks and the constant repetition of ideas, hunches, insights, poetic passages, and illustrations. Still, he approached the discipline of note-making with Benedictine zeal: "Working at what one can do is a sacrament," he writes at the beginning of Notebook 44 (CW 5: 102). Or again, "My whole life is words: nothing is of value in life except finding verbal formulations that make sense" (CW 5: 267).

Here and there Frye speaks of the intent of his notebook writing, as in this remark about the relation between his obsessive note-taking and the books that eventually emerge: "All my life I've had the notebook obsession manifested by what I'm doing at this moment. Writing in notebooks seems to help clarify my mind about the books I write, which are actually notebook entries arranged in a continuous form. At least, I've always told myself they were that" (CW 5: 172–3). In one of his marginalia to Coleridge, Frye observes that Coleridge's "mind moves in a series of crystallizations, like Homer trying to write an epic. We need a prose Poe to assert that a long prose structure is impossible."[4] The notebook entries can also be seen as a series of crystallizations, Frye's ideas suddenly emerging into discontinuous prose form. Continuity in Frye's published prose is sometimes difficult to discern, and when Frye is especially elliptical one wonders if he does not believe about prose what Poe said about the long poem. But the notebook entries are kernels of what he hopes can be incorporated into longer forms: "I keep notebooks because all my writing is a translation into a narrative sequence of things that come to me aphoristically. The aphorisms in turn are preceded by 'inspirations' or potentially verbal *Gestalten*. So 'inspiration' is essentially a snarled sequence" (CW 5: 226). While the notebook entries are ordinarily not as brief as an aphorism (they contain about seventy-five words on average), they do consist on the whole of discontinuous reflections. But, as "snarled sequence" suggests, the entries are by no means unrelated to each other. Frye will often devote a succession of paragraphs to a single topic, and he frequently refers to previous sections of the notebook in which he is writing at the time and occasionally to other notebooks.

Frye puts "inspiration" in quotation marks because the actual genesis of the notebook entries is often somewhat mysterious. "I think in cores or aphorisms, as these notebooks indicate, and all the labor in my writing comes from trying to find verbal formulas to connect them. I have to wait for the cores to emerge: they seem to be born and not made" (CW 5: 364). In one of his notebooks for *Anatomy of Criticism*, he speaks of these aphorisms as auditory epiphanies: they are, he says, "involuntarily acquired" and have "something to do with listening for a Word, the ear being the involuntary sense." If the birth of the aphorisms comes from things "heard," the connections among them come from things "seen." Realizing the potential of a "verbal *Gestalten*" or a pattern of continuous argument, Frye says, has something to do "with the spread-out panorama for the eye" (CW 23: 142). But, as the notebooks unequivocally reveal, the pattern of continuity is never achieved without a mighty struggle: once Frye got hold of the building-blocks, "the spread-out performance" was never necessary or even predictable. In his words, "Continuity, in writing as in physics, is probabilistic, and every sequence is a choice among possibilities. Inevitable sequence is illusory" (CW 5: 21). The sequence that Frye eventually achieved in his published work came only after revisions of numerous drafts, sometimes as many as eight or nine revisions. Some of the chapters in *Words with Power* were, in their early form, as long as one hundred pages, so Frye's revisions involved a great deal of cutting.[5] He would typically type three or four drafts himself before giving them, often with holograph additions and corrections, to his secretary Jane Widdicombe to type or, late in his career, to enter on a word processor. Once he received the draft back, he would revise again, and this process would be repeated as many as five times. But the notebooks themselves are by no means drafts: they reveal a stage of Frye's writing before, sometimes years before, he began even to work on a first draft.

As for the rhetoric of the notebooks, one can naturally detect features of Frye's style on every page: the wit, the koan-like utterances that capture some paradox, the attention to the shape of the periodic sentence, the grace and elegance of the prose, the ironic tone. But the difference between Frye's notebook entries and his published work is readily apparent, for in the notebooks Frye is wearing everything on his sleeve. He feels no need for the detachment that was almost always a feature of what he presented to the public, no need to create that sense of assurance that comes with a distanced academic presence. Frye did insist that the antithesis between the scholarly and unscholarly, between the personal and impersonal, was an antithesis that needed to be transcended. Still, the voice in the notebooks is not Frye's public voice. There is, on the one hand, the direct expression of convictions, often taking the form of beliefs. Frye's own beliefs were, of course, implicit in all his writing, from *Fearful Symmetry* on. But in the notebooks they are explicit, sometimes amounting almost to a confession of faith. On the other hand, at the level simply of diction, Frye's not infrequent use of coarse and indecent language may come as a surprise to some. But his four-letter words are used fairly innocently, serving as a kind of shorthand for referring to sex, which is one of his "primary concerns" (as in the male and female principles in Genesis 1 and 2 that are the starting points for his account of the mountain and garden archetypes in *Words with Power*), and to bodily functions. Still, Frye's language often deflates the most sober of reflections. Thus, while there is not so much as a whisper of the mock-heroic in the notebooks, there is a good measure of the Swiftian burlesque, which is one of the ways that Frye, never without a sense of irony, brings his soaring speculations back down to earth.

If we cannot always with assurance follow the sequence of the arguments in Frye's published work or always understand clearly why one paragraph follows the next, we nevertheless have the impression that *he* knew where he was going. But this confident sense of direction is often absent from the notebooks. "God knows," he writes at one point, "I know how much of this is blither: it makes unrewarding reading for the most part. But I have to do it: it doesn't clarify my mind so much as lead to some point of clarification that (I hope) gets into the book. Hansel & Gretel's trail of crumbs." Or again, when speculating on the relation between the dialogues of Word and Spirit and the four levels of meaning, Frye remarks, "I don't know if this is anything but bald and arbitrary schematism." Or still again, "I'm again at the point in the book where I wonder if I know what the hell I'm talking about" (CW 5: 346; CW 6: 427; CW 5: 331). Remarks such as these are sprinkled throughout the notebooks, and there are entries in which Frye begins to explore an idea but, by the time he gets to the end of the paragraph, forgets the point he was going to make. Over and over we see the persona of a Frye who is human, all-too-human. There is nothing particularly surprising in this: writing for Frye was a discovery procedure, and we should not expect that every aphorism that came to him should issue in a "verbal Gestalten." In this respect Frye's notebooks are like Nietzsche's own book of aphorisms, *Human All-too-Human*, an exercise in free thinking; and free thought, by definition, is under no obligation always to issue in certitude. The persona of the writer is revealed too in the occasional intemperate epithets ("fool," "idiot," and the like) that Frye hurls at himself for overlooking the obvious or for a lapse in memory, and in the self-deprecating remarks ("By the standards of conventional scholarship, *The Great Code* was a silly and sloppy book" [CW 5: 160]). Still, Frye's most explicit reference to the use readers might make of his notebook aphorisms, which follows on a remark about the metaphor of *sparagmos* (tearing to pieces) that runs throughout his writing, helps to explain the extensive use I make of the notebooks:

> The way I begin a book is to write detached aphorisms in a notebook, and ninety-five percent of the work I do in completing a book is to fit these detached aphorisms together into a continuous narrative line. I think that Coleridge worked in the same way, though he seems to have had unusual difficulty when it came to the narrative stage, and so instead of completing his great treatise on the Logos he kept much of the best of what he had to say hugged to his bosom in the form of fifty-seven notebooks. Holism is not only not the end of the critical enterprise: it is an axiom pursued for its own rewards which at a certain point may turn inside out. I may work hard enough to weld my books into a narrative unity, but it is possible that many of my readers tend to find their way back to the original aphoristic form, finding me more useful for detached insights than for total structures. However, if bits and pieces of me float down to Lesbos with the head still singing, it doesn't matter to me if some of those pieces (I'm mixing metaphors violently here, but the mixing seems to fit the context) get swallowed by someone and grow up again from inside him. (CW 18: 483)

In one of his early notebooks Frye expresses the fear that his speculations will not turn out to be definitive (CW 13: 70), but this is a fear that he is soon able to vanquish. The pace of the writing initially seems to be almost frenetic—the drive of a man possessed to record every nuance of the "obstinate questionings" of his active mind. But when we stand back from the notebooks as a whole, the mood they convey is neither fear nor frenzy. It is rather a process of speculative free play, "of letting things come & not forcing or cramping or repressing them" (CW 13: 49). Frye is in no panic to bring things to closure, moving as he does at a leisurely pace, releasing himself from all inhibitions, and not worrying that his schemes will "go bust immediately." "Perhaps that's the reason I have them," he muses (CW 13: 177). Sometimes anxieties about the efficacy of the incessant scribbling arise: "Why do I try to keep notes like this, when forty years of experience shows me they don't do me any good?" (CW 15: 86). At other times boredom sets in "because so much of what I put into [the notebooks] is just a form of masturbation: an empty fantasy life making the scene with beckoning fair charmers who don't exist" (CW 9: 332). But this sentence is followed by the single, telling word, "however," which signals, of course, that the doubts he might have about the value of recording his imaginative life do not deter him from moving on immediately to do just that.

In one of his notebooks from the 1960s, Frye issues these tactical instructions to himself: "In beginning to plan a major work like the third book, *don't eliminate anything*. *Never* assume that some area of your speculations can't be included & has to be left over for another book. Things may get eliminated in the very last stage ... but *never, never*, exclude anything when thinking about the book. It was strenuous having to cut down FS [*Fearful Symmetry*] from an encyclopaedia, but ... major works are encyclopaedic & anatomic: everything I know must go into them—eye of bat & tongue of dog" (CW 9: 74–5). Frye goes on to say that all of his major books are essentially "the same book with different centres of gravity: interpenetrating universes. Give me a place to stand, and I will include the world" (CW 9: 75). This "same book" theory means that we encounter many iterations and echoes of the same idea. Repetition was a feature of Frye's published work, which, as he said, assumed the shape of a spiral curriculum, "circling around the same issues" in a way that produced a gradual continuity over time (CW 27: 392). He justifies the repetition in his books and essays by noting that the principles he keeps returning to are the only ones he knows. Like thematic returns in music, the same ideas can be presented in different contexts, and repetition can be a sign of a consistency of conviction: "Repetition charges the emotional batteries & suspends the critical faculties. What I tell you three times is true. What I tell you three hundred times is profoundly true" (CW 13: 198).

The repetition in the notebooks, however, is of a different kind. Like Daedalus, who set his mind to unknown arts, Frye uses his notebooks for invention and discovery, returning again and again to the archetypes of his mental landscape in an effort to get the architecture and the verbal formulation right. The repetition can be vexing, but it is nonetheless an example of Frye's following the principle underlying his most important educational advice: develop the habit of Samuel Butler's practice-memory. "The repetitiousness of the Koran would drive a reader out of his mind if he were reading it as he would any other book" (CW 13: 195), and one could almost say the same thing about the discontinuity of Frye's notebooks: they contain little linear argument, even though there are many occasions where sequences of paragraphs focus on a single, obsessively pursued issue. Still, the entire notebook enterprise is based on a theory of verbal meaning that turns Aristotle's notion of causality upside down. Frye writes at one point that there is "a convergence causation founded on the analogy of space," as opposed to linear causation, which assumes that writing is a temporal sequence of effect following cause (CW 13: 255). Such convergent causation, which is close to the first-phase language of metaphor, is the kind that governs the notebooks.

If one abandons both linear causation and a concern for continuity, then the principles of the figurative use of words become more important than conceptual meaning. Frye's fertile and energetic mind is, as already said, always pursuing similarities or, as he is fond of calling them, links.[6] Perceiving likenesses requires the free play, not of the imagination, but of fancy, as Frye writes in one revealing entry:

> I am intensely superstitious; but there are two kinds of superstition, related as self-destructive melancholy is to penseroso melancholy. There is the superstition based on fear of the future: this is based also on my character as a coward & weakling, & is of course to be avoided. There is another kind which consists of removing all censors & inhibitions on speculation: it's almost exactly what Coleridge calls fancy. It may eventually be superseded by imagination: but if there's no fancy to start with there won't be any imagination to finish with. Let's call it creative superstition. It works with analogies, disregarding all differences & attending only to similarities. Here nothing is coincidence in the sense of unusable design; or, using the word more correctly, everything is potential coincidence—what Jung calls synchronistic. (CW 9: 211)

Once the similarities Frye observes begin to organize themselves into patterns, then the imagination has taken over: the schematic structures then take the form of the mental diagrams, one of the signatures of Frye's thinking.

Why all of this imaginative free play, with its incessant spatial projections and schematic doodling? As we have said, it is an uninhibited form of free writing that eventually distills itself into Frye's books and essays. But more importantly, it represents the many stages in his own religious quest. Frye remarks in Notebook 21 that his "particular interest has always been in mythology & in the imaginative aspect of religion.... The whole imaginative picture of the world which underlies both religion and the arts has been constant from the beginning" (CW 13: 157–8).

Notebook 21 begins by Frye's announcing that while his immediate object is to collect ideas for his 1971 Birks Lectures at McGill University, his ultimate aim is to work through his "thoughts on religion" (CW 13: 140). Religion for Frye is not a matter of belief, though it stems from the conviction that life has a point. "All attempts to find out what that point is are religious quests" (CW 13: 177), which is reminiscent of what Frye wrote in a student essay forty years earlier: "the most fundamental intellectual activity of the human race is ... an attempt to find a pattern in existence" (CW 3: 403).

If the ubiquitous spatial projections of the notebooks form the *dianoia* of Frye's critical and imaginative universe, the forthrights and meanders of his quest are its *mythos*. But a quest for what? Well, for the great code and words with power. "For at least 25 years," Frye writes in the early 1970s, "I've been preoccupied by the notion of a key to all mythologies" (CW 13: 198), and what he really wants to discover, he writes at one point, is "the myth of God, which is a myth of identity" (CW 9: 69). Identity is one of the central principles in Frye's universe, the principle he returns to again and again in his speculations on the paradoxes of literal meaning, metaphor, and the Incarnation. From the perspective of the imagination, the *telos* of knowledge comes from the ability to perceive not differences but identities. While knowledge is clearly not divorced from perception, Frye's quest has more to do with seeing than with knowing; hence, the centrality of light and sight, of recognition and vision and illumination. One telling feature of the present book is that eight of the twelve essays address the different meanings of identity in Frye (Aristotle, Longinus, Bruno, Reynolds, Kierkegaard, Carroll, Mallarmé, and Yates).

Frye often organized his categories in cyclical patterns, the most familiar of these being the specific forms of drama and the thematic convention of *epos* and lyric in *Anatomy of Criticism*, along with the phases of the four *mythoi*. The quest narrative, including Frye's own, can be seen as cyclical, but he distanced himself from some of the implications of the cycle, as I indicate in the chapter on Kierkegaard. To be able to see the possibilities in a new beginning is another way of formulating the goal of Frye's quest, but there are numerous other ways to phrase it: the Everlasting Gospel, Milton's Word of God in the heart, the interpenetration of Word and Spirit. An elaboration of the quest movement in Frye is explored further in the chapter on Mallarmé.

I have spoken of Frye's notebook entries as speculations, as he himself does. The word has parallels to its use in Keats's letters, though Frye's speculations ordinarily have more shape than those that come tumbling out of Keats's fertile brain. Keats distances his speculations from what he calls "consecutive reasoning," and Frye would agree that if there is any truth in his speculations, they belong to an order different from that of the "reflective" mode of truth in the descriptive writing that Keats has in mind. Underlying both "reflection" and "speculation" is, as Frye notes in *Words with Power* and elsewhere, the mirror metaphor:

> If we ask what the speculation is a mirror of, the traditional answer is being, a conceptual totality that transcends, not only individual beings, but the total aggregate of beings. Heidegger endorses the statement that the first question of philosophy is, "Why are there things rather than nothing?" But things are not what Heidegger means by being, and the question leads to another: "Why is there being beyond all beings?" (CW 26: 26)

The mirror metaphor naturally arises in my analysis of Aristotle's *mimesis*, but it turns out to be central as well in the chapters on Kierkegaard, Carroll, and Mallarmé. As for the being beyond all beings, it lies in the background of Frye's own quest, though his search for it typically relies on language different from Heidegger's Greek vocabulary. We hear a great deal of that language spread out across the entire Frye canon.

~

I first encountered Frye's work more than fifty years ago, and since then I have devoted a large portion of my professional life to reading and writing about him. I have a relatively clear memory of the encounter. Browsing the shelves of the University of Chicago bookstore in the early 1960s, I picked up a copy of *Anatomy of Criticism*, not because anyone had recommended it, but because a cursory glance made me feel that it might be interesting. I had decided by then that I would be doing my degree in the history and theory of criticism, and leafing through this book made me think it worth looking into, though I didn't actually read it until a couple of years later. That was after I was jerked out of my graduate studies in 1964 to serve in the army. I headed off to the Air Defense School at Ft. Bliss, Texas, where I was trained to be a battery commander for Nike Hercules rockets. As it turned out, I received orders to remain at the school and edit training manuals—a rather cushy job. The editing work took about a half-hour per week, so I more or less hid out in my office and read books.

One of the first ones I turned to was the *Anatomy*, which had been staring at me from my shelves for a couple of years. Well, I read it and remember thinking, "This is a real book." I had been more or less transported by its expansive scope, its structural ingenuity, its authoritative voice, and the incredible learning it displayed. Why hadn't they told me about this guy Frye in graduate school? I scurried over to the library at Texas Western University, as it was called in those days, to see if I could turn up anything on Frye. I naturally ran across a good deal. I made photocopies of two things I read—reviews of the *Anatomy* by Frank Kermode in *Review of English Studies* and by M. H. Abrams in *University of Toronto Quarterly*, dog-eared copies of which I've still got. Because Kermode had just written *The Romantic Image*—it was also published in 1957—he had the symbolist aesthetic on his mind, and so he read the *Anatomy* through that lens. He ended up calling the book a work of "sixth-phase Symbolism." The *Anatomy*, said Kermode, was "a work of criticism which has turned into literature." Like Kermode, Abrams praised the book, but he had his own misgivings. He concluded that the *Anatomy* was an example of wit criticism: it illustrated the free-play of a richly stored mind but its principles could not be confirmed. Kermode and Abrams were clearly very smart people, but I later came to see that they both had mistaken the means for the end. At the time, all I realized was that the views of Kermode and Abrams did not conform to my own view of the book, which was that it taught me a great deal about literary conventions.[7] In any event, that encounter with the *Anatomy* in the deserts of Texas was what began a long odyssey. Who knows what my professional career would have turned out to be had they given me a real job in the army? Or had I come to Frye by way of *Fearful Symmetry*, the path followed by my friend Michael Dolzani. In the years that followed, I spent a considerable amount of time trying to figure out the ends and means of the *Anatomy*, its arguments and taxonomies, its language and assumptions. When I returned to the University of Chicago in 1970 to complete my Ph.D., I was able to convince Wayne Booth to let me write a dissertation on Frye's critical method. My initial encounter with Frye goes back, then, fifty years. I was, as I say, at Ft. Bliss, Texas, where we would quip, "Ignorance is bliss. Welcome to Ft. Ignorance." I was very ignorant at the time, but I had a clear sense that by reading Frye's book I might become less so. My books and essays on Frye's work have been generally motivated by a desire to discover how his mind works and and why he says the things he does. The twelve chapters in the present collection are another episode in that quest.

I suspect my debt to Frye is as great as his was to Blake. For that propitious moment in the early 1960s when I picked up *Anatomy of Criticism*, I remain eternally thankful. Now that it has become a matter of rereading Frye, I find that the cadence of his prose continues to delight and the substance of his vision continues to instruct. I remain thankful as well for that large group of students of Frye's work who have afforded me a generous measure of assistance and goodwill over the years. I have acknowledged my debts to them on several occasions elsewhere, and I call out their names again: Michael Dolzani, Margaret Burgess, Ron Schoeffel, Jean O'Grady, and Alvin Lee. The acquisitions, production, and copy editors at the University of Ottawa Press who have shepherded the manuscript through the publication process deserve as special salute: Dominike Thomas, Elizabeth Schwaiger, and Susan James. To Rachel, my wife now for fifty-four years, I offer thanks for all her little, nameless, unremembered acts of kindness and of love—and for the remembered ones as well.

My own books and articles on Frye go back now more than forty years, and I have occasionally lifted sentences, even paragraphs from them. In this respect I am following in the footsteps of Frye, who freely borrowed from what he had previously written.

The essay on Frye and Longinus was delivered as a keynote address at a conference in honour of Northrop Frye's centenary, "Frye 100: A Danubian Perspective," Budapest, 8 September 2012, and I thank my dear Hungarian friends—Tibor Fabiny, Péter Pásztor, and Sára Tóth—for inviting me to their conference. The paper begins with an epigraph, not simply because it is about the sublime but because Ferenc Juhász is, so far as I can determine, the only Hungarian writer Frye ever referred to. This paper was published in *Northrop Frye 100: A Danubian Perspective*, ed. Sára Tóth, Tibor Fabiny, János Kenyeres, and Péter Pásztor (Budapest: L'Harmattan Kiado, 2014), 15–36. An earlier version of the paper appeared in "Northrop Frye for a New Century," a special issue of *English Studies in Canada* 37, no. 2 (June 2011): 87–109, and I thank the editor, Michael O'Driscoll, for permitting me to use it again. The essay on Frye and Colin Still was presented at "Educating the Imagination: A Conference in Honour of Northrop Frye on the Centenary of His Birth," Victoria University in the University of Toronto, 4 October 2012.

Emory, Virginia
December 2014

Abbreviations for Northrop Frye's Collected Works and Selected Letters

CW 1	*The Correspondence of Northrop Frye and Helen Kemp, 1932–1939.* Vol. 1. Ed. Robert D. Denham. Toronto: U of Toronto P, 1996.
CW 2	*The Correspondence of Northrop Frye and Helen Kemp, 1932–1939.* Vol. 2. Ed. Robert D. Denham. Toronto: U of Toronto P, 1996.
CW 3	*Northrop Frye's Student Essays, 1932–1938.* Ed. Robert D. Denham. Toronto: U of Toronto P, 1997.
CW 4	*Northrop Frye on Religion.* Ed. Alvin A. Lee and Jean O'Grady. Toronto: U of Toronto P, 2000.
CW 5	*Northrop Frye's Late Notebooks, 1982–1990: Architecture of the Spiritual World.* Ed. Robert D. Denham. Toronto: U of Toronto P, 2000.
CW 6	*Northrop Frye's Late Notebooks, 1982–1990: Architecture of the Spiritual World.* Ed. Robert D. Denham. Toronto: U of Toronto P, 2000.
CW 7	*Northrop Frye's Writings on Education.* Ed. Jean O'Grady and Goldwin French. Toronto: U of Toronto P, 2000.
CW 8	*The Diaries of Northrop Frye, 1942–1955.* Ed. Robert D. Denham. Toronto: U of Toronto P, 2001.
CW 9	*The "Third Book" Notebooks of Northrop Frye, 1964–1972: The Critical Comedy.* Ed. Michael Dolzani. Toronto: U of Toronto P, 2001.
CW 10	*Northrop Frye on Literature and Society, 1936–1989.* Ed. Robert D. Denham. Toronto: U of Toronto P, 2002.
CW 11	*Northrop Frye on Modern Culture.* Ed. Jan Gorak. Toronto: U of Toronto P, 2002.

CW 12	*Northrop Frye on Canada.* Ed. Jean O'Grady and David Staines. Toronto: U of Toronto P, 2003.
CW 13	*Northrop Frye's Notebooks and Lectures on the Bible and Other Religious Texts.* Ed. Robert D. Denham. Toronto: U of Toronto P, 2003.
CW 14	*Fearful Symmetry: A Study of William Blake.* Ed. Nicholas Halmi. Intro. Ian Singer. Toronto: U of Toronto P, 2004.
CW 15	*Northrop Frye's Notebooks on Romance.* Ed. Michael Dolzani. Toronto: U of Toronto P, 2004.
CW 16	*Northrop Frye on Milton and Blake.* Ed. Angela Esterhammer. Toronto: U of Toronto P, 2005.
CW 17	*Northrop Frye's Writings on the Eighteenth and Nineteenth Centuries.* Ed. Imre Salusinszky. Toronto: U of Toronto P, 2005.
CW 18	*"The Secular Scripture" and Other Writings on Critical Theory.* Ed. Joseph Adamson and Jean Wilson. Toronto: U of Toronto P, 2006.
CW 19	*The Great Code: The Bible and Literature.* Ed. Alvin A. Lee. Toronto: U of Toronto P, 2006.
CW 20	*Northrop Frye's Notebooks on Renaissance Literature.* Ed. Michael Dolzani. Toronto: U of Toronto P, 2006.
CW 21	*"The Educated Imagination" and Other Writings on Critical Theory, 1933–1963.* Ed. Germaine Warkentin. Toronto: U of Toronto P, 2006.
CW 22	*Anatomy of Criticism: Four Essays.* Ed. Robert D. Denham. Toronto: U of Toronto P, 2006.
CW 23	*Northrop Frye's Notebooks for "Anatomy of Criticism."* Ed. Robert D. Denham. Toronto: U of Toronto P, 2007.
CW 24	*Interviews with Northrop Frye.* Ed. Jean O'Grady. Toronto: U of Toronto P, 2008.
CW 25	*Northrop Frye's Fiction and Miscellaneous Writings.* Ed. Robert D. Denham and Michael Dolzani. Toronto: U of Toronto P, 2007.

CW 26 — *Words with Power: Being a Second Study of "The Bible and Literature."* Ed. Michael Dolzani. Toronto: U of Toronto P, 2008.

CW 27 — *"The Critical Path" and Other Writings on Critical Theory, 1963–1975*. Ed. Eva Kushner and Jean O'Grady. Toronto: U of Toronto P, 2009.

CW 28 — *Northrop Frye's Writings on Shakespeare and the Renaissance.* Ed. Garry Sherbert and Troni Y. Grande. Toronto: U of Toronto P, 2010.

CW 29 — *Northrop Frye on Twentieth-Century Literature.* Ed. Glen Robert Gill. Toronto: U of Toronto P, 2010.

Selected Letters — *Selected Letters, 1934–1991*. Ed. Robert D. Denham. West Jefferson, NC, and London: McFarland and Co., 2009.

Uncollected — *Northrop Frye's Uncollected Prose.* Ed. Robert D. Denham. Toronto: U of Toronto P, 2015.

I

Frye and Aristotle

Aristotle's *Poetics* is the most influential critical work in the Western tradition. Northrop Frye's *Anatomy of Criticism* is the most influential critical work of the last century. How are the two connected? Two of Frye's early theoretical essays—"A Conspectus of Dramatic Genres" (1951) and "Towards a Theory of Cultural History" (1953)—begin with Aristotle: the first quotes the opening paragraph of the *Poetics* (CW 21: 104), and the second refers us to what Aristotle says about character in chapter 2 (CW 21: 150). When Frye writes in "The Archetypes of Literature" that we need a "new poetics" (CW 21: 124), he clearly has Aristotle in mind: he wants to do for his own time what Aristotle had done for posterity. And at the very beginning of the *Anatomy*, Frye announces that by following in Aristotle's footsteps he is undertaking a twentieth-century *Poetics*:

> A theory of criticism whose principles apply to the whole of literature and account for every valid type of critical procedure is what I think Aristotle meant by poetics. Aristotle seems to me to approach poetry as a biologist would approach a system of organisms, picking out its genera and species, formulating the broad laws of literary experience, and in short writing as though he believed that there is a totally intelligible structure of knowledge attainable about poetry which is not poetry itself, or the experience of it, but poetics. One would imagine that, after two thousand years of post-Aristotelian literary activity, his views on poetics, like his views on the generation of animals, could be re-examined in the light of fresh evidence. Meanwhile, the opening words of the *Poetics*, in the Bywater translation, remain as good an introduction to the subject as ever, and describe the kind of approach that I have tried to keep in mind for myself. (CW 22: 16)

The *Poetics* comes to us circuitously—through an eleventh-century manuscript, now at the Bibliothèque Nationale, a thirteenth- or fourteenth-century manuscript, a Syriac translation from the Greek, and an Arabic translation from the Syriac, both from the tenth century. The earliest extant manuscript of the *Poetics*, then, is separated from its origin by more than a millennium. It is a fragmentary and corrupted text, and what has come down to us was composed perhaps by one of Aristotle's students, who, some have speculated, appears to have dozed off at certain key points. So the question of what Aristotle actually said or wrote cannot be answered with any certainty. But from the text we have (and we are naturally dependent on the agendas of the various translators), it is by no means clear that "poetics" for Aristotle, according to Frye, meant a "theory of criticism whose principles apply to the whole of literature and account for every valid type of critical procedure." The extant portions of the original text reveal a much more focused objective. The first paragraph sets the parameters. Aristotle proposes to discuss the art of poetry itself, as opposed to poetry in relation to other things. In other words, he brackets out a host of critical questions, such as those having to do with the poet's creative process or with the reader's response or with the social and political function of poetry. He believes there are various poetic species, each with its own particular power or quality (*dynamis*). He is interested in how poems are constructed, and in the making of poems, plot is singled out as especially important. He wants to enumerate the kinds of poetic parts, which, we discover, turn out to be both quantitative (prologue, exode, etc.) and qualitative (plot, character, thought, etc.). And he wants to begin with "the principles which come first," meaning apparently the antecedent conditions of making. Where Frye derives the idea that Aristotle's principles are intended to "apply to the whole of literature" is uncertain. In his second paragraph, Aristotle restricts his treatise to *most* forms of epic and dithyrambic poetry and of tragic and comic drama, and his subject is restricted even more to those that "happen to be imitations," the implication being that some poetic works happen not to be imitations.[8]

Frye is not unaware of most of these matters, having devoted a great deal of concentrated attention to the *Poetics* for more than sixty years. It seems unlikely that he knew much about Aristotle before arriving at Victoria College as a seventeen-year-old in 1929, but once he was accepted into the Honours curriculum in philosophy (English or history option) during his second year he would have read Aristotle in several courses. For his last three years he enrolled in courses in ethics (two courses), philosophical texts, history of philosophy, types of aesthetic theory, and modern philosophy. His transcript identifies his first course in Honours Philosophy only as "Phil.," so it is impossible to know from this record which of the first- or second-year courses (ethics, logic, history of philosophy) he elected. The University of Toronto Calendar does not provide reading lists for all of Frye's courses, but the lists that are supplied do naturally include Aristotle. And Frye would have encountered Aristotle in the secondary readings for these courses, listed as "references" in the Calendar. We know, for example, that Frye read Wilhelm Windelband's *History of Philosophy* the summer before his fourth year at Victoria, or at least began reading it (CW 1: 66), and he used Windelband in his fourth-year paper on Romanticism (CW 3: 477). His student papers also cite histories of philosophy by Ueberweg and Erdmann (CW3: 250). While we do not have a very complete record of which Aristotelian texts Frye read as a student, in the dozen-and-a-half references to Aristotle in the student essays that have survived, it is clear that he was familiar with the *Poetics* and the *Politics*. We also know that during his first year of teaching at Victoria (1937–38), Frye, who was twenty-five at the time, lectured on Aristotle to first-year students.[9] Five years later Aristotle crops up in one of Frye's many resolutions for intellectual self-improvement: "What I do now is learn some German and set up the seven pillars of wisdom—Homer, Aeschylus, Sophocles, Euripides, Aristophanes, Plato & Aristotle—in my own backyard" (CW 15: 15). In the early explorations for the shape of the book that would follow *Fearful Symmetry*, Frye planned to devote the seventh chapter of the book to Renaissance Platonism. This chapter, Frye writes in the late 1940s, would include material on "Plato as a dramatist & as a 'rhetorical' stick to beat the 'logical' Aristotle.... Aristotle himself transformed into a literary critic by the revival of the *Poetics*" (CW 15: 50). Frye's interest in the *Poetics* was no doubt spurred by his encounter with the Chicago Neo-Aristotelians. He had heard R. S. Crane lecture at Toronto in 1952, had reviewed the Chicagoans' *Critics and Criticism* and Crane's *The Languages of Criticism and the Structure of Poetry* in 1954, and in 1955 had lectured at Chicago, where he encountered Elder Olson and other members of the so-called Neo-Aristotelian school.[10]

In 1954 we find Frye teaching Aristotle's *Poetics* in a course in literary criticism. Margaret (née Kell) Virany's forty-two pages of class notes give a fairly detailed record of Frye's lectures in this course.[11] His reading of Aristotle over the years was fairly wide. Throughout his writing he either quotes from or refers to the *Poetics*, *Metaphysics*, *Nicomachean Ethics*, *Physics*, *Rhetoric*, *Politics*, *Analytics*, and *On the Soul*. He also refers to Aristotle's treatise on biology, apparently the *Parts of Animals*. One of the features of Frye's writing is the appearance of *aperçus* that he had picked up in his reading of poets or philosophers or critics. These insights, often signalled by a single word, then get repeated over and over in his writing. Examples include Kierkegaard's "repetition," Joachim of Floris's "three ages," Hegel's "*Aufhebung*," Plato's commonwealth as an allegory of the wise man's mind, and Samuel Butler's "practice-memory." There are scores of these catchwords and several are from Aristotle, such as "rhetoric is the *antistrophos* of dialectic"—a line that gets repeated a dozen times from 1954 to 1990. Similarly, such Aristotelian ideas as *proairesis* (moral character), *hexis* (state, disposition, habit), and *telos* (end, purpose) recur time and again.

"Literary criticism," Frye tells his students at the beginning of the 1954 course, "is one of the hardest types of all literary writing. The world has seen only a few good literary critics." The course was listed as Greek and Latin Literature, but apparently instructors could tailor the course to meet their own interests. In any event, Frye devoted the course to the major critical figures—Plato, Aristotle, Horace, Longinus, and Quintilian, with glances at Aristophanes, Theophrastus, Isocrates, Terence, Laertius, Lucilius, Neoptolemus of Parium, Philodemus of Gadara, Aristarchus of Samothrace, and Dionysius of Halicarnassus.[12] The course met one hour per week for twelve weeks. Frye allocated three full lectures and portions of two other lectures to Aristotle, which was close to a third of the course—about 30 percent of Virany's notes. Her notes on Aristotle are reproduced in the Appendix to the present chapter.

Lumpers and Splitters

My intent now is to examine Frye's debt to Aristotle as it manifests itself throughout his writing, using Virany's class notes when they can help to elaborate his views or define his own critical position.[13] Not long after he taught the literary criticism course, Frye wrote in one of his notebooks,

> Aristotle seems to me unique among philosophers, not only in dealing specifically with poetics, but in assuming that such poetics would be an organon of a specific discipline. Other philosophers, when they touch on the arts, deal in questions of general aesthetics which they make a set of analogies to their logical & metaphysical views; hence it is difficult to use the aesthetics of, say, Kant or Hegel without getting involved in a Kantian or Hegelian "position," which of course is the opposite of what I am here attempting to do. (CW 23: 267)

Frye's "here" refers to the notes he is making for *Anatomy of Criticism*. The distinction is between what George Simpson calls "lumpers" and "splitters." A lumper like Plato can bring any subject matter into whatever he or she happens to be discussing at the moment, so that it is completely appropriate in an account, say, of the ideal commonwealth to pose questions about the role of art. A splitter like Aristotle, on the other hand, seeks to separate questions according to the appropriate discipline or "science." In the passage just quoted, Frye is referring to Aristotle's principle, set down in the opening paragraph of his *Metaphysics*, of distinguishing each of the "sciences" according to its general area of inquiry and based on the kinds of questions each "science" or discipline asks. The theoretical sciences (metaphysics, physics) were concerned with knowing; the practical sciences (ethics, politics), with acting or doing; and the productive sciences (poetics, rhetoric), with making. While certain features of Aristotle's method (for example, his four-cause mode of inquiry) are used across his writings, he was careful to restrict the questions of poetics to the ways and means for constructing good poems, or rather, based on the truncated version of the *Poetics* we have, good dramatic tragedies. Frye makes this point about Aristotle's division of the sciences at the beginning of his first lecture in the criticism course.

In 1951, Frye's sabbatical year at Harvard, he set out in his diary a reading program that included Aristotle's *Ethics*, *Politics*, *Rhetoric*, and *Poetics* (CW 8: 455). Then in 1952, when he was struggling with his chapter on the theory of symbols (essay two of the *Anatomy*), he wrote, "More study of the *Poetics*, & especially of Aristotle's conception of metaphor, is indicated" (CW 23: 206). Perhaps part of that study came as he worked out his lectures on Aristotle for his students. He begins those by noting that, whereas Plato wanted people to live right, Aristotle wanted them to think straight. According to Virany, Frye said that the *Poetics* is the "basis of so much—so much in it"—a rather glib paraphrase, no doubt. Frye stressed that the *Poetics* was a difficult book, partly because it is fragmentary; that Aristotle was searching only for general principles, not final ones; and that he "didn't intend what he said about literature to be taken as absolute."

The *topoi* from the *Poetics* that keep appearing in Frye's work over a fifty-year period are these: the four-cause method of definition, *mimesis*, the qualitative parts of dramatic tragedy (*mythos*, *ethos*, *dianoia*, *melos*, *lexis*, *opsis*), *spoudaios* and *phaulos*, *catharsis*, *hamartia*, and *anagnorisis*. There are other Aristotelian subjects that interest Frye, such as metaphor, but these are the chief ones. How, then, did Frye present Aristotle to his students? The answer is by providing a fairly detailed commentary on the *Poetics*. He first divided the treatise into these sections:

Chapters 1–5. Introductory
Chapters 6–19. On tragedy
Chapters 23–24. Epic
Chapter 25. Objections against poetry and how they may be answered.[14]
Chapter 26. Disputes about the relative merits of epic and tragedy and their resolution.

Following this, Frye proceeds in an orderly way, beginning, like Aristotle, "with the principles that come first" (1447a).[15]

The Four-Cause Definition of Tragedy

At the beginning of his October 15 lecture, Frye introduces the idea of imitation, saying that Aristotle provides "general remarks on imitation as basis of all art." As we have already suggested, this is a contested interpretation: if "most" of the poetic forms "happen to be" modes of imitations, then there are apparently some forms that happen not to be. Frye next lists the three differentiae of imitations. According to Virany, he outlined these as follows:

(1) the object of imitation	what?
(2) the means of imitation	how?
(3) the reason of imitation	why?

What Aristotle's four-cause method actually produces in chapters 1 through 3 are the means of imitation, the objects of imitation, and the manner of imitation. The final cause, or the end of imitation, what Frye calls the "reason of imitation," does not occur until Aristotle's definition of dramatic tragedy in chapter 6. What Virany refers to as the means of imitation actually answers the question, out of what? What she omitted was the manner of imitation (chapter 3). Aristotle arrives at his definition of tragedy by applying the four-cause method to produce a series of *genera* and *differentiae*. The process might be diagrammed like this:

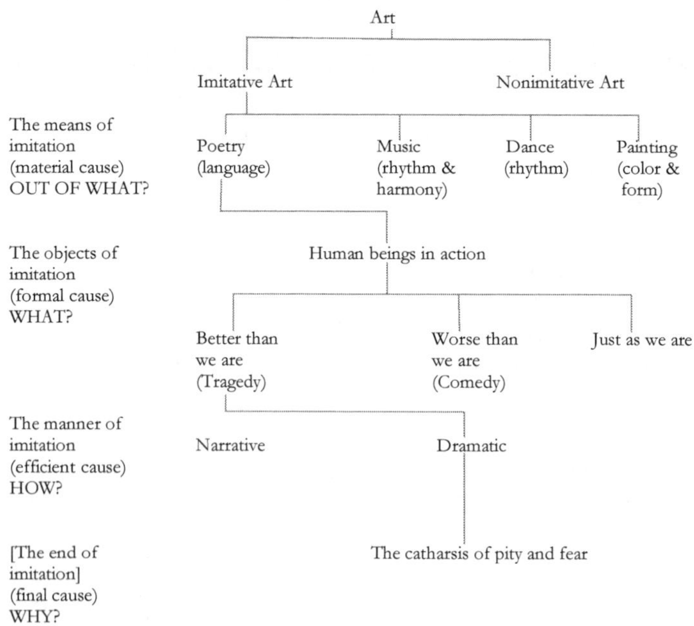

In short, the means of imitation permits Aristotle to distinguish the various arts on the basis of what they are made from (material cause): poetry from language, dance from rhythm, and so forth. Then the verbal arts are distinguished from each other on the basis of the objects imitated (formal cause). This imitation can be carried out either in narrative, as in epic poetry, or enacted in the theatre (efficient cause). This takes us through chapter 3 of the *Poetics*. In one of his notebooks, Frye has a very similar diagram:

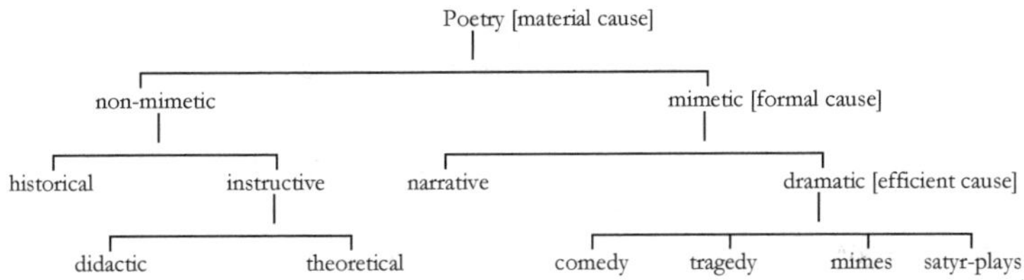

(CW 20: 211)

The left side of Frye's chart contains his own speculations on what Aristotle might have said about non-imitative art: it does not derive from the *Poetics*. The right side carries us through the first three chapters of the *Poetics*. But where is the chapter on the final cause? In chapter 6 Aristotle says that his formal definition of dramatic tragedy follows from "what has already been said": "Tragedy, then, is an imitation of an action that is serious, complete, and of a certain magnitude [formal cause]; in language embellished with each kind of artistic ornament, the several parts being found in separate parts of the play [material cause]; in the form of action, not of narrative [efficient cause]; through pity and fear effecting the proper purgation of these emotions [final cause]" (1449b). Aristotle says that this definition, which according to Frye "is undoubtedly the most celebrated sentence that has ever been written in the history of literary criticism" (CW 18: 470), results from "collecting" or "gathering up" what has come before.[16] But it is far from obvious how the final cause results from what has come before. This is no doubt why the final cause, the catharsis of pity and fear, is missing from Frye's own chart. Given the systematic way Aristotle has proceeded with the first three causes, we expect him to discuss the final cause in chapter 4, but it is at that point that he launches into a history of imitation. If the *Poetics* comes from student notes, is this the point where the student nodded, just as Virany appears to have nodded in confusing the means and the manner of imitation?

A great deal has been written to explain this apparent gap in the *Poetics*, none of which is completely satisfactory. But one possible explanation may be that Aristotle traces the history of imitation in chapter 4 in order to show how poetry developed from the instinct to imitate through the forms of poetry that had instrumental value (satires, panegyrics) and finally to that point where it achieved its "natural form," meaning that each poetic species developed to the point where it served no ends other than itself. Each poetic species, Aristotle has said in the preamble to the *Poetics*, has its own particular quality or power (*dynamis*). In the case of tragedy, this power is the catharsis of pity and fear as a final cause. Virany's class notes contain a hint that Frye may have been leaning in the direction of a similar explanation when he said, following the entry on the final cause, "Summary of the growth of tragedy and comedy [chapter 4] /—disputes regarding that / (Aristotle always looking for the essence—more easily seen when a thing is in growth)." In other words, tragedy achieved its "essence" when it moved away from practical ends of imitation, such as praising noble actions, satirizing "meaner" ones, or composing hymns to the gods, and came to stand on its own feet, having no end beyond the pleasure produced by the catharsis of pity and fear. However the missing link to the final cause might be explained, in his lectures Frye says that as a biologist Aristotle was "always dissecting things," and the four-cause method provided him a tool for such analysis, that is, breaking a whole (*synolon*) down into its parts. Frye does not refer to the four-causes in his Aristotle lectures, but he is aware that the four-part definition of tragedy does follow from the steps in the dissection Aristotle undertakes in chapters 1 to 3.

The four-cause method is put to work in Frye's early theoretical essays. In "The Archetypes of Literature," for example, he says, "The unity of a work of art, the basis of structural analysis, has not been produced solely by the unconditioned will of the artist, for the artist is only its efficient cause: it has form, and consequently a formal cause.... There is still before us the problem of the formal cause of the poem, a problem deeply involved with the question of genres" (CW 21: 125–6). And he describes the *Anatomy* as "the systematic study of the formal causes of art" (CW 22: 30), meaning what Aristotle meant—the form or arrangement of the poetic material.

The four causes make an appearance in Frye's work on more than 120 occasions, and, as just suggested, they tend to cluster in his earlier work. In 1948 he wrote:

> New Comedy has the blessing of Aristotle, who greatly preferred it to its predecessor, and it exhibits the general pattern of Aristotelian causation. It has a material cause in the young man's sexual desire, and a formal cause in the social order represented by the *senex*, with which the hero comes to terms when he gratifies his desire. It has an efficient cause in the character who brings about the final situation. In Classical times this

> character is a tricky slave; Renaissance dramatists often use some adaptation of the medieval 'vice'; modern writers generally like to pretend that nature, or at least the natural course of events, is the efficient cause. The final cause is the audience, which is expected by its applause to take part in the comic resolution. (CW 28: 5)

But as late as *The Great Code*, Frye sees typology "as an analogy of causality, a development of Aristotle's formal and final causes" (CW 19: 100), and in the last interview Frye gave he applied the four causes to education (CW 24: 1097–8). Frye is our great literary taxonomist, and Aristotle's method of analysis helps him classify the various forms and conventions of literature.[17]

Mimesis

Frye's literary theory lies firmly in the Romantic tradition, which replaced the Classical emphasis on *mimesis* as the underlying, defining category of aesthetics. In the post-Kantian world, imagination became the central category, displacing the views of art that had dominated criticism from ancient times up through the neoclassical period. Sidney is firmly in the Aristotelian camp: "Poesie therefore is an art of imitation, for so Aristotle termeth it in his word *mimesis*, that is to say, a representing, counterfeiting, or figuring forth—to speak metaphorically, a speaking picture; with this end, to teach and delight" (137–8). Similarly, the Aristotelian influence is apparent in Lisideius's definition of a play in Dryden's "Essay of Dramatic Poesy," which also has the Horatian tag trailing along: "a just and lively image of human nature, representing its passions and humours, and the changes of fortune to which it is subject; for the delight and instruction of mankind" (166). But with Kant's notion that the phenomenal world is created by the perceiving mind, the categories of poetic discussion were radically altered. Inheritors of the Kantian paradigm shift included Blake and the other British Romantics, and it included Frye as well.

Frye, nevertheless, did not abandon either the concept or the language of *mimesis*. In his literary criticism lectures Frye said, "Imitation is the basis of all art.—Plato gave imitation an unfavourable meaning. Aristotle wanted to rescue it. Sees in imitation the creation of something new. This means art imitates nature in the sense that both produce something new." This remark gets expanded in *Anatomy of Criticism* to include the ideas, frequently repeated throughout Frye's work, of "secondary imitation" and of the poetic action as the typical action, being more philosophical than history and more historical than philosophy. Here is one example of what Frye calls a "reconstruction" of this cluster of ideas:

> Here [with Sidney's view of the poem as having a "second nature"] we reach a more unified conception of narrative and meaning. Aristotle speaks of *mimesis praxeos*, an imitation of an action, and it appears that he identifies this *mimesis praxeos* with *mythos*. Aristotle's greatly abbreviated account here needs some reconstruction. Human action (*praxis*) is primarily imitated by histories, or verbal structures that describe specific and particular actions. A *mythos* is a secondary imitation of an action, which means, not that it is at two removes from reality, but that it describes typical actions, being more philosophical than history. Human thought (*theoria*) is primarily imitated by discursive writing, which makes specific and particular predications. A *dianoia* is a secondary imitation of thought, a *mimesis logou*, concerned with typical thought, with the images, metaphors, diagrams, and verbal ambiguities out of which specific ideas develop. Poetry is thus more historical than philosophy, more involved in images and examples. For it is clear that all verbal structures with meaning are verbal imitations of that elusive psychological and physiological process known as thought, a process stumbling through emotional entanglements, sudden irrational convictions, involuntary gleams of insight, rationalized prejudices, and blocks of panic and inertia, finally to reach a completely incommunicable intuition. Anyone who imagines that philosophy is not a verbal imitation of this process, but the process itself, has clearly not done much thinking. (CW 22: 76)

Frye extends the history and philosophy opposition with Sidney's distinction between example and precept, poetry being intermediate between both sets of oppositions—which is another of those *aperçus* that get repeated by Frye again and again.[18]

Mimesis, like *catharsis*, *hamartia*, and *spoudaios* and *phaulos*, is what W. B. Gallie calls an "essentially contested concept"—words about whose meaning and use there is widespread debate. In Plato's *Republic*, imitation refers to representation or copying: the carpenter imitates the ideal form of a bed and the artist comes along and imitates what the carpenter has made. Such imitations are of course viewed negatively by Plato, as they are two stages removed from the really real, the perfect Idea of the bed or the Idea of a perfect bed. Aristotle's imitation seems also to refer to representation, but not in the sense of copying. Aristotle's title is *Poietikes* or "things that are made or crafted." The first three words of the *Poetics* are "Concerning the art of making" or "Concerning the productive science." The reference is to the art or *techne* of doing something, not to the act or the product.

The sequence of ideas in chapter 1 seems to run from the general to the particular: from the art of making to imitative art and then to poetry.

In his entry on the term in the *Harper Handbook to Literature*, Frye himself differentiates the views of Plato and Aristotle regarding *mimesis*:

> [*Mimesis*] has been central to literary criticism since Aristotle's *Poetics*, which included, or at least implied, a critique of the conception of mimesis in Plato, more particularly in the last book of the *Republic*, that made Socrates exclude poets from his ideal state. The ordinary meaning of *imitation* as creating a resemblance to something else is clearly involved in Aristotle's definition of dramatic plot as mimesis *praxeos*, the imitation of an action. But there are many things that a work of literature may imitate, and hence many contexts of imitation.
>
> Socrates remarks in Plato's *Phaedrus* that a *logos*, or discourse, should resemble a zoon, or organism, a unity from which nothing can be taken away without injury. This organic conception of verbal structure recurs in Romantic criticism: in Coleridge, for instance, a literary work resembles or imitates nature in being an organic unity. At the same time there is a pervasive resemblance in the literary work as a whole to something in the external environment; otherwise, it would be impossible to understand. Similarly in the art of photography, the resemblance in the picture to its original "subject" is the first aspect of it to strike us, though this is reinforced by a corresponding sense of the differences between a photograph and an ordinary sense impression. Literature too may appear as "realistic," or like what the reader knows, though the differences created by its literary structure are at least equally important.
>
> In Aristotle himself *imitation* appears to mean, not an external relation of a copy to its original, but an internal relation of form to content: a tragedy, for example, is a form that has some aspect of "nature," or actual experience, for its content. From this point of view literature surrounds an aspect of experience and transforms it into its own shape. We are aware of the resemblance of the tragic action to human behaviour, but we are also aware of the containing conventions of tragic drama that differentiate that action from all other forms of action. (CW 18: 377)

As Frye's word "resemblance" indicates, *mimesis* implies an analogy (the principle underlying simile) rather than identity (the principle underlying metaphor). We will never encounter a Telemachus or a Stephen Dedalus in real life, but we may well encounter people who are very much like them.

The relation of mimetic theories of art to realism should not go unremarked. If we consider literature as a continuum, running from myth, fantasy, and romance at one extreme to realism at the other, the distinction between these extremes lies behind the theory of modes that Frye develops in the first essay of *Anatomy of Criticism*. *Mimesis* is the foundation of two of the modes, the high- and low-mimetic, in which things are represented as being more or less life-like. It is as if the nineteenth-century realists are holding a mirror up to nature. The mimetic tradition, then, plays a central role in Frye's outline of fictional modes, regardless of the fact that his sympathies lie with literary works at the other end of the continuum. His explanation of the cycle of stories moving historically from myth to irony, continually being displaced in the direction of plausibility, could not have been developed without *mimesis* as a foundational concept.

The Qualitative Parts of Tragedy

In his literary criticism lectures, Frye gives this summary of the qualitative parts of dramatic tragedy, introduced and initially defined in chapter 6 of the *Poetics*:

> Plot: synthesis of the individual acts
> Diction: synthesis, composition, of the verses
> Spectacle: stage appearances, costumes, scenery
> Character: anything in the play that left one in the position to make some conclusion about a type of individual
> Thought: that by which speakers sought to prove something
> Melody: no definition
>
> Three of these deal with the object you are imitating (plot, character, and thought)
> —diction and melody deal with the means
> —spectacle deals with the manner

Aristotle's words for the six parts of tragedy—*mythos*, *ethos*, *dianoia*, *melos*, *lexis*, and *opsis*—are omnipresent in *Anatomy of Criticism*, and they appear at other places in his work. In the *Anatomy*, Frye says that he is a "terminological buccaneer" (CW 22: 402), and his piracy of these terms is the clearest example of his taking over words from Aristotle and using them for his own purposes. In the *Poetics*, these terms have specific and limited definitions. Frye greatly expands the definitions, as we can see in the following comparisons, taken from chapter 6 of the *Poetics* and the glossary of the *Anatomy*, respectively:

Mythos (PLOT)
Aristotle: "imitation of the actions"; "arrangement of the incidents"
Frye: (1) The narrative of a work of literature, considered as the grammar or order of words (literal narrative), plot or "argument" (descriptive narrative), secondary imitation of action (formal narrative), imitation of generic and recurrent action or ritual (archetypal narrative), or imitation of the total conceivable action of an omnipotent god or human society (anagogic narrative). (2) One of the four archetypal narratives, classified as comic, romantic, tragic, and ironic.

Ethos (CHARACTER)
Aristotle: "that in virtue of which we ascribe certain qualities to the agents"
Frye: The internal social context of a work of literature, comprising the characterization and setting of fictional literature and the relation of the author to his reader or audience in thematic literature.

Dianoia (THOUGHT)
Aristotle: "required wherever a statement is proved, or, it may be, a general truth enunciated"
Frye: The meaning of a work of literature, which may be the total pattern of its symbols (literal meaning), its correlation with an external body of propositions or facts (descriptive meaning), its theme, or relation as a form of imagery to a potential commentary (formal meaning), its significance as a literary convention or genre (archetypal meaning), or its relation to total literary experience (anagogic meaning).

Melopiia (WHICH FRYE SHORTENS TO *melos*: SONG, MELODY)
Aristotle: not defined: "a term whose sense everyone understands"; one of the "embellishments"
Frye: The rhythm, movement, and sound of words; the aspect of literature which is analogous to music, and often shows some actual relation to it. From Aristotle's *melopoeia*.

Lexis (DICTION)
Aristotle: "metrical arrangement of the words"
Frye: The verbal "texture" or rhetorical aspect of a work of literature, including the usual meanings of the terms "diction" and "imagery."

Opsis (SPECTACLE)
Aristotle: "equipment" having an "emotional attraction"; "the production of spectacular effects depends more on the art of the stage machinist than on that of the poet"
Frye: The spectacular or visible aspect of drama; the ideally visible or pictorial aspect of other literature.

At the very beginning of the first essay of *Anatomy of Criticism*, we discover that "mode" is a category defined broadly in relation to what Frye calls the ethical elements, or the *ethos*, of a literary work. In this context *ethos*, an expansion of Aristotle's "character," refers on the one hand to literary heroes and their society and on the other to writers and their audience. The constant term, then, in Frye's definition of both fictional and thematic modes is *ethos*, though the meaning in each case is different, since the point of reference is either the hypothetical characters or the author–audience relationship. "Fictional" works are those in which the characters are internal, existing primarily as functions of a plot. And a "fictional mode" refers to the power of action that a character possesses. For works in the "thematic mode," the internal characters more or less disappear, having been subordinated to the *dianoia* of the writer's argument. Works in the thematic mode are therefore *external* fictions in which the dominant "ethical" relationship is between writers and their societies, rather than between heroes and their societies. "Poetry may be as completely absorbed in its internal characters," Frye remarks, "as it is in Shakespeare, or in Homer.... But as soon as the poet's personality appears on the horizon, a relation with the reader is established which cuts across the story, and which may increase until there is no story at all apart from what the poet is conveying to his reader" (CW 22: 49). The word *dianoia*, as Frye uses it in the first essay, means "theme" or "conceptual interest," which is again an expansion of its meaning in the *Poetics*, where it refers to "the faculty of saying what is possible or pertinent in given circumstances" (1450b).

Mythos, as Frye's glossary definition indicates, can mean any number of things, depending on the level of criticism one is engaged in (literal, descriptive, formal, archetypal, or anagogic), and just as *mythos* continues to expand in Frye's writing to include any aspect of literature that moves in time, so *dianoia* expands to mean the ways that literature is organized in space. At the beginning of the fourth essay of the *Anatomy*, Frye sets down a diagrammatic framework that recapitulates the view of art proposed in the *Anatomy*. It is based upon the ancient division of reality into three categories, described variously as thought, action, and passion, or truth, goodness, and beauty. In this division, Frye says,

> the world of art, beauty, feeling, and taste is the central one, and is flanked by two other worlds. One is the world of social action and events, the other the world of individual thought and ideas. Reading from left to right, this threefold structure divides human faculties into will, feeling, and reason. It divides the mental constructs which these faculties produce into history, art, and science and philosophy. It divides the ideals which form compulsions or obligations on these faculties into law, beauty, and truth. (CW 22: 225)

Using the method of analogy, Frye can conveniently fit *mythos*, *ethos*, and *dianoia* into this triadic framework. *Ethos*, as he has defined the term, stands at the centre, flanked on one side by the verbal imitation of action (*mythos*) and on the other by the verbal imitation of thought (*dianoia*). Similarly, the poetic symbol finds its place in the framework midway between event and idea, example and precept, ritual and dream—all of which were used in the second essay to define the phases of symbolism. Event, example, and ritual are aligned with *mythos*; idea, precept, and dream, with *dianoia*.

The second feature of this triadic scheme corresponds to the last three qualitative parts of Aristotle's analysis of tragedy: *melos*, *lexis*, and *opsis*. Frye develops this threefold division with another series of analogies:

> The world of social action and event, the world of time and process, has a particularly close association with the ear. The ear listens, and the ear translates what it hears into practical conduct. The world of individual thought and idea has a correspondingly close association with the eye, and nearly all our expressions for thought, from the Greek *theoria* down, are connected with visual metaphors. Further, not only does art as a whole seem to be central to events and ideas, but literature seems in a way to be central to the arts. It appeals to the ear, and so partakes of the nature of music, but music is a much more concentrated art of the ear and of the imaginative perception of time. Literature appeals to at least the inner eye, and so partakes of the nature of the plastic arts, but the plastic arts, especially painting, are much more concentrated on the eye and on the spatial world.... Considered as a verbal structure, literature presents a *lexis* which combines two other elements: *melos*, an element analogous to or otherwise connected with music, and *opsis*, which has a similar connection with the plastic arts. (CW 22: 225–6)

This second series of triads comprises what Frye sees as the rhetorical aspect of literature, one that "returns us to the 'literal' level of narrative and meaning" (CW 22: 226). We recall not only that Frye frequently equates rhetorical criticism with the procedures of the New Critics, but also that he establishes, in the Second Essay, a correspondence between these procedures and the literal phase of symbolism.

Frye also defines rhetoric by means of the traditional "trivium," locating it midway between grammar and logic. The definition arises from an analogy between *mythos* and grammar on the one hand and between *dianoia* and logic on the other. "As grammar may be called the art of ordering words," Frye observes, "there is a sense—a literal sense—in which grammar and narrative are the same thing; as logic may be called the art of producing meaning, there is a sense in which logic and meaning are the same thing" (CW 22: 226). In this view, grammar is "understood primarily as syntax or getting words in the right (narrative) order," whereas logic is "understood primarily as words arranged in a pattern with significance" (22: 226). Rhetoric, because of its central position in this framework, synthesizes grammar and logic, just as *lexis* performs the same function in relation to *melos* and *opsis*. Frye translates *lexis* as "'diction' when we are thinking of it as a narrative sequence of sounds caught by the ear, and as 'imagery' when we are thinking of it as forming a simultaneous pattern of meaning apprehended in an act of mental 'vision'" (22: 226). *Lexis*, in fact is rhetoric, or rather ornamental rhetoric as distinct from persuasive rhetoric. Similarly, if we consider grammar as the art of ordering words and logic as the art of producing meaning, then literature "may be described as the rhetorical organization of grammar and logic" (22: 226). The affinity between diction as a narrative sequence and *mythos*, on the one hand, and imagery as a pattern of meaning and *dianoia*, on the other hand, should not go unnoticed.

In Aristotle, *opsis* has a fairly restricted meaning. It refers to what theatre-goers could see on the stage, the *deus ex machina* and other "equipment" used to produce spectacular effects, including apparently such things as costumes and masks. Similarly, with *melos*, which refers to the melodies and harmonies in the chanting of the chorus, and *lexis*, the means of expressing thought, we have substantially expanded meanings. Frye's definitions of these terms are much more inclusive, operating at a high level of generality and functioning to delineate his theory of genres, differentiating, for example, among the four kinds of literary rhythm.

Altogether, Frye uses the Aristotelian names of the qualitative parts of tragedy more than 200 times in the *Anatomy*. The omnipresence of these terms reveals an Aristotelian debt, but it is essentially one of critical vocabulary. Frye annexes the language of the *Poetics*, but he redefines the terms according to his own purposes, even though there is in each of the terms a enduring conceptual residue from Aristotle.

Spoudaios and Phaulos

Another example of Frye's expanding on Aristotle is his appropriation of the words *spoudaios* and *phaulos*, about which Aristotle says, "Since the objects of imitation are men in action, and these men must be either of a higher [*spoudaios*] or lower [*phaulos*] type (for moral character mainly answers to these divisions, goodness and badness being the distinguishing marks of moral differences), it follows that we must represent men either as better than in real life, or as worse, or as they are" (1447a–1448a). Compare this with Frye's redefinition:

> In the second paragraph [chapter] of the *Poetics* Aristotle speaks of the differences in works of fiction which are caused by the different elevations of the characters in them. In some fictions, he says, the characters are better than we are, in others worse, in still others on the same level. This passage has not received much attention from modern critics, as the importance Aristotle assigns to goodness and badness seems to indicate a somewhat narrowly moralistic view of literature. Aristotle's words for good and bad, however, are *spoudaios* and *phaulos*, which have a figurative sense of weighty and light. In literary fictions the plot consists of somebody doing something. The somebody, if an individual, is the hero, and the something he does or fails to do is what he can do, or could have done, on the level of the postulates made about him by the author and the consequent expectations of the audience. Fictions, therefore, may be classified, not morally, but by the hero's power of action, which may be greater than ours, less, or roughly the same. (CW 22: 31)

Thus, whereas in Aristotle *spoudaios* and *phaulos* refer specifically to an ethical quality of the object imitated, indicating whether the agent is morally better or worse than ordinary people, in Frye the terms are used to refer quite generally to the relationship of a character to other people and to their environment. The distinction which serves as the basis of Aristotle's usage all but disappears in Frye, who, recognizing the *figurative* meaning of the two words, changes their reference from a moral application to one of natural law. In his literary criticism lectures, Frye defined *phaulos* figuratively as "of less consequence," and later in the *Anatomy* he equates *spoudaios* with Arnold's "high seriousness" (CW 22: 145). While *spoudaios* and *phaulos* are contested or at least ambiguous terms (Else devotes ten pages in an effort to explain them), Frye removes the moral reference altogether, using the terms in the first essay of the *Anatomy* to refer to the hero's power of action.

Catharsis

In his theology studies at Emmanuel College, Frye encountered the idea of purgative suffering in both the prophetic and New Testament traditions, as well as in Orphism, where it was attached to the idea of palingenesis. In his student paper from the mid-1930s on "The Jewish Background of the New Testament" Frye wrote, "the only possible explanation of the fact that tragedy produces a catharsis in the spectator ... implies, of course, that in the death of the soul man passes through suffering; and it is in the discovery of the purgative and redeeming nature of that suffering that the prophetic tradition fulfilled its mission" (CW 3: 149). And in a student essay from his final year at Emmanuel—"The Relation of Religion to the Art Forms of Music and Drama"—he contrasted the Orphics' concept of purification with Aristotle's more naturalistic view "as a purging or cleansing of the spirit by a powerful surcharge of emotions, which he specified as pity and terror" (CW 3: 333). *Catharsis* remained an important concept in Frye's consciousness, the word appearing more than 115 times in his writing over the next fifty years. In 1989 he wrote, "There must be at least fifty theories on the market about the meaning of *catharsis*" (CW 18: 470). This is obviously an overstatement, but *catharsis* is another contested concept. Three principal translations have been proposed: clarification, purification, and purgation.

The clarification view has been advanced by the classicist Leon Golden, who argues that the incidents in the tragic action are themselves clarified. What is revealed is how the fall of the noble protagonist can happen, thus giving to tragedy an educative function. Tragedy does not just delight: it teaches. Martha Nussbaum takes a similar view, arguing that in *catharsis* our emotions are educated rather than purged. The clarification view flies in the face of the idea that the *Poetics* is solely a productive science, concerned not with knowing but with making. The purification view, which begins with such Renaissance critics as Castelvetro and Robertello, maintains that tragedy tempers the emotions by revealing the proper objects of pity and fear to the audience. The purgation view, which is the oldest theory, argues that tragedy drives out the emotions of pity and fear. There are two variations on this theory: (1) we are so exhausted by having been gripped by pity and fear that all emotion is purged; and (2) once the play is over we are relieved of the emotional engagement and can stand back from the play, detach ourselves from it, and take pleasure in seeing something that was well made.

The only other place Aristotle uses the word *catharsis* in the context of the arts is in the *Politics*. The passage says in effect that music and poetry can relieve the unpleasant feelings experienced by people who have fallen into a religious frenzy: they are restored "as if they had undergone a curative and purifying treatment" (1341b). This raises the issue of how Aristotle's other works should be used to interpret the *Poetics*, which could have been written any time between 347 and 322 B.C. If the *Poetics* is a late work, written after Aristotle had detached himself from Plato's influence and had developed his own system, then we should probably exercise caution in using Aristotle's other works to explicate the meanings of particular words. This, in any case, is the position taken by those who argue that Aristotle's technical terms should be seen in relation to other terms within the "science" (theoretical, practical, or productive) where they appear. Since the *Politics* is a practical science, we can be led astray, so goes this argument, by the assumption that *catharsis* means the same thing in the *Politics* and the *Poetics*.[19]

How then did Frye view *catharsis*? Virany's class notes reveal that Frye proposed two principal theories about the meaning of this "common Greek word": the psychological, in which pent-up emotions would cause hysteria if not released; and the moral, which argues for the purifying of emotions. According to Virany, Frye preferred the psychological view, because "that's what he [Aristotle] meant in his *Ethics*" (Frye, or Virany, apparently meant to say here "*Politics*"), adding that "it is doubtless that he [Aristotle] thought catharsis was good for you." In his published work Frye translates *catharsis* as both purification (CW 18: 387) and as purgation (CW 14: 300, CW 18: 470, CW 24: 251).

In *Anatomy of Criticism*, the word *catharsis* takes on a more expansive meaning, coming to stand as a sign for one of the two principal ways of doing criticism. In "Towards Defining an Age of Sensibility," published a year before the *Anatomy* appeared, Frye wrote: "Where there is a strong sense of literature as aesthetic product, there is also a sense of its detachment from the spectator. Aristotle's theory of catharsis describes how this works for tragedy: pity and fear are detached from the beholder by being directed towards objects. Where there is a sense of literature as process, pity and fear become states of mind without objects, moods which are common to the work of art and the reader, and which bind them together psychologically instead of separating them aesthetically" (CW 17: 12). This gets elaborated in the *Anatomy*:

> [T]he difference in emphasis that we have described as fictional and thematic corresponds to a distinction between two views of literature that

> has run all through the history of criticism. These two views are the aesthetic and the creative, the Aristotelian and the Longinian, the view of literature as product and the view of literature as process. For Aristotle, the poem is a *techne* or aesthetic artefact: he is, as a critic, mainly interested in the more objective fictional forms, and his central conception is catharsis. Catharsis implies the detachment of the spectator, both from the work of art itself and from the author. The phrase "aesthetic distance" is generally accepted now in criticism, but it is almost a tautology: wherever there is aesthetic apprehension there is emotional and intellectual detachment. The principles of catharsis in other fictional forms than tragedy, such as comedy or satire, were not worked out by Aristotle, and have therefore never been worked out since. (CW 22: 62)[20]

In *The Well-Tempered Critic*, Frye calls these two critical emphases or approaches the hieratic and the demotic, the hieratic assuming an aesthetic emotional balance or detachment and the demotic assuming a psychological attitude of participation (CW 21: 382). This is the feature of catharsis that Frye stresses throughout his writing. In his entry on tragedy for the *Harper Handbook* he wrote: "According to Aristotle, a tragic action should, by raising pity and terror, effect a catharsis, or purification of these emotions. Whatever Aristotle meant by this, in dramatic experience this catharsis appears to be essentially a detachment of the spectator from feelings of attraction or repulsion toward the characters, particularly the hero" (CW 18: 387).

There is one further turn in the catharsis riddle, the result of a tendency we find everywhere in Frye—to take the discussion to another level. In a talk given at Mt. Sinai Hospital in 1989 ("Literature as Therapy") Frye said:

> If we are watching something in which [the] emotions of pity and terror predominate, if they are the leading features that we react to, we have something that is usually today called melodrama, rather than tragedy. Melodrama impels us, of course, to hiss villains and applaud heroes. But if these emotions of sympathy and repulsion, "pity and terror," are purged through catharsis, as they are in tragedy, then the response to tragedy is a response of emotional balance, a kind of self-integrating process. (CW 18: 471)

At the highest level of generality, "Literature as Therapy" is a reflection on catharsis, which, as Frye understands its implication in tragedy, results in a kind of restorative balance and harmony. This is another of Frye's many twists on Aristotle: self-integration rather than detachment now becomes for Frye the cathartic reward. Twenty-five years earlier, he had remarked that "the therapeutic power of the arts has been intermittently recognized ... but the fact that literature is essential to the mental health of society seldom enters our own speculations about it. But if I am to take seriously my own principle that works of literature are not so much things to be studied as powers to be possessed, I need to face the implications of that principle" (CW 27: 157). In "Literature as Therapy," Frye does draw out the implications of the principle, noting the restorative power, not simply of tragedy, but of ironic and comic modes as well. And the conjunction of body and mind in the literary experience leads Frye finally to argue that "the immense recuperative power of literature" (CW 18: 476) is a matter of vision, for literature is, in his words, a "controlled hallucination, where things are seen with a kind of intensity with which they are not seen in ordinary experience" (CW 18: 475). Literature is therapeutic, in short, because it provides a counter-environment to the illusions of ideology and the delusions of ordinary experience. We actually have an earlier version of this in the *Anatomy*, where the meaning of *catharsis* is extended to mean the liberated vision of exuberance: "The traditional theory of catharsis implies that the emotional response to art is not the raising of an actual emotion, but the raising and casting out of actual emotion on a wave of something else. We may call this something else, perhaps, exhilaration or exuberance: the vision of something liberated from experience, the response kindled in the reader by the transmutation of experience into mimesis, of life into art, of routine into play" (CW 22: 86).

With an emphasis on self-integration, exuberance, and seeing with an intensity of vision, we have moved some distance from catharsis as simply a pleasure triggered by the elimination of unpleasant emotions. We have moved beyond the moral and the psychological into the cosmological: "There is, according to Aristotle, a kind of excessive action on the part of the tragic hero, which Aristotle calls *hybris*. That is bound to lead to the restoring of balance in the natural order—what he calls nemesis. So the action of tragedy is almost physically intelligible, almost as intelligible in terms of a cosmos and the workings of nature as it is in moral or human terms" (CW 18: 471).

Hamartia

Another of Aristotle's terms that has generated considerable debate and that recurs scores of times throughout Frye's work is *hamartia*, a word that appears in the *Poetics* in the context of the most effective kinds of plots. In chapter 13 of the *Poetics*, Aristotle proposes four possibilities for the change in fortune of the hero: (1) a good person moving from happiness to misery: this, Aristotle says, is odious or repellent to us; (2) a bad person moving from misery to happiness: this is "most untragic" because there is no pity and fear; (3) a bad person moving from happiness to misery: this, again, generates no pity and fear; and (4) a good person whose misfortune is brought about by *hamartia*: this produces the most effective plot.

The root meaning of *hamartia* is "missing the mark" (from *hamartanein*). Bywater translates it as "error of judgment"; Butcher, as "error or frailty"; Golden, as "miscalculation"; Else, as "a big mistake"; Telford, as "some mistake"; and Grube as "flaw." It is clear from what Aristotle says about "vice and depravity" that *hamartia* has got nothing to do with moral evil or sin. Oedipus certainly doesn't suffer because he has done something wrong, even though he can be hot-headed and impulsive. Since Oedipus is one of Aristotle's examples, does *hamartia* refer to his lack of knowledge or ignorance? In his criticism lectures Frye presented a more or less textbook account of the *hamartia* debate, but he dismissed both the moral-fault and the error-in-judgment interpretations. He did not come up with a definitive interpretation himself, but he did circle around one. Virany records Frye's remarks as follows:

> —must keep it from being a case of justice / —hero gets just what is coming to him. On the other hand must avoid case of martyrdom, with the hero in no way to blame / The fault has to be something in a man which is very intelligible, very excusable, but yet not wholly justifiable. It is possible that the greatest dramatists hit upon this by instinct. No proof that Aristotle was able to see this. Perhaps he sensed it. Always a danger of reading into Aristotle things that have become articulate later. Another possibility would explain everything—Aristotle might have had in mind the famous Greek dictum "the doer must suffer." *Drasanti pathein*. The one who does something must suffer, irrespective of his intention.

In the *Anatomy* Frye amplifies his understanding of *hamartia* by saying that it "is associated with Aristotle's ethical conception of *proairesis*, or free choice of an end, and Aristotle certainly does tend to think of tragedy as morally, almost physically, intelligible" (CW 22: 196).[21] He adds that "*hamartia* or 'flaw' ... is not necessarily wrongdoing, much less moral weakness: it may be simply a matter of being a strong character in an exposed position, like Cordelia" (CW 22: 36).[22] Finally, whereas Aristotle seems intent on finding a cause for the tragic hero's fall, Frye thinks it may not be caused at all: "we come nearer the heart of tragedy when the catastrophe is seen, not as a consequence of what one has done, but as the end of what one is. The Christian original sin, the medieval wheel of fortune, the existentialist's 'dread' are all attempts to express the tragic situation as primary and uncaused, as a condition and not an act, and such ideas bring us closer than Aristotle's flaw (*hamartia*) does to the unconscious crime of Oedipus, the unjust death of Cordelia, or the undeserved suffering of Job. When we pass beyond *hamartia*, the tragic version of law shows itself to be a vision of the supremacy of the event (*mythos*)" (CW 21: 108–9). This, then, is another example of Frye's expanding a basic Aristotelian concept.

Anagnorisis

Anagnorisis means literally "knowing again," but like many other words having to do with knowledge, it is figuratively associated with seeing. Usually translated as "recognition," *anagnorisis* is a central category in Aristotle's theory of dramatic tragedy (chapters 10, 11, and 16), and it is a fundamental component of Frye's visionary world. In his definitive study of recognition as a poetic category, Terence Cave sees recognition as lying at the very centre of Frye's literary theory.[23]

In the third essay of *Anatomy of Criticism*, Frye represents his four central literary forms—comedy, irony, tragedy, and romance—as parts of a single, universal story or monomyth, which he calls the quest-romance. The central theme of this story is the killing of the dragon, and the ritual analogy to such a story is connected to the myth of the dying god. This myth has four aspects, which are connected with the four central *mythoi*:

agon (conflict)	the archetypal theme of romance
pathos (suffering or death)	the archetypal theme of tragedy
sparagmos ("tearing to pieces")	the archetypal theme of irony
anagnorisis (discovery or recognition)	the archetypal theme of comedy

We find this myth in a variety of forms in Western literature, but the myth always has the same general shape, having to do with the disappearance and return of a divine being. The various forms of literature are episodes, and all the episodes add up to the monomyth. In the Gospel narrative, for example, the tragedy of Christ's crucifixion is part of a larger comic structure which is resolved in the resurrection, the final rebirth and recognition scene: "the gospel is the world's great recognition scene" (CW 13: 324). And for Frye, one cannot "develop a serious belief in either a salvation or an enlightenment religion without accepting the validity of the comic structure" (CW 9: 29).

In *Anatomy of Criticism* and much of his other published works, Frye often uses *anagnorisis* in the conventional Aristotelian sense of an element in the plot whereby characters come to discover or recognize something about themselves they did not previously know, the discovery involving a movement from ignorance to knowledge. For Aristotle, the recognition, if properly handled, will evoke the emotions of pity and fear in the audience, but the recognition itself is something that happens to heroes and heroines. But more often than not Frye greatly expands the structural or centripetal usage in Aristotle, just as he does with his other adaptations of terms from the *Poetics*. Here, for example, is Frye's definition of *anagnorisis* from the *Harper Handbook to Literature*:

> *Oedipus Rex* begins with the king determined to discover why his land is suffering from a drought: the reader or audience assumes that his discovery of the reason will end the play. He eventually discovers that *he* is the reason; he has killed his father and lives in incest with his mother. Two things are involved here: one is "reversal" (*peripeteia*), or sudden change in fortune; the other is "discovery" (*anagnorisis*). The word *anagnorisis* could also be translated as "recognition," depending on how much of a surprise it is. In some plots, such as those of detective stories, the *anagnorisis* is a discovery, because it is a surprise to the reader; in others, such as those of most tragedies, it is a recognition by members of the audience of something they have come to realize long before, though it may still be a surprise to the chief character. (CW 18: 380)

In this definition we begin with the discovery of Oedipus and our assumption that his discovery will complete the parabolic shape of the story; we then move to our own discovery as readers or members of an audience, with the additional distinction, which Frye makes elsewhere: in the two usual translations, "discovery" refers to a new awareness by the audience and "recognition" to knowledge the audience has had all along.[24] Here, "recognition" has become an entirely functional and centrifugal concept, far removed from its structural sense in Aristotle. Frye, so to speak, recognizes this himself: "Functional analysis belongs to anagnorisis alone" (CW 23: 131). At one point Frye makes the connection between *anagnorisis* and the reader by speculating that *anagnosis*, the word ordinarily used in the New Testament for the reading of the Scriptures, "is derived from *anagnorisis*, which I believe also can mean reading" (CW 13: 364).[25] Another intriguing suggestion Frye makes, not found in Aristotle, is that the recognition in tragedy is individual and subjective and in comedy social and objective (CW 23: 106). This is still an internal distinction, referring to what happens in the plot, though it does not necessarily involve a movement from ignorance to knowledge. Frye, incidentally, says almost nothing about recognition in his criticism lectures—only that the *peripeteia* and *anagnorisis* point to "the reversal of intention" and that *anagnorisis* is "the recognition of what has happened."

When we turn to Frye's diaries and notebooks, where the word *anagnorisis* appears repeatedly, we find the meaning of "recognition" expanding in a number of directions.[26] In one diary reflection about the experience of hearing the Bach B Minor Mass, Frye uses *anagnorisis* to describe what in *Anatomy of Criticism* he calls the anagogic experience:

> The B minor Mass was a glorious performance.... Though a very Protestant mass, with the weight thrown on the Kyrie & the Credo, it's pure revelation, & that's why it's so brilliant & buoyant. It's such a contrast to the Beethoven mass, where the predominant feeling is mystery, & the big climax is the Messianic Benedictus, which is dependent on a violin solo. Bach takes mystery in his stride: the key word of the mass, for him, is "gloria," & he gives you pure mandala vision. He's also given the real meaning of sacrament, which is commedia, recognition, anagnorisis, epiphany. It's the exact opposite of sacrifice: in sacrifice, which is tragedy, something is killed: in sacrament something is brought to life. That something is the real presence of a single mind which contains both the Mass & the participating audience. No external God can be adored with music He did not compose. (CW 8: 324–5)[27]

Here the visionary or perceptive experience is an epiphany of the ear, but the recognition still is a matter of figuratively seeing. "Emblematic focus," he says, "seems to be the radical of recognition" (CW 15: 244). But recognition of the "real presence" is as paradoxical as the counterlogic of the Incarnation: "This doctrine of epiphany is important to me because the visibility or appearance of God, who is practically by definition invisible, seems to me a more momentous paradox than the alternative form of stating the same paradox: God becomes man in the Incarnation. Perhaps epiphany is to pneuma what incarnation is to logos: the everlasting gospel again" (CW 13: 322).

At times Frye speaks of *anagnorisis* as the reader's perception to the total shape of the tragic plot—a parabola formed by the rising action (the *desis* or complication) through the *peripeteia* and to the falling action (the *lysis* or solution) (CW 20: 291). "Recognition of *total shape* (anagnorisis)," he writes, "is crucial" (CW 23: 125), the linear experience of *mythos* now having become spatialized as *dianoia*. "Seeing" as a metaphor for what Frye calls the "final act of understanding the whole" is an observation about structure, but for the ideal presence of this final act, he says that he actually prefers the term *anagnorisis* to "structure" (CW 18: 315). Recognition is like interpenetration, he writes, because both involve the surrender of the ego (CW 15: 254). *Anagnorisis* is what gives coherence to a work of literature, but in life it is "the moment of truth" (CW 5: 356). Given Frye's boundlessly analogical habit of mind, it is an easy step for him to associate the structural coherence of the parabola with a cycle, for the *anagnorisis* takes us back to the beginning, as in the movement in the epic, which begins in the middle and moves back to the beginning, "which are, more or less, the same point" (CW 23: 199). Frye's next expansion—not quite so easy a step perhaps—is to see the recognition pattern in terms of renaissance, rebirth, and repetition: "both repetition & efflorescence seem to combine in *anagnorisis*, the recognition of the end as like the beginning" (CW 23: 199). Or again, Kierkegaard's "repetition is really Aristotle's *anagnorisis*," he writes in one notebook (CW 23: 234).[28] In another notebook, *anagnorisis* is said to be "the recovery of *memory*"—Plato's *anamnesis* (CW 23: 169). Frye was fascinated by the implications of Kierkegaard's "repetition," and in *The Great Code* he links the idea to Plato's *anamnesis*: "Kierkegaard's very brief but extraordinarily suggestive book *Repetition* is the only study I know of the psychological contrast between a past-directed causality and a future-directed typology. The mere attempt to repeat a past experience will lead only to disillusionment, but there is another kind of repetition which is the Christian antithesis (or complement) of Platonic recollection, and which finds its focus in the Biblical promise, 'Behold, I make all things new' (Revelation 21:5)" (CW 19: 101). Here Frye is moving toward the idea of *anagnorisis* as religious vision, and in a number of places he makes the identification explicit. In *The Return of Eden*, for example, he remarks that "Epiphany is the theological equivalent of what in literature is called 'anagnorisis' or 'recognition'" (CW 16: 130).[29] Similarly, the teleological movement of romance away from fantasy, which has no end beyond itself, is a movement of recognition that turns into revelation or epiphany:

> If I look at my circle of dramatic genres, I see four zones in it, epiphany, spectacle, mimesis & irony, the middle two being archetype & allegory. These are the Eden, Beulah, Generation & Ulro forms of art. Art begins in Beulah with the romance, & as it ages goes into realism & Generation. There are two ways of hypothesizing: fantasy, or the use of a let's pretend world, and selection, & these two give us the middle terms. But fantasy as an end in itself lacks a teleological point: this is anagnorisis or revelation (epiphany), the thing revealed being the infinite form of the innocent world, the form of work. The emergence of this from romance raises

> romance to scripture, & as the real presence of this world is the central teaching of all religions worth anything, we learn about it mostly from religious literature. The arrival at epiphany is the end of the quest, the consummation, a new birth, a marriage & a fertile fuck all identical with the burning of experience. (CW 23: 81–2)

Here *anagnorisis* marks the point of the movement from word to spirit, "raising" literature to the "real presence" found in scripture.

In Notebook 11b, Frye wrote:

> Recognition means both discovery of the new & *recognition* of the old. The latter is the total comprehension of the work or spectacular apocalypse; the former is the absorption into the personality. But this identifies recognition with imagery, not with narrative. Perhaps there's a stage of identification that bridges the gap between reversal (of *movement*) and recognition. I'm looking for a Mosaic or Pisgah view, the first or preliminary apocalypse. (CW 13: 354)

The Pisgah view is what Frye would later call the panoramic apocalypse, and this stage of *anagnorisis* is, as he remarks, "still incomplete without the rebuilding of Jerusalem" (CW 6: 715). He completes the pattern by postulating a second stage or level of *anagnorisis*, which is the participating or existential apocalypse. This second level is found in four different places in Frye's notes for his ogdoad project in the mid-to-late 1960s, when he was energetically formulating scheme after scheme for his projected "third book." The six and seventh books of this unfulfilled project were to be what he called "two gigantic anagnorisis summaries" (CW 9: 133). They are labelled "Anagnorisis I" and "Anagnorisis II" in an outline for the ogdoad that Frye jotted down on the inside front flyleaf of Notebook 45, and in a similar form of the outline that appears in Notebook 19, written about the same time (CW 9: 85). "Anagnorisis I" is associated with the encyclopaedic vision of plenitude and education as a quest myth, and "Anagnorisis II" with wisdom and religion. Twenty-three entries later, Frye worries about his use of the word, saying "the anagnorisis *has* to be literary, not with an eye swivelling out to education & religion" (CW 9: 89), though he immediately recurs to the two phases of *anagnorisis* with still another prospectus for the ogdoad, the six and seventh parts projected as follows:

> The Anagnorisis, Phase One ... The commedia of Eros in Plato & Dante; Shelley & Hegel; the symposium & the triumph of dialectic....

> The Anagnorisis, Phase Two ... The Bible & the final commedia: the double gyre with the dead; rephrasing of [the *agon*] in terms of total identity. (CW 9: 89)

In one of his eight-part compass diagrams, Frye locates apocalypse at the northern point of the circle, where it is coincident with the birth of God, and he comments that *anagnorisis* or recovery is connected with this stage of the hero's quest. This is also the stage of the rebuilding of Jerusalem, and "rebuilding the Temple is putting the body of Christ together again, making one body out of a society. But it must be a spiritual body" (CW 6: 716).

Frye eventually favoured "apocalypse" over *anagnorisis* for characterizing the penultimate and the ultimate stages of the quest, but the differences in language are not important; for in the vocabulary of Frye's religious speculations *anagnorisis* is interchangeable with apocalypse (as in CW 23: 111 and CW 20: 193), revelation and epiphany (as in CW 23: 81 and CW 13: 34), rebirth (as in CW 9: 114), the reversal into the vision of Logos (as in CW 5: 139), the place where death is destroyed (as in CW 9: 82), and where self-discovery is spiritual (as in CW 23: 106). What we have discovered about "discovery" is one of many examples of a movement from literature to religion. Frye's appropriation of Aristotle's poetic term moves up through a series of elaborations to the level of interpenetration, where poetic vision becomes spiritual vision, though, given the operation of the familiar *Aufhebung*, the Hegelian process of preserving, cancelling, and lifting to another level, the former stages are never negated. This is the vision embodied in *Oedipus the King*. At the level of literary *anagnorisis*, Oedipus discovers who murdered King Laius, and he comes to recognize that he is guilty of parricide and incest. But if we leave the story at that, we have only a detective story, and if Sophocles' play were only a murder mystery, then it would have long since disappeared into the dustbin of history. Something else in the play is compelling, and this something else is the vision Oedipus has at the moment of recognition and reversal—the moment he blinds himself and screams out against Apollo. This vision does not cancel our experience of the literary level: it lifts the detective story to another level, forcing Oedipus now into the role of a cosmic detective. What Oedipus *discovers* at this level is difficult to articulate, just as it is difficult for Frye to articulate the content of what he calls moments of intensified consciousness. But surely it has to do with his awareness of both the limitations of his own human power and with his hope, even when he feels most polluted and helpless, that genuine self-knowledge and social enlightenment might come to him if he patiently endures the suffering he must undergo. Although Frye does not use the word *paravritti* in connection with any of his speculations about *anagnorisis*, he would doubtless consider the recognition of Oedipus to be a *paravritti*—the complete conversion of Oedipus' mind and soul at the moment of his deepest desolation. Finally, recognition is connected with the vision of love: "If the ultimate reality in the world is love, there can be no love without recognition.... Every individual turns out to be a functioning community. And if everything is community, and love is reality, love must include recognition, which is also discovery, anagnorisis. Recognition is the 'moment of truth' in a real and not a slang sense" (CW 5: 356).

This survey of the different meanings that cluster around *anagnorisis*, especially as the word is used in the notebooks, can perhaps help us better understand Frye's remark, confirming the centrality of recognition in his own approach to literature: "Much of my critical thinking has turned on the double meaning of Aristotle's term *anagnorisis*" (CW 26: 16); better understand his comment in Notebook 24 about one of the reading assignments he had been given: "As always, my approach was through *anagnorisis*" (CW 9: 325); better understand his very early observation that while Milton and Bunyan were the great Protestant poets of the *agon*, Blake was the great Protestant poet of the *anagnorisis*" (CW 25: 166); and better understand, finally, the concluding sentences of Frye's last and posthumously published book, which take us far beyond Aristotle: "In the double vision of a spiritual and a physical world simultaneously present, every moment we have lived through we have also died out of into another. Our life in the resurrection, then, is already here, and waiting to be recognized" (CW 4: 235).[30]

Appendix: Margaret (née Kell) Virany's Class Notes on Aristotle from Frye's 1954 Course in Literary Criticism

Oct. 8.

Aristotle

- —born at Stagira in 384 BC Died 322
- —took up Plato's challenge
- —a biologist—always dissecting things
- —came to Athens when 17
- —tutor for Alexander—one of his pupils
- —set out to bring order to the existing sciences

  Plato wanted men to live right

  Aristotle wanted men to think straight

- —divided sciences into three main classes

(1) productive	poetry, rhetoric
(2) practical	politics, ethics
(3) theoretical	mathematics, physics, metaphysics

The productive and practical sciences dealt with the getting of knowledge and the application of knowledge to mutable, human, changeable things. All you can get from productive and practical sciences would be general. Might change.

Theoretical sciences dealt with knowledge and the contemplation of knowledge in itself. From this you got universal, final principles.

Aristotle wanted to bring logic into the sciences, which he felt were just a jumble of facts. He wanted to put some kind of order into poetry (all imaginative writing). All he hoped to get there were general, not final, principles. Yet later writers regarded everything Aristotle said as immutable as a dictum of Euclid.

Oct. 15.

Aristotle didn't intend what he said about literature to be taken as absolute and final.

Poetics

- —short
- —esoteric language

—text seems fragmentary. Perhaps the second book has been lost.
Therefore, a difficult book.

Widely divergent theories about its meaning

—introductory part—chapters 1–5

—general remarks on imitation as basis of all art

(1) the object of imitation	what?
(2) the means of imitation	how?
(3) the reason of imitation	why?

Summary of the growth of tragedy and comedy

—disputes regarding that

(Aristotle always looking for the essence—more easily seen when a thing is in growth.)

chapters 6–19 deal with tragedy

—definition: what are the parts of tragedy? (chapter 6)

—goes further into each of them

—deals with the epic and its relation to tragedy

—chapters after 19 of no particular use to us

—diction
—poetic diction
} language very different from ours

—chapters 23–24—epic

—chapter 25—objections brought against poetry and how they may be answered

—chapter 26—tries to resolve disputes about the relative merit of epic and tragedy

(1) Aristotle accepted existing Greek literature as if it were final. Do tragedy and comedy mark the end of the line? (brought this question up and then discarded it)

(2) Greek preoccupation with ethics

—goes through the whole thing. Teleology

(3) Answering Plato, who had bitterly attacked drama (especially tragedy)

(4) Current questions

—relative merits of art and genius, epic and tragedy; therefore, emphasizes the thing that tragedy has and the epic has not

Imitation is the basis of all art

—Plato gave imitation an unfavorable meaning. Aristotle wanted to rescue it. Sees in imitation the creation of something new. This means art imitates nature in the sense that both produce something new
—poetry—includes music and dancing as well as all imaginative writing. (Music = flute and lyre)
 —typical exhaustive Aristotelian approach
 —three things: rhythm, harmony, language
 —if you imitate by rhythm alone—dancing
 —if you imitate by harmony—music
 —if you imitate by language—lyric poet (together and consistent)
 —if you imitate by language—tragedy and comedy (varied)
—distinction between poetry strictly so-called and poetry that only did the work of prose
 What will a man imitate?
 —can imitate things as they are, as they are said to be, as they ought to be.
 Can imitate men as good as ourselves, men better and men worse. If we imitate men better than ourselves, by and by you have tragedy. If you imitate men worse than ourselves, by and by you have comedy.
 ("worse" = of less consequence)

Why do we have poetry, dancing, and music?
—traces it to the tendency to imitate that is deep in everybody
—man gets pleasure from imitation of others because of this tendency. Although the object itself may be repulsive, good imitation of it will gives us pleasure
—everybody has an innate sense of rhythm.
Literature is in contact with the universal. Cuts out the particular
 —what should happen according to the law of probability and necessity

Chapters VI–XIX
Tragedy was the crowning glory of Greek literature
Tragedy is an imitation of an action that is entire and that is serious and of a certain magnitude, in language made beautiful by different means in different parts, in dramatic not in narrative form, with incidents that arouse pity and fear so as to bring about a catharsis of these emotions.
Aristotle's words, in the definition, were chosen to distinguish tragedy from something else, in this case comedy
—"dramatic, not narrative form" distinguishes it from epic

Plot: synthesis of the individual acts
Diction: synthesis, composition, of the verses
Spectacle: stage appearances, costumes, scenery
Character: anything in the play that left one in the position to make some conclusion about a type of individual
Thought: that by which speakers sought to prove something
Melody: no definition

Three of these deal with the object you are imitating (plot, character, and thought)

- —diction and melody deal with the means
- —spectacle deals with the manner

- —great part is given to dealing with plot
- —Aristotle preoccupied with teleological ideas
- —did or didn't the Greeks believe in free will as we understand it?
  - —if not, they'd be more concerned with what a person does, not with why he did it

Anything entire must have a beginning, middle, and end.

The Greeks in their plays dealt with stories already known. Therefore, where you should begin became an important question.

—scene at the beginning would be something that didn't of necessity follow from something before. Would point to something that was naturally coming later. Middle would follow of necessity from the beginning and point to something later. End would follow from the middle and be self-conclusive. (Greeks didn't start with a corpse in a bag that followed of necessity from something.) Took it for granted the audience knew the story.

Oct. 22.

Aristotle—unity of action insisted upon.
—perfect cohesion of parts
—says in his day Greek tragedy tried to restrict itself to what would happen in one day or slightly more

- —he mentioned this simply as current practice
  - It wouldn't apply to several of the Greek plays

16th century—Castelvetro

- —*Poetics* of Aristotle popularized and explained
- —turned Aristotle's statement into a law of the unity of time

—if you have unity of time, must have unity of place
This is responsible for the three unities. They do not go back to Aristotle.

Aristotle didn't say much about the unity something received from one character
—everything should happen according to the law of probability and necessity, cause and effect
This was his way of bringing tragedy into contact with the universal

What plots should you use?
—in Greece they restricted their plots to a few noble houses.
Aristotle saw no need for staying entirely with the traditional plots.
—simple and complex plots
—desis and lysis in each play
(bind and loose)
—plot is complicated up to a certain stage and then begins to unravel. This brought about by the peripeteia and anagnorisis, i.e., the reversal of the intention.
A deed done in all good faith which produces the opposite result of what was intended
Peripeteia—intention
Anagnorisis—the recognition of what has happened
All these things must come about through cause and effect, and not with the use of a *deus ex machina*.
(such a device is used in Molière's *Tartuffe*)
—Aristotle warns against certain plots—to be avoided
—keep away from plots that don't excite pity and fear. Turn to those that will excite them.
(1) bad man who comes to an evil end is poetic justice
(2) bad man prospers—neither pity nor fear—disgust
(3) can't have a completely good man going from good fortune to bad fortune

Tragic hero
—model of saintliness, never a bad man
—goes from good fortune to bad fortune because of some mistake
What does he mean by a "mistake"?
—moral fault? error in judgment?
—hard to see a moral fault or an error in judgment in *Oedipus Rex*—what brought his downfall happened in a way [right?] outside the play

—must keep it from being a case of justice—hero gets just what is coming to him. On the other hand must avoid case of martyrdom, with the hero in no way to blame

The fault has to be something in a man which is very intelligible, very excusable, but yet not wholly justifiable. It is possible that the greatest dramatists hit upon this by instinct. No proof that Aristotle was able to see this. Perhaps he sensed it. Always a danger of reading into Aristotle things that have become articulate later. Another possibility would explain everything—Aristotle might have had in mind the famous Greek dictum "the doer must suffer." *Drasanti pathein*. The one who does something must suffer, irrespective of his intention.

Positive law, i.e., that made by a legislator is the kind of law that takes in cognizance of intention. Even here it is restricted.

Aristotle on Character

(above discussion is all included under plot)

(1) A character should be good, i.e. in the sense of useful

—there's goodness in everybody, even in a woman or a slave

—{Fontenelle, *Réflexions sur la poétique*

There is a perfection even in vice. Cruelty, when carried to perfection, is good in tragedy. The stage is not opposed to what is vicious, but what is low and trivial.}

(2) The character must be appropriate

—woman must not be represented as manly or brave or clever

(3) Character should have resemblance

i.e., like reality?

like their mythical prototypes?

in the same breath, he compares it to a painting; does he mean that a character is like the original but heightened somewhat?

(4) Character should be consistent. If you introduced an inconsistent character, keep him inconsistent all through

(5) Keep everything in the character according to the law of necessity and probability

Poetics, chapter XVI

—advice to the writer

—use your imagination—picture yourself in the audience, writing your own play

—try to enter into the feelings. Act out the part of your characters, even with the proper gestures. Unless you are able to enter into the feelings of the person you are putting before people you will never be successful in it.
—make an outline. Fill in the details.

Thought
—refers you to his account in the *Rhetoric*
Spectacle
—very simple in these [itself?]
—not of much concern
Didn't have a great deal to say about Chorus and Melody
—important aids in tragedy
—must come under unity of action law
—chorus must sing something connected with the play to further the action in which they appear
Diction
—recognized the distinction between prose and verse
—Greek and Latin are quantitative languages. Hard to compare with English

Comedy
—says it wasn't taken seriously in the beginning
—that which is painless to the victim, not harmful to others
(*Tractatus Coislinianus* is given in places as if it were Aristotle's ideas on comedy, but it is not)
Epic—epic doesn't have melody and spectacle. Can be as long as you want, different meter. Close connection to tragedy despite differences

Tragedy
—superior to the epic
—more refined
—epic can best be appreciated by being read, tragedy by being read and seen

Chapter 25
—very important from the point of view of ordinary criticism
—talks about errors that may appear in poetry
(1) it is better if all error can be avoided
(2) if errors do occur, they are not all of the same kind. Not every error is very serious. There are errors that touch the essence of poetry and there are errors that are only accidental

—poor imitation is the essential error
The standard of correctness is the same in poetry as it is in the other arts
(3) Do not be too hasty in postulating errors in great works.
—may have been a current belief in the time he wrote
—may be quoting something without vouching for its truth
—may be quoting things as they were said to be
—may be it serves an end (great thing through all Greek philosophy and literature, especially in Aristotle)
Must consider: who said it? when? for what purpose? to whom? by what means?

This chapter was hardly ever mentioned after the days of Aristotle. Yet it is one of the most important chapters in Aristotle from a practical point of view. Subsequent writers, e.g., Longinus and Horace, were to discover that all errors can't be avoided.

{Some reviewers go to great lengths to discuss trivial technical errors in a book; i.e., they don't distinguish between types of errors.}

When dealing with probabilities, remember that a great number of things happen contrary to probability
    —i.e., don't condemn a work of art because there is some improbability in it

Did Aristotle regard aesthetic pleasure as the end, the purpose of poetry?
—spoke of "the proper pleasure of poetry"
—but preoccupied with ethics
—all ethical standards must be satisfied
  i.e., ago-old dispute between art and morality
    —have to draw a line on morality somewhere
      Where should it be drawn? (from the point of view of art)

OCT. 29.
Inspiration in Aristotle
—believed poetry is inspired
—seemed to distinguish between poetic inspiration and frenzy
  —the text contains trouble here though
—Dryden—preface to *Troilus and Cressida*—takes the text that says poetry is the "work of a great mind *not* a madman." There is another text that reads "work of a great mind *or* a madman"

Meter

—incidental to poetry

—Aristotle went too far in his reaction against classification of poets according to meter

Aristotle becomes more lenient in his views as he goes on

—first he restricts poetry to the universal

(he brings it close to Aristotelian philosophy)

—later he realized that what is poetic art can divert attention from improbabilities and other elements you couldn't give a non-philosophical explanation for in a work

The Poetics

—basis of so much

—so much in it

NOV. 5.

Rhetoric—Aristotle

—influenced by Plato's attack on rhetoric and by Gorgias' school of highly rhetorical prose

—not writing on prose in general, but on prose in the orator, i.e., to be spoken, not just read.

Three things to consider

(1) speaker

(2) speech

(3) audience

—used this division for his three books

first draws line between rhetoric and other things

e.g., rhetoric and logic

—both try to convince others of their conclusions, but logic is abstract, rhetoric is concrete.

Different in method and proof.

The purpose of rhetoric

(1) to promote inquiry (2) to teach (3) to debate (4) to defend oneself

—must start from common ground in politics and ethics

politics—everything to do with the organization of the state

ethics—everything to do with man as an individual

—the basis would not be universals because it does not start with metaphysics—basis would be a generally accepted statement (probabilities) in which there is always the possibility of an exception

Three Classes of Rhetoric
(1) forensic—in the law courts
(2) deliberative—in the assemblies
(3) occasional—in speeches on great men, welcomes, funeral speeches

Speaker must have three qualities
(1) virtue—upright, decent man
(2) wisdom—or at least the appearance of it
(3) interest in audience

An orator must understand character if he is to appear wise (ethos)
—must show some emotion in order to show interest; therefore, must know about pathos or emotion
The audience is the final judge. It must therefore be considered. Various types—must mold speech to fit them
Speech—as a philosopher, Aristotle thought men should work by reason. A strong argument should be enough. Yet he realizes that a good cause may have to be decked out to please the less intelligent audience
—two essential qualities of style: (1) clearness (2) propriety
—audience must be able to understand what you are saying. Use ordinary words, clear metaphors, pure, idiomatic Greek. Avoid the abstract
—all classical prose contains propriety, i.e., suiting speech to theme and audience
—for all uses of ordinary words give talk a sort of dignity
Division of speeches
(1) finding the arguments
(2) their arrangement
(3) their delivery

Supposed indifference to style taken by the Stoics as the basis of their own style—very correct but devoid of ornament

2

Frye and Longinus

Dedicated to the memory of Domokos Pásztor

> *There he stood on the renewing crags of time, stood on the ringed summit of the sublime universe.* —Ferenc Juhász

The earliest reference to Longinus in Frye's work is in a 1953 review of books by Allen Tate, Herbert Read, and Francis Fergusson, where he says that the theme of Read's *The True Voice of Feeling* "is essentially the same as the problem of *ekstasis* or 'transport' in Longinus," adding that this "problem" had been "ably handled" by Tate. He is referring to Tate's "Longinus and the 'New Criticism'" from a collection of Tate's essays, *The Forlorn Demon* (1953). About the same time, Frye wrote this somewhat riddling entry in Notebook 37:

> Re the first lecture: sublime process as beautiful product (Longinus on sublime). Sublime includes *self*-identification (process). Interest in a *convention* ... more congenial to the aesthetic, especially in paradoxical forms of it like T. E. Hulme's. The *rhetorical* relation expects to instruct & delight. (CW 23: 126)[31]

The "first lecture" is most likely a reference to the first address Frye gave at Princeton in 1954. Invited by E. D. H. Johnson of the Special Programs in Humanities at Princeton to institute a new series, known as the Class of 1932 Lectures, Frye gave four talks at Princeton in 1954: "The Critic and His Public," "Symbols of Fact and Fiction," "The Language of Poetry," and "Myth and Society" (Ayre 244). In his Preface to *Anatomy of Criticism*, Frye notes that much of the substance of the book came from his Princeton lectures. In any event, Frye seems intent on exploring the connection between Longinus's emphasis on the sublime process and the Aristotelian "aesthetic" approach. The opposition between "convention" and "rhetorical relation" is apparently an opposition between final and instrumental value: the aesthetic needs no justification beyond itself, whereas rhetoric is concerned with the ways and means of instruction and delight. The reference to Hulme seems to be that his call for formal restraint and concrete imagery ("dry hardness"), along with his attacks on Romanticism, means he is a "classicist" and does not belong to the Longinian camp.

Fictional and Thematic

The notebook entry on "the first lecture" suggests that in his thinking about the beginning of the *Anatomy* Frye has in mind two approaches the critic might take to literature, one emphasizing process and the other product. And in fact this opposition turns up at the end of the *Anatomy*'s first essay, where Frye expands on the meaning of the terms "fictional" and "thematic" in his theory of modes. A "fictional" work for Frye, as we saw in chapter 1, is one that has internal characters, as in novels, epics, and plays. A "thematic" work is one in which there are no characters involved except the author and the reader, as in lyrics and essays, or in which the internal characters are subordinated to the writer's argument, as in allegories and parables. The foundational category in the first essay is Aristotle's *ethos*, or rather Frye's expansion of this term: even though the meaning of "character" in "fictional" works differs from its meaning in "thematic" works, *ethos* is the constant term in both. Here is the key passage at the end of the first essay:

> [T]he difference in emphasis that we have described as fictional and thematic corresponds to a distinction between two views of literature that has run all through the history of criticism. These two views are the aesthetic and the creative, the Aristotelian and the Longinian, the view of literature as product and the view of literature as process. For Aristotle, the poem is a *techne* or aesthetic artefact: he is, as a critic, mainly interested in the more objective fictional forms, and his central conception is catharsis. Catharsis implies the detachment of the spectator, both from the work of art itself and from the author. The phrase "aesthetic distance" is generally accepted now in criticism, but it is almost a tautology: wherever there is aesthetic apprehension there is emotional and intellectual detachment. The principles of catharsis in other fictional forms than tragedy, such as comedy or satire, were not worked out by Aristotle, and have therefore never been worked out since.... Just as catharsis is the central conception of the Aristotelian approach to literature, so ecstasis or absorption is the central conception of the Longinian approach. This is a state of identification in which the reader, the poem, and sometimes, at least ideally, the poet also, are involved. We say reader, because the Longinian conception is primarily that of a thematic or individualized response: it is more useful for lyrics, just as the Aristotelian one is more useful for plays. (CW 22: 62–3)

Thirty-three years later Frye is still appealing to the Aristotelian–Longinian dialectic. In *Words with Power* (1990), he writes: "Traditional critical theories, from Plato and Aristotle on, look at literature within a mimetic context. We are told in both the *Republic* and in the *Poetics* that the poet's work is imitative, though very different inferences are drawn from the principle in the two contexts. What the poet imitates is usually assumed to fall within either the phenomena of human society or the order of nature. But the Longinian conception of ecstatic response suggests another dimension of imitation" (CW 26: 108–9).

John Stuart Mill reports that "Coleridge used to say that everyone is born either a Platonist or an Aristotelian."[32] For Coleridge, there was no complementarity in this dialectic: if you are a Platonist, you cannot be an Aristotelian, and vice versa. "Dialectic" signals the presence of oppositions, and Frye is a dialectical thinker. He is forever moving back and forth between opposing poles of reference: knowledge and experience, space and time, stasis and movement, the individual and society, tradition and innovation, synthesis and analysis, engagement and detachment, freedom and concern, *mythos* and *dianoia*, the world and the grain of sand, immanence and transcendence, and scores, nay, hundreds of other oppositions. But in Frye there are few occasions that present us with an *either/or* choice, and the Aristotle–Longinus dialectic is no exception. Frye's world is a *both/and* world. The two perspectives complement each other, or at least they appear to do so.

As we saw in the previous chapter, the imprint of Aristotle is everywhere in Frye's work. He sets out in the *Anatomy* to develop a twentieth-century *Poetics*, and a number of Aristotelian *topoi* appear with regularity: *mythos*, *ethos*, and *dianoia* are the material cause for much of Frye's analysis in the first three essays of the *Anatomy*, and *melos*, *lexis*, and *opsis* serve the same function in the fourth essay. Frye frequently relies on the four-cause method of definition. As we have seen, Aristotelian terms—*mimesis*, *spoudaios* and *phaulos*, *catharsis*, *hamartia*, and *anagnorisis*—are scattered liberally throughout his writing. More often than not, Frye greatly expands the meanings that these terms have in Aristotle, as already suggested, but the *Anatomy* nevertheless would have been a very different book had there been no *Poetics*.

The occasions Frye has to consider Longinus are far fewer than the Aristotelian ones, but they are frequent enough to deserve our attention. I propose here to examine the influence of Longinus on Frye and to speculate on whether or not in his *both/and* world, where Aristotle complements Longinus and vice versa, he finally privileges one over the other. In studying the influence of Longinus on Frye, we have the class notes for his 1954 course in Literary Criticism, recorded by his student Margaret (née Kell) Virany,[33] a course in which he taught the major Classical critics: Plato, Aristotle, Horace, Longinus, and Quintilian.

The Sublime

Some uncertainty surrounds the translation of *Peri hypsous* as "On the Sublime." Most agree that it conveys the sense of height or elevation. The first English translation by John Hall in the seventeenth century was entitled *Of the Height of Eloquence*. Even the etymology of "sublime," which comes from the Latin *subl mis*, is uncertain. The OED speculates that *sublīmis* probably derives from *sub* "up to" plus *līmen* "lintel." G. M. A. Grube says that the "English translators and editors seem to be agreed that sublime is an unsatisfactory translation... but they continue to use it; few of them given any clear idea of what Longinus is writing about" ("Notes" 355). One of the implicit meanings of *hypsous* is that of movement or process. Emma Gilby maintains that "Longinus gives us to understand that 'hypsos' is best defined as a movement, and not just a movement upward (as one might expect from a term often translated as 'height') but also horizontally toward others" (23).

Etymology and the uncertainties of translation aside, Longinus is relatively clear about what he means by *hypsous*. In his opening paragraph he says to his correspondent Terentianus that the first requirement of a systematic treatise is "a statement of the subject," and he proceeds to provide just that in his opening chapter. Elder Olson is clearly correct in calling our attention to two contexts for the definition. One is that the ends and means of the sublime are contrasted with those of rhetoric; the other is that the definition is presented within the framework of the familiar triad of audience, author, and work.[34]

From the perspective of the *author*, sublimity is that which has constituted the greatest poets; it is what has given them their high place, their fame. "[S]ublimity is a certain distinction and excellence in expression, and that it is from no other source than this that the greatest poets and writers have derived their eminence and gained an immortality of renown" (1.3).[35]

From the perspective of the *audience*, the "effect of elevated language upon an audience is not persuasion but transport [*ekstasis*]" (1.4). Ecstasy is stronger than persuasion because the audience can resist persuasion, but it can't resist transport. The Greek stem for *ekstasis* means "a being put out of its place," and in late Greek it acquired the additional meaning, according to the OED, of "withdrawal of the soul from the body, mystic or prophetic trance."

From the perspective of the *work*, the excellencies of rhetoric are contextual: they emerge from the whole and are temporal. The excellencies of *ekstasis* emerge from the part and are instantaneous: "Sublimity flashing forth at the right moment scatters everything before it like a thunderbolt" (1.4).[36]

Thus, to summarize in a chart:

	Author	Work	Audience
Art of rhetoric	rhetorician	whole	persuasion
Art of the sublime	greatest poets & writers	part	transport

Longinus is a qualitative critic. Whereas Aristotle is interested in artistic wholes and the way the parts go to make up those wholes, Longinus is interested only in a particular literary quality, sublimity, which can be found in any number of genres, including nonliterary ones. There are parallels in contemporary criticism: Cleanth Brooks's concern, for example, with the qualities of irony and paradox or Mikhail Bakhtin's with the dialogical and carnivalesque—qualities they discover in a variety of literary forms.

Class Notes on Longinus from Frye's Course in Literary Criticism

Margaret Virany's class notes for Frye's lecture on Longinus, which are reproduced in the appendix, are mostly a rather matter-of-fact summary of the topics Longinus addresses. Frye does remark that Longinus "gets to the heart of great writing," says (in regard to chapter 2) that Longinus is noncommittal about whether the sublime can be taught, notes in regard to Longinus's section on periphrasis that Molière satirized circumlocution, comments regarding diction that "beautiful words are the light of thought (not realized in England until Coleridge) /—cf. stained-glass window and light /—words and thought must be correlated." He also says that Longinus was the first to point out that judicial literary criticism is difficult and can come only after long experience, and he notes that the passages Longinus cites are similar to Matthew Arnold's "touchstones." Finally, he observes that Longinus's requisites for sublimity—"words, thought, conception, imagination, feeling"—make for a "rare combination." Otherwise, Frye seems content simply to list the topics Longinus treats. These are marked with an asterisk on the following outline of *On the Sublime*:

Chapter Number

*1–2	Introduction [missing text]
*3–5	Instances of False Sublimity: Tumidity, Puerility, "Parenthyrsus"
6–7	Definition of Sublimity

8 Sources of True Sublimity

A. Sources that are innate: common to all art; independent of words

- *1. Great Thoughts, Conceptions
- *2. Strong Passion, Feeling

B. Sources that are acquired

3. Proper Handling of Figures
   (words in connection with thought)
4. Noble Diction
   (words in connection with one another)
5. Elevated Composition
   (words by themselves)

First Source: Thoughts (9–15)

*9 First mode for achieving sublimity: nurturing the soul to great conceptions requires the contemplation of great objects: gods, heroes, majesty of nature, etc. [missing text between 9.4 and 9.5]

10 Second mode: selection and integration of characteristics upon which a great subject's sublimity depends

*11 Third mode: Amplification or Magnification

12 (Third mode, continued)
[missing text between 12.2 and 12.3]

*13–14 Fourth mode: Imitation of Great Writers

15 Fifth Mode: Invention or Imagination

[Second source: Strong Passion, Feeling. Missing section]

*Third Source: Proper handling of figures (16–29)

16–17 Figures of thought: Adjuration (*apostrophe, oath, etc.)

18 Figures of thought: Questions
[missing section after 18.2]

19–29 Figures of Feeling

- 19 Asyndeton (omission of conjunction)
- 20–21 Anaphora (repetitions) and diatyposis (vivid descriptions)
- 22 Hyperbaton (inversions)
- 23 Polypota (accumulations, variations, climaxes)
- 24 Plural to Singular
- 25 Past to Present
- 26 Transposition of Persons

27 Change in Narrative Point of View

*28–29 Periphrasis (circumlocution)

*Fourth Source: Choice of Words (30–38)
30 Introduction to Diction
[missing text after 30.2 and before 31]
*31 Use of Common Language
*32 Metaphors
33–36 Digression on Genius (though not without fault) vs. the Commonplace
37 Similes
[missing text in 37 and beginning of 38]
38 Hyperbole

Fifth Source: Elevated Composition (39–43)
*39 Rhythm
*40 Shape of Sentence
*41–43 Features Antithetical to Sublimity: rhythmic affectation, "cut up" style, excessive concision, trivial expression
*Reasons for the decay of great literature (44)

The Aristotelian and Longinian Dialectic

If we assume that Margaret Virany gives a fairly complete account of Frye's lecture on Longinus, there is little evidence to suggest from his rather unexceptional summary of topics that Longinus would come to represent for him one of the two central approaches to literary criticism, first articulated in "Towards Defining an Age of Sensibility," a paper he presented in 1955, only a year after he gave his literary criticism lectures. Frye's thesis is that Aristotle and Longinus represent complementary approaches to literature. He returns to this proposition at the end of his theory of modes in the passage quoted above from *Anatomy of Criticism* (CW 22: 62–3), written about the same time, and then again in *The Well-Tempered Critic*, lectures delivered in 1961. From these three sources we can abstract the key elements in the opposition Frye sets up between Aristotle and Longinus. These are summarized in Figure 1. Except for what Frye says in his lecture about true sublimity involving a meeting between or a union of the poet and the reader, there is nothing in the class lecture that anticipates this broad critical dialectic.

We should note that the Longinian context for the sublime is different from the eighteenth-century one in which the sublime, distinguished from the beautiful, is identified by Shaftesbury, Dennis, Burke, Kant, and others with the picturesque in nature. This is the context in which Frye discusses Blake's view of the sublime, especially in reference to Burke, in *Fearful Symmetry*. The rhetorical context for the Longinian sublime emphasizes the effect of the qualities found not in nature but in thought and language.[37]

	Aristotelian (*Poema*)	**Longinian (*Poiesis*)**
View Of Literature	Aesthetic: literature as product ("hieratic")	Creative, psychological: literature as process ("demotic")
Nature Of Poem	*Techne* or artistic artifact; poem as product; imitation	Poem as process; expression; creation; locus of sublime passages
Central Conception	Katharsis	*Ekstasis*
Spectator	Detached from work of art and from author	Identification of reader, poem, and poet; individualized response, based on participation
Chief Interest	Fictional forms (more useful for plays)	Thematic forms (more useful for lyrics)
Typical Metaphors	Of objective order; *natura naturata*	Of organism, genesis, and elevation; *natura naturans*
Focus	Human society and order of nature; metaphors of imitation	Prophetic; metaliterary; metaphors of divine creation or inspiration; oracular "touchstones"
Nature of Text	Text as single form; unified story	Text as sequence of epiphanies; series of ecstatic moments or points of expanding comprehension
Emphasis	Classical	Romantic
Poetic Imagery	Images or order and purpose	Images of mystery and vagueness

Figure 1

As already said, Frye is a dialectical thinker, frequently seeking to unify the many oppositions contained in his criticism as a matter of course. In his late work, this is often achieved through the method of the great synthesizer, Hegel, who takes the contraries to another level through a process he calls *Aufhebung*. Frye almost always resists the Kierkegaardian *either/or* solution. But unity is not achieved at the expense of variety, and in his notebooks he never tires of insisting that opposites are never resolved by reconciliation, harmony, or agreement. Such terms relate to propositional language and are forms of what he calls "imperialistic compulsion" (CW 6: 653). In one of his notebooks from the mid-1960s, Frye wrote: "I have always distrusted what I call Reuben the Reconciler in thought: the syncretism that 'reconciles' Plato & Aristotle or St. Thomas & Marx. I think every great structure of thought or imagination is a universe in itself, identical with and interpenetrating every other, but not similar or harmonizable with any other" (CW 9: 39). At about the same time Frye wrote in his "Letter to the English Institute, "I wish we could throw away the notion of 'reconciling,' and use instead some such conception as 'interpenetration.' Literature itself is not a field of conflicting arguments but of interpenetrating visions" (CW 27: 216). Earlier—in the *Anatomy*—Frye had taken a different position regarding reconciliation. The Bible, he writes,

> may be examined from an aesthetic or Aristotelian point of view as a single form, as a story in which pity and terror, which in this context are the knowledge of good and evil, are raised and cast out. Or it may be examined from a Longinian point of view as a series of ecstatic moments or points of expanding apprehension—this approach is in fact the assumption on which every selection of a text for a sermon is based. Here we have a critical principle which we can take back to literature and apply to anything we like, a principle in which the "holism," as it has been called, of Coleridge and the discontinuous theories of Poe, Hulme, and Pound are reconciled. (CW 22: 305)

Complementarity, Ekstasis, and the Kerygmatic

To reconcile means to restore to a unity, or to make things compatible or agreeable with each other. After the *Anatomy*, did Frye change his mind about the possibility of reconciling the holistic approach of Aristotle with the discontinuous one of Longinus? It is difficult to see how the two ways of seeing a text—as an organic whole or as a series of ecstatic moments—can be brought together as a single "critical principle." Frye does say in an endnote in the *Anatomy* that the "conception of Aristotelian aesthetic catharsis and Longinian psychological ecstasis ... [are] complementary to one another" (CW 22: 411), complementarity suggesting that what is missing in one approach is supplied by the other. Whatever the reason for Frye's both affirming and denying the principle of reconciliation, it is clear that as he moved beyond the *Anatomy*, interpenetration did become an increasingly important principle for him. He uses interpenetration to define a kind of experience, a way of understanding, a process of enlightenment, a religious final cause, and a visionary perception. Around the word "interpenetration" cluster a host of additional verbal formulas that help to define it, and interpenetration is a function of the Hegelian *Aufhebung*.

"Complement" comes from the Latin meaning to fill up or complete. Two years after the *Anatomy* was published, Frye defined a "complete" theory of criticism in these terms:

> There are traditionally two main centres of emphasis in the theory of criticism, sometimes described by the words *poesis* and *poema*. The former, or Longinian, centre is primarily an interest in the psychological process of poetry, and in the rhetorical relation (often arrived at by indirection) set up between poet and reader. The latter, or Aristotelian, centre is primarily an interest in the aesthetic product, and is based on a specific aesthetic judgment, detached by catharsis from moral anxieties and emotional perturbations. Any complete theory of criticism needs both, but in a complete theory the aesthetic judgment takes precedence, for the Longinian interest is in enthusiasm, or what "carries us away," in other words in what uncritical feelings we may trust to afterwards. (CW 21: 277).

We encounter here Frye's privileging, in the 1950s, the Aristotelian over the Longinian approach: the aesthetic view takes precedence over the enthusiasm of *ekstasis*, as the feelings generated when we are transported are not subject to critical scrutiny. But as Frye continued to reflect on the complementary critical approaches, he leaned more and more in the Longinian direction. In one of his *Late Notebooks*, he has this reprimand to himself for not including Longinus in his account of the oracular, kerygmatic mode of language: "Longinus, you idiot. Why did you leave him out of chapter four? Most of him is the fragmentary, oracular, individualized, that's-for-me kerygma" (CW 5: 343). Frye is referring to chapter 4 of *Words with Power*. In chapters 2 and 3, he has been exploring the relation between the rhetorical and the poetic. He then turned to the relation between the poetic and kerygmatic, mending his omission by saying this about Longinus:

> [W]e need the guidance of a critic who understands what we have called the ecstatic state of response, and the difference, or contrast, between the ideological rhetoric that persuades and the proclamation that takes one out of oneself. The best of such critics is the first- or second-century writer whom we know only as Longinus. The title of Longinus' treatise,

> *Peri Hypsous*, is usually translated *On the Sublime*, which refers to an eighteenth-century adaptation of his ideas. The most effective part of *On the Sublime* deals with brief passages—"touchstones," as Matthew Arnold would call them—which stand out from their context. This we may call the oracular or discontinuous prophetic, the passage in the text where we suddenly break through into a different dimension of response. Longinus' examples come from Greek literature, but one—he was probably a Jew or a Christian—is the "Let there be light" verse from Genesis. (CW 26: 106)[38]

The "proclamation that takes one out of oneself" is what Frye calls kerygma, a term he introduced in *The Great Code*, meaning the rhetoric of proclamation. But in *Words with Power* he expands the meaning of kerygma far beyond what it had meant in *The Great Code*. It now becomes synonymous with the prophetic utterance, the metaliterary perception that extends one's vision, and the Longinian ecstatic response to any text, sacred or secular, that "revolutionizes our consciousness."[39] Kerygma takes metaphorical identification "a step further and says: 'you are what you identify with'" (CW 26: 110). We enter the kerygmatic realm when the separation of "active speech and reception of speech" merges into unity (CW 26: 111).

Frye's late work often focuses on ecstatic states and the revolutionizing and expanding of consciousness that results from the experience of *ekstasis*. Kerygma moves beyond the poetic, embracing the reader's existential experience. The highest states of this experience are a function of what Frye calls existential or, following Heidegger, ecstatic metaphor. In one of his *Words with Power* notebooks Frye writes: "Metaphor is the attempt to open up a channel or current of energy between subject and object. It begins in ecstatic metaphor (Stone Age painting and 'primitive' music), and literature develops in proportion as the sense of a split between subject and object becomes habitual. The link with religion is there because metaphor creates a 'Thou' world between the 'I' and the 'it,' and the god is the stabilized metaphor" (CW 6: 537). In *Words with Power*, Frye proposes three levels of metaphorical experience: the imaginative, the erotic, and the existential or ecstatic. As we move up the ladder of metaphorical experience, the difference between identity and difference continues to lessen until we arrive at the highest level, an ecstatic state in which, Frye says, "there is a sense of presence, a sense of uniting ourselves with something else" (CW 26: 85). Such a state is Longinian *ekstasis* or transport—a being put out of its place. "In the ecstatic state," Frye writes, "there is a sense of presence, a sense uniting ourselves with something else" (CW 26: 85).

Moments of intense consciousness for Frye move us beyond time and space into a world of pure identity that is an altogether different order of experience:

> Continued study of literature and the arts brings us into an entirely new world, where creation and revelation have different meanings, where the experience of time and space is different. As its outlines take shape, our standards of reality and illusion get reversed. It is the illusions of literature that begin to seem real, and ordinary life, pervaded as it is with all the phony and lying myths that surround us, begins to look like the real hallucination, a parody of the genuine imaginative world. The glimpses that I have had of the imaginative world have kept me fascinated for nearly half a century. (CW 7: 567)

If we step back from the total body of Frye's work, we can see how the Aristotelian and Longinian complementary approaches play out in his own career. The first phase, in which the *Anatomy* looms large, is schematic, analytical, systematic, and, like the first chapters of the *Poetics*, given to taxonomy. The *Anatomy* appropriates and redefines, as indicated above, a host of Aristotle's central terms. Its focus is on the conventions of the aesthetic product as an object. But once Frye turned his attention to the Bible, Longinian *ekstasis* became the focus of his attention. Frye himself notes the change in emphasis:

> [M]any of the most intense forms of human experience take some form of ecstatic metaphor. The hypothetical nature of literature, its ironic separation from all statements of assertion, was as far as I got in my *Anatomy of Criticism*, published nearly thirty years ago. The literary imagination seemed to me then, as in large part it does now, to be primarily a kind of model-thinking, an infinite set of possibilities of experience to expand and intensify our actual experience. But the *Anatomy* had led me to the scripture or sacred book as the furthest boundary to be explored in the imaginative direction, and I then became increasingly fascinated with the Bible, as a book dominated by metaphor throughout, and yet quite obviously not content with an ironic removal from experience or assertion. Clearly one had to look at other aspects of the question, and reconsider the cultural context of metaphor, as something that not only once had but may still have its roots in ecstatic experience. (CW 18: 348–9)

In his late work Frye repeatedly explores those moments of intense consciousness that move us beyond time and space into the mythical world of pure identity. The key issue here is the experience of myth and metaphor. It is possible, Frye feels, to recapture the intensity of perception that was available to people in Vico's age of the gods. These are what he calls "moments of ecstatic union," or what we refer to as peak experiences—epiphanic moments that take us away from ordinary waking consciousness. Here are two typical accounts of such experience.

> The poem or painting is in some respects a "hallucination": it is summoned up out of the artist's mind and imposed on us, and is allied to delirium tremens or pretending that one is Napoleon. Blake would say that such creative hallucinations are spiritual visions, and that what they present is more detailed, more vivid, and more accurate than anything that normal eyesight affords. In other respects a work of art is like a dream, but it does not introduce us to the ordinary dream world, where we retreat from reality into our withdrawn selves. It takes us into the world of social vision that informs our waking life, where we see that most of what we call "reality" is the rubbish of leftover human constructs. It speaks with authority, but not the familiar authority of parental or social conditioning: there will always be, I expect, some mystery about the real source of its authority. (CW 7: 566–7)

> Moments of ecstatic union ... may come and go, like flashes of lightning, but some moments are ... the frozen or simultaneously grasped aspects of a *mythos* or continuous narrative. Within the limitations of human life, the most highly developed human types are those whose lives have become, as we say, a legend, that is lives no longer contemplating a vision of objective revelation or imprisoned within a subjective dream. The New Testament presents the ultimate human life as a divine and human Logos, but the Logos has transcended its relation to logic and has expanded into mythos, a life which is, so to speak, a kind of self-narration, where action and awareness of action are no longer clashing with each other. (CW 18: 325)

Such ecstatic moments transport one into a purely symbolic world that is given to recording "portents or auguries of what life could be." "It is worth any amount of commonplace life," Frye says, "to purchase one of them" (CW 18: 336). He remarks that we try to capture the intensity of experience involved in the identification of metaphor with such words as "magical" and "religious" (CW 18: 294). These moments of intense perception are what Blake calls seeing with a twofold vision. When such perception takes place, Frye says, "the whole world is humanized" (CW 4: 183). Or again,

> Metaphor, as a bridge between consciousness and nature, is in fact a microcosm of language itself. It is precisely the function of language to overcome what Blake calls the "cloven fiction" of a subject contemplating an object.... Language from this point of view becomes a single gigantic metaphor, the uniting of consciousness with what it is conscious of. This union is Ovid's metamorphosis in reverse, the transfiguring of consciousness as it merges with articulated meaning. In a more specifically religious area this third order would become Martin Buber's world of "Thou," which comes between the consciousness that is merely an "I" and a nature that is merely an "it." (CW 18: 349)

Transport in Frye's Late Writings

Longinian *ekstasis* has a central role to play in what Frye refers to variously as the transfiguring, the intensifying, the revolutionizing, or the expanding of consciousness. Beginning in the late 1950s, he devoted a great deal of energy to designing a framework for the development of the stages of religious consciousness. He referred to these stages as the three awarenesses. He even contemplated writing a book about the topic, and he speculated about a somewhat mysterious fourth awareness.[40] Awareness as a category, however, tends to disappear from Frye's vocabulary in the 1980s. The fourth *awareness* of the notebooks is transformed into speculations about higher levels of *consciousness*. For Frye one of the central archetypal scenes of the intensity of consciousness that arises from the desire to identify is found in the Paleolithic cave drawings, references to which appear on more than thirty occasions in his work. The cave drawings represent "the titanic will to identify" (CW 18: 346).

> When one considers the skill and precision of these works, and the almost impossible difficulties of positioning and lighting surrounding their creation, we begin to grasp something of the intensity behind them to unite human consciousness with its own perceptions, an intensity we can hardly imagine now. Magical motives, such as maintaining a supply of game animals by picturing them on the cave walls, seem utterly inadequate: for one thing, many of the figures are evidently human beings in animal skins. In any case such caves are the wombs of creation, where

> conscious distinctions have no relevance and only pure identity is left. (CW 26: 215–16)

The cave drawings at Lascaux, Altamira, and elsewhere are an example of what Lévy-Bruhl called *participation mystique*, the imaginative identification with things, including other people, outside the self, or an absorption of one's consciousness with the natural world into an undifferentiated state of archaic identity.[41] In such a process of metaphorical identification the subject and object merge into one, but the sense of identity is existential rather than verbal (CW 6: 503).

But what does the intensity or expansion of consciousness entail for Frye? Answering this is something of a challenge, for Frye reflects on the implications of the phrase only obliquely. But let us take the clues Frye does provide and see how they align with the Longinian perspective.

1. Expanded consciousness is a function of *kerygma*. Ordinary rhetoric, "seldom comes near the primary concern of 'How do I live a more abundant life?' This latter on the other hand is the central theme of all genuine kerygmatic, whether we find it in the Sermon on the Mount, the Deer Park Sermon of Buddha, the Koran, or in a secular book that revolutionizes our consciousness. In poetry anything can be juxtaposed, or implicitly identified with, anything else. Kerygma takes this a step further and says: 'you are what you identify with.' We are close to the kerygmatic whenever we meet the statement, as we do surprisingly often in contemporary writing, that it seems to be language that uses man rather than man that uses language" (CW 26: 110).

This is a principle that Longinus affirms in his account of the excellencies of Demosthenes, "allied to the highest sublimity and perfected to the utmost." His "mighty gifts," which were "absorbed bodily within himself, ... we may deem heaven sent (for it would not be right to term them *human*)" (34.4)

2. Expanded consciousness does not necessarily signify religion or a religious experience, but it can be "the precondition for any ecumenical or everlasting-gospel religion" (CW 5: 17). Moreover, the raising of consciousness is revelation (CW 5:61). Longinus does not speak directly about religion, though he does say that the true sublime uplifts the soul (7.2) and elevates the spirit (33.4), and that sublimity raises human beings "near the majesty of God" and so "transcends the human" (36.1, 3).

3. Whatever the techniques used to expand consciousness (e.g., yoga, Zen, psychosynthesis, meditation, drugs), or whatever forms it takes (e.g., dreams, fantasies, the "peak experiences" described by Abraham Maslow, ecstatic music), the language of such consciousness always turns out to be metaphorical. Thus literature is the guide to higher consciousness, just as Virgil was Dante's guide to the expanded vision represented by Beatrice (CW 6: 717; CW 26: 40–1). Still, Frye believes that language is the primary means of "intensifying consciousness, lifting us into a new dimension of being altogether" (CW 6: 717). For Longinus, language is also one of the keys to the sublime—the third source for the poet who wants his work to transport the reader—and he devotes chapter 32 to metaphor. After an extensive catalogue of metaphors in Plato, he concludes that "figurative language contains great natural power, and that metaphors contribute to the sublime" (32.6).

4. *Vision* is the word that best fits the heightened awareness that comes with the imagination's opening of the doors of perception. What the subject sees may be "only an elusive and vanishing glimpse. Glimpse of what? To try to answer this question is to remove it to a different category of experience. If we knew what it was, it would be an object perceived in time and space. And it is not an object, but something uniting the objective with ourselves" (CW 26: 83). The "kerygmatic breakthrough," Frye writes, "always contains some sense of 'time has stopped.' The sequential movement has become a focus, or fireplace. In intensified consciousness the minute particular shines by its own light (or burns in its own life-fire)" (CW 5: 290).

Again, *ekstasis* means a being put out of its place, which Longinus eloquently captures in this passage:

> Nature has appointed us men to be no base nor ignoble animals; but when she ushers us into life and into the vast universe as into some great assembly, to be as it were spectators of the mighty whole and the keenest aspirants for honour, forthwith she implants in our souls the unconquerable love of whatever is elevated and more divine than we. Wherefore not even the entire universe suffices for the thought and contemplation within the reach of the human mind, but our imaginations often pass beyond the bounds of space, and if we survey our life on every side and see how much more it everywhere abounds in what is striking, and great, and beautiful, we shall soon discern the purpose of our birth. (35.2–3)

5. The principle behind the epiphanic experience that permits things to be seen with a special luminousness is that "things are not fully seen until they become hallucinatory. Not actual hallucinations, because those would merely substitute subjective for objective visions, but objective things transfigured by identification with the perceiver. An object impregnated, so to speak, by a perceiver is transformed into a presence" (CW 26: 87). This is analogous to Longinus's view that the sublime casts a spell over us (1.4).

6. Intense consciousness does not sever one from the body or the physical roots of experience. "The word spiritual in English," Frye writes,

> may have a rather hollow and booming sound to some: it is often detached from the spiritual body and made to mean an empty shadow of the material, as with churches who offer us spiritual food that we cannot eat and spiritual riches that we cannot spend. Here spirit is being confused with soul, which traditionally fights with and contradicts the body, instead of extending bodily experience into another dimension. The Song of Songs ... is a spiritual song of love: it expresses erotic feeling on all levels of consciousness, but does not run away from its physical basis or cut off its physical roots. We have to think of such phrases as "a spirited performance" to realize that spirit can refer to ordinary consciousness at its most intense: the *gaya scienza*, or mental life as play.... Similar overtones are in the words *esprit* and *Geist*. (CW 26: 119)

Or again, St. John of the Cross makes "a modulation from existential sex metaphor (M_2) to existential expanding of consciousness metaphor (M_1)" (CW 5: 120). As in *Aufhebung*, things lifted to another level do not cancel their connection to the previous level: "M_2" is still present at the higher level. Chapter 6 ("The Garden") of *Words with Power* "is concerned partly, if not mainly, with getting over the either–or antithesis between the spiritual and the physical, Agape love and Eros love" (CW 6: 451). Still again, "spiritual love expands from the erotic and does not run away from it" (CW 26: 195).

The best account in Longinus of the uniting of soul and body is his analysis of Sappho's "Peer of Gods" lyric: "Are you not amazed how at one instant she summons, as though they were all alien from herself and dispersed, soul, body, ears, tongue, eyes, colour? Uniting contradictions, she is, at one and the same time, hot and cold, in her senses and out of her mind, for she is either terrified or at the point of death. The effect desired is that not one passion only should be seen in her, but a concourse of the passions" (10.3).

7. Intensified consciousness is represented by images of both ascent and descent: "[I]mages of ascent are connected with the intensifying of consciousness, and images of descent with the reinforcing of it by other forms of awareness, such as fantasy or dream. The most common images of ascent are ladders, mountains, towers, and trees; of descent, caves or dives into water" (CW 26:138). These images, which arrange themselves along the *axis mundi*, are revealed with exceptional insight in some of Frye's most powerfully perceptive writing—the last four chapters of *Words with Power*. In these concentrated chapters, Frye illustrates how four central archetypes connect the ordinary world to the world of higher consciousness: the mountain and the cave emphasizing wisdom and the word, and the garden and the furnace emphasizing love and the spirit.

Longinus focuses on elevation, though he does remark on the sublimity of Ajax's silence in the underworld (9.2), and he notes that we admire the imagery of both the "celestial fires" and the "subterranean fire" of the craters of Etna (35.4)

The notion of expanded consciousness, which appears everywhere in Frye's late work, is related to many things other than Longinian *ekstasis*. It is linked to the thesis of his final book, *The Double Vision*, to Patanjali's yoga, to the German mystics (especially Eckhart and Boehme), and to other forms of the visionary and kerygmatic breakthrough that was the goal of Frye's quest. But of the two approaches to criticism—the Aristotelian and the Longinian—Frye ends up decidedly in the Longinian camp. This does not gainsay the insights of the *Anatomy*, which continues to have widespread interest and application. But the Longinian thrust of *The Great Code*, *Words with Power*, *The Double Vision*, *Myth and Metaphor*, and the three volumes of his notebooks on the Bible (CW 5, 6, and 13) suggest that Frye did not try to resolve the Aristotle–Longinus antithesis with still another of his many applications of the Hegelian *Aufhebung*. The two approaches remain complementary, but the final accent of Frye's own allegiance is to Longinus.

Appendix: Margaret (née Kell) Virany's Class Notes on Longinus from Frye's 1954 Course in Literary Criticism

DEC. 10.
Longinus
—minister of Zenobia, Queen of Palmyra in Africa—213–292 AD
—fragments only
—"Sublime"—this really means anything that can raise anything up
—written to Terentianus—to correct a lost work of Sicilius
—1–6 and 41–43—false sublimity
—7—grandeur of conception
—vehement, deep feeling
—17–29—careful manipulation of figures
—30–38—nobility of phrase
—39–40—word order
—42–43 (with 1–6)
—44–decay of eloquence
—he gets at the heart of great writing

Purpose of sublimity
—Not persuasion but transport. Appeal of writing is immediate, not reasoned out
—can it be used for teaching?
    —non-committal
    —need for some teaching
—missing section
    Defects of Style
    —puerility—learned trifling, insipid
    —parenthyrsus—uncalled for display of emotion
        —more in speaking than writing
    —comes from a craze for novelty
Needed for the Sublime
    —lofty thought and lofty words
    —submission to great predecessors
Figures of Speech
    —amplification
    —rhetorical treatment of the commonplace
        —images—writer has clear picture and gives it to readers

—no arbitrary devices
—artificial ring in figures—harmful
e.g., from Demosthenes and others
—apostrophe—emotional appeal

Periphrasis
—round about way of saying things
e.g., death = destined path
—warned that it could fall flat
—Molière satirized this. Popular in the eighteenth century

Diction
—lost section
*beautiful words are the light of thought (not realized in England until Coleridge)
—cf. stained-glass window and light
—words and thought must be correlated
—twenty metaphors could be good in a passage. One could spoil it; i.e., the number doesn't matter

Rhythm
—can be too pronounced

Literary Criticism
—difficult. First to point this out
"crowning fruit of long experience"—Can person get it by study? Thinking of criticism as judicial rather than historical. Fewer critics than creative artists.

False sublimity
—the true lifts up
—two minds meet—creator and reader
—immediate response of the reader
—what appeals to all men at all places and times. Universal appeal
"Men" = men of literary taste
—test—wanted to read it again
—suggestive powers
—test—lasting comparison with the recognized great
—e.g., Matthew Arnold's "touchstones"

Sublimity—words, thought, conception, imagination, feeling
—a rare combination
—prefers Iliad to Odyssey
—typical Greek fear of so much fantasy in the Odyssey

Faultlessness
—greatness not to be confused with accuracy. The former appeals while the latter never can. A touch of genius can overcome defects. "Faultless mediocrity" versus "genuine greatness." Perfection annoys us in life or literature. Great poet (1) ability—feel and experience (2) ability to communicate feeling (3) great soul—imagination. Faults come from within

3

Frye and Joachim of Floris

The Italian abbot Joachim of Floris (also Fiore or Flora) (ca. 1132–1202) makes more than three dozen appearances in Frye's published and unpublished writings, which suggests that the connections between the two might be worth exploring. In reading the few texts of Joachim that are available in English and in studies about him by the pre-eminent Joachimite scholar Marjorie Reeves and others (Bernard McGinn, Delno C. West and Sandra Zimdars-Swartz, Beatrice Hirsch-Reich, Morton Bloomfield), I have been struck by the number of parallels between the two visionaries.[42]

Who Was Joachim of Floris?

Joachim was a biblical exegete, mystic, and philosopher of history. Sometime before 1192 he founded the monastic order of San Giovanni in Fiore, whence his name derives. After a pilgrimage to the Holy Land in 1159, he underwent a spiritual crisis and conversion. For a time he was a hermit and an itinerant preacher in his native Calabria, but he eventually joined the Order of Cistertians and applied himself chiefly to biblical interpretation, seeking to uncover hidden meanings in Scripture, especially Revelation. Pope Urban appointed a deputy abbot so that Joachim might devote more time to his writings. Although he received the favour of three other popes, he was not an uncontroversial figure. The Cistertian order denounced him as a runaway. His work was condemned by the Fourth Lateran Council in 1215 and in 1255–56 by the special commission set up to review his interpretations of Scripture. His work was dismissed by both Bonaventura and Aquinas, yet Dante enshrines Joachim, "spirit-fired and prophet true," in the second sun canto of the *Paradiso* (canto 12:140–1).[43] In the twentieth century, Joachim's influence can be seen in Yeats and Jung—two writers who influenced Frye—and in Kandinsky.[44]

Joachim's three chief works—*Liber Concordiae Novi ac Veteris Testamenti* (*Harmony of the Old and New Testaments*, often called the *Book of Concordance*), *Expositio in Apocalypsim* (*Exposition of the Book of Revelation*), *Psalterium Decem Cordarum* (*Psaltery of Ten Strings*)—focus on scriptural prophecy, especially as it relates to the future of the Church. Joachim is best known for his view of the three states or ages of the world, based on his understanding of the Trinity. The age of the Father or the Old Testament order of worldly affairs was characterized by power and obedience to law and issued in the arousing of fear. It was the period of marriage, work, servitude, and slavery. The age of the Son was the New Testament age of faith instead of works. It was an age of the clergy, the organized church, and the sacraments. It begins with the birth of Christ and continues until 1260, the year of the advent, Joachim speculated, of the age of the Spirit, which would usher in the period of what Revelation calls the "everlasting gospel." The age of the Spirit was an age of autonomy, in which the absolute freedom contained in the gospel message would prevail. The age of the Spirit was the monastic age, so that the need for the Church and other constraining institutions would effectively disappear. All would be freed from the letter of the Gospel, and universal love, freedom, and justice would reign. Frye says that "Joachim of Floris has a hint of an order of things in which the monastery takes over the church & the world" (CW 13: 17), but Joachim's monastic ideal is certainly more than a hint. The age of the Spirit is a revolutionary and transformative process. As Eric Hobsbawm writes, Joachim "distinguished between the reign of *justice* or *law*, which is essentially an equitable regulation of social relations in an imperfect society, and the reign of *freedom*, which is the perfect society" (11). Joachim conceived his three major works as a unified Trinitarian sequence. The *Book of Concordance* centred on the Old Testament and was typologically connected to the Apocalypse of the risen Christ in the *Exposition of the Book of Revelation*. The *Psaltery of Ten Strings*, in turn, centred on spiritual understanding. "The Spirit," Frye writes, "is the voice of inspiration & prophecy, the Christian oracle, of whom the Mother is a hypostatic form: hence it's involved in all future-centered revolutionary constructs like that of Joachim of Floris" (CW 9: 198).

Frye's Knowledge of Joachim

Frye first encountered Joachim's idea of the three ages in Oswald Spengler's *The Decline of the West* (1:19–20), a book he discovered in the Hart House Library during the 1930–31 academic year. How much of the *Decline* the eighteen-year-old Frye read at the time is uncertain, but he could not have missed Spengler's remarks on Joachim toward the beginning of the introduction to volume 1:

> On the very threshold of the Western Culture we meet the great Joachim of Floris ... the first thinker of the Hegelian stamp who shattered the dualistic world-form of Augustine, and with his essentially Gothic intellect stated the new Christianity of his time in the form of a third term to the reli-

> gions of the Old and New Testaments, expressing them respectively as the Age of the Father, the Age of the Son and the Age of the Holy Ghost. His teaching moved the best of the Franciscans and the Dominicans, Dante, Thomas Aquinas, in their inmost souls and awakened a world-outlook which slowly but surely took entire possession of the historical sense of our Culture. (19–20)

Frye reports that during the summer of 1932 he read *The Decline of the West* in the YMCA in Edmonton ("one of the great nights of my life") (CW 25: 28).[45] As a twenty-year-old, then, Frye had encountered Joachim twice through at least one secondary source. Three years later we find Frye referring to Joachim in two papers he wrote during his final year at Emmanuel College, "The Augustinian Interpretation of History" and "The Life and Thought of Ramond Lull." In the former he wrote:

> In the Middle Ages the only contributions to a philosophy of history could come from thinkers addicted to mysticism, to reflection rather than systematization; that is, with sympathies not altogether given up to the development of systematic philosophy, yet enough influenced by it to work it into their thought. Such a figure, quasi-mystical and almost Oriental, was Joachim of Floris (1145–1202), whose interpretation was threefold. Augustine's view of the temporal progression (not the most important element of his philosophy of history) was flat, balanced, antithetical, and hinged on the Incarnation. The world of time, after its creation, was the scene of a dramatic change from comparative darkness to comparative light. This was the only essential alteration possible to the *civitas terrena*. The great medieval abbot visioned an organic development in which the age of the Father, or the reign of law, before Christianity, advanced to the age of the Son, or reign of the Gospel, to be finally fused in the age of the Spirit, a sort of Kantian kingdom of ends in which all hierarchical distinctions were to be abolished. The general progression was that of the liberation of the life of contemplation from that of action—the eternal struggle to make thought independent of being. (CW 3:210)

Frye went on to say that Joachim stands midway between Augustine's religious view of history and Hegel's philosophical view. "Joachim, partly religious and partly philosophical, superimposes one on the other in time, connecting them by the era ushered in by the Incarnation" (CW 3: 211). In his essay on Lull, Frye says only that Lull's prose romance *Blanquerna* is "a worthy connecting link between Joachim of Floris and the Grail legends of the Middle Ages and the great Utopian writers of the Renaissance" (CW 3: 223). Frye is clearly correct in saying that Joachim displaced Augustine's long-held view of history and the Book of Revelation. West and Zimdars-Swartz contend that to Augustine

> [t]he historical trend was one of deterioration. His vision was of that of a more perfect age in the past and of another yet to come. He was living in an age sure to decline until the end of the world order immediately preceding the Second Advent. He focussed in the Kingdom as a then-present reality that had begun with the First Advent.... [he] viewed the Apocalypse as instructional instead of prophetic. (12)

Joachim turned this view upside down.[46]

The sources of Frye's knowledge of Joachim are uncertain. He never cites the titles of any of Joachim's works, and there were no texts by Joachim in his own library. The secondary sources he lists at the end of his Augustine paper do not mention Joachim even in passing. Whatever sources were available to him were relatively few, as Frye was writing almost two decades before the virtual rediscovery of Joachim, beginning in the 1950s,[47] and even now scholars continue to use photographically reproduced copies of sixteenth-century Latin editions. Frye had a fairly extensive knowledge of Latin, and it is of course possible that he had access to the sixteenth-century Latin texts. What seems more likely is that his knowledge of Joachim came largely, if not entirely, from secondary sources. More than a decade after his student papers, Frye ran across the fairly comprehensive chapter on Joachim in Karl Löwith's *Meaning in History*, which he reviewed for the *Canadian Forum* in 1949.[48] The same year, in a lecture to students in English Poetry and Prose, 1500–1660 (English 2i) he wrote in his *Diaries* of "the monastic overtones in Utopia, of Joachim of Floris & the monastery militant, so to speak: the conquest of the world by the monastic ideal" (CW 8: 86). But the *Diaries* reveal nothing about his reading of Joachim.

Parallels

In my opening paragraph I mentioned the parallels between Joachim and Frye. Here are a dozen:

1. **Both are on a spiritual pilgrimage.** Reeves and Hirsch-Reich begin their book on Joachim's *figurae* by saying that the opening phrase of his *Book of Concord*, drawn from Hebrews 13:14, "strikes the keynote of the

mood in which he sets out on his labours: that of the spiritual quest which is the true life of Man. The traditional interpretation of these words from Hebrews is that of the pilgrimage from this earthly life to the world beyond. While accepting this, Joachim also looks toward the goal in this life, and for this purpose he will later use all the great Biblical images of the pilgrimage" (1).[49] In *Northrop Frye: Religious Visionary* I argued that Frye was on a spiritual pilgrimage and that his quest took three forms. First, there is a horizontal pilgrimage in pursuit of an object of desire. Frye begins with the literary universe of William Blake, and he seeks with unremitting energy the verbal formulations that will carry him to a double vision lying beyond the poetic. This is Frye's own horizontal quest. He calls it a purgatorial journey, and its goal is apocalyptic vision: an interpenetrating, kerygmatic universe in which all subject-object distinctions have been erased and lifted to another level. The shape of the journey is often, in the second place, projected cyclically, and the contour of Frye's career could be described as a cycle, beginning with *Fearful Symmetry* and coming full circle in *The Double Vision*. "The way or journey is a series of cycles (journey of course is from *journée*) where we get 'up' in the morning and 'fall' asleep at night. At a certain point the cycle stops for us—there's finally a winter-night-old age-sea point with no spring-dawn-birth-rain following. We all take that road; the question is whether (or when) an upward spiral moves against it. It does, of course, but there must be a point at which rebirth must give place to resurrection" (CW 5: 289). The journey assumes still a third shape in the last half of *Words with Power*, where the horizontal and cyclic quests are displaced by descending and ascending movements along the *axis mundi*: "ascent & descent are a verticalized journey" (CW 5: 315), the way down and the way up in the Heraclitean formula. Or in another formulation, the path or way of the journey becomes metaphorically a "reconstructed ladder" (CW 5: 23).

2. **Both experienced sudden illuminations,** which were less mystical experiences than epiphanies, in which they received a vision of some topic they were struggling with that suddenly came together as a coherent pattern that made sense. "The major images were given to [Joachim]," writes Richard Bauckham, "in moments of visionary illumination, acting as a kind of conceptual breakthrough at points where Joachim had found his thought obstructed" (109). Reeves recounts two of these experiences, in which "what was given was not a specific answer to a specific question but an inspiration which freed his mind to work out the problems" (*Joachim of*

Fiore 5). Frye had similar experiences, which he referred to as epiphanies, illuminations, intuitions, and enlightenments.[50]

3. **Both were primarily exegetes interested in finding the meaning of texts;** their projects were fundamentally hermeneutical. Joachim has been called a prophet, but not in the sense of one who foretells or predicts future events. He was an interpreter of prophetic literature. In *The Critical Path*, Frye says that one of the two large critical questions that interest him is "How do we arrive at poetic meaning?" (CW 27: 8). This is a hermeneutical question, and discovering poetic meaning involves exegesis.

4. **Both always favoured the spirit over the letter in scriptural interpretation.** "You ought also to note," writes Joachim, "that the letter of the Old Testament was committed to the Jewish people, the letter of the New to the Roman people. The spiritual understanding that proceeds from both Testaments has been committed to the spiritual men" (McGinn, *Apocalyptic* 128). The dialectic of Word and Spirit is the driving force behind Frye's *Words with Power*. In this dialectic, Spirit is a many-layered term, one that I examine in the last chapter of *Northrop Frye: Religious Visionary*, but it is the unifying force that leads toward the gospel of love. In the apocalypse of the Word and Spirit dialogue, the Creation is transformed and renewed and "the U-shaped comic ending reverses the cycles of history, where resurrection abolishes rebirth and revolution-culbute abolishes revolution-turning wheel" (CW 5: 329). The age of the Spirit, Frye notes, is the same as Milton's Word of God in the heart (CW 15: 163),[51] which he also identifies with the Everlasting Gospel and the interpenetration of Word and Spirit.

5. **Both were typologists,** interested in the relationship between the events in the Old Testament and the New. The concords between the Old and New Testament that Joachim discovers result in a more or less standard form of biblical typology. Typological readings, of course, lie at the heart of Frye's two books on the Bible, Frye's account of the typological method of reading most extensively set down in chapters 5 and 6 of *The Great Code*.[52]

6. **Both focused on the Apocalypse as a text and a teleological event of great importance.** Joachim's *Exposition* is devoted to the Book of Revelation, and the Apocalypse is one of seven phases of revelation Frye

postulates in *The Great Code*. His most complete account of Revelation is in his lectures "Symbolism of the Bible" (CW 13: 584–600), which are accompanied by an intricately constructed chart of the structure of Revelation (CW 13: 591–4).

7. Both place great weight on what the Book of Revelation calls "the everlasting gospel." The phrase, which comes from Revelation 14:6, meant for Frye what it meant for Blake: the religion of Jesus, which is the embodiment of Blake's "all religions are one" thesis. In his *Descriptive Catalogue*, Blake says, "All had originally one language, and one religion: this was the religion of Jesus, the everlasting Gospel. Antiquity preaches the Gospel of Jesus" (543). In the unfinished poem *The Everlasting Gospel* Blake turns the tables on John's use of the phrase in Revelation 14:6, where it points to the proclamation of the imminent judgment of God. For Blake, the everlasting gospel had to do with forgiveness rather than punishment for sins, and Jesus turns out to be a kind of Promethean rebel. As Frye explains in *Fearful Symmetry*, "Blake does not mean by one religion the acceptance of a uniform set of doctrines by all men: he means the attainment of civilized liberty and the common vision of the divinity and unity of Man which is life in Jesus" (CW 14: 332). In "Blake's Treatment of the Archetype," Frye refers to Joachim in the context of "the everlasting gospel": the Book of Revelation "deals with what it describes, in a phrase which has fascinated so many apocalyptic thinkers from Joachim of Fiore to Blake, as the 'everlasting gospel,' the story of Jesus told not historically as an event in the past, but visually as a real presence" (CW 16: 201–2). And in his *Late Notebooks* Frye writes that the "Joachim of Floris notion, that there's a coming age of purely spiritual Christianity, an everlasting gospel, has always been central to my own thinking" (CW 5: 202). For Paul Tillich, Joachim means by the "everlasting gospel" that "the presence of the divine Spirit [is] in every individual, according to the prophecy of Joel, which is often used in this context. It is a *simplex intuitus veritatas*, a simple intuition of truth which all can have without intermediate authority. Freedom means the authority of the divine Spirit in the individual" (*History of Christian Thought* 179). As one might expect, such a view posed a threat to ecclesiastical authority, and in the thirteenth century what is known in the Joachimite literature as the "scandal of the Eternal Evangel" blew up in Paris. From this "scandal," which was essentially another of the countless power struggles in the Church, Joachim's authority eventually managed to emerge unscathed.[53] On the place of the church in the Joachimite scheme, Frye writes:

> I think in this conception of a Word–Church dialogue in the N.T. I'm coming back to my old historical vs. everlasting gospel thesis. The purely spiritual gospel preached by Jesus is also known to what Augustine called the anima naturaliter Christiana [the soul is naturally Christian], to Buddhists and Stoics and what not. What isn't known to them is the specific historical development known as the Christian Church, which is useful to have around as long as it doesn't make absurd and blasphemous pretensions. It's one of many ways in which the Holy Spirit operates: one can renounce the church without sinning against that Spirit: in fact one may well be working for it. Otherwise, why do contemporary writers on religion keep quoting Nietzsche, Heidegger, Marx, Freud? Fold my ass. There is no such thing as a Holy Catholic Church, but a church that knows it isn't catholic and is sincerely trying to become so is certainly worthy of respect. So I'm back to Joachim of Floris again; the age of the Son is a historical growth establishing the primitive form of the matured religion of the age of the Spirit. And I question whether it would be possible to have the mature religion without a primitive embryo still present in society. If only it could remember that it is embryonic!. (CW 6: 630)

8. Both took the medieval theory of four senses or levels of meaning—the historical, the allegorical or doctrinal, the moral or tropological, and the anagogic or heavenly—as an important hermeneutical starting point, and both added a fifth sense to the conventional four. This means that they both argued for an allegorical approach to textual meaning. Joachim writes in his *Book of Concordance* that *concordia* is not allegorical interpretation: it means only that there is a parallel or likeness between two people or events in the Old and New Testaments. *Allegoria*, on the other hand, "is the similarity of any small thing to an extremely large one, for example of a day to a year, of a week to an age, of a person to an order, or a city, or a nation, or a people, and a thousand similar instances. By way of illustration, Abraham is a single man who stands for the order of patriarchs in which there are many men" (McGinn, *Apocalyptic* 122). Allegorical meaning is what Joachim called *spiritualis intellectus*—spiritual knowledge or understanding that allows him to discover the hidden meanings in

Scripture. Frye's view of allegory is more expansive than Joachim's, and as distinct from Joachim, he sees allegory as a part of typology or *concordia*. Still, the following account would be congenial to Joachim's view of allegory:

> To some extent the Old Testament had to be read allegorically by the Christian, according to the principle later enunciated by St. Augustine: "In the Old Testament the New Testament is concealed; in the New Testament the Old Testament is revealed." Certain Messianic passages in the Old Testament were held to refer specifically to Jesus; the Jewish law was abolished as a ceremony but fulfilled as a type of the spiritual life. St. Paul in Galatians, commenting on the story of Abraham, Sarah, and Hagar, explicitly says that the story is an allegory, though it later became more exact to say that such stories had or contained allegorical meanings. Hence a doctrine of multiple meanings in Scripture was elaborated which could be applied to religious literature as well. (CW 27: 174)

9. Both held an optimistic theory of history, one that pointed in the direction of a new creation. "Many passages on the third *status*," writes McGinn, "can be read as expressing hope in a coming historical era that, whatever its deep roots in the abbot's organic view of the past, was to be a form of new creation.... For Joachim history was the story of the gradual triumph of spirit over flesh, of contemplation over literal-mindedness" (*Apocalyptic* 103, 107). In an essay on Spengler, Frye writes:

> If the death to rebirth transition from Classical to Western culture happened once, something similar could happen again in our day, though the transition would be to something bigger than another culture. This would imply three major periods of human existence: the period of primitive societies, the period of the organic cultures, and a third period now beginning. Spengler ... attacks and ridicules the three period view of ancient, medieval, and modern ages with ... a good deal of justification. But he also remarks that the notion of three ages has had a profound appeal to the Faustian consciousness, from Joachim of Fiore in the thirteenth century onward. It is possible that what is now beginning to take shape is the real "Third Reich," of which the Nazis produced so hideous a parody. (CW 11: 313–14)

Reeves shows how Joachim rejected the pessimistic cyclical view of history in favour of a positive linear one. "Joachimism," she writes, "shows how strong was the urge to find a more positive affirmation about the meaning of history itself. The linear pattern of successive stages must lead to a final stage of achievement within history itself. Joachim's Trinitarian pattern supplied the theological basis for this" (*Influence of Prophecy* 506).

10. Both had a reformer's mentality and took a rather dim view of the future of the institutional church. They were revolutionary thinkers, going against the grain of the conventional paradigms of thought and action. In many respects, Frye's whole career, like Blake's, was to think otherwise. "At what point," Frye asks, "did Xy [Christianity] throw away Paul's spiritual-natural antithesis and pick up his dismal shit about a soul-body combination that separates at death, leaving us with a discarnate soul until God gives the order for the resurrection of the body? This evil notion was concocted to keep man under the priest-king hierarchy. I suspect the Filioque clause[54] was added to subordinate the Spirit to the Son and reduce the former to continuing the priest-king authority in time. Not that the Eastern Churches did any better with it. Even if you do this, as Joachim of Floris realized, you turn history revolutionary and go through a 'reformation'" (CW 6: 714). Paul Tillich says about Joachim's ideas that they "are important because they had a dynamic, revolutionary, explosive power. The extreme Franciscans used his prophecies and applied them to their own order, and on that basis they revolted against the church. Many sectarian movements, including the sects of the Reformation on which much of American life is dependent, were directly or indirectly dependent on Joachim of Floris" (*History of Christian Thought* 179–80). Tillich goes on to mention as examples of these influences the Enlightenment philosophers, the socialist movement, and American Utopianism.[55] Frye was always attracted to religious dissidents, believing that if they were accused of heresy they were on to something important: "As in all repressive cultures, most of the more penetrating thinkers of the Middle Ages were dissidents accused or at least suspected of heresy: they included Siger of Brabant, Scotus Erigena, Peter Abelard, John Wyclif, Roger Bacon, Nicholas of Autrecourt, Meister Eckhart, William of Occam, and Joachim of Fiore" (CW 4: 219). In *The Great Code*, Frye writes:

> The full thrust of New Testament typology goes in two directions: into the future and into the eternal world, the two things

> coinciding with the apocalypse or Last Judgment. The one thing that would naturally be resisted by a socially established Church by every means in its power would be the suggestion of a transcending of its authority within history. Such teachings as those of Joachim of Fiore about a third historical age of the Spirit, which would succeed the Jewish age of the Father and the Christian ecclesiastical age of the Son, consequently were regarded as heretical. (CW 19: 104)[56]

As for the ecclesiastical age of the Son, Frye says, "Joachim of Floris reveals the suppressed feeling that the contentious age of Christianity, refining militant dogmas, going on crusades, torturing heretics and the like, is still immature" (CW 6: 651).

11. Both had highly developed theories of symbolism, and both had an interest especially in the symbolism of numbers (see below). The most complete version of Frye's theory of symbols is in the Second Essay of *Anatomy of Criticism*. Two later variations on the theory are "Symbols" (CW 4: 287–9) and "The Symbol as a Medium of Exchange" (CW 18: 327–41). The most comprehensive study of Joachim's view of the symbol is McGinn, "Symbolism in the Thought of Joachim of Fiore."

12. Both had to retreat from the administrative and functionary duties they were called on to perform in order to devote time to their writing.

The Three Ages

The central focus of Frye's scattered remarks on Joachim has to do with the latter's principle of the three ages. The eminent Joachimite scholar Marjorie Reeves has this summary of the three-age theory:

> Joachim worked out his philosophy of history, primarily in a pattern of "twos"—the concords between the two great dispensations (or Testaments) of history, the Old and the New. But already Joachim's spiritual experience was creating in his mind his truly original "pattern of threes." If the *spiritualis intellectus* springs from the letter of the Old and New Testaments, then history itself must culminate in a final age of the spirit that proceeds from both the previous ages. Thus was born his trini-

tarian philosophy of history in which the three Persons are, as it were, built into the time structure in the three ages or *status* of the Father, Son, and Holy Spirit.

The third *status* was to be won by the church only after arduous pilgrimage and great tribulation, like the Israelites marching through the wilderness and crossing the Jordan River into the Promised Land. As guides through this crucial stage, Joachim prophesied the advent of two new orders of spiritual men, one of hermits to agonize for the world on the mountaintop and one a mediating order to lead men on to the new spiritual plane. Although the third age belongs par excellence to contemplatives, secular clergy and laymen are not shut out of it. In a strange diagram, a "ground plan" of the New Jerusalem, various categories of monks are grouped around the seat of God, but below, secular clergy and tertiaries (lay members) live according to their rule. ("Joachim of Fiore," pars. 4–5)

In an expansion of a passage about Joachim's monastery taking over the church and the world, Frye identifies militant monasticism with a form of Christian yoga and then goes on to express his desire for a secular monastery:

I've said that the monastic movement—at least that phase of it that ended with the great Benedictine period—was in a way Christian yoga, & as such the Church's conquest of it was perhaps a more remarkable assimilation than its conquest of local cults. Putting this beside my idea of orthodox Christian mysticism as a Bhakti Yoga, it's easier to understand the association of such mysticism with militant monasticism. In the tendency of great mystics to create rival holy orders there is something of revolt, something of sacrifice, when the rival order is laid on the Church's altar. Hence the number of saints produced by mysticism—saints in the cynical official Roman sense of those who have acquired a special cultic significance from the Church for having been remarkably useful to it. But Joachim of Floris has a hint of an order of things in which the monastery takes over the church & the world. That is the expanded secular monastery I want: I want the grace of Castiglione as well as the grace of Luther, a graceful as well as a gracious God, and I want all men & women to enter the Abbey of Theleme where instead of poverty, chastity and obedience they will find richness, love and *fay ce que vouldras*; for what the Bodhisattva wills to do is good.[57] (CW 13: 16–17)

In his notebooks for *The Great Code*, Frye sets down an organizing pattern of what he conceived at the time as part four of the book (CW 13: 276). As he is always wont to do, he anatomizes his categories into a schema, this one a tripartite framework that includes Vico and Joachim. The various categories of his schema can be arranged in columns.

	Father	Son	Spirit
Joachim's three ages	Age of the Father	Age of the Son	Age of the Spirit
Form of language	Hieroglyphic	Hieratic	Demotic
Conceptual form	Mythological	Theological	Politico–psychological
Vico's ages	Age of the gods	Age of heroes	Age of the people
Demonic parody	OT Yahweh	Avenging Son of Last Judgment	Destroying angel
Emanation	Daughter (Kore, Athene, Maat)	Mother	Bride
Demonic parody	Totalitarian state	Jung's terrible mother	Demonic bride (siren, Kali)
Dominating conceptions	Presence (male) and contract (female)	Substance (Catholic) and principle (Protestant)	Process and symbol
Historical stage	Biblical and Classical	St. Thomas through Hegel	Rousseau through Marx, Nietzsche, and Freud

Except for Vico's three ages, which organizes Frye's theory of language in *The Great Code*, his threefold set of categories in the notebooks disappear from the book, but the notebook exercise does show how Joachim's three ages are a part of his imaginative consciousness. Joachim figures in eleven of Frye's notebook entries for *Words with Power*, though he is absent from the book itself. As indicated above, Frye's central categories have become Word and Spirit: he has collapsed Joachim's Father and Son into the Word. If the age of the Spirit is to occur, Frye thinks it will be in a Protestant context:

> I don't look for it [Joachim's purely spiritual Christianity] in the future of time, but ideally it's always there. I should quite cheerfully write off Protestantism as a transitional phase to it. But Catholic converts who turn back from the wilderness to Egyptian civilized life will never see the Promised Land. The road to Jesus' spiritual kingdom runs through Luther, perhaps Calvin: it gets pretty dry and narrow there, as Jesus said it would, but the self-sufficient Church just won't do. The same thing is

> true of Xy [Christianity] itself: it's superstitious compared to Judaism and intolerably inhumane compared to the greatest of the Greeks—but it's higher in human scale. I don't know what I mean by "human" here: certainly not that Christians are more human than Jews or Greeks—I'm following Paul's phrasing.[58] (CW 5: 202)

Following a reference to Catholicism's condemnation of Joachim's doctrine of the three ages as heretical, Frye writes in *The Double Vision*:

> Just as the Protestant church subordinates itself to the impact of Scripture, so in temporal matters it subordinates itself to the "higher powers," without claiming temporal authority. This renunciation extrudes the society of power from the church itself, which thereupon builds itself up on the pattern of Christian liberty, forming an apostolic community in which members are made free and equal by their faith. Temporal authority must then come to terms with this free and equal community in its midst. (CW 4: 262)[59]

"Physically," Frye says, "history moves towards the resurrection of the body; spiritually, it moves toward Joachim of Floris's ideal of an age of the Spirit" (CW 6: 640). Frank E. Manuel describes the features of the three ages in these terms: "The *Concordia* tells us that in the first we were under the law, in the second we were under grace, and in the third we shall be under still richer grace. The first was knowledge, the second was the power of wisdom, the third will be the fullness of knowledge. The first was spent in the submission of slaves, the second in the obedience of sons, the third in freedom. The first in suffering, the second in action, the third in contemplation. The first in fear, the second in faith, the third in love. The first is starlight, the second at dawn, the third in broad daylight" (40–1).

Picture Thinking: Symbolic Diagrams and Numbers

Like Frye, Joachim was a schematic thinker. His main works are full of symbolic illustrations: the ten-stringed psaltery, trees, eagles, alpha and omega, and circles of various kinds, among others.[60] Perhaps the most famous of these is his Trinitarian diagram based on the tripartite splitting of the tetragrammaton—the Hebrew consonants of God's name: Yod, He, Vav, He. Joachim derived his diagram from Peter Alfonsi, who arranged his version of the tetragrammaton by changing the Hebrew consonants to vowels (IEUE) and organizing them in a triangular diagram of three interlaced concentric circles: IE (the Father), EU (the Son), and UE (the Holy Spirit). In the original, the circle of the Father is rendered in green; of the Son, in blue; and of the Holy Spirit, in red. In this ingenious formulation, the second half of each pair of vowels became the first half of the succeeding pair. Joachim abandoned Alfonsi's triangular shape, but retained the interlocking concentric circles, known as Borromean rings.

As Reeves and Hirsch-Reich say, "The Abbot Joachim had a visual imagination. For him spiritual understanding was an activity of seeing.... As he writes, the images constantly arrange and rearrange themselves, as in a rich and complex dance" (20, 21). Reeves describes him as a "picture thinker" ("*Liber Figurarum*" 65). Bauckham concurs: "One very striking result of Marjorie Reeves's work, with Beatrice Hirsch-Reich, on the *figurae* of Joachim of Fiore is considerable new insight into Joachim's remarkable visual imagination. It is now abundantly clear that far from being mere illustrations, the *figurae* function as central elements in Joachim's theological thought" (109). The same thing can be said about the ways in which Frye projected his speculations, especially in his notebooks, into innumerable spatial forms and diagrammatic patterns, such as the Great Doodle, the HEAP scheme, and ogdoad.[61] Frye's schema are not illustrations but are constitutive in that they help to shape his vision.

Similarly with the symbolic significance both Joachim and Frye attached to numbers. In addition to the numbers two and three, Joachim built up an elaborate schema based on the numbers five, seven, twelve, and forty-two. Frye is more cautious about number symbolism, numerology, and synchronicity. In Notebook 44 he wrote, "Recurrent numbers, seven & twelve & the like, are elements of design only: they represent no hidden mystery or numinousness in things. Not even the trinitarian three or the Jungian four. There are twelve signs in the zodiac, but it would be equally easy to see nine or eleven or fourteen and a half. Only fractions seem so *vulgar*" (CW 5: 157–8). But at other places Frye certainly seems to think that numbers do contain some hidden mystery. He says in another notebook that seven and twelve are in fact "sacred numbers" (CW 13: 258),[62] in which case they would necessarily, it seems, embody some sense of mystery or the numinous. Frye even has a notebook entry on gematria, the cabalistic practice of interpreting the Bible by counting the numerical value of the letters of each word and using the result to derive the meaning of a passage; in gematria, each letter of the Hebrew alphabet has a traditional numerical value assigned to it. Frye writes, "In gematria, the numerical value of the Tetragrammaton (or four-letter word) is 26, so that a Trinity would be 78. The word for salt also has that number. Don't know what Rabelais knew or cared about this: I should look at Revelation" (CW 9: 304). In another notebook he writes, "Re. numbers: one gets 28 either by adding 24 & 4 or by multiplying 4 & 7. For Blake it's important that 24 & 28 make 52. For Chaucer it may be important that 4 humors & 7 planets make 28 temperamental types, along with a 29th narrator who is, so to speak, interlunar. I must track down the moon-on-England reference in Dryden's AA [*Absalom and Achitophel*] & keep in mind Malory's association of 28 & the Round Table. As I've said, there are seven supports or pillars of wisdom, 7 branches of the tree of life, & 7 hills of the unfallen city (2 Esdras) as well as a sevenfold analogy" (CW 23: 20).

Frye pays a substantial amount of attention to the symbolic significance of numbers, a topic I have examined in more detail elsewhere.[63] The difference between Joachim and Frye is that the Calabrian monk is quite assured in the significance that numbers reveal, whereas for Frye one looks in vain throughout his writings for the meanings, like those of the Pythagorean mystics and *kabbalists*, which he seems to believe are inherent in numbers themselves.[64] Still, Frye is always attentive to the imaginative use he can make of numbers.

In conclusion, it is perhaps worth noting that Frye's reading of the Book of Revelation is very much in tune with Joachim's *spiritualis intellectus* (spiritual understanding). Frye's view of Revelation always hinged on his understanding of verse 17 from the final chapter: "And the Spirit and the bride say, Come. And let him that heareth say, Come. And let him that is athirst come. And whosoever will, let him take the water of life freely." About this appeal Frye writes, "The suggestion seems to be that the Bible reaches in its closing words, not an end, but a beginning. And that beginning is in the mind of the reader. So that the Apocalypse, in its turn, becomes a type. In that case, what is its antitype? ... There's only one thing it can possibly be, and that is where we started, with a new creation, which is how Paul describes the gospel in Romans and elsewhere" (CW 13: 589). Frye does not mention Joachim in any of his commentaries on Revelation, but this view of a new creation would have been altogether congenial to the Calabrian abbot.

Let us close with a final quotation from *The Double Vision* in which Frye speaks eloquently of the Joachimite three-age vision:

> I think immense changes could be brought about by a Christianity that was no longer a ghost with the chains of a foul historical record of cruelty clanking behind it, that was no longer crippled by notions of heresy, infallibility, or exclusiveness of a kind that should be totally renounced and not rationalized to the slightest degree. Such a Christianity might represent the age of the Spirit that the thirteenth-century Franciscan Joachim of Fiore saw as superseding the Old Testament age of the Father and the New Testament age of the Logos. Such a Christianity would be

neither an inglorious rearguard action nor a revolutionary movement creating suffering and death instead of life more abundantly. It would be a Christianity of a Father who is not a metaphor of male supremacy but the intelligible source of our being; of a Son who is not a teacher of platitudes but a Word who has overcome the world; and of a Spirit who speaks with all the tongues of men and angels and still speaks with charity. The Spirit of creation who brought life out of chaos brought death out of it too, for death is all that makes sense of life in time. The Spirit that broods on the chaos of our psyches brings to birth a body that is in time and history but not enclosed by them, and is in death only because it is in the midst of life as well. (CW 4: 212–13)[65]

4

Frye and Giordano Bruno

The doctrine of coincidentia oppositorum, *the interpenetration, interdependence and unification of opposites has long been one of the defining characteristics of mystical (as opposed to philosophical) thought. Whereas mystics have often held that their experience can only be described in terms that violate the "principle of noncontradiction," western philosophers have generally maintained that this fundamental logical principle is inviolable. Nevertheless, certain philosophers, including Nicholas of Cusa, Meister Eckhart and G.W.F. Hegel, have held that presumed polarities in thought do not exclude one another but are actually necessary conditions for the assertion of their opposites. In the 20th century the physicist Neils Bohr commented that superficial truths are those whose opposites are false, but that "deep truths" are such that their opposites or apparent contradictories are true as well.* — Stanford L. Drob

This essay explores the connection between Northrop Frye and Giordano Bruno, the sixteenth-century Dominican friar, philosopher, mathematician, astronomer, playwright, Copernican activist, hermeticist, excommunicant at the hands of both Calvinists and Lutherans, friend of Sir Philip Sidney, and madcap free-thinker who was burned at the stake in the Campo dei Fiori in 1600 for his heretical theological views.[66]

The earliest reference in Frye's work to Bruno is in his student essay, "The Life and Thought of Raymon Lull," written for a course in Christian Missions, which he took during his final year at Emmanuel College (1935–36). Frye includes Bruno among a list of thinkers for whom mathematics is the best approach for understanding the nature of God (CW 3: 229), and he notes that Bruno had been haunted by Lull's efforts to establish a genuine dialectic (CW 3: 230). In the early 1580s Bruno had lectured on Lull at the University of Paris and had written a treatise on his work. And then in a paper Frye wrote for Professor Kenneth Cousland, "Gains and Losses of the Reformation," Bruno is mentioned in passing as one whose scientific work was bitterly opposed by the Catholic Church (CW 3: 270). At the end of Frye's career, Bruno makes an appearance in *Words with Power* (1990). For fifty-five years, then, Bruno was lodged in Frye's consciousness. His own library contains annotated editions of *The Expulsion of the Triumphant Beast*, Bruno's harshest attack on the Catholic Church, and *On the Infinite Universe and Worlds*, one of his major philosophical dialogues. Frye owned a copy of Bruno's attack on Oxford professors, *The Ash Wednesday Supper*, and he read, or at least was familiar with, Bruno's comic play *Il Candelaio* (CW 29: 346). Whatever else by Bruno Frye read is uncertain. As for secondary sources, we know from his notebooks that he read Frances Yates's *Giordano Bruno and the Hermetic Tradition* (CW 6: 618), a book he cites in *The Great Code* (CW 19: 338 n. 11), and he no doubt also read the chapter on Bruno in Yates's *The Art of Memory*.[67] As we shall see, Frye was also influenced in his thinking about Bruno by Owen Barfield's *What Coleridge Thought*.

Frye's most extensive commentary on Bruno is in "Cycle and Apocalypse in *Finnegans Wake*" (CW 29: 332–49)[68] where his purpose is to untangle the influence of Bruno on Joyce's novel. Bruno was, for Frye, the stalwart defender of the new philosophy and the new science, which sought to replace the earth-centred view of the cosmos with a sun-centred one. His theological views, rather than his defence of the Copernican theory of astronomy, led to his martyrdom at the hands of an anxious Roman Inquisition.[69] Frye was fascinated by memory theatres, his knowledge of Bruno on memory theatres coming from Frances Yates's *The Art of Memory*. Yates's study of memory from classical times up through Robert Fludd had been triggered some years before by her interest in Bruno's works on memory, on which she was an expert. In another context, Frye devotes two notebook entries to a connection between the character Bruno in John Crowley's *Little, Big* and Giordano Bruno (CW 5: 190, CW 15: 330). But there are scores of other references to Bruno in Frye's writing and most of these focus on two related ideas—polarity and the *coincidentia oppositorum* (coincidence of opposites).

The Coincidence of Opposites in Nicholas of Cusa and Others

Coincidence is both a spatial and a temporal category, meaning either occupation in the same place or occurrence at the same time. Polarity, or the dialectic of opposites, is the antecedent principle for the coincidence of opposites: two contraries must be present for coincidence to occur. In "Cycle and Apocalypse in *Finnegans Wake*" Frye sees polarity as one of the two structural principles of the novel (the cycle is the other), and of course polarity is a primary feature of Frye's own thought. A dialectic of opposites permeates practically everything he wrote: knowledge vs. experience, space vs. time, stasis vs. movement, the individual vs. society, tradition vs. innovation, Platonic synthesis vs. Aristotelian analysis, engagement vs. detachment, freedom vs. concern, *mythos* vs. *dianoia*, the world vs. the grain of sand, immanence vs. transcendence, and hundreds of other oppositions. In the first essay of *Anatomy of Criticism* alone one can discover more than thirty polar categories.

The principle of polarity, meaning a mutual opposition between two attributes or ideas, can be traced back to Heraclitus. It is developed in the neo-Platonic thought of Nicholas of Cusa in the fifteenth century and is carried into the nineteenth century through Hegel's brand of German idealism. Frye had known of Cusa's work as an Emmanuel College student,[70] and he later read and annotated Cusa's *Vision of God* and selections from Cusa in Herman Shapiro and Arturo B. Fallico's collection, *Renaissance Philosophy*. Frye refers to Wilhelm Windelband's *History of Philosophy* as a source for some of his student essays, and it seems likely that his initial knowledge of both Cusa and Bruno derived from Windelband, who discusses their use of the *natura naturans–natura naturata* distinction, their appeal to the *coincidentia oppositorum* principle, and their views on the identity of the part and the whole, among other matters. Frye would also have known of Cusa through the writings of the philosopher most responsible for rediscovering Cusa, Ernst Cassirer, who delivered Cusa from his medieval context and established his work as the hallmark of Renaissance philosophy. Frye would have encountered Cusa in Cassirer's *The Individual and the Cosmos in Renaissance Philosophy*, a copy of which he owned, and in Paul Tillich's *Systematic Theology*. For Tillich, Cusa "represents the metaphysical foundations of the modern mind" (*History of Christian Thought* 373).

What Bruno took from Cusa was the basic idea that the two poles of any dialectic are united by a *coincidentia oppositorum* (coincidence of opposites). Cusa sets forth his notion of *coincidentia oppositorum* in *On Learned Ignorance* (1437–40). His arguments are somewhat mystical and abstruse,[71] but his intent is to seek a synthesis or unity between the oppositions he treats in *On Learned Ignorance*: maximum and minimum, being and nonbeing, cause and effect, universal and particular, motion and rest, human and divine, finite and infinite, divisible and indivisible, centre and circumference, beginning and end, lower and higher, temporal and atemporal, and humiliation and exaltation. Cusa sees the entire universe as tied to an identity of contraries.

Bruno's view of the *coincidentia oppositorum* was significantly influenced by Cusa, though Bruno's *On the Infinite Universe and Worlds* has less of a mystical accent:

> There are then an infinity of mobile bodies and motive forces, and all of these reduce to a single passive principle and a single active principle,

> just as every number reduceth to unity, and as infinite number doth coincide with unity; and just as the supreme Agent and supreme active power doth coincide in a single principle with the supreme potentiality, patient of all creation, as hath been shewn at the end of our book *On Cause, Origin and the One*. In number then, and in multitude, there is infinite possibility of motion and infinite motion. But in unity and singularity is infinite motionless motive force, an infinite motionless universe. And the infinite number and magnitude coincide with the infinite unity and simplicity in a single utterly simple and indivisible principle, which is Truth and Being. (*On the Infinite*, Fifth Dialogue)

> You see further that our philosophy is by no means opposed to reason. It reduceth everything to a single origin and relateth everything to a single end, and maketh contraries to coincide, so that there is one primal foundation both of origin and of end. From this coincidence of contraries we deduce that ultimately it is divinely right to say and to hold that contraries are within contraries, wherefore it is not difficult to compass the knowledge that each thing is within every other—which Aristotle and the other Sophists could not comprehend. (*On the Infinite*, Fifth Dialogue)

> You have heard more than once that some, in whose composition fire doth predominate, are by their own quality bright and hot. Others shine by reflection, being themselves cold and dark, for water doth predominate in their composition. On this diversity and opposition depend order, symmetry, complexion, peace, concord, composition and life. So that the worlds are composed of contraries of which some, such as earth and water, live and grow by help of their contraries, such as the fiery suns. This I think was the meaning of the sage who declared that God createth harmony out of sublime contraries; and of that other who believed this whole universe to owe existence to the strife of the concordant and the love of the opposed. (*On the Infinite*, Third Dialogue)

Bruno conceived the cosmos as an organic whole, and the *coincidentia oppositorum* in the cosmos as operating to achieve a unity or synthesis of the contraries, all opposites coinciding in an infinite and divine oneness. For all of the difficulties posed by his often hermetic arguments,[72] it is these notions of harmony, synthesis, identity, reconciliation, and unity that attracted Frye to Bruno. Frye was not alone in championing a *both/and* rather than an *either/or* dialectic. The principle of *coincidentia oppositorum* is found in Hegel, where Aristotle's law of contradiction is rejected in favour of a synthesis in which opposites are reconciled through a process known as *Aufhebung*. Frye would also have encountered the principle in Carl Jung and its repeated appropriation by Mircea Eliade. Jung, whose work is replete with such oppositions as animus–anima and persona–shadow, writes, "The self is made manifest in the opposites and the conflicts between them; it is a *coincidentia oppositorum*. Hence the way to the self begins with conflict" (*Psychology* 186).[73] According to Eliade, myths "express on the one hand the diametrical opposition of two divine figures sprung from one and the same principle and destined, in many versions, to be reconciled at some *illud tempus* of eschatology, and on the other, the *coincidentia oppositorum* in the very nature of the divinity, which shows itself, by turns or even simultaneously, benevolent and terrible, creative and destructive, solar and serpentine, and so on (in other words, actual and potential)" (*Myths, Rites, Symbols* 449).

The Idea of God

As for Bruno's idea of God, Frye writes that Samuel Butler's natural theology "brings us close to Bruno's doctrine *natura est deus in rebus*, that nature is an incarnation of God in whom 'all is in all'" and that in this respect Bruno "had anticipated something of Jung's 'collective unconscious'" (CW 29: 342). The reference is to Bruno's doctrine of immanence in *The Expulsion of the Triumphant Beast*, which sees the universe as an emanation of God within it:

> Jove: [T]his Nature (as you must know) is none other than God in things.
> Saul: So, natura est deus in rebus [nature is God in all].
> Sophia: "However," he said, "diverse things represent diverse divinities and diverse powers, which, beside the absolute being they possess, obtain the being communicated to all things according to their capacity and measure. Whence, all of God is in all things." (*Expulsion* 235)

> Divinity reveals herself in all things, although by virtue of a universal and most excellent end, in great things and general principles, and by proximate ends, convenient and necessary to diverse acts of human life, she is found and is seen in things said to be most abject, although everything, from what is said, has Divinity latent within itself. (*Expulsion* 242)

"All is in all" reminds us of the passage in 1 Corinthians that Frye on several occasions points to: "And when all things shall be subdued unto him, then shall the

Son also himself be subject unto him that put all things under him, that God may be all in all" (15:28).[74] In *Words with Power* Frye writes:

> The contemporary scientific vision of nature, in spite of its millions of galaxies, continues to speak of a universe, or "one-turning" totality which forms an infinite circumference enclosing us on all sides. Here the human being's natural place is the centre of an expanding sphere, instead of hanging between an upper and a lower world like the samphire-cutter in *King Lear*. The corresponding spiritual vision would be a vision of plenitude in which each human being is a centre and God a circumference, or "all in all," in Paul's phrase (1 Corinthians 15:28). The proverb says that God's centre is everywhere and his circumference nowhere, but in a human perspective the divine circumference would be everywhere too, as a centre has no identity without a circumference.
>
> The sense of allness, if there is such a word, transcends the totality of "all things," which suggests a number to be counted, however large a number, and is the basis for the conception of the spiritual world usually called pantheism. Traditionally, "all things" refers to the totality of created beings, as in Revelation 21:5 ("Behold, I make all things new"). "All in all" takes us further than statements of the "all is God" or "all is one" type, where the predicate "is" re-inserts the duality the statement itself attempts to deny. "All in all" suggests both interpenetration, where circumference is interchangeable with centre, and a unity which is no longer thought of either as an absorbing of identity into a larger uniformity or as a mosaic of metaphors. (CW 26: 165–6)

Lying behind this passage is the ghost of the geometrically minded Bruno, whose *On the Infinite Universe and Worlds* speaks to the point of obsession about the infinite universe whose centre is nowhere and whose circumference is everywhere.

Identity and Analogy

Frye associates Bruno with the principle of identity rather than analogy. In several somewhat cryptic juxtapositions in his "Third Book" Notebooks, where Frye is developing an outline of the conceptual displacements of myth, it appears that he takes Bruno's drive toward identity and unity as set over against the Thomistic *analogia entis*, the theological notion that while we cannot know God directly because his infinite and perfect nature transcends any names we could apply to it, we can have limited, indirect knowledge of his being through analogy with our own being or with the created world: it is the practice of drawing conclusions concerning God from the known objects and relationships of the natural order. Here is one of the notebook entries:

> I wonder if I can really exclude metaphysical displacements from the Third Book. Surely I need some of this essential & primary displacement. I start, after all, with the symbolic or schematic universe. This schematic universe is not the objective world, but a mythical analogy of it. Still, attempts to fit it to the objective world have been constant & generally accepted before our own time. The most important conceptions seem to me to be:
> a) Analogy, especially the Thomistic analogia entis. I've been fascinated by this ever since my "general note" to FS [*Fearful Symmetry*].[75]
> b) Coincidence of contraries, the doctrine of identity as manifested through the appearance of opposites: the Cusa-Bruno movement in the Renaissance and its Romantic revival. (CW 9: 69)

Here what Frye seems to be outlining is the opposition between analogy, as in Aquinas, and identity, as in Cusa and Bruno. For all of his analogizing, Frye will always come down on the side of identity (the principle behind metaphor) rather than analogy (the principle behind simile).[76] In this, Bruno is his confrère.

Frye refers to Bruno's *coincidentia oppositorum*, which is set over against the cyclical principle of Spengler and Vico, as "an interchange of opposites" (CW 15: 269), "coincidence of contraries" (CW 9: 69), "coincidence of opposites" (CW 9: 84), and "identity of polarized opposites" (CW 29: 48). Sometimes Frye recurs to the Latin phrase (CW 9: 70, 89). In his *Late Notebooks* he uses the phrase "unity of opposites," which he connects with Bruno, to describe the struggle-of-brothers theme in *Finnegans Wake*: "the union of the dreamer with the twin brother who's dreaming him" (CW 6: 430).[77]

The Coincidence of Opposites and Interpenetration

Frye's linking "all in all" with interpenetration lies at the heart of his anti-Cartesian efforts to get beyond either/or oppositions. I have written elsewhere about interpenetration as a key concept in Frye's late work.[78] Frye uses the word in historical, philosophical, social, and scientific contexts, but its primary context is religious. When in one of his notebooks Frye links Bruno with Hegel (CW 9: 84), he has in mind the process by which they resolve antitheses. In Hegel's case the antitheses are cancelled but the identity of each term in the opposition is preserved and then lifted to another level. Again, Hegel refers to this process as *Aufhebung*. Frye refers to it as interpenetration, which is the most important of the many verbal formulas he uses in his late work to push language toward expressing the ineffable or capturing the highest mode of thought. Frye discovered the historical analogue for interpenetration in Spengler; the philosophical in Whitehead, Plotinus, and Hegel; the scientific in David Bohm, Karl Pribram, and Fritjof Capra, and the religious in the Mahayana sutras, particularly the Avatamsaka Sutra. Although he never makes an explicit connection between Bruno's *coincidentia oppositorum* and interpenetration, the former is clearly an analogue of the latter.

Following his claim in one notebook that the whole-part antithesis is resolved by interpenetration, Frye inserts the parenthetical remark "Coleridge through Barfield" (CW 5: 179). The reference is to Owen Barfield's *What Coleridge Thought*, which provides a detailed exposition of Coleridge's understanding of interpenetration, a dynamic and generative process that does not reconcile polarities but recreates a new entity from them.[79] Coleridge, in fact, uses the word "interpenetration," maintaining that only through the imagination can one see the power "of interpenetration, of total intussusception, of the existence of all in each as the condition of Nature's unity and substantiality, and of the latency under the predominance of some one power, wherein subsists her life and its endless variety" (qtd. in Barfield 52–3).[80] Polarity, the two forces of one power, is, Coleridge says in the *Statesman's Manual*, "a living and generative interpenetration" (qtd. in Barfield 36). Barfield points to analogues of Coleridge's theory of polarity in Lull and Bruno, and Frye understands Coleridge as participating in a Romantic movement to revive the Renaissance *coincidentia oppositorum* (CW 9: 69). One also encounters interpenetration in Shelley's idea that the elevating delight of poetry "is as it were the interpenetration of a diviner nature through our Own" (*Defence* 31). Here is one of Frye's versions of polarity: "The revealed community would have to be based on some such conception as Christ, who is conceived metaphorically, as an interpenetrating force we're a part of and yet is also a part of us" (CW 20: 383). In his essay on Joyce, Vico, and Bruno, Frye writes that in *Finnegans Wake* "we are reminded of Bruno's personal motto, used at the beginning of his play *Il Candelaio* and elsewhere: *in tristitia hilaris, in hilaritate tristis* ["in sadness happy, in happiness sad," the Latin motto on the title page of Bruno's play]. The solemn and the gay are interchangeable aspects of the same thing, and this may well be the essence, for Joyce, of Bruno's theory of polarity" (CW 29: 346). In the same essay Frye reports that Joyce told Harriet Weaver that Bruno's philosophy "is a kind of dualism—every power in nature must evolve an opposite in order to realize itself and opposition brings reunion." He then adds that "[m]ost writers would be more likely to speak of Hegel in such a connection" (CW 29: 334). Frye himself would be one of those writers, and yet Bruno is clearly for him a precursor of what he found in Hegel.

The thrust of these observations, then, is to suggest that Frye's idea of interpenetration is rooted in and partially defined by Bruno's principles of polarity and the coincidence of opposites. The idea that two things are the same thing (as in metaphor) is for Frye better captured by "interpenetration" than by "identity"; for interpenetration, whether of unity and variety, wholes and parts, totality and particularity, self and other, human and divine, suggests more strongly than does identity that each half of the dialectic retains its own distinctiveness while each is also present in the other. This idea of preservation is contained within the process of Bruno's *coincidentia oppositorum* and of Hegel's *Aufhebung*. Unity, as Frye is fond of insisting, does not mean uniformity. Moreover, interpenetration is a more dynamic concept than identity, the former implying a free flow back and forth between, in Coleridge's phrase, the "two forces of one power." Bruno's speculations suggest that once we get beyond the assumptions of Cartesian coordinates and Aristotelian causality, the idea of the coincidence of opposites is not so inexplicable a paradox as it initially might seem.

5
Frye and Henry Reynolds

Blake being a mythological poet, Frye had to school himself early on in myth. The sources of his reading on myth are not wholly known, but we do have a fairly complete list of the mythographers that he began to explore at the beginning of his career. In *The Critical Path* he observed that "[s]tudents of mythology often acquire the primitive qualities of mythopoeic poets. I have read a good many of them, from medieval writers through Bacon and Henry Reynolds and Warburton and Jacob Bryant and Ruskin to our own time, and I have noted two things in particular. First, a high proportion of them are cranks, even nuts, and, second, they often show a superstitious reverence for the 'wisdom of the ancients'" (CW 27: 67). Bacon, Warburton, and Ruskin are well known, and S. Foster Damon describes Bryant as "the outstanding figure among the mythagogues who flourished in the late eighteenth and early nineteenth centuries" (61). But who was Henry Reynolds?

In the 1960s Frye wrote a preface to a collection of essays in myth criticism, covering the period from the fourteenth through the nineteenth centuries, the aim of which was "to relate the study of mythology to the criticism of literature" (CW 25: 327).[81] About this collection, Frye wrote to Richard Schoeck,

> You may know that Marshall [McLuhan] and Ernest [Sirluck] have asked me to do a collection of comments on myth and criticism as one of the Gemini books. I gather that their original idea was to collect contemporary essays on the subject, but I thought it might be more interesting and useful to go back into the history of the tendency. Things like Raleigh's *History*, the opening of Purchas, Camden, Reynolds' *Mythomystes*, Bacon's *Wisdom of the Ancients*, Sandys' Ovid, from that period; some of the "Druid" stuff from around Blake's time; some of the material used by Shelley and Keats, and so on down to Ruskin's *Queen of the Air* (*Selected Letters* 82).

Here Reynolds appears again, and his *Mythomystes* also shows up on a list of books in the mythological tradition that Frye provided for his 1956 course in Spenser.[82]

Very little is known about Reynolds. In 1628 he translated Tasso's pastoral drama *Aminta*, and his *Mythomystes* appeared in 1632. Michael Drayton dedicated an *Epistle* to him, "my most dearly-loved friend." Otherwise, the biographical information is scant: outside of his friendship with Drayton, no facts about his personal life are known.[83] J. E. Spingarn calls *Mythomystes* a "tropical forest of strange fancies" (xxi), and Donald Lemen Clark believes Reynolds's book offers little more than "wool-gathering" (39). Frye has a very different opinion. In one of his *Late Notebooks* he makes the extraordinary remark that Reynolds was "the greatest critic before Johnson" (CW 5: 236). He is apparently referring only to the English critical tradition, but if Frye thinks that the little-known Reynolds is greater than Bacon and Jonson, better than Hume and Burke, better than Campion and Sidney, better than Milton and John Dennis, better than Pope and Dryden, better than Samuel Daniel and Edward Young, then the matter is worth looking into. Outside of Spingarn, whose anthology is Frye's source for *Mythomystes*, one is hard pressed to find even passing references to Reynolds in the histories and anthologies of criticism.[84] In the Wimsatt and Brooks history of criticism he does not merit even a footnote, and he is absent from all of the standard anthologies of criticism, including Hardison's *English Literary Criticism: The Renaissance*. What then leads Frye to assert that so relatively obscure a mythographer is "the greatest critic before Johnson"?

What little Frye has to say about Reynolds can be briefly summarized. In addition to the two passages already cited, Frye remarks in his essay on *Lycidas* that "Milton and his learned contemporaries, Selden, for example, or Henry Reynolds, knew at least as much about the symbolism of the 'dying god' as any modern student could get out of *The Golden Bough*, which depends mainly on the same Classical sources that were available to them" (CW 16: 25). In one of his notebooks for *Anatomy of Criticism*, Frye includes Reynolds, along with John Selden, as one of writers he wants to treat in a study of the Elizabethan understanding of myth (CW 23: 344), and he says in his *Late Notebooks* that the fact that there is so much resistance to writers such as Samuel Purchas and Reynolds, whom Spingarn thinks of as "an idiot crackpot," means that Reynolds and Purchas are "supremely important," adding that he does not understand the reasons for the resistance (CW 5: 236). In Notebook 34, where Frye outlines an unrealized twelve-chapter book on anagogy "as a morphological study of the symbols of art," "Henry Reynolds & his tradition" are projected as part of chapter 10—on rhetoric. By "his tradition" Frye means the new theory of allegory that sprang from Renaissance Platonism, with its occult developments, primarily Kabbalism, found in Pico della Mirandola and others (CW 15: 49, 51). In *Fearful Symmetry* Frye notes that Reynolds makes an etymological connection between

"Eden" and "Adonis" (CW 14: 228).[85] Twice he mentions Reynolds in connection with Spenser, saying that he is one of "Spenser's earliest and acutest critics" (CW 21: 315) and that Reynolds thought "Spenser overdid the moral allegory" in *The Faerie Queene* (CW 20: 27). In the reference to Reynolds and others from *The Critical Path*, quoted above, Frye goes on to say about their crankiness and their reverence for the ancients, that

> [t]hese qualities are not hard to account for: their crankiness is partly the result of the intensely associative quality of myth, where almost any kind of analogy may be significant, and their respect for antiquity is connected with the fact that literature does not improve, but revolves around its classics. Even the greatest mythological explorers of the last generation, Frazer and Freud, are apt to sound dated as soon as they attempt to be rational. The modern critic's approach, however, is, in the terms of my opening section, not allegorical but archetypal: he seeks not so much to explain a poem in terms of its external relation to history or philosophy, but to preserve its identity as a poem and see it in its total mythological context. (CW 27: 67)

These quotations hardly provide sufficient grounds for the claim that Reynolds is the "greatest critic before Johnson." But there is one passage—from *Fearful Symmetry*—where we begin to get a sense of why Frye was attracted to Reynolds:

> Most of the Elizabethan methods of interpretation, deriving as they did partly from the Plutarchan attempt to varnish the gods into images of moral virtue and partly from the medieval homiletic tradition, were allegorical in the wrong sense, concerned with extracting moral platitudes and general ideas. But in Reynolds' *Mythomystes*, apart from much Cabbalistic pedantry of the sort that derives Bacchus from Noah by way of Boachus, there is a keen sense of myth as the "essential form" of poetry:
>
> > ... who can make that Rape of Proserpine,—whom her mother *Ceres* (that vnder the Species of Corne might include as well the whole Genus of the Vegetable nature) sought so long for in the earth,—to meane other then the putrefaction and suceeding generation of the Seedes we commit to *Pluto*, or the earth....
>
> Reynolds is generally thought to be an antiquarian curiosity, but this explanation of the Proserpine myth is at least as "modern," if that is the

> opposite of the obsolete, as anything we can find in Dryden. Subsidiary allegorical traditions, like Bacon's attempt to explain Classical myths as Baconian and the alchemists' to explain them as alchemic, helped to encourage contemporary readers to read all poetry in the same way that one must read Blake's Prophecies. (CW 14: 160)[86]

For Frye, then, Reynolds breaks from the Elizabethan tendency, derived from the Plutarchan and medieval traditions, which generally interpreted the ancient myths in moral terms. But for Frye the form of the ancient myths is poetic rather than moral, and they are to be read allegorically. To understand better what Frye means, we need to examine the argument of *Mythomystes*.

Mythomystes

"Mythomystes" is Reynolds's neologism, combining "myth" and "mists," the latter in the sense of obscuring something hidden. On one occasion, he uses the word in this sense: "Wee liue in a myste, blind and benighted" (163). It seems likely that Reynolds also wants to suggest "mystical."[87] As we will see, concealed meanings are central to his apology.

Mythomystes begins with a critique of the poetry of the time. Reynolds's contemporaries, he says, have focused on what he calls the accidents and adjuncts of poetry (extrinsic features such as rhetorical tropes, meter, and rhyme), which have little to do with "the Forme and reall Essence of true Poësy" (143). Reynolds spares little scorn in his attack on the "heresies" of his contemporaries who profess humane learning, and of these "none so grosse, nor indeed any so great scandall ... as in the almost generall abuse and violence offered to the excellent art of Poesye" by those who call themselves poets (145). He does exempt several Spanish, French, and Italian writers from his scathing attack, and among English writers he commends Chaucer, Sidney, Spenser, Daniel, and Drayton for the "fancy and imagination they possesse" and especially for their drawing on "the rich fountes of our reuerend Auncients" (147). They are, he says, the "children of obedience." Otherwise, "most of our ordinary pretenders to Poesy now a dayes are to their owne and diseased times ill habits, as the racke will not be able to make the most aduised among twenty of them confesse to haue further inquired or attended to more in the best of their Authours they haue chosen to read and study" (148). These "vngrounded rimers" produce, like Ixion, monsters. Reynolds can use only superlatives in honouring the ancient writers, who "deseruedly wore the name of Prophets and Priuy-counsellors of the Gods ... or Sonnes of the Gods" (149).

The central argument of *Mythomystes* is in three parts, each devoted to an area in which the ancients have acquired their knowledge of truth and in which we see the disparity between this knowledge and that of the moderns. The first is the ancients' devotion to celestial or intellectual love, the object of which "is the excellency of the Beauty of Supernall and Intellectual thinges: To the contemplation whereof, rationall and wise Spirits are forcibly raised and lifted aloft" (150). Such contemplation leads to a kind of rapture or divine frenzy characteristic of the rhapsode in Plato's *Ion*. It is not unlike the transport (*ekstasis*) of Longinus's sublime. Reynolds quotes one of his primary sources, Pico della Mirandola, on the Platonic contemplation that leads to an out-of-body experience: "they are but a few, who, separating themselves wholy from the care of the body, seeme thence oftentimes extaticke and as it were quite rauisht and exalted aboue the earth and all earthly amusements" (151). Pico's examples are the blinding of Homer on his seeing the ghost of Achilles and the blinding of Tieresias on seeing the naked Athena. Both fables illustrate for Pico—and for Reynolds—that contemplation of "intellectual things" leads to the loss of "corporall eyes," which in turn spurs inspiration—"Poeticke fury" in Homer's case and prophetic insight in Tieresias' (151). Both fables, in other words, are allegories of blindness leading to insight: the blind are released from the triviality of earthly things, and what ensues is a "rapture of the spirit" (151).

Reynolds finds analogues of "extaticke elevation" in Homer's fable of Ganymede, and he quotes with approval Natalis Comes's view that the ancient philosophers were really fabulists, once the husks of their fables are stripped away (152). Following his masters Pico and Alessandro Farra, Reynolds provides a catalogue of others whose work illustrates that poets and philosophers are "both professors of but one and the same learning" (153). Included here is Orpheus with his "mysticall doctrine of Numbers," which leads Reynolds to call on support from Farra's *Settenario dell'humana riduttione*. Farra says of the ancient poets (Linus, Orpheus, Musæus, Homer, Hesiod, *et al.*), "Their fables are full of most high Mysteries; and haue in them that splendour that is shed into the fancy and intellect, rauisht and inflamed with diuine fury" (153). None of this, alas, is to be found among the moderns—the "illiterate Empyricks and dogleeches," "the mont'ibank Rimers of the time" (154).

The second disparity between the ancients and the moderns is that the former took care to conceal their knowledge from the "vnworthy vulgar" (155). The hieroglyphics of the Egyptian priests were intended to prevent the "prophane Multitude" from sharing the "high and Mysticall matters" cloaked by "riddles and enigmaticall knots" (156). Examples given by Reynolds are Orpheus, who, "within the foults and inuoluements of fables hid the misteries of his doctrine and dissembled them vnder a poeticke maske" (156), and Homer, who, according to Farra, "under a curious and pleasing vaile of fable hath taught the world how great and excellent the beauty of true wisdom is" (157). Even Aristotle's works on supernatural subjects are said to be "Mystically or enigmatically written ... only knowne to our hearers or disciples" (157)—"our" meaning those like Reynolds in possession of "sacred and divine wits," as distinct from "unworthy minds" (158). Pythagoras and Iamblicus are summoned in support of this view. Communicating only to worthy minds means first of all communicating by word of mouth and then by that Cabbalistic "Art of mysticall writing by Numbers" (158), the knowledge of which will unlock the concealed meanings. Again, Reynolds calls forth authorities to confirm his numerological theory of meaning: his beloved Pico, Plato, Aristotle, Avenzoar, Rabanus Maurus. The "fabulous riddles" have descended from the Egyptians through the Greeks and Romans (Hesiod, Lucretius, Virgil, Ovid) down to Moses, the "great Secretary of God," who wrote in a "mysticall manner" (160, 162). The passage from 2 Esdras that Reynolds quotes could serve as an epigraph to this section of his survey: "Write ... all these things that thou hast seene, in a booke, and hide them, and teach them to the wise of the people, whose hearts thou knowest may comprehend and keep these secrets" (160).[88] Once again the moderns fail to measure up: "they possesse the knowledge of no such mysteries as deserue the vse of any art at all for their concealing" (162).

The third disparity is that the moderns are generally ignorant of "the mysteries and hidden properties of Nature" (162). How can poets become natural philosophers? By cultivating the knowledge and love of God. And how does one achieve that? First, "by laying his burden on him that on his Crosse bore the burthen of all our defects, and interpositions between vs and the hope of the vision of his blessed Essence face to face heerafter"; and second, "by a carefull searche of him here in this life (according to Saint Paules instruction) in his works; who telles vs, *those inuisible things of God are cleerly seene, being understood by the things that are made*" (164).[89] We can achieve such knowledge from the hands of the best teachers—first, from those of the ancients who developed a "*Theologica Philosophica*," as well the Church Fathers, and second, from the poets "*who liued nearest to the time of the gods*" (164–5). According to Pico, these include Homer, the Orphic hymns, the Psalms of David, Zoroaster, Hesiod, Linus, and Musæus. These have been the wisest expounders of "the Generation of the Elements, with their Vertues and Changes, the Courses of the Starres, with their Powers and Influences, and all the most important Secrets of Nature" (167). There is, Reynolds adds, a great deal of moral force in the "Religious Philosophy, or Philosophical Religion" of the ancients, especially in Zoroaster and the Orphic hymns. In one of the latter,

Orpheus says "O you that vertue follow, to my sense / Bend your attentiue minds; Prophane ones, hence!" (168). In other words, good people should pay attention; profane folks, who can never understand the enigmas, begone.

Reynolds recognizes that the ancients "mingled much doctrine of Morality (yea, high Diuinity also) with their Naturall Philosophy" (167), and so he has to confront the questions raised by moral allegory. The Greek and Roman myths reveal that sometimes virtue is rewarded and vice punished. But what about all the tales of murder, rape, riot, incest, and adultery? How can these be taken as fit examples of morality or of what Reynolds calls "Manners"? Reynolds's answer is to switch the issue from moral to natural allegory. In the Persephone myth, for example, the central feature is not the judgement about her rape but the fact that her mother Ceres is an earth goddess whose presence represents "the putrefaction and succeeding generation of the Seedes we commit to *Pluto* or the earth" (170)—a reading of the Persephone myth that Frye calls as modern as anything we find in Dryden. Similarly, Jupiter's blasting of Semele after he had seduced her and the subsequent birth of Bacchus, after having been sealed in Jupiter's thigh, means "the necessity of the Ayres heat to his birth in the generation" (170). Reynolds avoids the moral issues of these myths, which come to represent aspects of the vegetable world, corn and wine. In like manner, the adultery of Venus and Mars means the inseparability of the "two Metals that carry their names," copper and iron, and so this myth represents what Reynolds calls "truths in Nature" (170). He performs the same interpretative manoeuvre with the story of Hebe (which represents the cycle of nature) and with the myth of the incest of Myrrh and her father, from which conjunction issues Adonis (representing nature's sweetly flowing smells). Things that present "so foule a face to the eye," such as the contentious fights among the gods and goddesses in Homer, represent "the naturall Contrariety of the Elements, and especially of the Fire and Water" (171). The brawls between Jupiter and Juno mean that "those meteors occasioned by the vpper and lower Region of the Ayres [have] differing temperatures" (171). Reading the myths in this way is all in the service of understanding nature. Cinquemani refers to such interpretation as "physical allegory" (1041).

Reynolds next turns to catalogue a series of analogies between biblical and classical figures. Venus is Eve. Rhea is Eve. Homer's Ate is Eve. Hesiod's Pandora is Eve. Bacchus is Noah. Janus is Noah. *Adonis horti* (the Gardens of Adonis) are Eden. Some of Reynolds's evidence for such identifications is etymological. The Bacchus–Noah identification, for example, is based on the claim that Noah's name in Hebrew means wine. We will consider the legitimacy of these "poetic etymologies" shortly.

As an annex to *Mythomystes*, Reynolds appended "the Tale of Narcissus briefly mythologized" in which he interprets the myth again largely as an allegory of things in the natural world, but the Narcissus material is not included in Spingarn's edition of *Mythomystes*, and there is no evidence that Frye read the appendix elsewhere.

With this overview of *Mythomystes* before us, we can see more clearly why Frye was attracted to Reynolds, whom he calls a "sensitive & civilized student of allegory" (CW 20: 27). Reynolds and Frye share a number of assumptions—that poetry is closely related to mythology, that literature is made out of other literature, that poetic myth should be read allegorically, that Biblical and Classical myths are analogous to each other, that *ekstasis* is central to the poetic experience, and that poetic myth has religious import. The secrets of the myths of the ancients can be uncovered, Reynolds believes, given the proper attention to things other than superficial form. Armed with his neoplatonic and kabbalistic assumptions about the nature of the universe, the source of being, and the nature of the soul, he sets out to uncover the secrets. *Mythomystes* is steeped in the esoteric traditions, including numerology, which Reynolds assimilated from the works of Pico della Mirandola, Alessandro Farra, Zoroaster, and Iamblicus, among others. As Frye's notebooks reveal, he himself was no stranger to these and other strands of esoterica.

Allegory

Reynolds sees myths as allegories of ancient philosophical or mystical ideas, and Frye's understanding of allegory is in many respects congenial to Reynolds's. This understanding is best seen in Frye's essay on allegory (CW 27: 171–7) and in his account of the formal phase of criticism in the second essay of *Anatomy of Criticism*. In the latter, Frye calls the formal phase of criticism "commentary," which is "the process of translating into explicit or discursive language what is implicit in the poem" (CW 22: 79). More specifically, it tries to isolate the ideas embodied in the structure of poetic imagery. This produces allegorical interpretation, and, in fact, commentary sees all literature as potential allegory (CW 22: 82). The range of symbolism in the formal phase ("thematically significant imagery") can be classified according to the degree of its explicitness. All literature, in other words, can be organized along a continuum of formal meaning, from the most to the least allegorical:

Naïve ➛ Continuous ➛ *Freistimmige* ➛ Doctrinal ➛ Implicit ➛ Ironic ➛ Indirect

The criterion here is the degree to which writers insist on relating their imagery to precepts and examples. Naive allegory is so close to discursive writing that it can hardly be called literature at all. It "belongs chiefly to educational literature on an elementary level: schoolroom moralities, devotional exempla, local pageants, and the like" (CW 22: 83). Even though such naive forms have no real hypothetical centre, they are considered allegorical to some degree since they occasionally rely upon images to illustrate their theses.

The two types of actual or formal allegory, continuous and *freistimmige*, show an explicit connection between image and idea, differing only in that the former is more overt and systematic. Dante, Spenser, and Bunyan, for example, maintain the allegorical connections throughout their work, whereas in writers like Hawthorne, Goethe, and Ibsen the symbolic equations are at once less explicit and less continuous.[90] If the structure of the poetic imagery has a strong doctrinal emphasis, so that the internal fictions become exempla, as in Milton's epics, a fourth kind of allegorical relation is established. And to the right of this, located at the "centre" of the scale, are "works in which the structure of imagery, however suggestive, has an implicit relation only to events and ideas, and which includes the bulk of Shakespeare" (CW 22: 84). All other poetic imagery tends increasingly toward the ironic and paradoxical end of the continuum; it includes the kind of symbolism implied by the metaphysical conceit and *symbolisme*, by Eliot's objective correlative and the heraldic emblem. Frye refers to this latter kind of imagery (e.g., Melville's whale and Virginia Woolf's lighthouse) as ironic or paradoxical because as units of meaning the symbols arrest the narrative, and as units of narrative they perplex the meaning. Beyond this mode, at the extreme right of the continuum, are indirect symbolic techniques, like private association, Dadaism, and intentionally confounding symbols.

What Frye has done is to redefine the word "allegory," or at least greatly expand its ordinary meaning; for he uses the term not only to refer to a literary convention but also to indicate a universal structural principle of literature. It is universal because Frye sees all literature in relation to *mythos* and *dianoia*. We engage in allegorical interpretation, in other words, whenever we relate the events of a narrative to conceptual terminology. This is commentary, or the translation of poetic into discursive meaning. In interpreting an "actual" or continuous allegory like *The Faerie Queene*, the relationship between *mythos* and *dianoia* is so explicit that it prescribes the direction which commentary must take. In a work like *Hamlet* the relationship is more implicit. Yet commentary on *Hamlet*, for Frye, is still allegorical: if we interpret *Hamlet*, say, as a tragedy of indecision, we begin to set up the kind of moral counterpart (*dianoia*) to the events of its narrative (*mythos*) that continuous allegory has as a part of its structure. We should expect, then, that as allegory becomes more implicit, the direction that the commentary must go becomes less prescriptive. And this is precisely Frye's position: an implicit allegory like *Hamlet* can carry an almost infinite number of interpretations.

Frye notes that allegory is both a feature of literature and a method of criticism. As a feature of literature, the myth or story contains events, ideas, or names that refer to other events, ideas, or names. The latter can be historical or political events, moral or philosophical ideas, or physical or natural phenomena. As a technique of criticism, allegorical interpretation is, as just said, some form of commentary, which uncovers the meaning of the events or ideas (CW 27: 171–3). Reynolds does not use the word "allegory," but he follows the method, relating what he finds in the Greek and Roman myths to moral and philosophical ideas and, primarily, to natural phenomena.

Reynolds is naturally aware of the resemblance between biblical and Classical myths. He says that he wants to draw parallels between "the Sacred letter and Ethnick Poesyes" (175), by which he means the stories of the Bible and those of the "Ethnicks" (non-Christians and non-Jews). As already mentioned, he calls attention to the names of Classical and biblical characters that he claims are identical, but, after the manner of Sir James Frazer, he also points to the identity of certain stories. Noah's flood is analogous to the universal flood in Ovid, which was survived by Deucalion (175). Pandora's releasing from her jar all of the evils of humankind is analogous to the story of Eve and the forbidden fruit. The two-headed Janus is analogous to Moses, whom the biblical writers "also giue two faces to, for hauing seene both the old and the new world" (175). Reynolds supports this connection by claiming, incorrectly it turns out, that the Hebrew word for Janus is *Iain* (wine), thus linking him to Noah as the inventor of wine.

A whole library of commentaries had been built up from the Renaissance on, showing the similarities between Classical and biblical myths. Frye, who was no stranger to this literature, writes that in "early Christian centuries the main extra-Biblical source of mythology was the classical one, and some diehard Christians tried to regard all Classical myths as demonic parodies of the true Biblical ones. However, the myths moved from the position of demonic parody to that of positive analogy—Gentile 'types' added to the Old Testament ones—as it gradually dawned on the poets that 'gods' were not really in competition with the God of a monotheistic religion, but had much more in common with human beings themselves" (CW 26: 130–1). Frye's analysis in *Words with Power* of an eight-line stanza from Giles Fletcher's *Christ's Triumph over Death* shows how the resemblances worked themselves out. In Fletcher's stanza there are parallels between Deucalion and Noah, Nisus and Samson, Phaeton and Adam, and the descent of

Orpheus and the harrowing of hell (CW 26: 134). Reynolds is actually locating what Frye calls the positive analogies.

Poetic Etymology

Earlier we referred to Reynolds's etymological identifications: Noah is the same as Bacchus, the Gardens of Adonis are the same as Eden, and so on. His etymological speculations are perhaps creative, but both of these examples are based on faulty etymology. "Noah" actually derives from the Hebrew *nuah*, meaning "rest" or "settle down," not the Hebrew word for wine. As for the Adonis–Eden connection, Reynolds writes, "What can *Adonis horti* among the Poets meane other than *Moses* his *Eden*, or terrestriall Paradise,—the Hebrew *`Eden* being *Voluptas* or *Delitiæ*, whence the Greeke ηδονη [*hēdonē*] (or pleasure) seems necessarily deriued?" (176). There is warrant, at least in the exegetical tradition, for the pun that links the Garden of Adonis to Eden, the Greek *hēdonē* and the Hebrew *`Eden* both meaning "pleasure." But the linking of Adonis with *hēdonē*, which has subsequently been made by others,[91] is a false etymology: "Adonis" derives from the Phoenician *adōn* meaning "lord" or the title of a Phoenician divinity. In Hebrew *ādōn* also means "lord"; ηδονη does mean "pleasure" but it is unrelated etymologically to *ādōn*. But false etymologies do not gainsay, according to Frye, the importance of such poetic linkages for criticism.

In the late 1940s Frye devoted a substantial portion of one of his notebooks to investigating poetic etymologies. He begins by saying, "It seems to me that there [are] two kinds of etymology: one, historical & genetic, with very accurate & predictable laws, is what is now called etymology. But there is another kind, now called fanciful, but universally accepted down to the 16th c. & beyond, & going back to *Cratylus* & the pre-Socratics, of *lucus a non lucendo* etymology [i.e., an absurd etymology], which is fundamentally an attempt to evolve synthetic concepts out of words by associating groups of words together which sound alike. Whether this form of cabbalism will turn out to be entirely useless or not I don't know, but I'm going to look into it" (CW 15: 56). And look into it he did, devoting a good portion of Notebook 3 on to his speculations. By the time he came to write *Anatomy of Criticism* Frye had determined that poetic etymology was not useless:

> We remember that a good deal of verbal creation begins in associative babble, in which sound and sense are equally involved. The result of this is poetic ambiguity, the fact that, as remarked earlier, the poet does not define his words but establishes their powers by placing them in a great variety of contexts. Hence the importance of poetic etymology, or

> the tendency to associate words similar in sound or sense. For many centuries this tendency passed itself off as genuine etymology, and the student was taught to think in terms of verbal association. He learned to think of snow as coming etymologically as well as physically from clouds (*nix a nubes*), and of dark groves as derived from sunlight (the derivation by opposites which produced the famous *lucus a non lucendo*). When real etymology developed, this associative process was discarded as mumbo-jumbo, which it is from one point of view, but it remains a factor of great importance in criticism. Here again we meet the principle that an analogy between A and B (in this case two words) may still be important even if the view that A is the source of B is dropped. Whether or not one is etymologically justified in associating Prometheus with forethought or Odysseus with wrath, the poets have accepted such associations and they are data for the critic. Whether or not "new" critics make mistakes or anachronisms in explicating the texture of earlier poetry, the principle involved is defensible historically as well as psychologically. (CW 22: 313)

Frye makes a similar point in his *"Third Book" Notebooks*: "When I say in AC [*Anatomy of Criticism*] that animal imagery of the analogical cycle is based on the choice of animal (deer in *Endymion*, rats in *The Waste Land*), I imply a 'humor' or character theory of nature (cypress melancholy, oak sanguine) which, like 'poetic etymology,' is superstition as fact and a structural principle in criticism" (CW 9: 49–50). Similarly, Frye says, "The Elizabethan etymologists were right: Adonis is Adam" (CW 9: 118). But as "Adam" derives from the Hebrew *ā-dām*, meaning "man," whereas *ādōn* means "lord," Frye is speaking of "poetic etymology," the study of which has become a small industry in biblical and Classical studies.[92] The point is that for both Reynolds and Frye poetic etymology is a critical technique for discovering the meaning of a text rather than being just word-play. If the context is changed from the meaning of words as established by genuine linguistic derivation to the meaning of words as they have been taken to be by the poetic tradition, then such meanings are fair game for critical analysis, not "mumbo-jumbo." Frye refers to poetic etymology as a philosophical synthetic critical approach, rooted in Plato's *Cratylus*, that goes beyond a purely historical and philological one (CW 23: 114). In this respect, he and Reynolds would affirm the same exegetical principle.

Poetic etymology depends on the accidents and coincidences of language. It is a form of punning and so can involve a good measure of playfulness. Except for a touch of humour in creative name-calling that Reynolds directs toward the unenlightened modern poets, he is otherwise completely sober and stone-faced.

Frye, on the other hand, takes delight in the wit produced by linguistic accidents, as in this notebook entry:

> From the historical point of view most verbal coincidences are accidents: Kunst nach Gunst; Der Mensch ist, was er isst; God is good; the Italian version of "a translator is a betrayer,"[93] and so on. From my point of view I am not so sure. The whole crisis in Christian doctrine over whether Christ was an allegory or a reality, of like or of the same substance, was fought over literally one iota of difference: homoousios vs. homoiousios that seems to me the historical crisis of the whole argument. Again, cabbalism based on YHWH may have been foolish, but is not the sound identical with Iove, which does not seem to be etymologically related? And what about Christ & Krishna? In English there is one "l" of a difference between the Creator & the Creature, the Word & the World. Dante's whole allegory, political & moral, rests on a palindrome: Amor–Roma, just as Parmenides' philosophy of being rests on the ambiguity of "is" as copula & verb of existence. That sort of thing. (CW 15: 57)

That sort of thing makes Reynolds and Frye like-minded critics.

Ekstasis

In chapter 2, we observed that Frye distinguishes between two complementary approaches to criticism, the Aristotelian and the Longinian. The Aristotelian approach takes the poem to be a product or artistic artefact, from which the reader is detached; the Longinian, as process or expression, to which the reader is engaged. The central Aristotelian concept is *katharsis*; the Longinian, *ekstasis*. The metaphors associated with the Aristotelian view are of objective order (*natura naturata*); with the Longinian view, of organism (*naturata naturans*), genesis, and elevation.

As we have seen, in the 1950s Frye tended to privilege the Aristotelian over the Longinian approach: the aesthetic view takes precedence over the enthusiasm of *ekstasis*, as the feelings generated when we are transported are not subject to critical scrutiny. But as Frye continued to reflect on the complementary critical approaches, he leaned more and more in the Longinian direction, as the essay on Frye and Longinus in the present collection seeks to demonstrate.

Frye's late work often focuses on ecstatic states and the revolutionizing and expanding of consciousness that results from the experience of *ekstasis*. What Frye refers to as "kerygma" moves beyond the poetic, embracing the reader's existential experience. The highest states of this experience are a function of what Frye calls existential or, following Heidegger, ecstatic metaphor. With this emphasis on intensified and expanded consciousness in his late work, Frye aligns himself with Longinian transport (*ekstasis*).

Although Longinus became known in the Renaissance after *On the Sublime* was published by Francesco Robertello in 1554, there is no evidence that Reynolds knew Longinus. Still, there are a half-dozen or so places in *Mythomystes* where Reynolds sounds very much like a Longinian:

> The object of this Celestiall or Intellectuall Loue ... is the excellency of the Beauty of Supernall and Intellectuall thinges: To the contemplation whereof, rationall and wise Spirits are forcibly raised and lifted aloft ... and so full fraught with the delight and abondance of the pleasure they feele in those their eleuations, raptures, and mentall alientations, wherein the soule remains for a time quite seperated as it were from the body ... in an Extaticke manner, and ... cry out with the intraunced *Zoroaster*, *Ope thine eyes, ope them wide, raise and lift them aloft*. (150–1)

Reynolds quotes his much adored Pico, in his discourse on Plato, as saying that those who persevere in the elevation of the mind "seeme thence oftentimes extaticke and as it were quite rauisht and exalted aboue the earth and all earthly amusements" (151). About the ancients, Reynolds writes, "such their neglect of the body and businesse of the world! Such their blindnesse to all things of triuiall and inferiour condition: And such, lastly, were those extaticke eleuations, or that truly *diuinus furor* of theirs" (152). All of this is quite similar to Frye's idea that in expanded consciousness the reader is transported to another level of awareness and becomes a being out of its ordinary place.

Esoterica

As we have seen, Reynolds speaks frequently about mystical knowledge, hidden secrets, matters "hid from the vulgar," and "the mysticall doctrine of Numbers." He quotes with approval the neoplatonic and kabbalist Alessandro Farra on "the most high Mysteries" of the ancients' fables (153). He writes of the Egyptian hieroglyphics as always dissimulating and of the priests' admonition "that high and Mysticall matters should by riddles and enigmaticall knots be kept inuiolate from the prophane Multitude" (156). All of this is what Spingarn refers to as "strange fancies" (xxi). He dismisses Reynolds's mystical and hermetic speculations as based on grounds "utterly repugnant to neoclassicism,—not their superior portrayal of the fundamentals of human nature, but their defter manipulation of the cabalistic mysteries" (xxii). But for those, like Frye, who believe that neoclassicism and its representation of human nature do not represent the last word about the ends and means of poetry, other assessments are possible.

Frye's liberal and democratic sensibility makes him much less elitist than Henry Reynolds, Esquire, for whom there is a small coterie of those in the know to which the profane crowd need not seek admittance. But Frye's knowledge of the esoteric tradition was substantial. Of the 273 books in his personal library that deal with the various strands of the esoteric, 254 are annotated by Frye. I have written in some detail elsewhere about Frye's interest in esoterica, hermeticism, and the occult, traditions that include alchemy, astrology, Gnosticism, gnosis, magic, mysticism, the occult, the *philosophia perennis* in religious studies, Renaissance hermeticism, the Kabbalah, theosophy, numerology, and secret societies.[94] Antoine Faivre maintains that we can distinguish Western esoteric thought by four "intrinsic characteristics": 1. The belief that there are correspondences between all aspects of the visible and invisible worlds which are meant to be decoded. Correspondences can be (a) within nature itself (e.g., the seven metals and seven planets of astrology), or (b) between nature, history, and sacred texts (e.g., Jewish and Christian Kabbalah). 2. Nature is felt to be essentially alive in the cosmos (e.g., Paracelsianism, *Naturphilosophie*). 3. The imagination is the faculty for revelation and mediation. 4. Transmutation, metamorphosis, "second birth" (Introduction).[95] The first, second, and third of these features can be found in *Mythomystes*. Spingarn claims that Reynolds's method is "a negation of science" (xxii). But if criticism is conceived of as mythical and symbolic discourse rather than simply a rational mode of knowing, then Frye and Reynolds are in the same camp.

Frye and Reynolds read the ancient fables in mythical and metaphorical terms, and what results is not knowledge in any conceptual sense but knowledge as *anagnorisis*, which is an imaginative category rather than a discursive one. The point can be made by considering Frye's relation to A. E. Waite (1857–1947), a student, translator, and popularizer of numerous occult texts, and essentially self-taught scholar of mystical philosophies. Waite grew up under the influence Eliphas Lévi (Alphonse-Louis Constant), whose *History of Magic* he translated. He became a Freemason, joined the Order of the Golden Dawn, established several orders of his own, and poured forth a stream of ponderously written books. A friend of Arthur Machen, he is best remembered today for his Tarot pack, produced in art-nouveau style by his devotee Pamela Colman Smith. The scholarly establishment would consider Waite to be something of a crackpot, similar to

Spingarn's attitude toward Reynolds, whose "method implies the negation of science."

Frye read at least eight of Waite's books, including *The Quest of the Golden Stairs*, which is a faerie-world romance—a less sophisticated version of George Macdonald's prose fantasies. Frye includes it in a catalogue of books that are to be his main sources for the essay on faeries and elementals, which he intended to write. About this book he says only that it is "superficially off-putting" (CW 5: 190). But about Waite's book *The Holy Grail* Frye writes,

> I've been reading Loomis and A.E. Waite on the Grail. Loomis often seems to me an erudite ass: he keeps applying standards of coherence and consistency to twelfth-century poets that might apply to Anthony Trollope. Waite seems equally erudite and not an ass. But I imagine Grail scholars would find Loomis useful and Waite expendable, because Waite isn't looking for anything that would interest them. It's quite possible that what Waite is looking for particularly doesn't exist—secret traditions, words of power, an esoteric authority higher than that of the Catholic Church—and yet the kind of thing he's looking for is so infinitely more important than Loomis' trivial games of descent from Irish sources where things get buggered up because the poets couldn't distinguish cors meaning body from cors meaning horn. Things like this show me that I have a real function as a critic, pointing out that what Loomis does has been done and is dead, whereas what Waite does, even when mistaken, has hardly begun and is very much alive. (CW 6: 460)

"Loomis" is Roger Sherman Loomis, author of *The Grail: From Celtic Myth to Christian Symbol*. This and several other books by Loomis on Arthurian and other medieval romances established him as an early authority on the subject. As Frye suggests, his work was influential with other Grail scholars, even though now his thesis about the development of the Grail legend has been called into question. But for Frye the philological and historical matters treated by Loomis are dead, whereas Waite's probing of secret traditions, words of power, and the like is alive.[96] The question of why it is alive is part of the larger question of why Frye devoted so much energy to exploring the various forms of esoterica.

The esoteric tradition for Frye was finally a visionary tradition, analogous to other creative traditions, and analogies were the architectural blueprint for Frye's spiritual world.

> People think they're being iconoclastic & realistic when they ask me if there aren't differences as well as similarities in the patterns I put together. Of course there are, but that again is confusing imaginative & conceptual processes. In imaginative thought there is no real knowledge of anything but similarities (ultimately identities): knowledge of differences is merely a transition to a new knowledge of similarities. In conceptual thought analogy is tricky & misleading beyond the heuristic stage: in imaginative thought it's the *telos* of knowledge. The great ocean into which all analogy empties is the *via negativa* approach to God, which the Incarnation reverses into spring rain, the identity of God & Man. (CW 13: 215)

Henry Reynolds may not be "the greatest critic before Johnson," but by considering the several ways that *Mythomystes* connects with several of the central features of Frye's work—his views on allegory, poetic etymology, *ekstasis*, and esoteric meaning—we can perhaps better understand the attraction that Reynolds held for Frye as a kindred spirit.

6

Frye and Robert Burton

> *From my point of view the greatest book ever written at Oxford is the* Anatomy of Melancholy. *(CW 13: 132)*

In his interview with David Cayley, Frye reveals the very high estimate he has of Robert Burton's *The Anatomy of Melancholy*. Responding to Cayley's question about the use of the word "anatomy," Frye said,

> The word *anatomy* in Shakespeare's day and a little later meant a dissection for a synthetic overview. One of my favorite books in English literature—there are times when it is actually my favorite—is Burton's *Anatomy of Melancholy*. Of course, there were four humors then, but for Burton there was only the one, melancholy. That was the source of all mental and physical diseases in the world. So he writes an enormous survey of human life. It ranks with Chaucer and Dickens, except the characters are books rather than people. It was both an analysis of the causes and cures and treatment of melancholy and a kind of synthetic overview of human nature before it gets melancholy. On a much smaller scale there was Lyly's *Euphues: The Anatomy of Wit*, which has given us the word *euphuism*, meaning that if you're too bright and don't know enough you can get into trouble. That use of the term *anatomy* was one that I thought exactly fitted what I was doing." (CW 24: 936–7)[97]

The title *Anatomy of Criticism* is obviously indebted to Burton, but the title was assigned to the book late in the publication process. John Ayre reports that Frye's earliest working title for the book was *A Defense of Poetics* (253), though this is not a title Frye ever uses in his notebooks or diaries of the time. When he sent the manuscript off to Princeton in June 1955, it was called *Structural Poetics: Four Essays*. After Princeton issued a contract four months later, Frye's editor at Princeton, Benjamin Houston, asked him to consider changing the title and adding a conclusion and a glossary. Frye assented, suggesting that the book be called *Structure as Criticism*. But after the editorial staff at Princeton registered its strong opposition to that, he eventually settled on *Anatomy of Criticism*, one of the thirteen titles that Houston had offered as possibilities.[98]

It seems likely that Frye first encountered Burton's *Anatomy* in Herbert Davis's course on satire that he signed up for during his second year at Emmanuel College (1934–35).[99] Almost sixty years later—in *The Great Code*—Frye remarks: "I retain my special affection for the literary genre I have called the anatomy, especially for Burton's *Anatomy of Melancholy*, with its schematic arrangements that are hardly those of any systematic medical treatment of melancholy, and yet correspond to something in the mind that yields a perhaps even deeper kind of comprehension. Such books as Burton's have an extraordinary pulling power: I understand very well what Samuel Johnson meant by saying that Burton's was the only book that got him out of bed earlier than he wanted to" (CW 19: 15).[100]

What Is an Anatomy?

Frye's interest in the anatomy as a form of prose goes back to his teenage years. He reports that during the summer after his third year at Victoria College—the summer of 1932—"an embryonic anatomy theory began to shape itself in my notes" (CW 25: 28).[101] By the time he came to write "An Inquiry into the Art Forms of Prose Fiction" (CW 3: 383–400), he had Burton's *Anatomy* firmly in his possession. The date of this paper is uncertain, but it seems likely it was written for Davis's satire course (1934–35), just mentioned. Frye's ideas on the anatomy continued to gestate during his Oxford years (1936–37, 1938–39): in a 1937 letter, he wrote to Helen Kemp that he had read his "anatomy paper" to his Merton College tutor Edmund Blunden" (CW 2: 693). This paper was doubtless "An Inquiry into the Art Forms of Prose Fiction," or a portion of it.[102] Then in 1942, ten years after the "anatomy theory" had begun to take shape, Frye published his second major essay, "The Anatomy in Prose Fiction" (CW 21: 23–38), in which Burton plays a central role. This was followed eight years later by "The Four Forms of Prose Fiction" (CW 21: 77–89), part 3 of which is devoted to the anatomy. Meanwhile, Frye was teaching Burton's *Anatomy* in English 2i: English Poetry and Prose, 1500–1660. "The Four Forms" in turn got incorporated into the fourth essay of *Anatomy of Criticism*, where Frye's "discovery" of the prose form received much wider attention. In short, Frye developed his ideas about the anatomy over the course of some twenty years. His discovery was assisted by Dryden's account of Varronian and Menippean satire in his *Discourse Concerning the Original and Progress of Satire* (1693), selections of which Frye quotes in "The Anatomy in Prose Fiction" (CW 21: 25–6).

In "An Inquiry into the Art Forms of Prose Fiction" Frye sees the anatomy as related to fiction and drama but differing from them in its effort to build up an argument or attitude. It is similar to the essay in its interest in ideas: the essay develops an idea, while the anatomy interweaves a number of ideas. Because *anatomy* is a literary term, it can apply to any kind of writing in any field that has survived because of its literary value. Anatomies reveal the interests or outlooks of the author, as in satires and Utopias or other abstract, conceptual, or generalized attitudes to human personality or society. Such interests are prior to the strict requirements of philosophy or psychology. Anatomies always reveal an intellectual interest, and they display their authors' erudition. They begin, Frye writes, in the Renaissance with Cornelius Agrippa's *Vanity of the Arts and Sciences*, followed by Erasmus's *Encomium Moriae*, More's *Utopia*, and Castiglione's *Courtier*. On the continent, the culminating development is Rabelais's *Gargantua and Pantagruel*, and in England Burton's *Anatomy of Melancholy* (CW 3: 390–1).

The extension of the word *anatomy* from its literal zoological context (dissection of the body) to its figurative sense of an analysis of nonzoological things goes back a long way. The OED notes that Aristotle used *ἀνατομή* for logical analysis. Today, of course, the use of *anatomy* in the sense of detailed analysis or examination is widespread. A title search for "anatomy of" in WorldCat turns up more than 31,000 book references. Burton gives "honorable precedents" for his *Anatomy*, citing Anthony Zara's *Anatomy of Wit* (orig. *Anatomia ingeniorum et scientiarum*, 1615), and in a note he lists three more "anatomies": *The Anatomy of Popery*, *The Anatomy of Immortality*, and Angelus Sala's *Anatomy of Antimony* (1609) (*Anatomy of Melancholy* 16). During Burton's lifetime (1577–1640) at least fourteen other "anatomies" appeared.[103] Although the immediate end of the anatomy is dissection or analysis, its ultimate end is synthesis. It "depends far more [than the novel] on rhythmic integration; it is essentially a synthetic form of art, as the emphasis is thrown on construction rather than analysis" (CW 3: 394).

Frye was in his early twenties when he wrote "An Inquiry," and the features of the anatomy outlined there were not substantially altered in his subsequent treatments of the form, culminating in his expanded definition of the genre in the *Anatomy*. What does appear in his subsequent treatments is an effort to trace the beginning of the anatomy back beyond the Renaissance to the Classical Menippean satire, which is a kind of proto-species of the anatomy. But as Frye reflected on the features of the anatomy from 1934 to 1957, his several discussions do introduce variations in his accounts of these features.[104] Here is a summary account of those features, along with a brief commentary on Burton from each of Frye's four expositions of the anatomy:

A. "An Inquiry into the Art Forms of Prose Fiction" (1934–35)

Features of the anatomy

1. individualistic
2. generalized characters and narrative; story and character subordinated to argument or attitude
3. ordered arrangement of a subject or point of view; presents a thesis
4. a synthesis of ideas
5. whatever its disciplinary thrust, survives through literary value
6. builds up author's attitude to a subject (*Religio Medici* or *Areopagitica*) or works out author's attitude to society (satire or Utopia)
7. displays erudition

BURTON'S ANATOMY

"[T]he anatomy in England reached its culmination with Burton. *The Anatomy of Melancholy* is not a book of Burton; it is Burton's book; the complete expression of his personality. Needless to say, all the characteristics of the anatomy we have noted are in it: Utopian scheme, erudition, view of mankind through the generalized technique provided by the theory of humours, ordered presentation of a subject, and the rest, except that what we find partial in other anatomists we find complete in him. It is perhaps noteworthy that the anatomy in its largest and most highly developed and concentrated forms tends to become *the* book of its author rather than one of many; Burton, Rabelais, perhaps Sterne, being examples. *The Anatomy of Melancholy* is divided like a prelude and fugue; the prelude, the introduction of Democritus to the reader, being free in style, and the anatomy being capable of exhaustive analysis on a general threefold scheme. The metaphor is not altogether an irresponsible one, for both the anatomy and the contemporary fugue in music are, in different arts, the working out of the implications of a given subject and the organizing of them into a rhythmic unit" (CW 3: 392).

B. "The Anatomy in Prose Fiction" (1942)

Features of the anatomy

1. sets ideas, generalization, theories, dogmas over against the life they are intended to explain
2. a professional, scholarly, clerical "criticism of life"
3. bookish and filled with quotes from anatomist's predecessors
4. stylized, stereotyped characters
5. analogous to the dialectic method
6. develops the quality of creative detachment

7. skeptical about religious ideas
8. attacks social conventions
9. encyclopaedic farrago; compendium of erudition
10. frequent use of obscenity; riotous chaos

BURTON'S *ANATOMY*:

"[N]ot until Burton's *Anatomy of Melancholy* did the Menippean satire become an integral part of English literature.

The connection of this book with the encyclopedic farrago is obvious enough, but the absence of any *cena* setting, dialogue, or narrative might lead us to suspect Burton's literary claims. A closer examination will soon undeceive us. Burton's title of 'Democritus Junior,' borrowed from Erasmus, marks his Menippean ambitions clearly enough, and in the love-melancholy section, the most revised and expanded of all, quotations from Athenaeus, Lucian, Erasmus, and Agrippa pour off his pen. His introduction contains a Utopia: his digressions illustrate scholarly distillations of the main features of the tradition: the digression of air, of the marvellous journey; the digression of spirits, of the ironic use of the occult; the digression of the miseries of scholars, of the clerical satire. His lists of diseases and manias are not exactly obscene, but they contain enough of the material of obscenity to achieve much the same artistic effect as the catalogues of torcheculs and epithets of codpieces in *Gargantua*. The long lists of articles of diet take us back to Athenaeus, and there is a good deal, such as the string of consolatory phrases in the *Remedies of Discontents* section, which reflects only the magpie impulse to collect that we have found to be related to the form. In all cases, of course, the method is that of the exhaustive catalogue of conflicting authorities also used by Rabelais.

In short, *The Anatomy of Melancholy* is not a medical treatise which has accidentally survived in literature because of its style: it is not a freak of fantastic erudition; it is not a scholar's crib or vade-mecum. It is exactly the same kind of encyclopedic survey of a mad world we have found *The Praise of Folly* and *The Vanity of the Arts and Sciences* to be, except that it is longer and more comprehensive. Not a single feature of our form is missing from it: not even the dialogue, for quotations from books can speak as eloquently of the confusion of the wise as table talk. *The Anatomy of Melancholy* is as truly prose fiction as a tale of Poe or a novel of Thackeray. Hooker's *Ecclesiastical Polity* and Bacon's *Advancement of Learning* may be works on theology and philosophy of great literary merit; but *The Anatomy of Melancholy* is literature itself, and it is high time that Burton was dragged into the central and commanding literary position he ought to hold. He is our greatest prose artist between Malory and Swift; his book is to Elizabethan prose what *The Faerie Queene* is to its poetry; he put the most comprehensive criticism of life into one book that English literature had seen since that Chaucer whom he delights to call 'our English Homer'" (CW 21: 34–5).

C. "The Four Forms of Prose Fiction" (1950)

Features of the anatomy

4. deals with people as mental attitudes (humours)
5. concerned with abstract ideas and theories
6. sees evil and folly as diseases of the intellect
7. is a loose-jointed narrative form
8. relies on free play of intellectual fancy and humorous observation that produces caricature
9. conceives of the world in terms of a single intellectual pattern
10. contains violent dislocations of narrative logic
11. piles up an enormous mass of erudition

BURTON'S ANATOMY:

"This creative treatment of exhaustive erudition is the organizing principle of the greatest Menippean satire in English before Swift, Burton's *Anatomy of Melancholy*. Here human society is studied in terms of the intellectual pattern provided by the conception of melancholy, a symposium of books replaces dialogue, and the result is the most comprehensive survey of human life in one book that English literature had seen since Chaucer, one of Burton's favourite authors. We may note in passing the Utopia in his introduction and his 'digressions,' which when examined turn out to be scholarly distillations of Menippean forms: the digression of air, of the marvellous journey; the digression of spirits, of the ironic use of erudition; the digression of the miseries of scholars, of the satire on the *philosophus gloriosus*. The word "anatomy" in Burton's title means a dissection or analysis, and expresses very accurately the intellectualized approach of his form. We may as well adopt it as a convenient name to replace the cumbersome and in modern times rather misleading 'Menippean satire'" (CW 21: 86).

D. *Anatomy of Criticism* (1957)

Features of the anatomy

1. intellectualized and extroverted form
2. dominant role of theoretical interest

3. stylized characters that represent mental attitudes they express
4. loose-jointed narrative form
5. relies on free-play of intellectual fancy
6. contains humorous observation that produces caricature; thus, tends toward satire

Burton's *Anatomy*. In *Anatomy of Criticism* Frye incorporates the paragraph above about Burton's *Anatomy* from "The Four Forms of Prose Fiction" (CW 22: 291–2).

Varieties of the Anatomy

The anatomy as a form of prose fiction is much less extensive than, say, the novel or the romance, but as Frye continued to spot anatomies and anatomists over the years the class expanded substantially, as we see in the followings lists:

Works Designated as Anatomies and Writers as Anatomists by Frye

Agrippa, Cornelius, *Vanity of the Arts and Sciences* (1530)
Amory, Thomas, *The Life of John Buncle* (1756–66)
Athenaeus, *Deipnosophists* (2nd cent. CE)
Berkeley, George, *Siris* (1744)
Blake, William, *Island of the Moon* (1784)
Boethius, *Consolation of Philosophy* (ca. 524)
Browne, Sir Thomas, *Religio Medici* (1642); *Urn Burial* (1658)
Burton, Robert, *Anatomy of Melancholy* (1621)
Butler, Samuel, *Erewhon* (1872); *Erewhon Revisited* (1901)
Carroll, Lewis, *Alice's Adventures in Wonderland* (1865); *Through the Looking-Glass* (1871)
Castiglione, Baldassare, *The Book of the Courtier* (1528)
Earle, John, *Microcosmography* (1628)
Erasmus, Desiderius, *In Praise of Folly* (1511); *A Fish Diet* (1526)
Flaubert, Gustave, *Bouvard et Pécuchet* (1881)
Huxley, Aldous, *Brave New World* (1932); *Chrome Yellow* (1921); *Antic Hay* (1923); *Point Counter Point* (1928)
Kingsley, Charles, *The Water-Babies* (1863)
Landor, Walter, *Imaginary Conversations* (1824)
Lucian, *Sale of Lives*; *Symposium*; *Alexander the False Prophet*; *Kataplous*; *Charon* (2nd cent. CE)
Lull, Ramon, *Blanquerna* (1283–84)

Lyly, John, *Euphues: The Anatomy of Wit* (1578)
More, Sir Thomas, *Utopia* (1516)
Macrobius, *Saturnalia* (5th cent. CE)
Peacock, Thomas Love, *Headlong Hall* (1816); *The Misfortunes of Elphin* (1829); *Crochet Castle* (1841)
Petronius, *Satyricon* (1st cent. CE)
Sidney, Sir Philip, *Arcadia* (1581–84)
Southey, Robert, *The Doctor* (1834–47)
Stubbes, Philip, *Anatomy of Abuses* (1583)
Swift, Jonathan, *The Battle of the Books* (1704); *Gulliver's Travels* (1726); *A Tale of a Tub* (1704)
Voltaire, François Marie Arouet de, *Candide* (1759); *Diatribe of Dr. Akakia* (1753); *L'Ingénu* (1767)
Varro
Walton, Izaak, *The Compleat Angler* (1653)
Wilson, John, *et al.*, *Noctes Ambrosianae* (1822–35)

Short form: dialogue or colloquy, as in Erasmus, Voltaire; *cena* or symposium

Hybrid Forms

Novel–Anatomy
- Borrow, George, Lavengro (1851); The Romany Rye (1857)
- Briffault, Robert Stephen, *Europa* (1935)
- Bunyan, John, *Grace Abounding* (1666)
- Disraeli, Benjamin
- Eliot, George, later novels
- James, Henry, *The Ambassadors* (1903)
- Lawrence, D. H., *The Plumed Serpent* (1926)
- Meredith, George, *The Egoist* (1879)
- Peacock, Thomas Love
- Sterne, Laurence, *Tristram Shandy* (1759–67)
- Proletarian novels of the 1930s

Romance–Anatomy
- Melville, Herman, *Moby Dick* (1851)
- Rabelais, François, *Gargantua and Pantagruel* (1532–35)

Confession–Anatomy
- Carlyle, Thomas, *Sartor Resartus* (1833–34)
- Kierkegaard, Søren, *Either-Or* (1843)

Montaigne, Michel Eyquem de, *Essays* (1580–95)
Novel–Romance–Anatomy
Cervantes, Miguel de, *Don Quixote* (1605–15)
Novel–Confession–Anatomy
Proust, Marcel, *Remembrance of Things Past* (1913–27)
Romance–Confession–Anatomy
Apuleius, *The Golden Ass* (2nd cent. CE)
Novel–Romance–Confession–Anatomy
Joyce, James, *Ulysses* (1922)

Congeners

Works, including poems, not strictly anatomies by one or more of Frye's definitions of the form but which have certain family resemblances to the Menippean satire or anatomy:

Barclay, John, *Euphoprmionis Satyricon* (1603)
Bellamy, Edward, *Looking Backward* (1888)
Borrow, George, *The Bible in Spain* (1843); *Wild Wales* (1862)
Browning, Robert, *Sludge the Medium* (1864)
Bunyan, John, *The Pilgrim's Progress* (1678–84)
Dostoevsky, Fyodor, *The Brothers Karamazov* (1879–80)
Doughty, Charles Montagu, *Travels in Arabia Deserta* (1843)
Dryden, John, *Absalom and Achitophel* (1681); *MacFlecknoe* (1682); *Religio Laici* (1682)
Erasmus, Desiderius, *Adagia* (1500); *Colloquies* (1516)
Fletcher, Phineas, *The Purple Island* (1633)
Galsworthy, John, *The Forsyte Saga* (1922)
Gellius, Aulus, *Attic Nights* (2nd cent. CE)
Mann, Thomas, *Joseph and His Brethren* (1933–43)
Martianus Capella, *On the Marriage of Philology and Mercury* (5th cent. CE)
Morris, William
Pithou, Pierre, *et al.*, *Satire Menippée* (16th cent.)
Plato, *Symposium* (ca. 385–380 BCE)
Rolland, Romain, *Jean-Christophe* (10 vols., 1904–12)
Romains, Jules, *Men of Good Will* (14 vols., 1932–46)
Voltaire, François Marie Arouet de, *Dictionnaire Philosophique* (1764)
Wells, H. G.

Frye on Burton's *Anatomy*

Burton represented for Frye the kind of "slightly nutty fantasy" that had been a characteristic of Oxford's eccentric bachelors for centuries: "when one examines," he wrote in 1972, "the great imaginative productions of Oxford, such works as *The Anatomy of Melancholy* and *Alice in Wonderland*, one sees ... a hyper-logical fantasy which teeters on the brink of normal mental processes. That, of course, throws a flood of light on a number of other Oxford geniuses, such as Pater and Hopkins" (CW 7: 470). But Burton represented for Frye much more than an example of Oxford's *genius loci*. He was also attracted to Burton because of his verbal exuberance, his style (including the easygoing lilt of his musical rhythm), his encyclopaedism, his sense of humour, and his creative and pensive melancholy. Burton's *Anatomy* for Frye was inexhaustible in its breadth and depth, and it became another of those many books, such as Frazer's *Golden Bough* or Gibbon's *Decline and Fall of the Roman Empire*, that have undergone in time a change in genre. In Burton's case, what began as a medical treatise evolved into a literary one. This is not a function of its style, although Frye describes the features of Burton's style in some detail, but the result of the features it shares with other Menippean satires.

Several similarities between Frye and Burton suggest themselves. Both were clergymen. Both spent their entire professional lives in a single university. Both had very bookish minds. Both had a keen sense of humour.[105] And both saw their work, in Montaigne's phrase, as consubstantial with themselves,[106] each being possessed by what Frye calls a "dream of all one's work forming a single structure," "a speaking or written double of himself" (CW 6: 555). Burton continued to revise and expand the original 1621 version of his book. He issued five different editions during his lifetime, and a sixth, published after his death, incorporated further additions and emendations. Frye's "single structure" was somewhat different. He produced a number of separate books, but they all took their place in an eight-part framework he called his ogdoad, a dream that gave a schematic direction to his life's work. Both, moreover, were given to what Frye calls "verbal outline": "the quality I so admire in Burton and struggle for myself is verbal *outline*, a verbal analogy of powerful sketching that contains a great mass of facts" (CW 9: 25). Finally, both Burton and Frye suffered from melancholy. In response to David Cayley's question about whether he had experienced melancholy, Frye replied: "To the extent that I was poor and very much thrown back on myself, yes. But there are two sides to that, the side of alienation and the side of self-reliance. If there's nobody else but yourself, you have to depend on yourself. Burton has a long episode on miseries of scholars, which I certainly reacted to at one time" (CW 24: 937).

In a 1962 address to the American Psychiatric Association, "The Imaginative and the Imaginary," Frye examines the theme of melancholy in *Hamlet*, the "most fascinating" play of the Renaissance, and then he turns to Burton, whom he is fond of quoting at length. Here we can let them both speak (at some length), Frye's own quotations from Burton describing first the lover's mistress and then a case of hysteria:

> Not only the most fascinating play of the period [*Hamlet*], but its greatest prose work (in England), has melancholy for its theme. Burton's *Anatomy of Melancholy* is an exhaustive analysis of the causes, symptoms, treatment, and cure of melancholy, with two enormous appendices on love melancholy and religious melancholy. Burton was an Oxford don, and his chief amusement is said to have been going down to the Isis river and listening to the bargemen swear. The story may be true, or it may have been invented by someone who noticed that the qualities of Burton's prose, with its vast catalogues, piled-up epithets, Latin tags, allusiveness, and exhaustive knowledge of theology and personal hygiene, are essentially the qualities of good swearing. Burton assumes rather than discusses the connection of melancholy with creative power: being a scholar himself, like Hamlet, he associates it rather with the scholarly temperament, and includes a long digression on the miseries of scholars. On religious melancholy his position is simple: one can best avoid it by sticking to the reasonable middle way of the Church of England, avoiding the neurotic extremes of papist and puritan on either side. But in love there is no reasonable ground to take, for its very essence is illusion. On this point we had better let Burton speak for himself:
>
>> Every lover admires his mistress, though she be very deformed of herself, ill-favoured, wrinkled, pimpled, pale, red, yellow, tanned, tallow-faced, having a swollen juggler's platter face, or a thin, lean, chitty face, have clouds in her face, be crooked, dry, bald, goggle-eyed, blear-eyed, or with staring eyes, she looks like a squis'd cat, hold her head still awry, heavy, dull, hollow-eyed, black or yellow about the eyes, or squint-eyed, sparrow-mouthed, Persian hook-nosed, have a sharp fox-nose, a red nose, China flat, great nose, *nare simo patuloque*, a nose like a promontory, gubber-tushed, rotten teeth, black, uneven, brown teeth, beetle-browed, a witch's

> beard, her breath stink all over the room, her nose drop winter and summer, with a Bavarian poke under her chin, a sharp chin, lave-eared, with a long crane's neck, which stands awry too, *pendulis mammis*, "her dugs like two double jugs," or else no dugs, in that other extreme, bloody-fallen fingers, she have filthy, long unpared nails, scabbed hands or wrists, a tanned skin, a rotten carcass, crooked back, she stoops, is lame, splay-footed, "as slender in the middle as a cow in the waist," gouty legs, her ankles hang over her shoes, her feet stink, she breed lice, a mere changeling, a very monster, an oaf imperfect, her whole complexion savours, an harsh voice, incondite gesture, vile gait, a vast virago, or an ugly tit, a slug, a fat fustilugs, a truss, a long lean rawbone, a skeleton, a sneaker (*si qua latent meliora puta* ["think that what is not seen is better," Ovid, *Metamorphosis*, 1.502]), and to thy judgment looks like a mard in a lanthorn, whom thou couldst not fancy for a world, but hatest, loathest, and wouldest have spit in her face, or blow thy nose in her bosom, *remedium amoris* to another man, a dowdy, a slut, a scold, a nasty, rank, rammy, filthy, beastly quean, dishonest peradventure, obscene, base, beggarly, rude, foolish, untaught, peevish, Irus' daughter, Thersites' sister, Grobian's scholar; if he love her once, he admires her for all this, he takes no notice of any such errors or imperfections of body or mind, *Ipsa haec Delectant, veluti Balbinum polypus Agnae* ["Or is even charmed, like Balbinus with Hagne's mole," Horace, *Satire III*]; he had rather have her than any woman in the world.[107]

[In Burton's time] scientific and occult explanations could be given of the same phenomena, and hysteria and hallucination might be explained either as mental disorders or as caused by witchcraft or diabolical suggestion. Burton gives a good deal of attention to such matters, though with a detachment toward them unusual in his age. He has read all the books about devils and witches, and has gathered from them that there is more theorizing than solid knowledge of the subject. He drops a hint that belief in their existence is convenient for an organized priestcraft, and continues:

> Many such stories I find amongst pontifical writers, to prove their assertions; let them free their own credits; some few I will recite in this kind out of most approved physicians. Cornelius Gemma,

> *lib. 2 de nat. mirac. cap.* 4, related of a young maid, called Katherine Gualter, a cooper's daughter, *anno* 1571, that had such strange passions and convulsions, three men could not sometimes hold her; she purged a live eel, which he saw, a foot and a half long, and touched himself; but the eel afterwards vanished; she vomited some twenty-four pounds of fulsome stuff of all colours, twice a day for fourteen days; and after that she voided great balls of hair, pieces of wood, pigeon's dung, parchment, goose dung, coals; and after them two pound of pure blood, and then again coals and stones, of which some had inscriptions, bigger than a walnut, some of them pieces of glass, brass, etc., besides paroxysms of laughing, weeping and ecstasies, etc. *Et hoc (inquit) cum horrore vidi*, "this I saw with horror." They could do no good on her by physic, but left her to the clergy.[108]
>
> Burton is aware that he is describing a case of hysteria; what he is not sure of is whether it was the doctor or the patient who had it, and the reader is left with the feeling that Burton regards hysteria as a highly contagious illness. (CW 21: 424–7)

While Frye clearly takes great delight in reproducing Burton's exuberant catalogues, does he see *The Anatomy of Melancholy* as also yielding instruction? Even more, does it have any instrumental value medically or psychologically? Does it have therapeutic significance? Frye's answer is yes. In "*Rencontre*" he writes:

> Burton's *Anatomy of Melancholy* adopts the position of a university lecturer, the conductor of a vast orchestra of "authorities" which he can call up one by one. He pretends to be analyzing the causes, symptoms, and cures of the disease known as melancholy, but his attitude to his audience is a rhetorical one: he is out to persuade more than to expound. That is, having written one of the most delightful books in the language, he knows that reading that book would be a much better cure for melancholy than most of the remedies he prescribes. So he links himself with the ethical tradition of rhetorical prose. (CW 10: 54)

In "Literature as Therapy" Frye raises the possibility, at least, that reading Burton may indeed be cathartic: "Burton does not say that literature is a therapy for melancholy, except in a wider context of recreation generally. On the other hand, he begins his book by saying that he wrote the book because he was melancholy himself. In other words, it was a form of autotherapy that inspired him to write it. The other reason for writing it is that *we* are: everybody suffers from melancholy. Consequently, the book itself may have a therapeutic value" (CW 18: 467).[109]

THE FINAL CAUSE OF THE ANATOMY

The question naturally arises: What does it mean to say that Frye's *Anatomy* belongs to the same category as Burton's *Anatomy*? Frye's book is obviously not a work of prose fiction, but it does contain a number of characteristics of the anatomy as a literary form: it is an intellectualized form and thus focuses on *dianoia* rather than *ethos*; it builds up integrated patterns; it has a theoretical interest; it embraces a wide variety of subtypes; it displays considerable erudition; its schematic form is an imaginative structure, born of an exuberant and creative wit; and whatever dramatic appeal it has comes from the dialectic of ideas. Frye's *Anatomy* is of course not Menippean satire, which combines fantasy and morality often with the deprecating quality as found in, say, Lyly's *The Anatomy of Wit*, but embedded in its Utopianism is a clear moral attitude. If Frye, as an implied author, might appear to be obsessed with his entire intellectual project, he does not qualify as a *philosophus gloriosus* or a learned and pedantic crank—often the object of satire in the anatomy.

The main difference between Frye's *Anatomy* and other anatomies, however, is in their differing final causes. Frye always insisted that the lines between the critical and the creative should not be sharply drawn, and he remarks in one of his *Anatomy* notebooks, "In poetics we often have to speak poetically" (CW 23: 172). But for all of its aesthetic appeal—its creativity and ingenuity, its wit and stylistic charm, its inventive taxonomies—the *Anatomy* remains a work of criticism, in spite of those, such as M. H. Abrams and Frank Kermode, who claim otherwise, mistaking, it seems to me, the means for the end.[110] The *Anatomy* comes to us primarily in what Frye would later call second-phase language, the continuous prose of abstraction and reason and of analogical and dialectical thinking. Its aim is the analysis of literary conventions and the synthesis of these into comprehensive order.

Burton's *Anatomy of Melancholy* was ostensibly a medical discourse. In Frye's terminology, it was centrifugal, meaning that it referred to something outside itself. Today it is read less for instruction into the cures of the psychiatrically sick than for its delight, and so it has become centripetal like other works of literature. Readers of the future will determine whether Frye's *Anatomy* follows the course of Burton's. So far, almost sixty years after its publication, it is still read primarily as a work of literary theory, and most of its applications have been in the interest of description, explanation, and interpretation. This is not to gainsay its wit and eloquence, the aesthetic appeal of its formal structure, and its engendering of delight. But none of these things is the final cause of a book Frye saw as *a* new criticism that went beyond *the* New Criticism.

In conclusion, it is perhaps worth noting that Frye is an anatomist in another sense—as a writer of fiction himself. He had a number of fantasies about becoming a fiction writer and in fact wrote a substantial portion of a more or less realistic novel. But the anatomy tradition shows through in eight pieces of short fiction he wrote, six of which he published over a five-year period beginning in 1936. These hardly qualify as short stories, at least in the main tradition of that form as practiced by Chekhov and Maupassant or James and Mansfield.[111] The genre is admittedly difficult to define, and in *Anatomy of Criticism*, Frye's analysis of the genre amounts mostly to pointing out the forms that are shorter versions of his four forms of fiction: the tale, of the kind that Poe wrote, is a short form of romance; the short story, a terse form of the novel; the essay, a short version of the confession; and the dialogue or colloquy, a brief Menippean satire or anatomy. This means that the dialogue or colloquy, which Frye sometimes refers to as the *cena*, is, like the anatomy, an extroverted and intellectualized form. His stories are fundamentally brief anatomies. He has no interest in character development and very little in plot: *ethos* and *mythos* are displaced almost completely by *dianoia*. The point of Frye's little anatomies, four of which he called "dialogues,"[112] is to *make* a point. He remarked to David Cayley that he was attracted to satire at an early age and that when he wrote the stories he "knew more about ideas than ... about people," adding that "[i]f somebody like Borges had been known to me at the time, I would have tried to pick up that kind of tradition (CW 24: 938). As a young person, Frye immersed himself in Shaw, with his theatre of vital ideas and his comic and ironic tone. While the Blakean vision replaced the Shavian one as the point around which his literary universe revolved, he never discarded the ironic and satirical mask.[113]

In 2002 Thomas Wright named Burton's *Anatomy* as the first of his top five cult writers, one of the characteristics of cult writing being that it inspires other writers, such as Borges. A year before, on the occasion of Burton's *Anatomy* having been released as a *New York Review of Books* Classic, Nicholas Lezard declared it "the best book ever written." While Frye eschewed value judgments, he nevertheless could not hide his admiration for Burton's masterpiece, and it could be that his longstanding and repeated attention to Burton caused him, like it did Samuel Johnson, to get out of bed earlier than he wanted to.

7
Frye and Søren Kierkegaard

The roots of Frye's expansive vision of culture have often been remarked. Blake and the Bible are obviously central to the development of his ideas, and much has been written about Frye's debts to both. Much has been written as well about other significant influences on Frye: Nella Cotrupi's book on Frye and Vico, Glen Gill's study of Frye and twentieth-century mythographers (Eliade, Jung, and others), Ford Russell's account of the influence of Spengler, Frazer, and Cassirer on Frye. Still other studies have looked for points of contact between Frye and Buber (Sára Tóth) and Frye and Rousseau (Monique Anne Gyalokay). But no one, so far as I know, has considered the ways that Kierkegaard helped to shape Frye's thought. As the impact of Kierkegaard on Frye is relatively substantial, the purpose of this essay is to examine Frye's use of Kierkegaard. Direct influence is sometimes difficult to demonstrate, but parallels between and similar ideas held by the two can be instructive. Kierkegaard helps to define, illustrate, and develop Frye's thought. Along the way, we will also glance at Frye's critique of certain Kierkegaardian ideas.

Frye was attracted to Kierkegaard for the same reason he was attracted to Spengler and a host of other visionaries who wrote what he called "kook books." "I was well aware," he writes,

> all the time I was studying [Spengler and Frazer] that they were rather stupid men and often slovenly scholars. But I found them, or rather their central visions, unforgettable, while there are hundreds of books by more intelligent and scrupulous people which I have forgotten having read. Some of them are people who have utterly refuted the claims of Spengler and Frazer to be taken seriously. But the thinker who was annihilated on Tuesday has to be annihilated all over again on Wednesday.... This is not merely my own perversity: we all find that it is not only, perhaps not even primarily, the balanced and judicious people that we turn to for insight. It is also such people as Baudelaire, Rimbaud, Hölderlin, Kierkegaard, Dostoevsky, Nietzsche, all of them liars in Wilde's sense of the word, as Wilde was himself. They were people whose lives got smashed up in various ways, but rescued fragments from the smash of an intensity that the

> steady-state people seldom get to hear about. Their vision is penetrating because it is partial and distorted: it is truthful because it is falsified. To the Old Testament's question, "Where shall wisdom be found?" there is often only the New Testament's answer: "Well, not among the wise, at any rate." (CW 4: 39–40)[114]

Frye had more than a passing acquaintance with the writings of Kierkegaard. His library contained fourteen books by the existential Dane, twelve of which he annotated: *The Concept of Dread*, *The Concept of Irony*, *The Diary of Søren Kierkegaard*, *Either/Or* (vol. 1), *Fear and Trembling*, *The Journals of Søren Kierkegaard*, *Of the Difference between a Genius and an Apostle*, *The Point of View for My Work as an Author*, *The Present Age*, *Repetition*, *The Sickness unto Death*, and *Stages of Life's Way*. Frye also owned Kierkegaard's *Edifying Discourses: A Selection* and volume 2 of *Either/Or*; in his essay "Blake's Bible" he refers to *Attack upon Christendom* (CW 16: 423); and in *The Great Code* he mentions a translation of *The Present Age* different from the one he owned. As Frye quotes a phrase from *Concluding Scientific Postscript*, he may have read that work as well.[115] On the evidence we have, then, Frye was familiar with a substantial number of the books by Kierkegaard that were available in translation during his lifetime.

In his 1949 diary Frye reports that he has begun reading Kierkegaard's *Concept of Dread* again (CW 8: 189). This would have been Walter Lowrie's translation of the book, which appeared in 1944 (the translations into English of Kierkegaard by Lowrie, Alexander Dru, and David and Lillian Swenson began to appear in the early 1940s). So Frye's reading of Kierkegaard had begun at least by the late 1940s and perhaps earlier. There is a steady stream of references to Kierkegaard—more than 250 altogether—in Frye's writings, beginning in 1949 and continuing in his published and unpublished work through the posthumous *The Double Vision* (1991). He began to reread Kierkegaard in the late 1980s, and he gives a fairly extensive account of this rereading in Notebook 50 (CW 5: 255–418).

Although Kierkegaard did not use the word "existentialism," he is widely considered to be the father of this philosophical movement. Frye's own attention to existentialism in general followed closely on the post-World War II manifestations of the movement. He reports using the word "existentialist" in a January 1949 discussion with his Victoria College colleagues, and by 1950 he is lecturing on the "existential movement" (CW 8: 100, 282). Several dozen instances of his use of the word can be found in his diaries from the late 1940s and early 1950s.[116] Frye wrote nothing extensive about existentialism, but two thumbnail accounts of the movement can be found in "Speculation and Concern" (CW 7: 254–6) and "The University and Personal Life" (CW 7: 367).

The central Kierkegaardian *topoi* that make their way into Frye's writing relate to his understanding of the myths of freedom and concern; the either/or dialectic; the principle of repetition; Kierkegaard as a prophetic, kerygmatic, metaliterary writer; and his role in the revolutionary explosion in nineteenth-century thought, which Frye characterizes by the metaphor of the drunken boat. The present essay will examine what Frye says about these subjects in turn. It is often best to let Frye speak for himself, so the generous supply of quotations from his published and unpublished work results in a kind of Kierkegaardian anthology.

The Myth of Concern

The OED gives twenty-one meanings for "concern" as a noun. In common parlance the word refers to an active interest or an important relation to some matter. In the mid-1960s Frye began to use the word in a special way. Rather than recurring to the common distinction between fact and value, Frye says in a 1965 essay entitled "Speculation and Concern" that the existential terms "concern" and "engagement" are touchstones for what the humanities create. Three years later in reflecting on the history of his interest in the Bible, Frye writes,

> I was beginning to see that the language of religion and the language of literature were closely connected, but the reason for the connection did not really become clear to me until the existentialist people came along after the war and I began reading Kierkegaard and his followers. The reason for the connection is that myth is the language of *concern*. Man is in two worlds: there is a world around him, an objective world, which it is the business of science to study. But there is also the world that man is trying to build out of his environment, and this is the world which depends on man's view of himself and his destiny, or his concern about where he came from and where he is going to, and all his hopes and his ideals, his anxieties and his panics, come into his view of the society that he wants to build. (CW 27: 274)

In *The Critical Path* (1971), Frye expands the meaning of the word "concern," setting up an elaborate dialectic between the myths of freedom and concern. In *The Great Code*, "existential concern" enters into Frye's account of kerygma, and eight years later "concern" is given another twist in chapter 2 of *Words with Power*, entitled "Concern and Myth."

Frye never points to a source in Kierkegaard for his appropriation of the word "concern," but in the senses just specified (*Bekymring*—concern, care, interest, worry) the word appears throughout the Danish theologian's works. He writes, for example, "Not until the moment when there awakens in his soul a concern about what meaning the world has for him and he for the world, about what meaning everything within him by which he himself belongs to the world has for him and he therein for the world—only then does the inner being announce its presence in this concern." What this awakened concern yearns for is "a knowledge that does not remain knowledge for a single moment but is transformed into action the moment it is possessed" (*Eighteen Upbuilding Discourses* 86). Or again: "There is a truth whose greatness, whose sublimity we are accustomed to extol by saying that it is an *objective* truth, that it is equally valid whether one accepts it or not.... There is another kind of truth, or if this is more unassuming, another kind of truths, which we might call the *concerned* truths" (*Edifying Discourses* 87).[117]

Although Frye read Kierkegaard before he read Paul Tillich, the appeal of the word "concern" might also be traced to the first volume of Tillich's *Systematic Theology*, which appeared in 1951. Tillich had been significantly influenced by Kierkegaard during his student years at the University of Halle. "The word 'concern,'" Tillich writes,

> points to the "existential" character of religious experience. We cannot speak adequately of the "object of religion" without simultaneously removing its character as an object. That which is ultimate gives itself only to the attitude of ultimate concern. It is the correlate of an unconditional concern but not a "highest thing" called "the absolute" or "the unconditioned," about which we could argue in detached objectivity. It is the object of total surrender, demanding also the surrender of our subjectivity while we look at it. It is a matter of infinite passion and interest (Kierkegaard), making us its object whenever we try to make it our object. (*Systematic* 1:12)

As we will see in chapter 11, Frye had heard Tillich lecture at the University of Toronto in February 1950,[118] and he owned and annotated four of Tillich's books.[119]

Speculation and Concern

In Frye's essay of this title, which aims to differentiate between the sciences and the humanities, "speculation" is his shorthand for the detached mode of inquiry of the sciences. "Concern," on the other hand, is what we find in the containing forms of myths: "it is in these myths that the nature of man's concern for his world is most clearly expressed" (CW 7: 256). One version of "concern" is found in existentialism, particularly in Kierkegaard's notion of "ethical freedom." Existentialism, Frye writes, "insists that if we think of the external world as a human world, certain elements become primary that are carefully kept out of science: the imminence of death, the feeling of alienation, the pervading sense of accident and of emptiness, and the direct confrontation with something arbitrary and absurd." Kierkegaard's "ethical freedom" refers to the person, in Frye's words, "who has passed beyond speculation. It would be better to use the existential terms engagement or concern to express the contrast between a reality which is there to begin with and the greater reality which, like religious faith or artistic creation, does not exist at all to begin with, but is brought into being through a certain kind of human act" (CW 7: 254, 256). The parallel between speculation and concern, on the one hand, and Kierkegaard's "aesthetic" and "ethical" stages, on the other, will be considered shortly. The point here is that "concern" in the sense of committed or engaged derives from Kierkegaard and his twentieth-century followers.

"Concern" can mean a troubled state of mind, uneasiness, or anxiety (Kierkegaard's *Angst*), and this is the meaning it occasionally has for Frye. In his radio talk, given as a prelude to a performance of Auden's *For the Time Being*, Frye writes, "Kierkegaard says that all human activity, without exception, is the product of concern or anxiety about human life, so from one point of view all human activity is hysterical, compulsive and neurotic." Frye then advises his audience to "[l]isten for the word 'anxiety' in Auden's play: it's a very important word. The neurotic can't get at his neurosis or become conscious of it without the help of a psychoanalyst. But for anxiety, which defeats all of us equally, there aren't any psychoanalysts. To try to become conscious of this takes us into the mystery of what theologians call original sin and whatever it is that makes all human life grow out of a tense and frightened dissatisfaction. We can no more see inside this than we can see our own backbones" (CW 25: 298–9).[120]

The Myths of Freedom and Concern

In *The Critical Path*, Frye claims that the process of interpreting the social myths of culture is "very similar to criticism in literature" and that "the different forms of critical interpretation cannot be sharply separated, whether they are applied to the plays of Shakespeare, the manuscripts of the Bible, the American Constitution, or the oral traditions of an aboriginal tribe. In the area of general concern they converge, however widely the technical contexts in law, theology, literature or anthropology may differ" (CW 27: 84). This is the main assumption on which the book is based: while literary critics are not qualified to handle all the "technical contexts" of culture, they are especially prepared, particularly if they are archetypal critics, to interpret the cultural phenomena that form the social environment of literature. "The modern critic," Frye says, "is ... a student of mythology, and his total subject embraces not merely literature, but the areas of concern which the mythical language of construction and belief enters and informs. These areas constitute the mythological subjects, and they include large parts of religion, philosophy, political theory, and the social sciences" (CW 27: 67).

The Critical Path treats a wide-ranging body of such subjects, including the difference between oral and writing cultures, Renaissance humanism, the critical theories of Sidney and Shelley, Marxism and democracy, the idea of progress, advertising and propaganda, social contract theories and conceptions of Utopia, contemporary youth culture, McLuhanism, and theories of education. What holds these diverse subjects together is the dialectical framework that Frye establishes: whatever issue he confronts, it always is set against the background of what he sees as the two opposing myths of Western culture, the myth of concern and the myth of freedom.

The myth of concern comprises everything that a society is most concerned to know. It is the disposition which leads one to uphold communal rather than individual values. It exists, Frye says, "to hold society together.... For it, truth and reality are not directly connected with reasoning or evidence, but are socially established. What is true, for concern, is what society does and believes in response to authority, and a belief, so far as a belief is verbalized, is a statement of willingness to participate in a myth of concern. The typical language of concern therefore tends to become the language of belief" (CW 27: 23). "Concern" is basically a social category: a society's body of concerns are all those religious, political, cultural, and economic presuppositions that the members of society generally assent to and that therefore make communication possible. Concerns spring from humanity's desire to know where it came from, what its nature is, and where it is going.

A myth of concern has its roots in religion and only later branches out into politics, law, and literature. It is inherently traditional and conservative, placing a strong emphasis on values of coherence and continuity. It originates in oral or preliterate culture and is associated with continuous verse conventions and discontinuous prose forms. And it is "deeply attached to ritual, to coronations, weddings, funerals, parades, demonstrations, where something is publicly done that expresses an inner social identity" (CW 27: 29). Concerns, can of course, compete with one another, and the monopoly of Christian concern in Western culture started to give way in the eighteenth century so that a plurality of myths of concern, including secular ones, began to arise (CW 27: 33).

The myth of freedom, on the other hand, is committed to a truth of correspondence. It appeals to such self-validating criteria as "logicality of argument or (usually a later stage) impersonal evidence and verification." It is inherently "liberal," helping to develop and honouring such values as objectivity, detachment, suspension of judgment, tolerance, and respect for the individual. It "stresses the importance of the non-mythical elements in culture, of the truths and realities that are studied rather than created, provided by nature rather than by a social vision" (CW 27: 29). It originates in the mental habits which a writing culture, with its continuous prose and discontinuous verse forms, brings into society.

The way Frye uses this broad dialectic of freedom and concern can be illustrated by his treatment of two classic defences of poetry, Sidney's and Shelley's. Placing Sidney's view of poetry against the background of Renaissance humanism, Frye concludes that Sidney accommodates the role of the poet to the values of a reading and writing culture, to the norms of meaning established by writers of discursive prose. "The conception of poetry in Sidney," he says, "is an application of the general humanistic view of disciplined speech as the manifestation or audible presence of social authority" (CW 27: 44). For Sidney, "what is most distinctive about poetry is the poet's power of illustration, a power which is partly an ability to popularize and make more accessible the truths of revelation and reason" (CW 27: 45). In other words, poetry is not qualitatively distinct from the other verbal disciplines. What actually occurs in Sidney's view of poetry, according to Frye, is that the original characteristics of the myths of freedom and concern are interchanged: "The myth of concern takes on a reasoning aspect, claiming the support of logic and historical evidence; the myth of freedom becomes literary and imaginative, as the poet, excluded from primary authority in the myth of concern, finds his social function in a complementary activity, which liberalizes concern but also ... reinforces it" (CW 27: 51).

In Shelley's defence, on the other hand, we return to a conception of poetry as mythical and psychologically primitive.

> Shelley begins by neatly inverting the hierarchy of values assumed in Sidney.... Shelley puts all the discursive disciplines into an inferior group of "analytic" operations of reason. They are aggressive; they think of ideas as weapons; they seek the irrefutable argument, which keeps eluding them because all arguments are theses, and theses are half-truths implying their own opposites.... The works of imagination, by contrast, cannot

> be refuted: poetry is the dialectic of love, which treats everything it encounters as another form of itself, and never attacks, only includes.... This argument assumes, not only that the language of poetry is mythical, but that poetry, in its totality, is in fact society's real myth of concern, and that the poet is still the teacher of that myth.... [I]n Sidney's day, it was accepted that the models of creation were established by God: for Shelley, man makes his own civilization, and at the centre of man's creation are the poets, whose work provides the models of human society. The myths of poetry embody and express man's creation of his own culture, rather than his reception of it from a divine source. (CW 27: 64, 65)

There is no denying the fact the Frye's sympathies lie on the side of Shelley, for both of them believe that the language of literature represents the imaginative possibilities of concern. And both of them are opposed to the constrictive view of Sidney which makes the critic an evaluator and which makes poetry subservient to whatever established framework of concern an elite society happens to be championing at the moment. To say that literature contains the imaginative possibilities of concern means, for Frye, that it displays "the total range of verbal fictions and models and images and metaphors out of which all myths of concern are constructed" (CW 27: 67). Frye's conclusion is that while Shelley's (and his own) view of poetry takes us back to the areas of concern expressed in primitive and oracular mythology, the critic's approach to the values expressed by a myth of concern must derive from the myth of freedom. "The critic *qua* critic," Frye says, "is not himself concerned but detached" (CW 27: 67).

The merging of freedom and concern, however, is what produces the social context of literature. If there is a central thesis to *The Critical Path*, it is the dialectical tension Frye seeks to establish between the myths of freedom and concern. This tension comprises his own central myth, as it were, and the cultural phenomena he examines throughout the book are interpreted from the perspective of this tension. A corollary to the tension is the necessity for a pluralism of myths of concern, which can only occur in societies with open mythologies.

> The basis of all tolerance in society, the condition in which a plurality of concerns can co-exist, is the recognition of the tension between concern and freedom.... Concern and freedom both occupy the whole of the same universe: they interpenetrate, and it is no good trying to set up boundary stones. Some, of course, meet the collision of concern and freedom from the opposite side, with a naive rationalism which expects that before long all myths of concern will be outgrown and only the appeal to reason

> and evidence and experiment will be taken seriously.... I consider such a view entirely impossible. The growth of non-mythical knowledge tends to eliminate the incredible from belief, and helps to shape the myth of concern according to the outlines of what experience finds possible and vision desirable. But the growth of knowledge cannot in itself provide us with the social vision which will suggest what we should do with our knowledge. (CW 27: 73–5)

This is where Frye's view of the social function of criticism enters the argument; the literary critic, or at least Frye's ideal critic, is prepared to see that myths of concern in society are like those in literature in that they represent the range of imaginative possibilities of belief. There are parallels between Frye's myths of freedom and concern and the two stages that Kierkegaard in *Either/Or* calls the "aesthetic" and the "ethical." *Either/Or* is the chief source of the existentialist tradition and, for Frye, the "classical statement of the relation of concern and freedom" (CW 27: 88).[121] We will examine the either/or dialectic shortly.

As for the social function of art, Frye thinks that Kierkegaard's position on that issue is essentially wrongheaded:

> The whole argument (over the social function of art) today is confused by the "existential" views of S.K. [Søren Kierkegaard] (through Auden), which oppose a theatrical or "aesthetic" view of reality to an ethical or active one, & then go through that to repetition. But S.K.'s repetition is really Aristotle's anagnorisis, and the fallacy of both aesthetic & ethical attitudes is in the common objectification of reality. I'm not talking about idolizing works of art, & S.K. shouldn't be talking about an external substantial reality *as well as* existence, or rather, as characteristic of the existential situation. Real existential thinking is hypothetical: that's the first use of art that goes beyond *quid agas*. At a certain point all ethical situations become unreal: that's why casuistry is a dismal & illiberal science. Art trains us in the vision of the unmodified, unimprovised existential situation. (CW 23: 234)[122]

Concern and Myth

This is the title of chapter 2 of *Words with Power*, and in that book, as well as in *The Double Vision* and a number of essays from the 1980s, Frye distinguished between primary and secondary concerns. Frye first used the phrase "primary concern" in *The Critical Path* (1971): "For Kierkegaard the detached, liberal, and impersonal attitude fostered by the study of an objective environment, and which flowers into comprehensive intellectual systems like that of Hegel, is an 'aesthetic' attitude. It is fundamentally immature because with this attitude man tries to fit himself into a larger container, the general outlines of which he can see with his reason, but forgetting that his reason built the container. The crisis of life comes when we pass over into the commitment represented by 'or,' take up our primary concern," escape from our psychological defences (what Kierkegaard calls "shut-upness" in *The Concept of Dread*), "and thus enter the sphere of genuine personality and ethical freedom" (CW 27: 88). A decade later Frye began to define "primary concerns" and to set them in opposition to "secondary concerns." His attention to the distinction becomes a frequently sounded refrain in his late work: almost 200 instances of his use of the two phrases occur in *Late Notebooks* alone, and some fifty instances appear in his essays from the 1980s.

Primary concerns are the universal, individual, and physical needs and desires of human beings. In his *Late Notebooks*, Frye engages in uninhibited speculation about the primary concerns, letting his mind play freely with the basic things essential for our survival and noting a number of analogues and links with other categories in his thinking about his second book on the Bible. The following chart can be taken as a summary of the chief features in this expansive free-play:

The Primary Concerns

The Four Concerns	Food and drink and related bodily needs	Sex	Property: money, possessions, shelter, clothing, & everything that constitutes property in the sense of what is "proper" to one's life; structure; property, in the Aristotelian sense of the material extension of the personality; money	Freedom of movement; play
Mythographer	Frazer: linked mythology with anxiety about food supply	Graves: linked mythology with anxiety about sex; Freud	G.R. Levy: linked mythology with anxiety about shelter	Gadamer, Huizinga, Havelock Ellis
Presiding God or Informing Presence	Hermes	Eros	Adonis	Prometheus

Chain-of-Being Level	animal, vegetable	human	mineral	mineral
Blakean Analogue	Tharmas	Orc	Urizen	Urthona
Central Archetype	Cave	Garden	Mountain	Furnace
Expanded Mode	Bodily identity	Love	Construction, creation	Free energy that work is aimed at
Double Gyre	Separation ending in union; separation aspect: excretion	Union followed by separation; excretory organs for union	Embryo within another body	Separation at the beginning of life
Parody or Demonic Forms	Eating and drinking the God-Man	Exploiting the genital machinery: whoring	Tomb of the dead God-Man	Work (penal)

Frye eventually settles on food, sex, property, and freedom of movement as the four primary concerns but not before wondering if they do not form a quincunx, with breathing in the middle,[123] and he vacillates on whether Tillich's "ultimate concern" might not be primary.[124] There are other qualifications—"Actually food, like breathing, while it's a primary concern, isn't one on quite the level of the others. Sex can expand into unity with nature, property into creativity, and freedom of movement into freedom of thought, but eating and drinking, along with breathing, have to remain on a more or less allegorical level" (CW 6: 641)—and permutations: "I don't include health in my four concerns, but it could come under property (Job's boils are an attack on his property in the Aristotelian sense) or freedom of movement (note how often those cured by Jesus are sick of the palsy)" (CW 6: 660). These qualifications, which come from Frye's notebooks, disappear from his accounts of the primary concerns in *Words with Power* and *The Double Vision*, where the variations are resolved into the four concerns just mentioned. "The axioms of primary concern," Frye says in a repeatedly sounded refrain, "are the simplest and baldest platitudes it is possible to formulate: that life is better than death, happiness better than misery, health better than sickness, freedom better than bondage, for all people without significant exception" (CW 26: 51–2).[125]

Secondary concerns are ideologies arising from the social contract. They have to do with religious beliefs, patriotic attachments, class systems, gender status, communal structures of authority, and various other forms of identity politics. Historically, secondary concerns have almost always trumped primary ones:

> We want to live and love, but we go to war; we want freedom, but depend on the exploiting of other peoples, of the natural environment, even of ourselves. In the twentieth century, with a pollution that threatens the supply of air to breathe and water to drink, it is obvious that we cannot afford the supremacy of ideological concerns any more. The need to eat, love, own property, and move about freely must come first, and such needs require peace, good will, and a caring and responsible attitude to nature. A continuing of ideological conflict, a reckless exploiting of the environment, a persistence in believing, with Mao Tse-Tung, that power comes out of the barrel of a gun, would mean, quite simply, that the human race cannot be long for this world. (CW 4: 170)[126]

This is why Frye says that primary concerns had better become primary again, or else.[127] In Frye's theory of language in chapter 1 of *Words with Power*, he calls the third mode of language "ideological" or "rhetorical," the function of which is to rationalize authority, and "ideological language supports the anxieties of social authority" (CW 26: 47). Of course the myths that spring from primary concerns are most often less about the satisfaction of these concerns than about the anxieties associated with their not getting satisfied. Sexual frustration, for example, is a universal theme of romance.

Anxiety

Anxiety as a psychological and existential state is a regular part of Frye's critical vocabulary. The word itself, along with its synonyms "dread" and "*Angst*," appears well over 900 times in Frye writings. As already noted, in the 1940s Frye read and then reread Kierkegaard's *The Concept of Dread* (or *Anxiety* or *Angst*, depending on the translation). Frye was also doubtless influenced by Paul Tillich's *The Courage To Be* (1952), a copy of which he owned. Tillich distinguishes three kinds of existential anxiety: ontic (brought on by a sense of fate and death), moral (resulting from guilt or condemnation), and spiritual (caused by feelings of emptiness and meaninglessness). And Frye was naturally familiar with Freud's various theories of anxiety as both caused by and causing repression. But Kierkegaard's *The Concept of Dread* appears to be a more seminal influence.

Frye's most extensive consideration of anxiety is in the first chapter of *The Modern Century*, where he examines the dilemma of alienation and anxiety in contemporary society, associated in large measure with the idea of technological progress.

> [F]or most thoughtful people progress has lost most of its original sense of a favourable value judgment and has become simply progression, towards a goal more likely to be a disaster than an improvement. Taking thought for the morrow, we are told on good authority, is a dangerous practice. In proportion as the confidence in progress has declined, its relation to individual experience has become clearer. That is, progress is a social projection of the individual's sense of the passing of time. But the individual, as such, is not progressing to anything except his own death. Hence the collapse of belief in progress reinforces the sense of anxiety which is rooted in the consciousness of death. Alienation and anxiety become the same thing, caused by a new intensity in the awareness of the movement of time, as it ticks our lives away day after day. This intensifying of the sense of time also, as we have just seen, dislocates it: the centre of attention becomes the future, and the emotional relation to the future becomes one of dread and uncertainty. The future is the point at which "it is later than you think" becomes "too late." (CW 11: 18)

Then, changing his image from the clock to the mirror, which also focuses the issue on the response of consciousness to time, Frye writes:

> Looking into the mirror is the active mind which struggles for consistency and continuity of outlook, which preserves its memory of its past and clarifies its view of the present. Staring back at it is the frozen reflection of that mind, which has lost its sense of continuity by projecting it on some mechanical social process, and has found that it has also lost its dignity, its freedom, its creative power, and its sense of the present, with nothing left except a fearful apprehension of the future. (CW 11: 26)

Flash forward twenty-three years to the seventy-eight-year-old Frye giving his final series of lectures at Emmanuel College, six months before he died, when the consciousness of death was very much on his own mind:

> Reverting to our remark about the God of promises, all our conditioning is rooted in our temporal existence and in the anxiety that appears in the

> present as the passing of time and in the future as death. If death is the last enemy to be destroyed, as Paul tells us [1 Corinthians 15:26], the last metaphor to be transcended is that of the future tense, or God in the form of Beckett's Godot, who never comes but will maybe come tomorrow. The omnipresence of time gives some strange distortions to our double vision. (CW 4: 235)

These reflections on time and anxiety have their parallels in Kierkegaard's often intractable speculations about time in chapter 3 of *The Concept of Dread*.[128] After defining time as "infinite succession" (76), Kierkegaard says that our tendency to divide time into the past, present, and future, which he calls spatialized time, is fraught with difficulties. "If in the infinite succession of time one could in fact find a foothold which would serve as a dividing point, then this division would be quite correct. But precisely because every moment, like the sum of moments, is a process (a going-by) no moment is a present, and in the same sense there is neither past, present, nor future. If one thinks it possible to maintain this division, it is because we *spatialize* a moment, but thereby the infinite succession is brought to a standstill" (76–7). Here is Frye's similar version of the idea:

> In our ordinary experience of time we have to grapple with three dimensions, all of them unreal: a past that is no longer, a future that is not yet, and a present that is never quite. We are dragged backwards along a continuum of experience, facing the past with the future behind us. The centre of time is "now," just as the centre of space is "here," but "now," like "here," is never a point. The first thing that the present moment does is vanish and reappear in the immediate past, where it connects with our expectation of its outcome in the future. Every present experience is therefore split between our knowledge of having had it and our future-directed fears or hopes about it. The word "now" refers to the spread of time in between. (CW 4: 198–9)[129]

When we experience time horizontally in this manner, Frye says, the primary emotion is anxiety (CW 29: 235). For Kierkegaard, however, dread enters the discussion only after he has posited the category of the eternal—the fullness of time in Christianity that makes all things new. "The possible corresponds precisely to the future. For freedom the possible is the future; and for time the future is the possible. Corresponding to both of these in the individual life is dread" (82). Frye's account of going beyond the temporal is less riddling, but the concluding lines of *The Double Vision* have a similar accent:

> The omnipresence of time gives some strange distortions to our double vision. We are born on a certain date, live a continuous identity until death on another date; then we move into an "after"-life or "next" world where something like an ego survives indefinitely in something like a time and place. But we are not continuous identities; we have had many identities, as babies, as boys and girls, and so on through life, and when we pass through or "outgrow" these identities they return to their source. Assuming, that is, some law of conservation in the spiritual as well as the physical world exists. There is nothing so unique about death as such, where we may be too distracted by illness or sunk in senility to have much identity at all. In the double vision of a spiritual and a physical world simultaneously present, every moment we have lived through we have also died out of into another order. Our life in the resurrection, then, is already here, and waiting to be recognized. (CW 4: 235)

Frye's notion of the physical and the spiritual being simultaneously present is similar to Kierkegaard's saying "the eternal is the present...the eternal is annulled (*aufgehoben*) succession" (77). *Aufgehoben* is the Hegelian triple pun, meaning cancellation (or annulment), preservation, and elevation to another level. To lift to another level is one version of making all things new, which is Frye's interpretation of what Kierkegaard means by repetition (examined below). What Kierkegaard does not see is "that angst is the state of Blake's Spectre of Urthona: the egocentric or proud desire to *possess time*, the revolt against the consciousness of death" (CW 8: 222).

Either/Or

We have already mentioned the "aesthetic" and the "ethical" stages in the either/or choice. The "aesthetic" attitude for Kierkegaard is, in Frye's view, "the detached, liberal, and impersonal attitude fostered by the study of an objective environment...which flowers into comprehensive intellectual systems like that of Hegel" (CW 27: 88). It conceives of art as "a permanently detached object of contemplation" (CW 27: 152). It takes its name from the fact that Kierkegaard saw a similarity between this attitude and the place of art in society, and its archetypal character is the medieval Don Juan, "the universal lover surrounded by a mass of attractive objects" (CW 27: 54). The pursuit of intellectual and physical pleasures creates dread and eventually leads to despair. *Either* we remain trapped in the "aesthetic" mode, seeking ways to relieve our boredom, *or* else we pass over into the realm of the "ethical." This is the realm of genuine subjective personality, characterized by commitment, freedom, and the acceptance of faith.

Although the parallels are not exact, Frye's myth of freedom with its disinterested detachment has its counterpart in Kierkegaard's "aesthetic" attitude, and his myth of concern is aligned with Kierkegaard's "ethical" attitude, with its emphasis on radical engagement and individual freedom. There is a parallel, too, in the model of the tragic Neigung-Pflicht conflict, the conflict between inclination and duty, as in Kant's *Foundation for the Metaphysic of Morals* (CW 5: 19).

But as we know from *Anatomy of Criticism*, Frye rejects all either/or choices. He will not be cornered into accepting the Kierkegaardian "either-or" position. He wants the best of both possible worlds: the detached, liberal, impersonal values of the "aesthetic" attitude which Kierkegaard rejects and the values of commitment which come from the primacy of concern. He, of course, does not think Kierkegaard's own solution is satisfactory: "If we stop with the voluntary self-blinkering of commitment, we are no better off than the 'aesthetic': on the other side of 'or' is another step to be taken, a step from the committed to the creative, from iconoclastic concern to what the literary critic above all ought to be able to see, that in literature man is a spectator of his own life, or at least of the larger vision in which his life is contained" (CW 27: 88–9).

This is Frye's answer as to how one can be detached yet joined to the community of concern at the same time. It is an answer in which the visionary imagination becomes the ultimate criterion, for only in the world of imagination can the tension between freedom and concern be properly maintained. It is out of this tension, Frye concludes,

> that glimpses of a third order of experience emerge, of a world that may not exist but completes existence, the world of the definitive experience that poetry urges us to have but which we never quite get. If such a world existed, no individual could live in it.... If we could live in it, of course, criticism would cease and the distinction between literature and life would disappear, because life itself would then be the continuous incarnation of the creative word. (CW 27: 117)

Frye comes to a very similar conclusion in *Anatomy of Criticism*, where the "aesthetic" perspective of art as autonomous must be complemented by "ethical" criticism. But because art can never be subservient to the external goals of truth and beauty, ethical criticism must be complemented in turn by archetypal criticism, which relates literature to civilization, or "a vision of the goals of human work" (CW 22: 105).[130] Finally, archetypal criticism must be complemented by anagogic criticism—which focuses on a completely visionary verbal universe.[131] The parallel in Kierkegaard is his movement from the aesthetic to the ethical in *Either/Or*, followed by the discovery that he must get beyond the ethical to the religious stage, which he proceeds to do in *Fear and Trembling* and *Stages on Life's Way*. The real either/or turns out to be a choice between the aesthetic and the ethical on the one hand, and the religious on the other. Kierkegaard says we move to the religious sphere, the ultimate subjective action, by a leap of faith and by, in his famous phrase, "the teleological suspension of the ethical" (*Fear and Trembling* 59). Kierkegaard wants to transcend the speculative and disinterested in favour of the commitment of ethical freedom, but the either/or dilemma can itself be transcended. In *The Critical Path*, Frye puts the Kierkegaardian position in these terms:

> What applies to a Christian commitment in Kierkegaard applies also to commitments to other myths of concern, where Kierkegaard's "aesthetic" would be replaced by "escapist" or "idealistic" or what not. Kierkegaard is saying, in our terms, that concern is primary and freedom a derivation from it, as the present discussion has also maintained. The individual who does not understand the primacy of concern, the fact that we belong to something before we are anything, is, it is quite true, in a falsely individualized position, and his "aesthetic" attitude may well be parasitic. But Kierkegaard, like so many deeply concerned people, is also saying that passing over to concern gives us the genuine form of freedom, that concern and freedom are ultimately the same thing. This is the bait attached to all "either or" arguments, but it does not make the hook any more digestible.
>
> It is worth pausing a moment on this point, because Kierkegaard is not really satisfied with his own argument. He clearly understood the fact that freedom can only be realized in the individual, and sought for a Christianity that would escape from what he calls "Christendom," the merely social conformity or *religio* of Christianity. He speaks of the personal as in itself a subversive and revolutionary force, and sees the threat of what we should now call the totalitarian mob in the "impersonal." For him the highest form of truth is personally possessed truth, and he is not afraid to face the implications of what I think of as the "paranoia principle." This is the principle, lurking in all conceptions of a personal truth transcending the truth of concern, that it is only what is true only for me that is really true. This principle brings us back to the conception of a

> definitive experience ... as an unattained reality of which literature appears to be an analogy. (CW 27: 89)[132]

In *The Great Code*, Frye suggests that the disinterested and committed dialectic can be transcended by an *Aufhebung*; and similarly, by a process of cancelling, preserving, and lifting to another level, Kierkegaard's either/or dilemma can be transcended as well (CW 19: 244–5). As I have argued elsewhere, Frye makes a similar move to the religious sphere, especially in his late work. The teleological becomes the ultimate recognition scene for the reader, described by Frye as apocalypse, epiphany, revelation, spiritual self-discovery, a reversal into the vision of the Logos, and similar religious-laden phrases. Both writers are engaged in efforts to get *beyond*. For Kierkegaard, the move is beyond the aesthetic and the ethical—"the leap into the existential" (CW 23: 164). For Frye, it is beyond the poetic, the hypothetical, myth, time and space, language, and death. The leap into the existential takes one into the realm of faith:

> The relating of one's "literal" understanding of the Bible as a book to the rest of one's knowledge, more particularly of the Bible's "background" in history and culture, thus creates a synthesis that soon begins to move from the level of knowledge and understanding to an existential level, from Dante's "allegorical" to his "tropological" meaning, from Kierkegaard's "either" to his "or." Such an intensification, whether it has anything to do with the Bible or not, takes us from knowledge to principles of action, from the aesthetic pleasure of studying a world of interesting objects and facts to what Kierkegaard calls ethical freedom. This shift of perspective brings us to the word "faith." (CW 19: 250)

As regards Hegel, Kierkegaard levels an attack on the systematic philosophy of Hegel and replaces it with one more closely attuned to human needs. Kierkegaard has been called a radical Christian theologian, a religious thinker in the Augustinian tradition, the father of existentialism, an ethicist, a social and psychological critic, a metaliterary writer, and an early postmodernist, but he was also a staunchly anti-Hegelian philosopher.[133] Frye had a very different view of Hegel. In his late work Frye embraced the dialectical transition described by Hegel as an *Aufhebung*, a term used to embody the idea, as indicated above, that oppositions can be transcended without being abolished. Again, the verb *aufheben* has a triple meaning: "to lift or raise," "to abolish or cancel," and "to keep or preserve."

Both Frye and Hegel are climbing a spiralling ladder to a higher level of being, except that Frye is moving upward by way of the language of myth and metaphor. "If Hegel had written his Phenomenology in mythos-language instead of in logos-language," Frye remarks in one notebook, "a lot of my work would be done for me" (CW 5: 192). In Frye's notebooks Hegel often becomes a preoccupation. Hegel's use of *Begriff* or concept in his journey up the ladder of being and his view of dialectic as *Aufhebung* get mentioned in passing in *The Great Code* and *Words with Power*, but Hegel and Hegelianism are referred to in the notebooks more than 220 times, and Frye declares in Notebook 53, "The rush of ideas I get from Hegel's Phenomenology is so tremendous I can hardly keep up with it" (CW 6: 631). Elsewhere, Frye gives an eloquent testimony to Hegel as "the great philosopher of anabasis" (CW 9: 89) and to *Phenomenology of Spirit* as the "tremendous philosophical masterpiece" that through its upward thrust finally abolishes the gap between subject and object (CW 4: 194).[134]

Thus, while Kierkegaard offered a critique of the Hegelian system because it was removed from the lived existential experience of everyday life, Frye mined Hegel's system for insights he could appropriate for his own use. Still, as Merold Westphal argues, Kierkegaard was never simply an anti-Hegelian. While he critiques Hegel, at the same time he "incorporate[s] Hegelian insights so that the critique [is] an *Aufhebung*, a cancellation that preserves and a preservation that cancels" (103).

Repetition

The earliest reference to Kierkegaard's *Repetition* is in Frye's diary entry of 26 January 1952, where he says that he is reading the book for the second time, adding wryly that "one wouldn't expect a book with a name like that to yield much on the first reading" (CW 8: 488). He is mostly interested in identifying the book's genre, which he decides is a combination of the nineteenth-century existential anatomy and the confession, after the manner of Carlyle's *Sartor Resartus*.[135] Frye is not immune to the difficulties that everyone faces in reading Kierkegaard, especially the "aesthetic" works with their layers of pseudonymous speakers: "The trouble is that he disguises the confession & approaches the anatomy quizzically, so it's hard to figure out just what the hell he does mean. Like his Victorian contemporaries in England, he has a stentorian censor at his elbow ready to roar down any irony it doesn't feel it can control. By that I mean that one has to distinguish irony within a convention from irony that threatens the convention. Or humor, perhaps, even more than irony" (CW 8: 488–9). But Frye concludes by remarking that *Repetition* "deals with my epic circle idea, that the essential quest is cyclic, but returns, not to the same point, but to the same point renewed and transformed. As opposed to recollection, it's the Protestant justification by faith as opposed to the Catholic sacramental repetition of substantial presence. At least I think it is: whether he [Kierkegaard] knows it or not is another matter" (CW 8: 489).[136] Less than a week later, Frye reports that in his graduate seminar he "tried to bring in Kierkegaard, equating looking down the spirals of the tower with his 'recollection' and looking up with his repetition or anagogical vision of all things new" (CW 8: 495).

Here Frye picks up on the central distinction with which Kierkegaard's book opens—the difference between recollection in Plato's sense of *anamnesis* and repetition. In his first paragraph Kierkegaard writes,

> *repetition* is a crucial expression for what "recollection" was to the Greeks. Just as they taught that all knowing is a recollecting, modern philosophy will teach that all life is a repetition. The only modern philosopher who has had an intimation of this is Leibnitz. Repetition and recollection are the same movement, except in opposite directions, for what is recollected has been, is repeated backward, whereas genuine repetition is recollected forward. (*Fear and Trembling / Repetition* 131)[137]

This distinction makes its way into *Anatomy of Criticism*:

> Kierkegaard has written a fascinating little book called *Repetition*, in which he proposes to use this term to replace the more traditional Platonic term anamnesis or recollection. By it he apparently means, not the simple repeating of an experience, but the recreating of it which redeems or awakens it to life, the end of the process, he says, being the apocalyptic promise, "Behold, I make all things new" [Revelation 21:5]. The preoccupation of the humanities with the past is sometimes made a reproach against them by those who forget that we face the past: it may be shadowy, but it is all that is there. Plato draws a gloomy picture of man staring at the flickering shapes made on the wall of the objective world by a fire behind us like the sun. But the analogy breaks down when the shadows are those of the past, for the only light we can see them by is the Promethean fire within us. The substance of these shadows can only be in ourselves, and the goal of historical criticism, as our metaphors about it often indicate, is a kind of self-resurrection, the vision of a valley of dry bones that takes on the flesh and blood of our own vision. The culture of the past is not only the memory of mankind, but our own buried life, and study of it leads to a

> recognition scene, a discovery in which we see, not our past lives, but the total cultural form of our present life. It is not only the poet but his reader who is subject to the obligation to "make it new." (CW 22: 321)[138]

The Platonic view, then, is that knowledge is recollected from the past. Kierkegaard's Christian position is that repetition, which is both a contrast and a complement to Plato's view, finds its final apocalyptic formulation in the verse from Revelation. Kierkegaard does not actually quote or otherwise point to the biblical passage.[139] The warrant for Frye's using "Behold, I make all things new" is apparently this passage from *Repetition*:

> The dialectic of repetition is easy, for that which is repeated has been—otherwise it could not be repeated—but the very fact that it has been makes the repetition into something new. When the Greeks said that all knowing is recollecting, they said that all existence, which is, has been, when one says that life is a repetition one says: actuality, which has been now comes into existence. (149)

Frye thinks that Kierkegaard may have derived the idea of repetition from biblical typology, but even if he did not, the two are related, as what is prophesied in the Old Testament is fulfilled in the New. Frye makes this observation in *Creation and Recreation*, where he is arguing against the notion of eternal recurrence in the natural religion of pagan mythology and in Nietzsche (CW 4: 73), and he repeats it in *The Great Code*:

> Kierkegaard's very brief but extraordinarily suggestive book *Repetition* is the only study I know of the psychological contrast between a past directed causality and a future directed typology. The mere attempt to repeat a past experience will lead only to disillusionment, but there is another kind of repetition which is the Christian antithesis (or complement) of Platonic recollection, and which finds its focus in the Biblical promise, "Behold, I make all things new" (Revelation 21:5). Kierkegaard's "repetition" is certainly derived from, and to my mind is identifiable with, the forward moving typological thinking of the Bible. Perhaps his book is so brief because he lived too early to grasp the full significance of his own argument, as typological rhetoric was then only beginning to take on many of its new and remarkable modern developments. (CW 19: 101)

Kierkegaard's repetition, then, buttresses the quarrel Frye always had with the implications of the cycle. The treadmill of endless repetition, the dull sameness in the myth of the eternal return, the Druidic recurrences of natural religion, the doctrine of reincarnation—all these backward-looking cyclic myths were antithetical to Frye's belief in the Resurrection, one of his firmest religious convictions. The cycle never permitted what he called the revolutionary *culbute* or overturn in individual and social life—the possibility for a genuine reversal and a new beginning. "In literature there's the cyclical quest where we either come home again (Sam in Tolkien) or attain Kierkegaard's repetition, recreating the original form" (CW 5: 261). As noted in the essay on Joachim of Floris, another powerful verse from Revelation for Frye was 22:17: "And the Spirit and the bride say, Come. And let him that heareth say, Come. And let him that is athirst come. And whosoever will, let him take the water of life freely." These words at the very end of the Bible signal for Frye a new beginning, a new creation, and this new beginning is in the mind of the reader. All of this relates directly to the goal of Frye's quest in his late work—his effort to discover the Everlasting Gospel, Milton's Word of God in the heart, and the interpenetration of Word and Spirit.

In one of his notebooks Frye also draws a connection between, on the one hand, Platonic recollection and what Blake calls the inhibiting memory that has nothing to do with imagination, and on the other, Kierkegaard's repetition and the kind of "habit or practice memory that makes imagination expressible" (CW 13: 109–10). Frye's notion of practice memory (*habitus*) was derived from another of his nineteenth-century heroes, Samuel Butler. Practice memory is unconscious memory developed from habit that gives us the freedom to create. In that sense, it is always future-directed, like repetition. Frye does not mention Kierkegaard in his essay on Butler's *Life and Habit*, though he does make the Kierkegaard–Butler connection in two other notebook entries:

> Repetition develops, in a Hegelian way, spirally & through *aufhebung*, in three stages. In the first stage freedom, existing in pure experience, dreads repetition as the thing that would spoil it; in the second it comes to terms with it, and as it were harnesses its energy (this is the *habitus*-repetition I got from Butler, though S.K. [Søren Kierkegaard] doubtless wouldn't think so); in the third freedom & repetition are identified, where repetition is eternity and a new creation. It's heaven, in short, just as Nietzsche's recurrence is hell, the place Antichrist goes to prepare for his disciples. (CW 5: 363)

> Kierkegaard's "repetition" image ... is founded on ... the habit-memory of practice rather than the straight anamnesis memory. (CW 9: 236)

Another analogue for Kierkegaard's repetition that Frye sees is in Irenaeus' *recapitulatio*. Irenaeus held recapitulation to be the "summing up" of human history in Christ as the epitome of redemption (Irenaeus, bk. 5, chap. 20), and this, Frye says, is "the 'repetition' of Kierkegaard, the new heaven and earth, the restated myth" (CW 5: 169).

In sum, Kierkegaard's *Repetition*, which Frye returned to repeatedly over the course of forty years, provided a foundation for and helped to define his principle of recreation.

The Metaliterary Mode

In *The Great Code*, Frye adopts the word "kerygma" to indicate that while the Bible has obvious poetic features, it is more than literary because it contains a rhetoric of proclamation. "Kerygma," the form of proclamation made familiar by Bultmann, thus designates the existentially concerned aspect of the Bible, as opposed to its purely metaphoric features. Bultmann sought to "demythologize" the New Testament narrative as an initial stage in interpretation: the assumptions of the old mythologies, such as demonic possession and the three-storied universe, had to be purged before the genuine kerygma could be "saved," to use his word. Frye, of course, has exactly the opposite view of myth: "myth is the linguistic vehicle of kerygma" (CW 19: 48).

But having made his point about kerygma, Frye drops the word altogether from the rest of *The Great Code*, except for a passing reference toward the very end of the book (CW 19: 252). In *Words with Power*, the word "kerygma" disappears completely from Frye's analysis in the "sequence and mode" (or "language") chapter; we have to wait until chapter 4, where we learn that the excluded initiative—what lies hidden in the background of the poetic—is what leads to kerygma, even though Frye does not initially put it in these terms. He begins by saying, "Our survey of verbal modes put rhetoric between the conceptual and the poetic, a placing that should help us to understand why from the beginning there have been two aspects of rhetoric, a moral and a tropological aspect, one persuasive and the other ornamental. Similarly, we have put the poetic between the rhetorical and the kerygmatic, implying that it partakes of the characteristics of both" (CW 26: 105–6). The *Aufhebung* process now begins its lifting operation, as Frye expands the meaning of kerygma far beyond what it had meant in *The Great Code*. It now becomes synonymous with the prophetic utterance, the metaliterary perception that extends one's vision or the Longinian ecstatic response to any text, sacred or secular, that "revolutionizes our consciousness." Kerygma takes metaphorical identification "a step further and says: 'you are what you identify with'" (CW 26: 110). We enter the kerygmatic realm when the separation of "active speech and reception of speech" merges into a unity (CW 26: 111).

In one of his notebooks from the late 1980s, Frye reports that he is trying to reread Kierkegaard but that he does not "find him an attractive personality, because he seems to play the same cat-and-mouse game with his reader that he did with poor Regina—and that God played with Abraham and Job. He's a trickster writer, in short, and interests me because a literary critic sees him as doing the opposite of what he thought he was doing, obliterating the barriers between the aesthetic, the ethical, and the religious. That is, he's clearly a 'metaliterary' writer, like Dostoievsky, Kafka and perhaps Nietzsche (well, Mallarmé too)" (CW 5: 361).[140] Frye finds the most valuable insights in works where Kierkegaard assumes the mask of one of his many pseudonymous authors and gets beyond the aesthetic–ethical–religious stages or spheres of existence. These insights Frye calls "metaliterary," and his most extended discussion of this feature of Kierkegaard's prose is found in Notebook 50 (CW 5: 361–6):

> Oh, God, if Kierkegaard had only carried through his "repetition" scheme, instead of sneaking it out ... in the course of abusing a harmless reviewer for not reading what he hadn't written! I'm not clear why his three stages are related only by transcendence, or why Hegel's logic of immanent mediation has to be rejected. But I'm sure he did, at that point, though he lost his grip on it soon afterward.... It doesn't matter that the context is one more ow-oo about Regina: that's the right context, a myth with enough "existential" urgency to push it in a metaliterary direction, a Vita Nuova in reverse. (CW 5: 365)

Even though Frye finds the really valuable works by Kierkegaard are his "aesthetic" books—those signed with pseudonyms—the metaliterary mode has its drawbacks: "The ability to write very well very easily may lead to Kierkegaard's disease: the esthetic barrier against the kerygmatic" (CW 5: 342). So not all of the pseudonymous works are kerygmatic. In his *Late Notebooks* Frye writes:

> *Sickness unto Death* is a work of casuistry, an existential rhetorical form which is not kerygmatic, except in so far as it uses the Lazarus myth. It's another example of pre-mythical rhetoric usurping the post-mythical kerygmatic. *Fear & Trembling* is also casuistry, though in a less concen-

> trated form. Casuistry means that the ethical area is not one of freedom: it's a labyrinth. S.K. realized this, or came to realize it, in theory; but he never found a genuinely kerygmatic style: his "aesthetic" style is much the closest to it, but one in which a Socratic irony enters. (CW 5: 364)

Kierkegaard struggled to go beyond the "aesthetic," Frye writes, "but could produce only dialectical & rhetorical forms (he says this in his diary, but I can't find the reference)" (CW 5: 365–6).[141] This notebook entry gets expanded in *Words with Power* as follows:

> The existential movement of the 1940s, also, revolved around a number of figures—Dostoevsky, Kierkegaard, Nietzsche, Kafka, Sartre—who were primarily literary figures, the word "existential" referring to tendencies in them that were metaliterary, trying to get past the limitations of literature into a different kind of identity with their readers. Kierkegaard divided his works into the "aesthetic" or literary, which he published under pseudonyms, and the "edifying," where he spoke in his own name as an "ethical" writer and teacher. He realized that there was a prophetic dimension on the other side of the aesthetic, but evidently did not realize that it was only in his aesthetic writings that he came anywhere near expressing it. The edifying writings revert to standard dialectical and rhetorical forms, one book on the boundary line between the two, *The Sickness unto Death*, being essentially a work in the seventeenth-century rhetorical genre of casuistry. The implications for the conception of the kerygmatic are, first, that kerygmatic writing normally demands a literary, that is, a mythical and metaphorical, basis; second, that the kerygmatic does not, like ordinary rhetoric, emerge from direct personal address, or what a writer "says." (CW 26: 109–10)

In the kerygmatic world, one is released from the burden of speech and writing: "The gospels are written mythical narratives, and for casual readers they remain that. But if anything in them strikes a reader with full kerygmatic force, there is, using the word advisedly, a *resurrection* of the original speaking presence in the reader. The reader is the logocentric focus, and what he reads is emancipated both from writing and from speech. The duality of speaker and listener has vanished into a single area of verbal recognition" (CW 26: 108). We do not speak in the kerygmatic world, but God does, which is why the voice of revelation is "rhetoric in reverse" (CW 6: 660). When Frye uses kerygma in the sense of the prophetic or metaliterary utterance, human speech or writing does enter the picture, and while there is no metaliterary style, there is a metaliterary idiom which takes the kerygmatic as its model (CW 5: 369). It is because of this idiom that Kierkegaard is one of "the forerunners of the new spiritual emancipation of man" (CW 13: 296). Frye even projects his own kerygmatic anthology. He says, without commentary, that it would include Blake's *The Marriage of Heaven and Hell*, Buber's *I and Thou*, and selections from Dostoevsky, Kafka, Rimbaud, and Hölderlin (CW 5: 366). As we have seen, it would include Kierkegaard's "aesthetic" works as well, and we could add to the list some of Northrop Frye's more visionary and oracular pronouncements—those that issue from what he refers to as heightened or expanded consciousness.

For Frye, one of the central archetypal scenes of the intensity of consciousness that arises from the desire to identify is found in the Paleolithic cave drawings, references to which appear on more than thirty occasions in his work. The cave drawings at Lascaux, Altamira, and elsewhere represent "the titanic will to identify" (CW 18: 346). They are an example of what Lévy-Bruhl called *participation mystique*, the imaginative identification with things, including other people, outside the self, or an absorption of one's consciousness with the natural world into an undifferentiated state of archaic identity. In such a process of metaphorical identification, the subject and object merge into one, but the sense of identity is existential rather than verbal (CW 6: 503).

But what does the intensity or expansion of consciousness entail for Frye? This is a difficult question to answer with certainty, for Frye reflects on the implications of the phrase only obliquely. But we do know, first, that it is a function of kerygma; second, while it does not necessarily signify religion or a religious experience, it can be "the precondition for any ecumenical or everlasting-gospel religion" (CW 5: 17); third, the language of such consciousness always turns out to be metaphorical; fourth, "vision" is the word that best fits the heightened awareness that comes with the imagination's opening of the doors of perception; fifth, the principle behind the epiphanic experience that permits things to be seen with a special luminousness is that "things are not fully seen until they become hallucinatory. Not actual hallucinations, because those would merely substitute subjective for objective visions, but objective things transfigured by identification with the perceiver. An object impregnated, so to speak, by a perceiver is transformed into a presence" (CW 26: 87); sixth, intensified consciousness is represented by images of both ascent and descent; seventh, expanded consciousness is both individual and social, it amounts to revelation (CW 5: 61).

Kierkegaard helped Frye to define the kerygmatic utterance, and though Kierkegaard may have failed to get beyond the dialectical and rhetorical thrust of his prose in the late works, in some of his early ones he does write in a metaliterary mode.

The Drunken Boat

Kierkegaard plays a seminal role in the "drunken boat" metaphor, which Frye uses to characterize the great nineteenth-century revolutionary figures. The others are: Schopenhauer, Darwin, Freud, and Marx. The image derives from Rimbaud's *Le Bateau ivre*, which depicts the poet's boat tossed perilously upon the waves like a cork. The battering sea threatens the little boat, representing the enduring values and structures of civilized society. Whether the boat can survive the forces that lie below depends on the optimism of the mythographer. The dialectic might be summarized like this, the undulating lines representing the sea, separating what is present above from what lies below:

	Schopenhauer (1788–1860)	**Darwin & Huxley** (1809–82) (1825–95)	**Freud** (1856–1939)	**Kierkegaard** (1813–55)	**Marx** (1818–83)
All the Values of Civilization	world as idea morality; structure of civilization	consciousness & ego; ethics; morality is an accidental sport	consciousness; ego	higher impulses; something like the ego	ascendant class
≈≈≈≈≈≈≈≈	≈≈≈≈≈≈≈≈	≈≈≈≈≈≈≈≈	≈≈≈≈≈≈≈≈	≈≈≈≈≈≈≈≈	≈≈≈≈≈≈≈≈
The World of Power Beneath, Threating the Values of Civilization	world as will; moral indifference; evolutionary force	ruthlessly competitive; evolution	unconscious, libidinous impulse; the id; repressed Orc	dread; angst	excluded proletariat

What lies below the surface of the sea corresponds to the demonic level of the pre-Romantic great chain of being. Frye sometimes refers to the boat as an ark: "the boat is usually in the position of Noah's ark, a fragile container of sensitive and imaginative values threatened by a chaotic and unconscious power below it" (CW 17: 89). What is "above" are the human values of intelligence and morality, of social and cultural tradition. Below the *bateau ivre*, writes Frye, is "[o]ften an innocent world, the sleeping beauty of nature & reason in Rousseau, Blake's Orc & buried Beulah, Shelley's Mother Earth & Asia. From Schopenhauer on, it becomes increasingly inscrutable: menacing to conservatives & redeeming to revolutionaries; the world as will, Darwin's evolution, Kierkegaard's dread, Freud's libido-id, Marx's proletariat" (CW 23: 290). What lies below can be both a support (Marx, Darwin) and a threat (Kierkegaard, Freud, Schopenhauer). It can also lead to a creative descent.

The earliest account we have of this revolutionary topocosm is in Frye's description of a 1950 lecture he gave in his course on Nineteenth-Century Thought:

> I started Huxley, but got off on the general anti-Cartesian or existential movement which, I said, produced in Darwinism a reversal of the Cartesian derivation of existence from consciousness. I went on to show the connection of this with Schopenhauer's will & idea, Nietzsche's will to power & the "all too human," Marx's ruling-class & dispossessed, Freud's ego & libido & the whole psychological conception of that which is mental & yet not conscious (I linked the anti-Freudian French existentialist doctrine of conscious freedom with the Cartesian tradition) & Kierkegaard's "spiritless" natural reason & dread (which, as I saw for the first time, links both with the Nietzsche-Marx revolutionary pattern & with Bergson's identification of the subconscious will with duration: the existential is always the Spectre of Urthona). (CW 8: 282)[142]

This gets elaborated in Frye's 1952 essay, "Trends in Modern Culture," where he writes that in the Romantic movement,

> [in] nearly all branches of culture, the conscious mind is seen as deriving its strength from a subconscious reality greater than itself. Hence the importance of suggestion and evocation in Romantic art, of the surrender of conscious intelligence to spontaneous mythopoeia. After Schopenhauer, this subconscious world becomes evil, sinister, and yet immensely powerful, and visions of nightmarish terror begin increasingly to creep into the arts. No matter where we turn in the culture of the immediate past, the same picture meets us, a picture reminding us less of the harassed boat than of the young lady of the limerick who smiled as she rode on a tiger. In Schopenhauer the world of conscious idea thus rides on a cruel (except that it is unconscious) and inexorable world of will with the whole power of nature behind it. In Freud, the conscious mind attempts, with very partial success, to hold in check a mighty libidinous desire. In Darwin, the conscious mind is the sport of an unconscious evolutionary force. In Marx, civilization is the attempt of a dwindling minority to keep

> a vastly stronger majority away from its privileges. In liberal thought, freedom is the possession of integrity by a small group constantly threatened by a mob. In Kierkegaard, the consciousness of existence rests on a vast shapeless "dread" as big and real as life and death together. There is hardly a corner of modern thought where we do not find some image of a beleaguered custodian of conscious values trying to fend off something unconscious which is too strong to be defeated. It seems the appropriate cultural pattern for a period in which the tiny peninsula of Western Europe was encircling the world. (CW 11: 260–1)[143]

Frye's thesis is later expanded in "The Drunken Boat: The Revolutionary Element in Romanticism" (1963), which is further developed into the first chapter of *A Study of English Romanticism* (1968). Here Frye argues that in Romanticism we have a profound change in the spatial projection of reality. This means that the old hierarchy of existence (the great chain of being), with its divine, human, and natural levels, was turned upside down. The metaphorical structure of the Romantic writers tended to move inside and downward instead of, as in the older model, outside and upward. Romanticism, then, was primarily a revolution in poetic imagery.

Kierkegaard also plays a role in Frye's expansive vision of the four levels of meaning. In one twist on Dante's four levels (literal, allegorical, moral, and anagogic), Frye relates the levels to both their Blakean analogues and their corresponding revolutionary thinkers.[144]

Levels of Meaning	**Blakean Analogue**	**Revolutionary Sources**
Psychological	Urthona	Jung
Historical	Luvah	Spengler
Mythological	Tharmas	Frazer
Theological	Urizen	Kierkegaard (CW 23: 64)

In our own time, the structures of Romantic imagery are carried over into Auden's *For the Time Being*, Auden having been very much influenced by Kierkegaard. Auden's play, in which the word "anxiety" is sprinkled liberally throughout,

> develops a religious construct out of Kierkegaard on the analogy of those of Marx and Freud. The liberal or rational elements represented by Herod feel threatened by the revival of superstition in the Incarnation, and try to repress it. Their failure means that the effort to come to terms with

> a nature outside the mind, the primary effort of reason, has to be abandoned, and this enables the Paradise or divine presence which is locked up inside the human mind to manifest itself after the reason has searched the whole of objective nature in vain to find it. The attitude is that of a relatively orthodox Christianity; the imagery and the structure of symbolism is that of *Prometheus Unbound* and *The Marriage of Heaven and Hell*. (CW 17: 89)[145]

Frye sometimes speaks of the drunken boat complex as a "vortical explosion" (CW 23: 37–8, 39, 81; CW 18: 168; CW 20: 168–9). "Vortex" is a word that Kierkegaard uses in *The Concept of Dread* (18), *Repetition* (222), *Either/Or* (Penguin ed., 1992, 168), and elsewhere. Frye may have recalled the image of the sailor in *Edifying Discourses* "who is out to sea, when everything is changing about him, when the waves are constantly born and die" (16), but his chief source for "vortex" is Blake, who uses the word in both *The Four Zoas* and *Milton*. The central passage for Frye comes from the latter: "The nature of infinity is this: That everything has its / Own vortex; and when once a traveler thro Eternity. / Has passed that Vortex, he perceives it roll backward behind / His path, into a globe itself infolding; like a sun / Or like a moon, or like a universe of starry majesty" (bk. 1, pl. 15, ll. 21–5). Here is Frye's gloss on the passage:

> Blake says that everything in eternity has what he calls a "vortex" (perhaps rather a vortex-ring), a spiral or cone of existence. When we focus both eyes on one object, say a book, we create an angle of vision opening into our minds with the apex pointing away from us. The book therefore has a vortex of existence opening into its mental reality within our minds. When Milton descends from eternity to time, he finds that he has to pass through the apex of his cone of eternal vision, which is like trying to see a book from the book's point of view; the Lockian conception of the real book as outside the mind on which the vision of the fallen world is based. This turns him inside out, and from his new perspective the cone rolls back and away from him in the form of a globe. That is why we are surrounded with a universe of remote globes, and are unable to see that the earth is "one infinite plane." But in eternity the perceiving mind or body is omnipresent, and hence these globes in eternity are inside that body. (CW 14: 341)[146]

Vortex for Frye is an active or moving geometric shape, an image that helps him to visualize different events, particularly transformative ones, in the structure of literary and religious narrative and meaning. In his published writing the word appears only occasionally: in *The Secular Scripture* he uses it to describe the passage of the action through a recognition scene in Terence's *Andria*, and in *Words with Power* to characterize the pattern of creative descent in Melville. But in his notebooks he repeatedly calls upon the vortex to assist him in visualizing, particularly, passages from one state to another, as in Blake's account of Milton's descent. Vortexes can move in two directions: they can whirl upward or spin downward. They can attach themselves to each other at the point of the cone or they can expand outward into an apocalyptic or demonic universe. In the drunken boat complex, the vortex is an image of revolutionary change, a change in consciousness that enters the modern world with Kierkegaard, Marx, Nietzsche, Freud, and Darwin. Revolutionary changes can be individual moments of transformation, recognition, or enlightenment, or they can be social. Along with the "vortical explosion" of Kierkegaard, we have the central examples for Frye of Dante's two vortices, the swirling descent into the inferno and the circular climb up the purgatorial mountain. Similarly with Yeats's double gyres in *A Vision*. But Frye writes about the vortex mostly in relation to a sudden awareness that moves one from a lower state of being to a higher one. *Opsis* is the underlying category. One bursts through to a new awareness where things can now be *seen* differently. "When the action passes from one level to the other through the recognition scene, we have a feeling of going through some sort of gyre or vortex" (CW 18: 62), and recognition scenes are often accompanied by reversals, as in the case of *Oedipus the King*, where the central metaphors are light and darkness, blindness and sight. The reversal in *Oedipus the King* is, of course, closely connected with the ironic reversal of the central metaphors: Teiresias (the seer) is literally blind but can figuratively see; Oedipus can literally see and is renowned for his knowledge and insight but is figuratively blind to his own situation; and then at the reversal Oedipus is able figuratively to see only after he has literally blinded himself.

Nothing, however, is ever purely visual in Frye: there is always a dialectic of space *and* time, and the vortex can apply to both categories, as we see in this notebook entry, which is an abstract parallel to what Milton experienced in Blake's poem:

> The cycle of the Word is a series of epiphanies—creation, law, prophecy and apocalypse--and the cycle of the Spirit is a series of responses—exodus, wisdom, gospel and participating apocalypse. The true response is the historical one turned inside out. Not just upside-down: that's the other half of the Word cycle. But the Bible uses the up-down metaphors in the crucial first two chapters of Acts [the descent of the Spirit, the ascent

> of the Word]. What gets turned inside-out, as I said in GC [*The Great Code*] and have been stumbling over all my life, are the categories of time and space. At present we tend to think of eternity and infinity as time and space indefinitely extended, which they are anyway, and they have to go into a real reverse, another vortex. (CW 6: 462).

Frye's vortices do not interpenetrate like Yeats's, but they can come together at their apexes to form an hour-glass figure. This point of contact takes place in the human mind, and after the vortical explosion has occurred, we can look back from where we have come, as if in a mirror. Blake's *Jerusalem*, Frye says, "attempts to show that the vision of reality is the other one inside out. The poem shows us two worlds, one infinite, the other indefinite, one our own home and the other the same home receding from us in a mirror" (CW 12: 372–3). Frye writes about the vortex in more than forty notebook entries, some of which are as cryptic as Kierkegaard's difficult speculations.[147] But the effect of the whole is another of Frye's verbal formulas, this one a dynamic image, for trying to grasp what happens when one bursts through to a moment of "illumination." Frye's theory of the vortical explosion among nineteenth-century revolutionary figures, in which Kierkegaard plays a defining role, is one of the keys to his visionary poetics. Another key, as I have tried to show, is his concordant and antithetical relationship to Kierkegaard.

8

Frye and Lewis Carroll

Oxford people are extremely proud of their record of eccentric bachelors ... when one examines the great imaginative productions of Oxford, such works as The Anatomy of Melancholy *and* Alice in Wonderland, *one sees exactly this kind of thing, that is, a hyperlogical fantasy which teeters on the brink of normal mental processes. (CW 7: 470)*

*At Oxford, two years ago [1970], I pondered the question of a genius loci. The great imaginative productions of Oxford—*The Anatomy of Melancholy, Alice in Wonderland, *the development taking place there when I was a student around C.S. Lewis, Charles Williams and Tolkien, all suggest a slightly mad fantasy. (CW 25: 34)*

Frye read Lewis Carroll's Alice books as a child, and they made a deep impression on him. "There [are] a number of key works in English literature," he writes. "A person is simply deprived of part of his or her social context by not knowing them. If I hadn't had the Alice books at an early age, it would have been like a couple of front teeth missing!" (CW 24: 465). But, he notes, like *Huckleberry Finn* and *Gulliver's Travels*, the Alice books can be read at any stage of life (CW 10: 165). Frye summons Carroll in scores of different contexts throughout his published and unpublished writings—more than 140 references to Carroll altogether. This suggests that the role Carroll played in Frye's vision of literature is worth exploring.[148]

The earliest reference Frye makes to Carroll is in a 1934 letter to Helen Kemp where, after lecturing his girlfriend on the qualities of good writing, he concludes his little homily with this admonition: "always, strive for arrangement, balance, proportion, symmetry, soundness. And remember that that is your religion, and that all art rests on two purely moral qualities—sincerity and economy. This doesn't mean to take your work too solemnly or pretentiously, of course—Alice in Wonderland is a far better work of art than East Lynne" (CW 1: 287), *East Lynne* being a best-selling Victorian novel by Ellen Wood. The earliest reference to Alice in Frye's published writing is in *Fearful Symmetry*, where, referring to chapter 2 of *Through the Looking Glass*, he compares Thel's "world of dissolving and arbitrary fantasy" to "a looking-glass world of talking flowers" (*Annotated Alice* 199–213) (CW 14: 233).

Descending and Ascending Journeys

The narrative pattern of the journey in literature and in life takes different forms in Frye's understanding of *mythos*. Sometimes it follows a linear or horizontal movement from point A to point B. At other times the journey is projected cyclically. The journey assumes still a third shape in the last half of *Words with Power*, where the horizontal and cyclic quests are displaced by descending and ascending movements along the *axis mundi*: "ascent & descent are a verticalized journey" (CW 5: 315), the way down and the way up in the Heraclitean formula. Or in another iteration, the path of the journey becomes metaphorically a "reconstructed ladder" (CW 5: 23). The anabasis is a movement from Thanatos, at the bottom of Frye's circular diagram of the literary universe, to Logos at the top. But the katabatic movement down the ladder is equally important for Frye: in his later writings it appears to be even more important. "Everybody," Frye writes, "has a fixation. Mine has to do with meander-and-descent patterns. For years in my childhood I wanted to dig a cave & be the head of a society in it—this was before I read Tom Sawyer. All the things in literature that haunt me most have to do with katabasis. The movie that hit me hardest as a child was the Lon Chaney Phantom of the Opera. My main points of reference in literature are such things as The Tempest, P.R. [*Paradise Regained*], [Blake's] Milton, the Ancient Mariner, Alice in Wonderland, the Waste Land—every damn one a meander-&-katabasis work" (CW 9: 76). Frye's interpretation of the down and up movements along the *axis mundi* in *Words with Power* is anticipated in his account of the descending and ascending themes in chapters 4 and 5 of *The Secular Scripture*. In one of his notebooks for *The Secular Scripture* he speculates how the two Alice books might fit into his account of the descent and ascent themes:

> I'm still perhaps not ready for the Alice books, but it's beginning to look as though the first book were a descent theme, what with the cards, the red and white, Alice as invariably awkward and unwelcome, and the final trial scene which turns into an attack on her by what are usually agents of fatality. Note the curious dove (pigeon) and serpent episode,[149] where Alice is identified with the latter. The second book is an ascent to the "queen" stage, chess being more usually an Eros game; the white knight as the old man who turns back at Pisgah, the mirror business as going through the Narcissus progress in reverse. The episodes in this book are supplied by

> nursery rhymes, but don't overlook the twin theme in Tweedledum and dee. (CW 15: 229)

Frye's most focused reflections on the Alice books are found in the chapters on "Themes of Descent" and "Themes of Ascent" in *The Secular Scripture:*

> It is possible never to get out of this lower world, and some may not even want to. For it may also assume the form of a false paradise, like Spenser's Bower of Bliss. Of those turned into animals by Circe, some might refuse to return to human shape—this theme was a popular Renaissance paradox. Or there may even be genuine paradises in the lower world, descending from the Classical Elysium, or at least places of contentment, like the underworld community that we meet in the last part of Herbert Read's *The Green Child.* Sometimes, too, the descent imagery is merely playful, as in many children's stories.
>
> Yet even in *Alice in Wonderland* the tone is curiously ambiguous. Alice descends in pursuit of a rabbit preoccupied with the dial of his watch: she is not, like Dante in the *Inferno*, traversing a cone from base to apex, but a spiral-shaped poem, ending in the word "death," appears later in the story.[150] There is a good deal of alienation in Alice's world: she is never quite sure of her own identity, and the continuity with her previous life is broken when her carefully memorized poems turn into grotesque parodies. Giants and dwarfs, we saw, inhabit the lower world: Alice is always either too big or too small, hence often a nuisance or an unwanted guest. She feels estranged from her body by her changes of size, and falls into a pool of what a post-Victorian reader would simply call her liquid excretions. A sinister beheading queen makes her appearance, and the theme of metamorphosis is introduced in the witches' kitchen of the ugly duchess, where a little boy turns into a pig, not that Lewis Carroll would have considered that much of a metamorphosis. The story ends in a trial in which all the characters present turn on the heroine. We notice the prominence of cards in the story: cards and dice are common in descent narratives, because of their overtones of fatality and chance. (CW 18: 82–3)

And then in the chapter on "Themes of Ascent":

> We saw that *Alice in Wonderland*, for all its lightness and humour, preserved some of the traditional imagery of a lower-world descent. Alice passing through the looking-glass into a reversed world of dream language is also

> going through a descent; the incidents are largely suggested by nursery rhymes, but we may note the twin theme in Tweedledum and Tweedledee. Before long however we realize that the journey is turning upwards, in a direction symbolized by the eighth square of a chessboard, where Alice becomes a Psyche figure, a virginal queen flanked by two older queens, one red and one white, who bully her and set her impossible tasks in the form of nonsensical questions. Cards and dice, we said, have a natural connection with themes of descent into a world of fatality; chess and other board games, despite *The Waste Land*, appear more frequently in romance and in Eros contexts, as *The Tempest* again reminds us. As Alice begins to move upward out of her submarine mirror world she notes that all the poems she had heard have to do with fish, and as she wakes she reviews the metamorphoses that the figures around her had turned into.... In traditional romance, including Dante, the upward journey is the journey of a creature returning to its creator. In most modern writers, from Blake on, it is the creative power in man that is returning to its original awareness. The secular scripture tells us that we are the creators; other scriptures tell us that we are actors in a drama of divine creation and redemption. Even Alice is troubled by the thought that her dream may not have been hers but the Red King's. Identity and self-recognition begin when we realize that this is not an either-or question, when the great twins of divine creation and human recreation have merged into one, and we can see that the same shape is upon both. (CW 18: 103–4)

Frye relates the ascent theme with the mature daughter-figure, and in one notebook entry he links the ascent with the *I Ching*. "Sun & Tui [I Ching trigrams] are the human creature as the full-grown daughter of Logos, breaking away as Eve & returning as Sophia, Alice the queen.... Tui is Psyche also, of course. This association of the upper world with a daughter-figure clears up a point or two: the descent of innocence, Alice & the Dickensian girl-child, Marvell's drop of dew.[151] It would be wonderful if I could see AW [*Alice in Wonderland*] consistently as an Adonis descent, or parody of one, with the red & white roses, the beheading queen, the cards, & the final trial, & ATLG [*Alice Through the Looking-Glass*] as an Eros descent, I mean ascent, with chess, red & white queens, & the white knight as the melancholy Virgil-guide who can't go all the way. Even the mirror fits, Tui being a lake" (CW 9: 209–10).

Do the Alice books constitute a genuine descent or a parody of one? Frye is not altogether sure. He says that the "Alice books seem to me to be 'innocent' parodies of descent themes" (CW 9: 194) and he sees the trial scene at the end of Alice's *Adventures in Wonderland* as a demonic parody of the Last Judgment (CW 15: 228–9). But the trial is also a parody of the banquet symposium at the end of *Through the Looking Glass* (CW 5: 332). The primary parodic effect, however, comes from the mockery of the lyrics of Wordsworth and the ten other Romantic and Victorian poets lampooned by Carroll throughout both books. Frye seems to think that in the Alice books parody applies to several parts but not to the whole. Parody is not a feature of the anatomy as a form of prose fiction, but it can be a powerful tool of satire, which is a feature of the anatomy. And *Alice in Wonderland* is, as we shall see, one of the examples of the anatomy that Frye gives in *Anatomy of Criticism* (CW 22: 290).

The Chaste-Child Archetype

The magical world of romance is often held together by "the spell of chastity or purity, which sexual experience would instantly destroy. Wonderland depends on an unawakened Alice" (CW 17: 181). It's not so much that she represents innocence, but that she is inexplicable by ordinary means—"what seven-year-old girls would have been like without the Fall" (CW 13: 244). "Alice," Frye writes, "is a preternatural child, and an astonishing achievement: I know of nothing in all literature remotely like her. But she belongs to another world than the world of our seven-year-olds, though she is utterly real in her own terms" (CW 5: 47). Frye keeps returning to the chaste-child archetype. In one of his *Late Notebooks*, he remarks that "Alice couldn't have held Wonderland if she'd got even as far as the menarche, to say nothing of intercourse" (CW 5: 257), an observation that also appears in *Words with Power*.[152] Still, Alice is an archetype, and Frye links her with other young girls: Psyche, Perdita in *The Winter's Tale*, Miranda in *The Tempest*, Marina in *Pericles*, the girl-child among grotesques in Dickens (e.g., Nell Trent, Florence Dombey, Maggie in *Little Dorrit*), Henry James's Maisie, Valéry's *La Jeune Parque*, Joyce's Issy, Swift's Vanessa (CW 17: 302; CW 13: 247; CW 5: 123–4; CW 9: 222; CW 29: 340; CW 25: 291). The chaste-child archetype belongs to Blake's world of Innocence, and the process of Alice's moving toward maturity as she awakens from her dream at the end of *Through the Looking Glass* signals the end of innocence and the beginning of her entry into Blake's world of Experience.

The Genre of the Alice Books

Frye says that *Alice in Wonderland* is a "masterpiece of its kind" (CW 27: 324), but what is its kind? On several occasions he points out that, given the fact that the history of prose fiction is primarily a history of realistic novelists, the historian of fiction hardly knows how to account for the radical and experimental tradition of such works as Bulwer-Lytton's occult novel *Zanoni*, George MacDonald's *Phantastes*, or Rider Haggard's *She*, William Morris's *The Wood Beyond the World*, and *Alice in Wonderland* (CW 10: 69–70, 255–6; CW 9: 342; CW 18: 30; CW 4: 347; CW 15: 185, 202). Such works lean in the direction of romance, and insofar as they are stories told for fun, they differ from the allegorical seriousness of the great realists (e.g., Eliot, Austen, Thackeray). But although the Alice books are connected by way of dream to Victorian romance (CW 19: 70), they are not finally romances, even though at one point Frye does call *Alice in Wonderland* a romance (CW 10: 261). He speaks of the anatomic features of the Alice books (CW 15: 145), meaning features of the anatomy as a prose form. While the Alice books have features of the romance, the dream-vision, and allegory, in his analysis of the forms of prose fiction, Frye finally places them in the category of the Menippean satire:

> In the Menippean satires we have been discussing, the name of the form also applies to the attitude. As the name of an attitude, satire is, we have seen, a combination of fantasy and morality. But as the name of a form, the term satire, though confined to literature (for as a mythos it may appear in any art, a cartoon, for example), is more flexible, and can be either entirely fantastic or entirely moral. The Menippean adventure story may thus be pure fantasy, as it is in the literary fairy tale. The Alice books are perfect Menippean satires, and so is *The Water-Babies*, which has been influenced by Rabelais. The purely moral type is a serious vision of society as a single intellectual pattern, in other words a Utopia. (CW 22: 290)

Although Frye admits that the Menippean satire, which he renames the anatomy, is a "loose-jointed narrative form" (CW 22: 290), he nevertheless characterizes it, as we saw in the chapter on Burton, as having these features: it is intellectualized and extroverted; it has a strong theoretical interest; its stylized characters represent mental attitudes; it relies on free play of intellectual fancy; and it contains humorous observations that produce caricature; thus, it tends toward satire. About the humour and the stylized characters in the Alice books, Frye writes,

> The humour of pure fantasy, the other boundary of satire, belongs to romance, though it is uneasy there, as humour perceives the incongruous, and the conventions of romance are idealized. Most fantasy is pulled back into satire by a powerful undertow often called allegory, which may be described as the implicit reference to experience in the perception of the incongruous. The White Knight in Alice who felt that one should be

> provided for everything, and therefore put anklets around his horse's feet to guard against the bites of sharks [*Annotated Alice* 298], may pass as pure fantasy. But when he goes on to sing an elaborate parody of Wordsworth [*ibid.* 307–13] we begin to sniff the acrid, pungent smell of satire, and when we take a second look at the White Knight we recognize a character type closely related both to Quixote and to the pedant of comedy. (CW 22: 210)

The other features of the anatomy, which we glanced at in the essay on Burton, are less easy to discern. In his account of prose fiction in *Anatomy of Criticism*, Frye differentiates among four forms, the differentiation based on two pairs of categories: extroverted / introverted and personal / intellectualized. These pairs are based upon different principles. "Personal" refers to *ethos* or characterization and "intellectualized" to *dianoia* or content, whereas the extroverted-introverted dichotomy is essentially a matter of rhetorical technique, the latter terms describing whether a writer's manner of representation tends more toward objectivity or subjectivity. These are not the only categories, however, which Frye uses to define his fictional forms. The bulk of his argument consists of drawing certain distinctions between the two forms of "personal" fiction (novel and romance) and between the two "intellectualized" forms (confession and anatomy). The confession, a specialized form of autobiography, presents a writer's life in such a way as "to build up an integrated pattern" (CW 22: 287). But even though the subject is ostensibly the author himself, "some theoretical or intellectual interest" nearly always plays a dominant role. This is what distinguishes the confession from the novel proper, where the theoretical interest is always subordinated to the technical problem of "personal relationships" (CW 22: 288). The anatomy is also an "intellectualized" form, similar to the confession in its ability to represent theoretical statements and abstract ideas. It differs in being one step further removed from a concern with ethos. Its characters are more stylized than realistic, not so important in themselves as in the mental attitudes they express. In Frye's words, the anatomy "presents people as mouthpieces of the ideas they represent" (CW 22: 289–90). It embraces a wide variety of subtypes, which range from pure fantasy at one extreme to pure morality at the other. It differs from the romance in that it "is not primarily concerned with the exploits of heroes, but relies on the free play of intellectual fancy and the kind of humorous observation that produces caricature" (CW 22: 290); thus the tendency of the anatomy toward various kinds of satire.

Carroll's annotators (Martin Gardner and others) are fond of noting the connections to Carroll's life in the Alice books, as if they were a hidden confession, but such notes are anything but essential in our reading experience. Carroll seems not at all interested in representing theoretical statements and abstract ideas, as we find them in such an intellectualized form as Burton's *Anatomy of Melancholy*. Perhaps Frye would say that reality and appearance, the worlds of dream and waking consciousness, innocence and experience, and other such dialectical opposites constitute a subtext of abstract ideas in the Alice books.

The Alice Books as a Key to the Mythological Universe

"I've often said," Frye writes in one of his notebooks, "that if I understood the two Alice books I'd have very little left to understand about literature" (CW 9: 329). In another notebook entry, we find this twist: "I have a feeling that if I thoroughly understood the Alice books I'd have the key to the whole of mythology" (CW 9: 312). We naturally wonder about the substance of the understanding Frye wished for, but he never explicitly pursues the ways that the Alice books might provide the key to the mythological universe. Still, a number of features of the Alice books struck a chord with Frye's central preoccupations. Outside of the descent theme and the chaste-child archetype, the codes and conventions that absorbed Frye from the beginning recur throughout his scattered comments on Carroll: the principles of space and time (*dianoia* and *mythos*) as the basic structures of literary experience; the mirror-world of play, which, as Huizinga says, has a beginning and an end[153] and, related to this, the symbolism of cards and chess, with their overtones of fatality and chance; the nature of language and meaning; the convention of the double (mirror world, Tweedledum and Tweedledee); fantasy as the contrary of realism; the fascination with law in British fiction (the trial and courtroom scene at the end of Wonderland); the riddle, with its fusion of sensation and reflection; parody, demonic and otherwise; puns; Blakean composite art forms (our experience of the Alice books is tied to the illustrations of such artists as John Tenniel, Arthur Rackham, Peter Newell, Ralph Steadman, Willy Pogany, Harry Furniss, Salvador Dali, and Barry Moser); the garden archetype; the subconscious dream-world; the search for identity and self-recognition; the centrality of folk and fairy tales in our literary experience; the alchemical red and white symbolism; the Narcissus and Psyche myth; the theme of death; the Fall archetype; and so on. Because the Alice books embody so many of the themes and conventions that preoccupied Frye, one begins to realize that perhaps they did hold a key to the literary universe. At least they indicate the variety of entrances to and exits from the worlds of magic and childhood innocence.

Finally, the Alice books are such a part of Frye's consciousness that Carroll becomes for him a repository of images for clever similes, sententiae, asides, and aphorisms, and of ideas to illustrate or clarify or reinforce a point. In *The Great Code*, Frye writes:

> In Shakespeare's day there was much more emphasis, in studying literature in school, on the importance of sententiae, the epigrammatic comments on the human situation in, for example, a comedy of Terence: these were often copied into commonplace books and memorized. What is happening here is that the work of literature is acquiring the existential quality of entering into one's life and becoming a personal possession. The capacity to take on this quality of being quotable in a variety of situations is unpredictable: there is far more of it in *Alice in Wonderland*, for example, than there is in Thackeray or Browning, and it correlates with no system of value. But it indicates that literature can acquire the same decentralizing element that we have been discussing in connection with the Bible. The man who could not enjoy Hamlet because it was so full of quotations was responding to this quality in Shakespeare, if not in a very well-informed way" (CW 19: 238).

A Carroll Chrestomathy

Frye's memory was legendary, and one has the clear impression that he did not have to consult his edition of the Alice books (the Modern Library *Complete Works of Lewis Carroll*)[154] to cite Carroll. The lines simply popped into his head and flew trippingly off his tongue because the Alice books were a "personal possession." The following chrestomathy illustrates, by way of conclusion, the wide scope of Carroll's influence on Frye, who is our great analogical critic, able to discover likeness between two things. Similarity is not as important a principle, finally, as identity, but as Aristotle says in chapter 22 of the *Poetics*, the ability to discover similarities is a sign of genius. I mention this because fully a third of the following extracts centre on things in the Alice books that are like other things—the principle of simile at work.

- Edward Young's verse is seen as "placidly ambling, like a middle-aged Alice, through a wonderland of Oriental splendours and demonic terrors" (CW 16: 223).
- In a review of Earle Birney's *The Trial of the City and Other Verse*, Frye writes, "The time is the future, the setting the kind of pseudolegal kangaroo court which is the main instrument of McCarthyism, as packed and framed as a shipment of pictures, where everything is conducted on

the crazy Alice in Wonderland principle of sentence first, verdict afterwards"[155] (CW 12: 106).

- Frye describes P. K. Page's *Arras* as "a somewhat elliptical treatment of the Alice through the mirror theme" (CW 12: 132).
- About Joyce Cary's quotations from Blake in *The Horse's Mouth*, Frye says that two of them "were, as the White Knight says in Alice, his own invention"[156] (CW 8: 317).
- In his *Diaries*, Frye notes that in a Ph.D. committee meeting he and his colleagues sat "in the manner of suppressing applause described by Lewis Carroll"[157] (CW 8: 379).
- About time as the enemy of communication, Frye writes, "He is in Shakespeare, too. I mean time, which is him, not it, as the Mad Hatter said"[158] (CW 8: 511–12), the point being apparently that we need a fourth-person pronoun for the fourth dimension.
- "For long it was felt that the religious mind, like the White Queen in Alice, specialized in believing the impossible"[159] (CW 7: 282).
- In Dickens, the old curiosity shop "is a kind of threshold symbol of the entrance into the grotesque world, like the rabbit hole and mirror in the Alice books" (CW 17: 302).
- "Most of us feel that there is something else in Dickens [besides representational skill], something elemental, yet unconnected with either realistic clarity or philosophical profundity. What it is connected with is a kind of story that fully gratifies the hope expressed, according to Lewis Carroll, by the original of Alice, that "there will be nonsense in it"[160] (CW 17: 308).
- "To reverse a well-known phrase from Lewis Carroll, it took all the staying in the same place she [Emily Dickinson] could do to keep running. The intensity of her ordinary consciousness left her with few reserves to spend on a social life"[161] (CW 17: 250). "As an educational program, the recapitulation of the events of the decade a year ago gives a curious sense of running at top speed to stay in the same place, like Alice in Wonderland" (CW 10: 283).
- "The digging clam must finally reach some kind of antipodes, like Alice"[162] (CW 13: 269).
- "In the poetic structure as such there is no direct criterion of truth, as Aristotle explained: the writer of poetry or fiction says only 'Let this be,' and adopts postulates that may be as far away from ordinary experience as those of *Alice in Wonderland*. We do not argue about the postulates: we accept them and ask only what is done with them" (CW 19: 78).

- Like Blake's work, Carroll's is a composite art, and the Alice books, Frye says, "are like a number of other children's books in that Tenniel's illustrations can hardly be separated in our memory" (CW 16: 403). "I wouldn't accept anybody else's Mock Turtle at all" (CW 24: 195–6).
- "On the T. S. Eliot principle that every writer creates his own tradition, the success of Tolkien's [*Lord of the Rings*] helped to show that the tradition behind it, of George MacDonald and Lewis Carroll and William Morris, was, if not 'the great' tradition, a tradition nonetheless" (CW 18: 31).
- Regarding the insomniac reader of *Finnegans Wake*: "Such a reader is the closest we can come to Lewis Carroll's Humpty Dumpty, HCE before he fell off his wall, who could explain all the poems that had ever been written, along with a number that hadn't been written yet" (CW 29: 348).
- In discussing the breaks in consciousness of the heroes and heroines of romance, breaks that may involve "a change so drastic as to give the sense of becoming someone else altogether," Frye points to Alice, who, when "pressed to recount her adventures by the Mock Turtle and Gryphon, says she can tell them her adventures of that day, 'but it's no use going back to yesterday, because I was a different person then'" (*Annotated Alice* 138) (CW 18: 67–8).
- "But the indispensable axiom that, as long as we are talking about art, nature is inside art as its content, not outside it as its model, was written once for all into the critic's handbook by Longinus when he identified the 'sublime,' not with size, but with the mental capacity that appreciates the vastness of nature and, in the stock but expressive phrase, 'takes it in.' Thus art is, unlike Alice, as natural as life, but twice as large" (CW 21: 257). Alice, befuddled by the Gryphon and Mock Turtle, wonders "if anything would ever happen in a natural way again" (*Annotated Alice* 139).
- "Lewis Carroll's Sylvie & Bruno, one of the most off-putting books in the language. But its conception of a 'fairy' world close to children, dreams, and everything related to what the theosophists call the 'astral' will bear a good deal of thinking about. I suppose Bruno's relentless & nauseating cuteness is his way of coming to terms with little boys: Alice is never cute: that's one of the things that's so wonderful about her, and neither really is Sylvie" (CW 5: 190).
- In a review of Jung's *Psychology and Alchemy*, Frye writes that "most of its readers will want to hold it up to a mirror, like Jabberwocky. That is, the way that Jung has approached myth, working outwards from his own practice as a doctor, has had the result of turning every mythopoeic

structure he has studied into a vast allegory of his own techniques of psychotherapy"[163] (CW 21: 211).

- Allegorical criticism, Frye says, calls for tact, and "tact is violated ... when *Alice in Wonderland* is discussed in terms of her hypothetical toilet training" (CW 27: 10).[164]
- "[T]here is hardly an important nineteenth-century British novelist who does not make a major character out of the law: even *Alice in Wonderland* ends with a trial and a court room scene" (CW 27: 303).
- "Anyone reading *Finnegans Wake* thinks he can see at a glance that *Alice Through the Looking-Glass* was a major formative influence on it, especially the figure of Humpty Dumpty and his portmanteau words. Yet we learn that Joyce had not in fact known what was in that book until it was called to his attention by others" (CW 27: 318).[165]
- "[T]he riddle, in particular, illustrates the association in the human mind between the visual and the conceptual. What is understood must, at least metaphorically, be spread out in space: whatever is taken in through the ear has to form a series of simultaneous patterns (Gestalten) in order to be intelligible. Factors which inhibit this, such as too high a speed of utterance, prevent understanding. We may illustrate by a dialogue in *Through the Looking Glass*:

  > 'Can you do Addition?' the White Queen asked. 'What's one and one and one and one and one and one and one and one and one and one?'
  >
  > 'I don't know,' said Alice. 'I lost count.' (*Annotated Alice* 320)

  The White Queen is not employing a charm, but she illustrates the overwhelming of sense by sound, which is where charm starts" (CW 27: 370).
- "[V]erbal media internalize the imagery they use, so that the reader is compelled to build up his own structure of visualization. The illustration relieves the strain of this by supplying a ready-made equivalent for the reader's mental picture: hence its proverbial vividness, as expressed in the journalistic cliché that 'one picture is worth a thousand words.' In the nineteenth century books were illustrated to an extent hardly conceivable today, when the development of film and television has obviated the need for most of it. What's the use of a book, inquires Lewis Carroll's Alice, without pictures or conversations?" (*Annotated Alice* 25) (CW 18: 402).
- From Frye's summary of part 5 of "Rencontre": "Victorian fascination with law—the complicated legal situations behind the most unexpected

novels—*Pride and Prejudice, Wuthering Heights*. Even *Alice in Wonderland* ends in a trial scene and discussions about the rules of evidence" (CW 10: 129).

- In Blake's *Jerusalem* "we reach a climax of confused imagery, like the grotesque gods of the early world, half imaginative, and half nightmares, an elderly Adam and Eve trying to work with an amorphous mass of mutating life, like Alice in Wonderland trying to play croquet with flamingoes for mallets" (CW 10: 200).
- "The assimilating of external nature to human life is most clearly marked in myths, folk tales, fairy tales and legends. This is a class of literature which we instinctively feel to be 'good for the imagination' because it restores to the mind the sense of the primitive function of literature. The greatest producers of these genres, such as Lewis Carroll and Hans Christian Andersen, seem to drop into the very centre of our literary experience even when they come late in the history of literature" (CW 10: 240).
- "The cosmic voyage, as a journey through space, is finished as a form.... The world is cleared up, & in general the possibilities of space journeys were pretty well exhausted by Dante anyway. The same goes for Utopias in space. The possibilities remain of a new form, the journey through states, in which through some accident a hero finds himself in another phase of being. The principle is, if looking-glass reality is Alice's dream, why isn't our reality the red king's dream?"[166] (CW 25: 149).
- "In literature alone anything can be true; one hypothesis is as good as another. The hypothesis of *War and Peace* and the hypothesis of *Alice in Wonderland* are equally literary" (CW 4: 162).
- "Surely to see Protestantism as liberal is to admit the force of the 'butter-slide' argument, that Catholicism and atheism are the only logical positions, and that the Protestant can only slither down the intervening stages of Reformed theology, the Broad church, emotional pietism, deism, and ethical rationalism, and try to decide which one he will stop at. Even so, he will be troubled by the lesser dialectic between a liberalism which is afraid of theology, and so is merely secular, and a theology which is afraid of liberalism, and so is merely obscurantist. If this is really the Protestant's dilemma, then Protestantism has been left far behind by the march of history, like the empty jar that Alice put on a shelf while she was falling from one world to another" (*Annotated Alice* 27) (CW 4: 263).
- From an unpublished set on notes on Morris's *The Wood beyond the World*, Frye notes that "Walter's awake and headed for dreamland; the Maiden is dreaming and headed for waking: the point where they cross is the

union of the two. I'm not clear about all this, but the Alice and Red King business is somehow involved, I think."

- "I don't think I need anything more on the six Court of Love knights, but the fact that they are somewhat violently described as 'shadows' introduces another aspect of the symbolism, Britomart's going from Britain to Fairyland, which means that, like Alice, she is going into the same world reflected. The reflection is symbolized not only by her mirror, but by the whole sun and moon imagery which is not tied up until the Isis episode of book V" (CW 28: 42).
- "Re the hat & rabbit, if, or rather at, the way Alice gets into the magic world, how she meets a rabbit & a hatter at a party, & emerges with a rain of cards that turn into leaves. The hat symbolizes the magician, & thus a vortex" (CW 20: 150).
- "It is this solid core of moral reality in the middle of Quixote's illusion that makes him so ambiguous a figure. As with Alice's Wonderland, where we feel that no world can be completely fantastic where such Victorian infantile primness can survive intact, we feel that the humanity of Quixote is much more solidly established than the minor scholastic quibble about whether the windmills are really windmills or not" (CW 28: 16).
- "The second period of confusion and sexual licence [in Shakespearean comedy] is a phase that we may call the phase of temporarily lost identity, like the wood of no names that Alice passed through on her journey from pawn to queen" (*Annotated Alice* 225–7) (CW 28: 174).
- In *A Midsummer Night's Dream*, "Hermia speaks of the moon breaking through to the antipodes and joining the sun there [3.2.52–5], somewhat in the spirit of Lewis Carroll's walrus and carpenter poem"[167] (CW 28: 416).
- "In dealing with Cuchulain, Yeats is not always clear, like Alice, whether he is dreaming or the Red King, & seems to think of the word as reflecting instead of creating the deed. Yeats has no full belief in the creative Word" (CW 15: 114).
- "In the 19th c. there are a lot of stories, like Macdonald's *Phantastes*, where this complementary underworld is a fairy world. As such it has both ideal & demonic aspects. Ghost stories usually follow the same pattern. Alice's wonderland is a dream world, closer to Eros than Adonis, except for a few curious things like painting white roses red" (*Annotated Alice* 105) (CW 15: 168–9).

- "I've left out a great many demonic parodies like the final trial scene as a parody of the Last Judgement. This is in Arcadia, humorously in Alice, and Ivanhoe again" (CW 15: 228–9).
- "The folktale people say that only European stories run in threes: the North American Indians ones go in fours. Still I wonder. Why do we have two evil sisters and one good one: Psyche, Cinderella, Cordelia, Two-Eyes, etc.? I get a strong impression of the heroine emerging from the snapping jaws of two-hinged monsters, passing between the clashing rocks. It's perhaps a modulation of my old figure-in-the-doorway archetype, the Samson between the pillars, Christ between the thieves, etc. Same thing with three sons, of course, down to Ruskin's story.[168] Alice is also a Secunda between two other sisters,[169] who possibly, get metamorphosed as the Duchess and the Queen, or the Red and White Queens in the other one" (CW 15: 271).
- "*Through the Looking Glass*—chess normally an ascending symbol, like alchemy" (CW 15: 272).
- "Note that the penseroso figure is a speculative, or mirror-gazing, philosopher, except that he's really coming out of a mirror. Alice's return to the eighth square. Twin theme in the looking-glass book (nursery rhymes of course account for most of the incidents). Poems all about fish; riddle language of Jabberwocky, the dragon-killing in reversed mirror-writing" (CW 15: 273).
- Alice's pool of "tears" is piss: something else I've read on this, not the Irish Enir. Herodotus? (I, Mandane)"[170] (CW 15: 293).
- "Lewis Carroll's *Sylvie and Bruno* (which the Duffy woman doesn't mention)[171] is probably the most off-putting book in the language. And yet I may have to go through it, seeing at what points the fairy world of the two children affects the stupid behavior of the adult characters. I suppose the nauseating cuteness of Bruno is his way of coming to terms with little boys. Alice is never cute: that's one of the things that's so wonderful about her, and in fact neither is Sylvie. But while the book is a trifle sick-making the actual idea, set out in the preface, has a good deal of interest, as I suspect a fairy world closely related to dreams and children, closely beside us and occasionally breaking into our actions and influencing our behavior, is one of the things I'm looking for" (CW 15: 329).
- "In the first chapter [of *What Maisie Knew*] HJ [Henry James] remarks: 'it was to be the fate of this patient little girl to see much more than she at first understood, but also even at first to understand much more than

any little girl, however patient, had perhaps ever understood before.' That's an astounding remark when you look at it: he's saying she's one of the great archetypes in literature, on a level with, say, Alice in Wonderland, who's more obviously a preternatural child" (CW 15: 345).

- "Huizinga makes a good deal of the fact that play has a beginning and an end:[172] there comes a point at which the show is over. Work & seriousness themes relate to life's unending continuum of energy. The mirror of play has a frame: cf. the map in Sylvie & Bruno"[173] (CW 15: 292).
- "Alice books: the rabbit taking out his watch; the March Hare doing the same later: the discussion of Time as 'him' with the Hatter; lessons 'lessoning' for eleven days: the grinning old man in LG [Looking-Glass]"[174] (CW 9: 164).
- On Colin Wilson's *The Mind Parasites*: "As I say, the book is silly, but he does touch on significant themes. Descending into the mind & seeing all one's memories there, not examining them closely because each is a world in itself, is described in language recalling Alice's descent down the rabbit-hole. Of course this is really an Eros journey into the past; this is part of that difficult interchangibility principle" (CW 9: 215–16).
- "Alice goes into the mirror world & hears poems about fish: asks why & is given a riddling answer about undishcovering the fish or dishcovering the riddle" (*Annotated Alice* 333) (CW 9: 221–2).
- "But if the world is indifferent to the poet's nostalgia, it is still more unimpressed by the critic's adherence to his standards, however dogged. The poet can always write another book to console himself; the critic can only, like Alice, weep himself a pool of self-pitying tears and run the risk of being deflated and drowned in it afterwards" (CW 29: 28).
- As in *Alice through the Looking Glass*, to which it owes so much, the final question left with the reader of *Finnegans Wake* is, "Which dreamed it?"[175] (CW 29: 106–7).

Frye appears to have so completely assimilated the Alice books that he could, without effort or hesitation, call up incidents, quotations, themes, and tropes and apply them to any number of initiatives in his writing projects, hyperlogical fantasies included.

9
Frye and Stéphane Mallarmé

In 1985 Frye wrote in one of his notebooks, "The 'subject' swallows everything objective to it: hence the pan-historical critics of today, the Hegelian pan-philosophical absolute knowledge, the pan-literary universe which only three people understand: Blake, Mallarmé, and myself. The *final* answer, naturally, is interpenetration" (CW 5: 247). Five years later Frye gave an expanded version of the same extraordinary claim:

> I find it difficult to buy the panhistorical visions of so many contemporary literary scholars. They seem to me to operate only within history as such: when you're studying history you're inside a historical cosmos where everything is historical. If you're studying philosophy, you're inside a philosophical cosmos where what you do is climb a philosophical mountain, like Hegel, to find yourself on a pinnacle of absolute knowledge where you know everything except where to get the oxygen for the next breath. Similarly there seems to me to be a total cosmos of literature, within which everything is literary. So far as I can see, only three people have been inspired by that last vision. Two of them were Blake and Mallarmé; the third has learned what he knows about it from them. But of course these are not differing universes, and they have no boundaries; they are interpenetrating. (CW 18: 479–80)

The third person here, the one who takes his cues from the panliterary universe is, of course, Frye himself. The passages have a slightly different focus. In the first, the panliterary universe is an object of understanding; in the second, a source of inspiration. But the presence of Mallarmé in Frye's idea of a total literary cosmos will doubtless strike many of his readers as extraordinary, or at least unexpected. The place of Blake in this triumvirate needs little commentary. Frye told an interviewer on two occasions, "I've learned everything I know from Blake" (CW 17: 271; CW 24: 739), and a great deal has naturally been written about the Blake–Frye connection. But what about Mallarmé, a poet about whom Frye never wrote an extended commentary but who, as we know from Frye's published and unpublished works, is unusually important for him? The numerous references to

Mallarmé suggest that the Frye–Mallarmé connection is worth exploring, and the present chapter is an attempt to do just that, glancing at the role he played in the Frye's theory of symbols and then focusing on the work that Frye calls on most frequently, the enigmatic *Igitur*. He is clearly captivated by the poet, he confesses at one point, whom he "has spent so much time on" (CW 5: 142).[176]

Theory of Symbols

When Frye first read Mallarmé is uncertain,[177] but we know that in 1952 he bought Roger Fry's translation of the poems shortly after it was published (New Directions, 1951) (CW 8: 570). Four months earlier he had begun to take a serious look at Mallarmé in preparing a paper on symbolism that Henri Peyre had asked him to submit to *Yale French Studies* (*ibid.* 465).[178] Although he confesses in early January 1952 that he is "only guessing at what Mallarmé means" (*ibid.*), by the time he completed his paper, published later in the year, he writes with some assurance that Mallarmé is an important key to the connection between literature and religion. This passage from "Three Meanings of Symbolism" (1952) is, Frye says, practically a paraphrase of Mallarmé:

> The word ... is a symbol which turns away from its sign meaning in the material world, not to point to something in the spiritual world, for this would still make it representational, but to awaken other words to suggest or evoke something in the spiritual world. This something is occasionally called by Mallarmé an Idea, but he usually speaks of it simply as a mystery, because it is manifested only in the poem, and the mind can gain no direct contact with it. It is rather a sense of spiritual unity suggested by words. Poetry leads us from the material thing through the verbal symbol as sign, into the verbal symbol as image, and thence into an apprehension of the Word, the unity of poetic experience. It follows that the relation of the material thing to the spiritual mystery of the Word is a kind of sacramental relation. Thus *symbolisme*, like the Courtly Love convention before it, resolves into an elaborate analogy of religion. The poet's attitude to his public is not democratic but catholic. He should avoid anything like rhetoric, or the market-place view of words as like coins, to be exchanged, not for their own sakes, but as a medium for actions toward things. So far from being introspective or solipsistic, however, the poet as a personality is not in his poem at all. He is a priest of a mystery; he turns his back on his hearers, and invokes, chanting in a hieratic tongue, the real presence of the Word which reveals the mystery. It is only within that presence that

> he and his hearers communicate, and the experience is always new, for the Word is of a virgin birth. The poet brings about an apocalyptic separation of the pure Word from the sub-intelligent fact or thing, and his emblem is the swan, which sings at the death of its material self. (CW 21: 139–40).[179]

Five years later Mallarmé came to play a key role in Frye's theory of symbolism. In the account of the literal and descriptive phases of symbolism in *Anatomy of Criticism*, Frye establishes the distinction between the centrifugal and centripetal forms of reference. When the symbol is a sign, the movement of reference is centrifugal, as in descriptive or assertive works; and when the symbol is a motif, the movement is centripetal, as in imaginative, or in what Frye calls "hypothetical" works. This relation can be represented by a continuum running from documentary naturalism at one pole to *symbolisme* and "pure" poetry at the other. Although every work of literature is characterized by both of these phases of symbolism, there can be an infinite number of variations along the descriptive-literal axis, since a given work tends to be influenced more deeply by one phase than the other. Thus when the descriptive phase predominates, the narrative of literature tends toward realism, and its meaning toward the didactic or descriptive. The limits, at this end of the continuum, would be represented by such writers as Zola and Dreiser, whose work "goes about as far as a representation of life, to be judged by its accuracy of description rather than by its integrity as a structure of words, as it could go and still remain literature" (CW 22: 73). At the other end, as a complement to naturalism, is the tradition of writers like Mallarmé, Rimbaud, Rilke, Pound, and Eliot. Here the emphasis is on the literal phase of meaning: literature becomes a "centripetal verbal pattern, in which elements of direct or verifiable statement are subordinated to the integrity of that pattern" (CW 22: 74). Criticism, says Frye, was able to achieve an acceptable theory of literal meaning only after the development of *symbolisme*, which, he adds,

> as expressed for instance in Mallarmé, maintains that the representational answer to the question, "What does this mean?" should not be pressed in reading poetry, for the poetic symbol means primarily itself in relation to the poem. The unity of a poem, then, is best apprehended as a unity of mood, a mood being a phase of emotion, and emotion being the ordinary word for the state of mind directed toward the experiencing of pleasure or the contemplating of beauty. And as moods are not long sustained, literature, for *symbolisme*, is essentially discontinuous, longer poems being held together only by the use of the grammatical structures more appropriate to descriptive writing. Poetic images do not state or point to anything, but, by

> pointing to each other, they suggest or evoke the mood which informs the poem. That is, they express or articulate the mood. The emotion is not chaotic or inarticulate: it merely would have remained so if it had not turned into a poem, and when it does so, it is the poem, not something else still behind it. Nevertheless the words "suggest" and "evoke" are appropriate, because in *symbolisme* the word does not echo the thing but other words, and hence the immediate impact *symbolisme* makes on the reader is that of incantation, a harmony of sounds and the sense of a growing richness of meaning unlimited by denotation. (CW 22: 74)

On eight occasions throughout his work, Frye refers to Mallarmé's dictum that poets do not name things or point to objects that are external to the poem.[180] The touchstone passage Frye had in mind was this, from "Crisis of Verse":

> As opposed to a denominative and representative function, as the crowd first treats it, speech, which is primarily dream and song, recovers in the Poet's hands, of necessity in an art devoted to fictions, its virtuality. Verse, which out of several vocables, makes a total word, entirely new, foreign to the language, and almost incantatory, achieves that isolation of speech; negating, with a sovereign blow, despite their repeated formulations between sound and sense, the arbitrariness that remains in the terms, and gives you the surprise of never having heard that fragment of ordinary eloquence before, while the object named is bathed in a brand new atmosphere. (*Divigations* 210–11)

The Pan-Literary Universe and the Katabatic Journey

Fast forward from the *Anatomy* and we find, thirty-three years later, that Mallarmé is still very much on Frye's mind. He makes a half-dozen appearances in *Words with Power*, and Frye turns to him not infrequently in his essays from the 1980s. In Frye's notebooks, Mallarmé appears in almost a hundred entries, chiefly in the *Late Notebooks* and mostly in connection with Frye's fascination with *Igitur*, *Cantique de Saint Jean*, *Un Coup de Dés*, and Mallarmé's letters to Henri Cazalis.

A key passage about Mallarmé is in Frye's "The Symbol as a Medium of Exchange," a talk he gave at the Royal Society of Canada meeting in 1984 (CW 18: 327–41). Here it is clear that Frye's attraction is to Mallarmé's belief in a single, symbolic verbal universe, which is fundamentally a spiritual world. The "single, symbolic literary universe" is the "pan-literary universe" or the "total cosmos of literature" referred to in the two passages quoted at the beginning. Or again, "[J]ust as mathematics exists in a mathematical universe which is at the circumference of the common field of experience, so literature exists in a verbal universe, which is not a commentary on life or reality, but contains life and reality in a system of verbal relationships. This conception of a verbal universe, in which life and reality are inside literature, and not outside it and being described or represented or approached or symbolized by it, seems to me the first postulate of a properly organized criticism" (CW 18: 73). The verbal universe, which, Frye says, comes from Mallarmé,[181] is a world containing a symbolic death and resurrection, a world where divinity can be expressed only by the poetic word, a world in which chance (where we've got no choice) and choice (where chance does not operate) become the same thing, and a world where rebirth can only occur from the ashes of Nothingness. Mallarmé serves as the backbone of this essay on the symbol, and Frye finds in Mallarmé something that's almost like, perhaps even is, a mystical vision. Frye's punch line in this essay, by way of Heraclitus, is about the interpenetration of the up and down movement. As is the case always in Frye, the emphasis is on unity. Metaphor is the ultimate unifying principle, saying as it does that one thing is another thing. Frye's examples are from the Christian doctrine of the Incarnation, Poe's *Eureka* (another of his favourite works, which is about the experience of Self and not Self), and the enlightenment of Zen koans. The up and down movement is the anabatic and katabatic journey along the *axis mundi* that figures so importantly in Frye's late work. The image of the *axis mundi* is also an important part of our analyses of Carroll, Still, Longinus, Joachim of Floris, Kierkegaard, and Yates.

The quest movement in Frye typically moves toward the top and bottom of a vertical axis in his mental diagram of his literary universe. At the top is the point of epiphany of the Logos vision, the transcendent moment of pure illumination. There is a strong tendency for Frye, especially in his later work, to move up the *axis mundi* to the point where Word and Spirit are identical, a place where space and time interpenetrate. The answer for Frye is not to be found in history, which he saw mostly as a series of repeating nightmares. In the dialectic of his thought, the search for the moment of pure illumination, the anagogic vision, represents his Platonic, Longinian, and Romantic inclinations. The movement is from Thanatos, at the bottom of Frye's circular diagram of the literary universe, to Logos at the top.[182] But the katabatic movement down the ladder is equally important for Frye: in his later writings it appears to be even more important. A passage quoted in the essay on Carroll (above) is worth quoting again: "Everybody has a fixation. Mine has to do with meander-and-descent patterns.

For years in my childhood I wanted to dig a cave & be the head of a society in it—this was before I read Tom Sawyer. All the things in literature that haunt me most have to do with katabasis. The movie that hit me hardest as a child was the Lon Chaney Phantom of the Opera. My main points of reference in literature are such things as The Tempest, P.R. [*Paradise Regained*], [Blake's] *Milton*, the Ancient Mariner, Alice in Wonderland, the Waste Land—every damn one a meander-&-katabasis work. I should have kept the only book Vera kept, *The Sleepy* [*Sleeping*] *King*" (CW 9: 76).[183]

The study of archetypes in part 2 of *Words with Power* begins with the mountain and the garden, and it concludes with the cave and the furnace. Thus, the last part of the last book published in Frye's lifetime treats the archetypes on the lower half of the *axis mundi*. In chapter 8, Frye calls on Mallarmé to help define the cluster of katabatic images that characterize the *mythos* and *dianoia* of the lower world archetype of the furnace. The last four chapters of *Words with Power* are an outline of four groups of images on the *axis mundi*. The first two are associated with the different accounts of creation we get in Genesis—the ladder imagery of the Priestly account (Frye's chapter 5) and the garden imagery of the Jahwist account (chapter 6). Chapters 7 and 8 are expansive treatments of the reversals of the mountain (or ladder) and garden themes in chapters 5 and 6. The imagery of the fall, associated with the Jahwist account, comes under the archetypal heading of "The Cave." In the final variation—"The Furnace"—Frye traces the demonic parodies, the ideological adaptations, and the authentic myths associated with the furnace archetype. "The *demonic parody* is the descent into nothingness, and may involve only an individual life or a whole society.... The *ideological adaptation* to this is the realization that power always corrupts, but that nothing can be done about the ascendancy of such corrupt power in human society.... The *creative descent* to a lower wisdom is a descent to the sources of genuine human power, and the ascent from there is the authentic myth" (CW 26: 249–50; italics added).

Mallarmé enters Frye's discussion of the various forms of creative descent, and at one point Frye proposes that *Igitur* will serve as his "central model in modern literature" of the creative descent theme (CW 5: 312). Because Mallarmé is central to Frye's understanding of the creative descent, his commentary is worth quoting in full:

IGITUR

> The human poet does not create out of nothing; he creates out of his previous experience of literature. But he stares at nothing, so to speak, and negates himself as a subject as well as negating the objective environ-

ment. He is in the position of Wallace Stevens's observer looking at "The Snow Man," who is "nothing himself," and sees both "Nothing that is not there and the nothing that is." Hence, like Donne's geographer painting a map of the world on a globe, he "can quickly make that which was nothing, all," or at least potentially all. It is also Donne who introduces the theme of negating nothing, in an alchemical context, in his *Nocturnal upon St. Lucy's Day*. Mallarmé, who was fascinated with such words as "aboli," is preeminently the poet of the nothingness of the world the descending poet enters. The celebrated poem usually called the "sonnet in yx" describes how Dread or Angst ("L'angoisse") inhabits a deserted room, deserted because its master has left for the lower world ("Styx"), taking with him "ce seul objet dont le Néant s'honore" ["this sole object that Nothingness attains"], a "ptyx" which could mean fifty things and also means nothing.[184]

In *Igitur* the central character descends a staircase, commanded by his ancestors to take a candle with him which he blows out at midnight, recalling the "chapel perilous" image of medieval romance, then throws (or perhaps merely shakes) dice, and lies down on the ashes of his ancestors, described as the "ashes of stars," for the stars seem to keep recurring in Mallarmé with a Dantean persistence. In *The Ancient Mariner* a throw of dice accompanies the victory of Life-in-Death over Death; in Mallarmé the dice represent a world where, in Yeats's phrase, choice and chance are one.[185] Throwing dice is a commitment to chance that does not abolish chance, but is in itself a free act, and so begins a negating of negation that brings something, perhaps ultimately everything, into being again. A connection has been suggested between Mallarmé's word "Igitur" and the Vulgate text of Genesis 2:1, *igitur perfecti sunt coeli*.[186] This has been discredited for lack of evidence, but it is a most penetrating comment nonetheless.[187] For Mallarmé was also preoccupied by the opposite of his "Néant" world, speaking of a kind of definitive book that would contain the entire verbal cosmos and would be in literature what the "Great Work" was to "our ancestors, the alchemists" (CW 26: 248).

"Mallarmé fascinates me," Frye writes, "because he shows that as soon as poetry becomes pure it's abolished as poetry, and something transcendent (what 'would have been the truth,' as he said) appears that the pure poem is a symbol of. It's not for nothing that 'aboli' is one of his favorite words" (CW 5: 202).[188]

> [A]lthough Mallarmé speaks of God as an old scarecrow whom he has at last overcome,[189] he also speaks in his letters of a symbolic death and resurrection that he has attained through his search for a pure poetry, and speaks also of the poet who creates in the teeth of *the* creation, so to speak, as though he were the vehicle of a holy spirit. "Man's duty," he says, "is to observe with the eyes of the divinity; for if his connection with that divinity is to be made clear, it can be expressed only by the pages of the open book in front of him."[190] He also describes himself, in a letter to Cazalis, as "one of the ways the Spiritual Universe has found to see Itself, unfold Itself through what used to be me."[191]

The Passage from Oracle to Wit

To understand the meaning of the opposite of Mallarmé's *Néant* world, we need to put it in the context of one of Frye's several epiphanies—what he calls his Seattle illumination, which he defines as the passage from oracle to wit. It was an epiphany he had when he was teaching summer school at the University of Washington in 1951. Frye understood that his Seattle intuition was linked to Mallarmé's *Igitur* (CW 5: 399, CW 6: 480, 510, 535). The oracle was one of Frye's four or five "kernels," his word for the seeds or distilled essences of more expansive forms. Oracle for him is almost always a lower-world kernel. It is linked with *thanatos*, secrecy, solitude, intoxication, mysterious ciphers, caves, the dialectic of choice and chance, and the descent to the underworld. The locus of the oracle is the point of demonic epiphany, the lower, watery world of chaos and the ironic vision. The central oracular literary moments for Frye include Poe's Arthur Gordon Pym's diving for the cipher at the South Pole, the descent to the bottom of the sea in Keats's *Endymion*, Odysseus in the cave of Polyphemus, the visit to the cave of Trophonius, the oracle of the bottle in Rabelais, and Mallarmé's *Igitur*. As for wit, in the context of the Seattle illumination it is related to laughter, the transformation of recollection into repetition, the breakthrough from irony to myth, the *telos* of interpenetration that Frye found in the Avatamsaka Sutra, new birth, knowledge of both the future and the self, the recognition of the hero, the fulfilment of prophecy, revelation, and detachment from obsession.[192] The oracular and the witty came together for Frye in the finale of Verdi's *Falstaff*[193] and in *Igitur*.

Frye calls the Seattle illumination a "breakthrough,"[194] and the experience, whatever it was, appears to have been decisive for him. He was thirty-nine at the time, literally midway through his journey of life. One can say with some confidence that the Seattle epiphany was a revelation to Frye that one need not surrender to what he spoke of as the century's three A's: alienation, anxiety, absurdity; that there was a way out of the abyss; that life can have a purgatorial shape; that, in short, the invitation of the Spirit and the Bride in Revelation 22:17 is available to all. "The door of death," Frye writes, "has oracle on one side & wit on the other: when one goes through it one recovers the power of laughter" (CW 9: 162). And laughter, for Frye, is the "sudden release from the unpleasant" (CW 15: 73). Oracles are, of course, ordinarily sombre, and wit, in one of its senses, is lighthearted. Pausanius tells us that the ritual of consulting the oracle in the cave of Trophonius was so solemn that the suppliants who emerged were unable to laugh for some time: but they did recover their power to laugh.[195] There is a "porous osmotic wall between the oracular and the funny," Frye writes in Notebook 27 (CW 5: 15). Similarly in *Gargantua and Pantagruel*, when Panurge and Friar John consult the oracle of the Holy Bottle, there is, if not literal laughter, an intoxicating delight that comes from the oracle's invitation to drink; and we are told that the questers then "passed through a country full of all delights" (711). But laughter here is more than a physical act. It is a metaphor for the sudden spiritual transformation that is captured in the *paravritti* of Mahayana Buddhism. *Paravritti* literally means "turning up" or "change," and according to D. T. Suzuki it corresponds to conversion in religious experience. (*Lankavatara*, Introduction, xvii). In the *Lankavatara Sutra* we are told that in his transcendental state of consciousness the Buddha laughed "the loudest laugh," and in his marginal annotation of this passage Frye notes that "the laugh expresses a sudden release of Paravritti" (*Lankavatara* 13–14).[196]

In *Anatomy of Criticism*, Frye describes the oracular mind as lying beneath the conscious one, the original archetype of which is the cave of Trophonius (CW 22: 329). This is the world of the *perseroso* mood—the return to the womb or the imaginative withdrawal that we get in sixth phase romance. To escape from what Frye calls the "oracular cave" (CW 9: 198) is to enter the world of the "awakened critical intelligence" or wit (CW 22: 173). It is, as described in Notebook 21, "the passage from dream to waking" (CW 13: 227). To leave the dream-cave is to turn one's back on what in the *Anatomy* Frye refers to as the *reductio ad absurdum*, "which is not designed to hold one in perpetual captivity, but to bring one to the point at which one can escape" (CW 22: 218). This means that the movement of oracle to wit is the movement from the world of magical nothingness to full awareness or recognition.[197] In *Beyond the Body: The Human Double and the Astral Planes*, Benjamin Walker concludes that what ultimately happens to the soul is that it loses its body on earth and loses its sense of individuality in the celestial abodes. Reacting to this conclusion, Frye wrote in the margin of Walker's book, "you don't *lose* anything: you lose the lower sphere, or nothingness" (194).[198] What you gain, by contrast, is self-knowledge and creative energy. In one of his more revealing commentaries on oracle, this one on the oracle at Delphi, Frye writes,

> The motto of Delphi was "know thyself," which suggests that the self intended was a conscience far below the ego with its anxieties of self-interest, far below all social and cultural conditioning, in short the spiritual self. For that self to "know itself" would constitute the unity of Word and Spirit in which all consciousness begins and ends. Such a spirit could produce its own oracles, and they would be not only genuinely prophetic but genuinely witty. *Finnegans Wake* is the only book I know which is devoted entirely to this hidden intercommunion of Word and Spirit, with no emergence into the outside world at any point, but of course the creative energy involved has produced all literature. (CW 26: 216–17)

Wit is both an efficient and a final cause of satire. One of the differences between irony and satire is that the former represents humanity in a state of bondage, whereas the effort to escape from bondage marks the latter. In one of his notebooks for *Anatomy of Criticism* Frye writes, "satire goes up the ladder of laughter, through the low norm of the experiential & the high norm of the innocent, to participating in the laughter of the gods at the fallen state of man (which is sadistic if God & man are not mutually involved). That gives me a Lankavatara quote" (CW 23: 178–9), the Lankavatara quote being the "loudest laugh" passage, mentioned above, that Frye annotated in his copy of the *Lankavatara Sutra*. This is apparently what Frye means when he writes that by moving in a Lankavatara direction he hopes "to bust the supremacy of the existential" (CW 23: 208), with all of its ritual bondage and poker-faced *Angst*. By the time he came to write *The Secular Scripture*, some twenty-five years after the Seattle experience, Frye put the *axis mundi* movement in these terms in his chapter on "Themes of Ascent":

> As the hero or heroine enters the labyrinthine lower world, the prevailing moods are those of terror or uncritical awe. At a certain point, perhaps when the strain, as the storyteller doubtless hopes, is becoming unbearable, there may be a revolt of the mind, a recovered detachment, the typical expression of which is laughter. The ambiguity of the oracle becomes the ambiguity of wit, something addressed to a verbal understanding that shakes the mind free. This point is also marked by generic changes from the tragic and ironic to the comic and satiric. Thus in Rabelais the huge

> giants, the search for an oracle, and other lower-world themes that in different contexts would be frightening or awe-inspiring, are presented as farce. *Finnegans Wake* in our day also submerges us in a dream world of mysterious oracles, but when we start to read the atmosphere changes, and we find ourselves surrounded by jokes and puns. Centuries earlier, the story was told of how Demeter wandered over the world in fruitless search of her lost daughter Proserpine, and sat lonely and miserable in a shepherd's hut until the obscene jests and raillery of the servant girl Iambe and the old nurse Baubo finally persuaded her to smile. The Eleusinian mysteries which Demeter established were solemn and awful rites of initiation connected with the renewal of the fertility cycle; but Iambe and Baubo helped to ensure that there would also be comic parodies of them, like Aristophanes' *Frogs*. According to Plutarch, those who descended to the gloomy cave of the oracle of Trophonius might, after three days, recover the power of laughter. (CW 18: 85)

"The moment of illumination," Frye writes in one of his marginalia to the *Rigveda*, is "humorous & not pompous" (Macnichol 32). A further gloss on the movement from oracle to wit is Frye's juxtaposition, in one of his sets of typed notes for *The Secular Scripture*, of the recovery of laughter in the cave of Trophonius, located at the south point of his mandala, with "Blake's boy born in joy" (CW 15: 231). This is a reference to the boy in *The Mental Traveller* who "was begotten in dire woe"—another example of the gleeful release arising from the gloomy, oracular depths. Or, as Frye says in Notebook 21, "Laughter means hostility in the ironic direction and assimilation in the paradisal one" (CW 13: 231).

Finally, the oracle–wit opposition is parallel to a number of Frye's other bipolar distinctions. By collapsing the distinctions we experience in ordinary waking reality, the oracular is metaphorical. The process is like that of condensation in Freud's account of dream-work, accidental slips, allegories, and the like: a single word or image comes to represent two or more ideas, memories, or feelings. In contrast, the witty, having to do with recognition, is metonymic: one thing is put for another, as in Freudian displacement, and so is accommodated to waking experience once we have ascended from the oracular cave. Condensation occurs in a pre-recognition state. Displacement belongs to the daylight world where one recognizes the point of the joke—the "oh-I-see" moment of release and illumination. Similarly, to use another of Frye's distinctions, oracle represents a centripetal movement into the identities of metaphor, as in the interrelationship of words in *Finnegans Wake*; and wit, a centrifugal movement out into the world of realistic awareness, as in the continuous narrative of *War and Peace*, where myth has been adapted to the canons of plausibility.[199]

As oracle belongs to the complex of ideas Frye associates with metaphor, and wit with those ideas associated with myth, perhaps the oracle–wit distinction had to do with the realization that these two principles would become the backbone of the *Anatomy*. In any case, there is no difficulty in accepting Frye's judgment that the Seattle intuition was a breakthrough: it certainly helps to explain his treatment of the themes of romance in the secular scripture and the last four chapters of his second book on the sacred scripture. Nor is there difficulty in understanding what he means when he says, "I've spent nearly eighty years trying to articulate intuitions that occupied about five minutes of my entire life" (CW 6: 636). The Seattle illumination involved not only laughing in the face of irony—the telling moment that Frye saw in Trophonius and Rabelais and in the pure detachment of the Buddha's laugh. It also involved, in the passage quoted above, the vision of dice-throwing in Mallarmé's *Igitur* (CW 26: 248). The dice-throwing is also to be linked (one of Frye's favourite words) with the metaphorical-game tradition, which explores the metaphorical foundation of discursive prose and which Frye sees as characterizing some of his own work. "The word game," he writes, "is linked to the fact that its centre of gravity is that mysterious area I've talked so much about, where the oracular and witty seem different aspects of the same thing" (CW 13: 301).

Recognition and Creative Descent

In *The Secular Scripture*, Frye writes that in comedy the device that breaks the spell of death or paralysis is the recognition scene, and the word "recognition," as Aristotle and *Oedipus the King* remind us, has to do with figurative seeing, whether comic or tragic. And here again the recognition scene "transforms a story into a kind of game" (CW 18: 85).[200] The point of all this for Frye is that the abyss must be entered and the nightmare vision confronted before a triumphant reversal can occur.[201] It may not be for Frye, as it was for Heraclitus, that the way up and the way down are one and the same, but he sometimes comes close to suggesting that: "The principle of the higher or unfallen world is harmony or concord; the principle of the lower world is metamorphosis, the passing out of one state of being into another. But perhaps a sufficiently penetrating wisdom could see in metamorphosis itself a kind of harmony, a principle of change moving in correspondence with the worlds above" (CW 10: 103). To pass through the door of wit permits one to embark on the purgatorial journey, that journey of spirit-making that figures so importantly in Frye's notebooks and finally gets articulated in the chapters 4 to 8 of *Words with Power* and in *The Double Vision*. In any event, moving both directions on the *axis mundi* is part of the double movement of the spiritual vision that defines and is defined by Frye's religious quest.

Creative descent begins with the experience of nothingness. "God's creation," Frye writes in one of his *Words with Power* notebooks, "is involved in nothingness: when the conception of creation shifted from a divine product to a human process, nothingness became the dark half, so to speak, of human creation." This, he adds, is symbolized by Mallarmé's remark about "the white paper the poem is written on" (CW 5: 392). What Frye has in mind is the statement in the preface to *Un Coup de Dés*, where Mallarmé says that the blank spaces on the page "assume importance and are what is immediately most striking; versification always demanded them as a surrounding silence" (*Collected Poems* 121). Similarly, in *Brise Marine* he writes, "O night, / Nor the lone splendor of my lamp on the white / Paper which the void leaves undefiled" (*ibid.* 21).[202] The silence and the void are signatures of the *via negativa*. "In Mallarmé," Frye writes, "you start with a sheet of blank paper with nothing on it. The minute you write the word 'nothing' on it poetry begins" (CW 5: 417). Analogues of the journey downward, often a whirlpool or spiral movement, are found in the descent to the underworld in the *Aeneid* (book 6), Lucian's *Cataplus* (*Voyage to the Lower World*), the Troy dance,[203] St. John of the Cross, the descent to the Mothers in *Faust*, Boehme's *Urgrund*, the fall of Demogorgon and Jupiter in Shelley's *Prometheus Unbound*, and the journey to the chapel perilous in Eliot's *The Waste Land*. More abstract forms of nothingness are Heidegger's *Das Nichts*, Yeats's "where there is nothing, there is God" (*Unicorn from the Stars*), and Stevens's *Snow Man*: "Nothing that is not there and the nothing that is" (CW 5: 41, 350). All of these variations on Nothingness occur in the world below. But, Frye says, what the human process "creates below now keeps reshaping what is above" (CW 5: 392).[204]

How then does Mallarmé transform the demonic parody of nothingness in *Igitur* into a creative descent? *Igitur* is a fragmentary work, never published by Mallarmé and apparently never intended to be published. It is also a hermetic work, and its narrative frame, summarized by Frye above, is slight. Igitur descends a spiral staircase of "the human mind" with a candle, having been commanded to do so by his ancestors. He blows the candle out at midnight. When he reaches the abyss, he tosses the dice and lies down on the ashes of his ancestors. All of this is presented to us as if in a dream state in which the dreamer is suffering from impotence and boredom. Along the way, he encounters a series of recurring objects (furniture, drapery, a mirror, a clock, a book, a glass flask) and a series of often baffling metaphysical meditations on the Absolute, the Idea, the Infinite, the Shadow, Necessity, the Act. It is tempting to read *Igitur* as a work of pure irony or a demonic parody, to use the language of *Words with Power*. Here we have a hero who ends up in the world of Thanatos. Some have even suggested that Igitur commits suicide, the ultimate ironic gesture. But as a number of Mallarmé's commentators have proposed, the movement is, in Frye's terms, from oracle to wit.

There is no narrative logic in *Igitur*. In fact, Frye says on two occasions that the Latin "igitur" ("therefore") is not the logical *donc* (CW 6: 487, 535), and that it should be translated rather as "wherefore" or "whereupon." Both words can be used in the context of causality to mean as a consequence, but the meaning for Frye is apparently "for what purpose" or "at which point," which suggests an "osmosis between the oracular and the witty" (CW 6: 535). In the choice-versus-chance conundrum, one has a choice to throw the dice and in so doing arrives at the point at which chance is abolished. When one of the possible thirty-six results turns up, then the issue of chance becomes moot. Choice and chance are identified with each other, as Yeats says. "Mallarmé tells us," writes Frye, "that a dice-throw does not abolish chance, meaning, roughly, that human creation does not deliver us from death, though it is all that we have to fight death with" (CW 18: 115). Similarly, "Mallarmé's is a world where human creation comes to be, where meaning is, where chance is not abolished but where a world that within itself is not chance has taken shape" (CW 6: 602).

Frye is fascinated by the mirror into which Igitur stares on his journey into the interior of his psyche. "[S]eeking himself in the mirror becomes boredom" writes Mallarmé; "... seeing the mirror horribly null" (*Selected Poetry and Prose* 98). "Internalizing," Frye writes, "is voluntarily plunging into the prison of hell and demonic parody, and then the deeper prison below that & which produces it really: the prison of Narcissus, the *stade du miroir*. Mallarmé, of course, tried in Igitur to hit the real bottom, & says in a letter that he had to go through all that just to get a vision of the universe, the only alternative being left shut up in one's self" (CW 5: 300). The letter was to Henri Cazalis, written on 14 May 1867: "I floated downward until finally one day I looked again in my Venetian mirror. And saw the person I had been several months before.... I still need to see myself in this mirror in order to think: and that if it were not in front of me here on the table as I write you, I would become Nothingness again. Which means that I am impersonal now" (*Selected Letters* 74–5). The *stade du miroir* or mirror stage is Jacques Lacan's phrase for that period in a child's psychological development when the subject becomes separated from itself, that is, the reflection in the mirror is a model of the relation that exists between the self and the image of the self.[205] Frye interprets the phrase "to mean that one cannot become a genuine 'subject' in our subject-object world of ordinary experience until one has become an object to oneself. There must be a split within the subject, and the sense of the subject as bound up with something alien is thereby formed" (CW 18: 394).[206] The subject peers into a mirror and what is reflected back is both the self and not the self. The prison of Narcissus is the world that Igitur enters at the end of his downward journey. Once Igitur realizes that there is an identity of subject and object, he can break out of his prison. When he becomes impersonal, the Word takes over and the kerygmatic breaks through. He has become the medium through which, to quote again from one of his letters to Cazalis, "the Spiritual Universe has found to see itself, unfold itself in what used to be me" (*Selected Poetry and Prose* 87).[207] For Frye, one can escape the prison of Narcissus only by an expansion of consciousness (CW 6: 515), and heightened consciousness, which is the state reached by Igitur as he lies down on the "ashes of the stars," is an insistent theme in Frye's late work.

In the void or the abyss, Igitur encounters death but, according to Frye's view, he encounters life and death as well, which is "the intuition I got from Mallarmé about the dice-throw followed by the Igitur of a new creation" (CW 6: 459). The descent of Igitur, Frye writes, "is a stage one passes through on the way to something deeper.... Something connected with (a) nothingness (b) the cave where oracle meets wit" (CW 6: 480). Similarly, the Igitur descent "takes me into the oracular-laughter Rabelais climax I've been stewing over since Seattle days" (CW 6: 491). On this reading, Igitur's book becomes the sealed hermetic "Great Work," had he been able to write it, and the ashes he lies down in are those of the reborn phoenix. At one point in his *Words with Power* notebooks, Frye refers to Igitur's descent into nothingness as "a kenosis [emptying out] followed by an unwritten plenosis [filling up]" (CW 5: 207). In still another notebook entry Frye writes, "Igitur's name ["whereupon"] is one thread of continuity in the descent to nothingness.... The descent to nothingness reduces reality ('verité') to 'rien,' and one is left with the creation of a fiction that is real because it is a fiction. It's Vico's *verum factum* in a world without God—other than creative man, that is. This for Mallarmé is the birth of the Spirit, and is described in Resurrection terminology—and he would know that resurrection is not rebirth" (CW 5: 42).

Frye is not alone in his claim that *Igitur* is not a demonic parody. Wallace Fowlie says that by "divesting himself of the various costumes of his personality, he undergoes a reaction of a psychic chemistry by which all the manifestations of night surrounding him are metamorphosed into Eternity.... When Igitur lies down in the tomb over the ashes of his ancestors the work is really born" (115–16). Bettina Knapp argues that the end of *Igitur* signals "the beginning of a new orientation.... *Igitur*, therefore, is not to be considered as Mallarmé's suicidal journey, but rather an iconographic and verbal expression of the artist's heroic struggle to give birth to a new unknown" (189). For Yves Bonnefoy, *Igitur* is finally about the redemption of the word: "To write 'Igitur' is necessary as the preliminary act ensuring language its new fecundity, the words a future, and poetry poems" (338). Guy Michaud sees the roll of the dice as an act by which, at the end, Igitur identifies with the Absolute (77). And Robert Greer Cohn, the author of nine books on Mallarmé, writes that *Igitur* "is the spiritual adventure described by, among others, Carl Jung in *Psyche and Symbol* and Joseph Campbell in his *Hero with a Thousand Faces*; a descent into the dark womb of the unconscious, eternal night, and reemergence, rebirth to a vision of undying light and truth" (*Mallarmé: Igitur*, 2). While each of these readings is unique, they are similar insofar as they point to a creative descent. As Mallarmé says of *Igitur* in the brief coda ("He Lies Down in His Tomb"), "Nothingness having departed, there remains the castle of purity" (*Selected Poetry and Prose* 101).

As for Mallarmé's other poems, the *Cantique de Saint-Jean*, which is set at the summer solstice, appears in seven of Frye's notebook entries,[208] where Salome with the prophet's severed head is seen as standing over against the infant Jesus at the Virgin's breast. Thus, the *Cantique* is a kind of Nativity Ode: the summer solstice is St. John's Feast Day, marking the nativity of St. John the Baptist. Saint John's story for Mallarmé has to do with the paradox of time out of time (*kairos*) or the divided state of consciousness and what eludes consciousness. In *Words with Power*, Frye places Mallarmé's *Cantique*, not in the cluster of archetypes he associates with the furnace, but as a variation on the double theme or the divided state of life in his account of the cave archetype. The notebook entries get condensed to this observation:

> The presence of a clock suggests again that the gap between the conscious and subconscious has much to do with the way we observe time. This last aspect of the situation comes out in several poems and stories that reflect the curious nineteenth-century fascination with the story of Salome, Herodias, and the severed head of John the Baptist. In one of the most condensed poems ever written, Mallarmé's "Cantique de Saint-Jean," the image of the severed head is linked with the position of the sun in the zenith, suggesting the paradoxical timeless moment that never quite exists. (CW 26: 230)

It is perhaps worth reminding ourselves that Frye's remarks on Mallarmé reveal what is evident in his writing everywhere else: that he is the great discoverer of links. Mallarmé naturally suggests to him a number of connections—likenesses as well as differences within single poems, within Mallarmé's work as a whole, and within the myths and metaphors of the entire tradition. We have already remarked how Igitur's descent, from the perspective of its narrative macrostructure, has its analogues in the *Aeneid*, Lucian, *Faust*, and others. But on the microstructure level, Frye never tires of finding analogues and parallels. He connects Mallarmé's window and mirror imagery with Paul's "riddle in a mirror" (1 Corinthians 13:12). He contrasts the lace of *Une dentelle s'abolit* with the mandolin and the belly (*ventre*) in that poem. The swan stuck in ice in *Le vierge, le vivace*, he says "turns on the word *glace* that connects ice & mirrors," and in the first sonnet of this sequence, *Quand l'ombre menace*, the luxury of the ebony hall "recalls the Egyptian burying of everything precious in the king's tomb" (CW 5: 43). He links Mallarmé with Rimbaud and Shelley, all three of whom were "brooders on water" (*ibid.*). As already noted, he likens Mallarmé's treatment of nothingness to the same theme in Stevens and Donne (CW 26: 248). The resurrection by faith in myth that Frye finds in Mallarmé has its counterpart on Dylan Thomas's *A Winter's Tale*. The old man (*vieillard*) and infant (*ombre juvenile*) theme in *Un Coup de Dés* has its parallels in *The Tempest* and Keats's *Endymion*. The black bird in *Igitur* is a version of Poe's raven, and the flask from which Igitur drinks a drop of pure nothingness recalls similar bottles in Poe, de Vigny, and Rabelais (CW 5: 43). Frye links the final line of *Un Coup de Dés*—"All thought emits a throw of the dice"—with the same analogical metaphor in Heraclitus and Wyatt (CW 5: 45). And so on.

These parallels and analogies are no different from what Frye would find in the myths and metaphors of any poet. But Mallarmé's work is of a higher order because of his belief in a completely verbal universe, where Word and Spirit interpenetrate. Frye was attracted to Mallarmé, then, because, like Blake, he has the imagination of a religious visionary. Mallarmé is a poet, Frye writes, "who will take me through the third great crisis of the birth of the spirit out of the depth of fallen spirits," who sometimes talks "as though literature was a 'substitute' for religion," who sees the pure poem as a symbol of "something transcendent," who "tries to sink himself in myth & metaphor so completely that the kerygmatic will speak through," and who believes "there really is some kind of resurrection by faith in myth" (CW 5: 41, 182, 202, 303, 43). Yves Bonnefoy describes the kerygmatic breakthrough as "the horizon glimpsed beyond words" (340). This sounds very much like the project Frye set for himself in *Words with Power*. They were both on a quest to discover the mysteries of the verbal universe, and there is perhaps even a connection between Frye's vision of writing the one great, eight-part book, which he struggled mightily to formulate for a twenty-five year period after the *Anatomy*, and Mallarmé's equally unrealized dream of writing the one "Great Work."[209] "Tout, au monde," says Mallarmé "existe pour aboutir à un livre"—a line that Frye quotes three times.[210] In Notebook 44, Frye expresses the hope that perhaps his second study on the Bible and literature might provide a critical framework for what Mallarmé was not able to provide: "Mallarmé's 'great work' certainly wasn't written, but maybe a comparative study of the Bible and the literature we have may give critics, *in critical terms* only, some notion of what it would be like in outline" (CW 5: 216). Frye laboured ceaselessly to outline the panliterary universe, and this effort, now contained in twenty-nine large volumes, suggests that he also believed that everything can be contained in a book.

10

Frye and Colin Still

In *Anatomy of Criticism*, Frye notes that critics often break forth into an "oracular harrumph" when they encounter references to alchemy, the Tarot, or Rosicrucianism. Even today, one encounters readers here and there who, having discovered that Frye thought highly of Colin Still's book on *The Tempest* or that he had read some esoteric work, recoil in amazement, as if it automatically followed that Frye was a card-carrying member of some mystery cult or was engaging in the ritual practices of Freemasonry.

In the late 1970s, I was invited to a party in Toronto by a friend at York University, where the assembled party-goers turned out to be McLuhanites. When they discovered that I had an interest in Frye, they began to pepper me with questions about his having been a Mason. I naturally asked what evidence they had for this claim, but none was forthcoming, their assumption being that this was common knowledge. The rumour, apparently, was initiated by Marshall McLuhan, or at least perpetuated by him. McLuhan's biographer Philip Marchand writes that McLuhan "certainly never abandoned his belief that his great rival in the English department of the University of Toronto, Northrop Frye, was a Mason at heart, if not in fact" (*Marshall McLuhan* 105). In a later book review, Marchand removes the qualification, saying flatly that "McLuhan thought Frye was a Mason" ("Frye's Diaries"). He goes on to say that it's no wonder that McLuhan suspected that Frye was a Mason because he was interested in the occult, used diagrams, and, most damning of all—get this—took Colin Still's Shakespearean criticism seriously.

"Colin Still," Marchand declares, "was a crackpot," whose book on *The Tempest* "[m]ost academics would have been embarrassed to be seen reading." All this got picked up by *Maclean's* blogger Colby Cosh, who went Marchand one better: "McLuhan ... despised Frye because he thought he was dabbling in dark occultic forces and perhaps messing about with Freemasonry.... Marchand has discovered a new and major source for Frye's thinking in Colin Still, a hitherto undistinguished flake who believed *The Tempest* was a disguised representation of some sort of pagan initiation rite."

Still as a Mainstream Shakespearean Critic

Although Frye occasionally comments on Freemasonry,[211] there is not a shred of evidence to indicate that he was a Mason or ever entertained the slightest thought of becoming one. As for Still's being a "crackpot" and an "undistinguished flake," no less a critical intelligence than R. S. Crane speaks of the "pioneering work" of Still in reading Shakespeare allegorically, discovering in the play "the double theme of purgation from sin and of rebirth and upward spiritual movement after sorrow and death" (132). Peter Dawkins refers to Still as an "eminent scholar" (xxv), and Michael Srigley has defended Still's thesis. In a detailed examination of Still's argument, Michael Cosser says, "Certainly it is not stretching credulity to see a close parallel between the play and what can be pieced together from classical sources as to the training received in the Mystery-centers of old." In his study of the sacerdotal features of *The Tempest*, Robert L. Reid takes seriously Still's view that the play is a "universal purgatorial allegory." Howard Nemerov calls *Shakespeare's Mystery Play* an "interpretive masterpiece" (470). These critics, like Bishop Warburton before them, are far from being crackpots and flakes. In the eighteenth century, Warburton, as both Still and Frye were aware, had proposed the theory that book 6 of the *Aeneid*—the descent to the underworld—corresponds to the ancient rites of initiation.[212] In other words, observations about parallels between literary works and Greek initiation rites had been around for some time: noting such parallels was a common critical practice.

Still's books, listed in all the bibliographies, were also celebrated by the distinguished Shakespearean G. Wilson Knight, who calls *Shakespeare's Mystery Play* an "important landmark" (*Shakespeare and Religion* 201). As an undergraduate at Victoria College, Frye had known Knight, who taught at Trinity College at the University of Toronto in the 1930s.[213] T. S. Eliot referred to Still in his preface to Knight's *The Wheel of Fire*,[214] and it is possible that Frye ran across this reference even before he checked Still's book out of the Toronto Public Library during his sophomore year—the same year that *The Wheel of Fire* was published (1930). In *The Wheel of Fire*, Knight writes, "Since the publication of my essay, my attention has been drawn to Mr. Colin Still's remarkable book *Shakespeare's Mystery Play*.... Mr. Still's interpretation of *The Tempest* is very similar to mine. His conclusions were reached by a detailed comparison of the play in its totality with other creations of literature, myth, and ritual throughout the ages" (16).[215] Knight regards Still's book as confirmation ("empirical proof," he says) of his own view that *The Tempest* is a mystical work (*ibid.*). A year later Knight wrote that his view of *The Tempest*

> is most interestingly corroborated by a remarkable and profound book by Mr. Colin Still, *Shakespeare's Mystery Play*.... Mr. Still analyses *The Tempest* as a work of mystic vision, and shows that it abounds in parallels with the ancient mystery cults and works of symbolic religious significance throughout the ages. Especially illuminating are his references to Virgil (*Aeneid*, VI) and Dante. His reading of *The Tempest* depends on references outside Shakespeare, whereas my interpretation depends entirely on references to the succession of plays which *The Tempest* concludes. We thus reach our results by quite different routes: those results are strangely—and, after all, I believe, not strangely—similar. ("Mystic" 67–8)

Because they have no sense of allegory and no sense of the difference between the reading of a text and the use to which that reading is put, Marchand and friends will doubtless continue to dismiss the interpretations of Still, Knight, and Frye, though one wishes that their dismissals had been based on actually having read what Frye and Still had to say about the parallels between Shakespeare and ancient myth and ritual.

Still's allegorical interpretation of *The Tempest* seeks to demonstrate four things: that *The Tempest* has the same form as the medieval miracle and mystery plays, that it is an allegorical account "of those psychological experiences" referred to by the mystics as initiation, that its features are like those of the ritual and ceremonial rites of initiation, and that these resemblances are "consistent and exact" (*Shakespeare's Mystery Play* 8–9). His method is a comparative one: he works out the analogies between *The Tempest* and myths and rituals of the past. In this regard, Still's work stems from the work of the so-called "Cambridge school," which, following the publication of the final edition of Sir James Frazer's *The Golden Bough* in 1915, gave shape to the ritual view of drama. These scholars—most prominently Frazer himself, Jane Ellen Harrison, F. M. Cornford, Gilbert Murray, and, earlier, E. K. Chambers—produced book after book applying the ritual view of drama to culture. Colin Still, therefore, is not some eccentric on the margins of the literary establishment. He belongs to a very large group of critics who have expanded our view of literature by applying the myth and ritual approach. This group would include Jessie Weston, F. M. Cornford, Lord Raglan, Gertrude Levy, Joseph Campbell, Francis Fergusson, Theodor Gaster, C. L. Barber, Herbert Weisinger, O. B. Hardison, and of course Frye himself, to name some of the most prominent. The point is that in the field of literary criticism Still is very much an establishment figure. Thus, we need not concern ourselves overmuch with Marchand's dismissive judgments, other than to say a little learning is a dangerous thing. But if Frye and Still belong in the same general critical matrix, it is perhaps worthwhile to explore the connections between them and to consider the reasons that Frye was attracted to Still's reading of *The Tempest*.

STILL'S PLACE IN THE OGDOAD

First of all, Still played an important role in what Frye called his ogdoad—an eight-book vision that he used as a kind of road map for his life's work. As with all of his organizing patterns, the ogdoad was never a rigid outline, but it did correspond to the chief divisions in his conceptual universe over the years. Throughout his notebooks, he repeatedly uses a code to refer to the eight books he planned to write. The original plan was actually eight concerti he dreamed of writing—a dream he had at age nine. At about the same time, after reading Scott's novels, he imagined writing a sequence of historical novels, and after he had made his way through Dickens and Thackeray, this modulated into "a sequence of eight definitive novels." When he was fourteen, each of these novels acquired a one-word descriptive name (Liberal, Tragicomedy, Anticlimax, Rencontre, Mirage, Paradox, Ignoramus, and Twilight), and these names, along with their symbolic codes, remained with Frye over the years, appearing hundreds of times in his notebooks, as a shorthand designation for his books, both those completed and those anticipated. In the 1940s the eight books were reduced to what Frye called his Pentateuch, but they expanded shortly after that into the eight once again.

Frye himself provides several keys to the ways that the ogdoad shaped his preoccupations over the years. Michael Dolzani has given us as good an explanation of the ogdoad as we are likely to get. And in the "Introduction" to Frye's *Late Notebooks*, I have provided a summary of the various permutations of the ogdoad (xlii–xliii). Now in one of his autobiographical reflections, Frye indicates that in the development of his central preoccupations Still played a decisive role:

> I have long had a sense that the four books [i.e., the first four books of the ogdoad] had some kind of connexion with the four years of my undergraduate career here, though of course nobody can understand how except me. My first year [1929–30] was bits and pieces academically, and in retrospect the New Testament Greek course was pretty central to it: anyway the Bible book is connected in my mind with that year. The second year [1930–31] brought Pelham [Edgar] teaching Shakespeare, the stock company at the Empire Theatre, and my discovery of Colin Still on The Tempest. That's the bedrock of Tragicomedy. The third year [1931–32] was

> the discovery of Blake, and I'm just beginning to realize that Anticlimax is in many respects a book revolving around Blake: my treatment of Blake was, after all, very largely a conceptual and Urizenic treatment. The fourth year [1932–33] was the year of the Romanticism essay, and that has always seemed to have some relation to Rencontre. (CW 15: 308–9)[216]

If, as it seems likely, this was written in 1972, Frye's recollection about links between his four undergraduate years and the first four "books" of the ogdoad takes us back some forty years. All of these influences are summarized in the chart that follows, which adds Spengler (summer of 1932) and Frazer (Emmanuel College years) to the mix.

Frye's Critical Beginnings: A Summary of the Chief Influences from His Victoria and Emmanuel College Years

FIRST YEAR (1929–30): Interest in the Bible, developing from a course in New Testament Greek. The foundation for Liberal.

SECOND YEAR (1930–31): Interest in the patterns of drama, developing from (1) Pelham Edgar's course in Shakespeare, (2) plays presented by a repertory company at the Empire Theatre, and (3) the discovery of Colin Still's book on *The Tempest*. The foundation for Tragicomedy.

THIRD YEAR (1931–32): The discovery of Blake. The foundation of Anticlimax.

SUMMER OF 1932: Interest in the anatomy and in Spengler.

FOURTH YEAR (1932–33): Interest in Romanticism. The foundation of Rencontre.

EMMANUEL COLLEGE (1933–36): Interest in biblical typology; Frazer, and with Frazer the key to drama.

(CW 15: 308–9 and CW 25: 28)

We note that of the influences that Frye lists, only one is a literary critic—Colin Still. We note also that of the relations Frye sees between his seven years at

Victoria and Emmanuel Colleges and certain texts that he came to focus on, he wrote at least one extended piece on all but Colin Still. What then can we determine about Frye's attraction to Still from his scattered references to Still's two books on *The Tempest*? And why was Still such a seminal influence on Frye's views about Shakespeare and drama in general?

Frye reports that he discovered *Shakespeare's Mystery Play* not in the Victoria College Library but in the Central Circulating Library, which had been added to the Toronto Reference Library in 1930. During the summer of that year Frye had a job of pasting labels into new books at the Central Reference Library. It was here, he reports, that he ran across Still's book by accident, putting "accident" in quotation marks, as if it were somehow destined that *Shakespeare's Mystery Play* would fall into his hands (CW 9: 296). In any event, Frye eventually bought a copy of Still's book, along with its companion, *The Timeless Theme*, a revised version written fifteen years later and described by Still as an "enlarged and clarified restatement" of *Shakespeare's Mystery Play* (*Timeless* [1]).[217] *The Timeless Theme* remained on his shelves unread for many years. In the early 1970s, Frye wrote that he was now "reading the second book for the first time & it's a bit disconcerting to see how much of it is already part of my makeup. And my diagram" (*ibid.*).

In the papers he wrote during his Emmanuel College years Frye called on *Shakespeare's Mystery Play* on two occasions. In the first, on "St. Paul and Orphism," Frye wrote, "In general, it may be said that the great contribution to art made by the Orphics was the art form of the katabasis, or descent to the underworld. This theme, which in painting develops into the danse macabre in the Middle Ages, is developed from Odyssey XI by Virgil in the great sixth book of the Aeneid, and from him by Dante. Probably Shakespeare's *Tempest* belongs to the same tradition" (CW 3: 181). At this point Frye inserts as note, "Vide Colin Still: *Shakespeare's Mystery Play*." The second reference, from Frye's essay on "The Relation of Religion to the Art Forms of Music and Drama," is this: "As for the last play of all, *The Tempest*, that has now been fairly proved to be an extraordinarily faithful presentation of the Greek ideas of initiation and of the ritual that accompanied them. And, as we have seen, these initiation symbols are logical developments of fertility symbolism, with which they were, both in the Eleusinian rites and in Shakespeare's play, explicitly associated" (CW 3: 337). The reference here is to Still's book, and Frye inserts a note citing it. Still of course knew that Shakespeare had no direct knowledge of the Eleusinian rites. The symbolic coincidences between the ancient rituals and Shakespeare's plays are a reflection of the permanent and universal realities of what Still calls the collective genius.

Natural Symbolism and the Ladder of Elements

In the *Late Notebooks*, Frye reports that he was first attracted to archetypal criticism by Still's book on *The Tempest* (CW 5: 46), and he certainly has Still in mind as he is developing some of the implications of the ladder symbolism in chapter 5 of *Words with Power*. He does not mention Still in *Words with Power*, but he does in the *Late Notebooks*, where he says that the central conception of Still's book is its conception of the ladder of elements (CW 5: 46). This is a reference to Still's account of what he calls "natural symbolism," the tradition that has associated the four elements (earth, water, air, fire) with the physical, emotional, rational, and divine features of the composition of life. The four elements, ranging from the earthly to the divine, remind us of the four-storied universe that appears everywhere in Frye. One version appears in *Words with Power* in the form of a chart, which is reproduced in the first three columns of the chart below. The fourth column, which equates the four elements with the four bodies, is from Still's *Shakespeare's Mystery Play* (88). Frye picks up the idea of the four elements in chapter 5 of *Words with Power*, and the distinction between the second and third rungs on Still's ladder—the natural body (*soma psychikos*) and the spiritual body (*soma pneumatikos*) from 1 Corinthians 15—is a familiar one in Frye's late work, occurring in his writing more than a dozen times. He even says in a notebook that the oldest idea he had for *Words with Power*, "the two levels of nature, now seem to be hooking onto the two somas of Paul" (CW 5: 282), and in a notebook for *The Double Vision*, he remarks that the two components of this vision "are, of course, the vision of the soma psychikon, the conscious soul-body unit, and the vision of the soma pneumatikon, the spiritual vision" (CW 6: 617). There is no direct evidence that Frye's encounter with the Greek terms for the two bodies Paul speaks of came from Colin Still. It may have come from his first-year course in New Testament Greek, or it may have come from one of his Emmanuel College courses—not from the lectures (Frye didn't attend those) but from his reading. But we do know that he read Still in the 1930–31 academic year, and it seems highly unlikely that he could have missed the *soma psychikos* and *soma pneumatikos* placed directly in the middle of Still's ladder of elements. And Frye does refer to the *psyche* and the *pneuma* in the paper on Romanticism he wrote during his fourth year at Victoria College.[218]

FRYE'S FOUR-STORIED UNIVERSE AND STILL'S LADDER OF ELEMENTS

Cosmic Level	Time	Space	Colin Still's Ladder of Elements	Archetypes in Chap. 5–8 of Words with Power
Heaven. Blake's Eden	Time as total "now" or real present	Space as total "here" or real present	Aether or fire as heaven; St. Paul's "heavenly body" (*soma epouranios*)	Mountain; Ladder
Unfallen world. Blake's Beulah	Time as exuberance or inner energy (music, dance, play)	Space as home or "natural place"	Air as Paradise; St. Paul's "spiritual" body (*soma pneumatikos*)	Garden
Fallen world of experience. Blake's Generation	Time as "then" (linear and cyclical)	Space as "there" (objective environment)	Water as experience; St. Paul's "natural body" (*soma psychikos*)	Cave; Ark
Demonic world. Blake's Ulro	Time as pure duration and power of annihilation	Space as alienation	Earth as the demonic (oracular); the physical body	Furnace

With regard to the fifth column in the chart, given that Frye is the great analogist, is there an analogy between the four elements and the four archetypes that Frye treats in chapters 5 to 8 of *Words with Power*? Perhaps. One can see a connection between earth and the demonic furnace, air and the paradisal garden, fire and the heaven at the top of the *axis mundi*, and water and the ark and cave archetypes. By "axis mundi" I mean that vertical, cosmological ladder along which the various elements in the chain of being have their place. The ascending and descending movements along the *axis mundi* are the basis of the second half of *Words with Power*.

On the flyleaf of his copy of *The Timeless Theme*, Frye sketched another of his many circular diagrams with its Nomos to Nous horizontal axis and its Thanatos to Logos Vision vertical one. The circle however, is divided into four parts according to Still's four elements, beginning with fire at the top and running through air and water to earth at the bottom. In addition, the dividing lines that separate the four parts are Still's rainbow, mist, and mire axes. Frye adds some of his own categories to the diagram (e.g., point of demonic epiphany at the bottom and point of epiphany at the top), but the diagram is otherwise drawn almost exclusively from Still's account of the four elements. The diagram is another example of the *axis mundi* metaphor—the path along which the soul or spirit falls and rises.[219]

Finally, Still is very much drawn to the movement in *The Tempest* and in the Greek initiation rites from the *katabasis*, or downward journey, to the *anabasis* at the top of the ladder. These are the descent and ascent themes that play such a large role in the last half of *Words with Power*. It is the movement from Ulro to Eden, passing through the fallen world to the unfallen one. There are, of course, a number of sources in Frye for this archetypal narrative, Blake being an obvious one. Frye sometimes describes this narrative as the movement from oracle to wit, which we examined in the essay on Mallarmé (chapter 9, above), and I think that Still had something to do with Frye's embracing this narrative, a narrative that makes him an *Odyssey* rather than an *Iliad* critic. *The Tempest* illustrates this movement from oracle to wit, and I suspect that Still helped to condition Frye early on to be an *Odyssey* critic. The underworld journey, as Frye says, "seems to be an initiation, a learning of mysteries" (CW 29: 227). The emphasis on spiritual rebirth in *The Tempest* suggests initiation rites, and this is why Colin Still figures in all three of the extended essays Frye wrote on the play, explicitly in two and implicitly in the third.[220] He was a foundational figure in Frye's critical universe.

11

Frye and Paul Tillich

In his 1950 diary, when he is worrying about his understanding of the dialectic of both Thomism and Marxism, Frye speculates that Paul Tillich, who would shortly be coming to the University of Toronto to lecture, might have a solution (CW 8: 237). Ten days later Tillich spoke to a large crowd at Wycliffe College, where, Frye says,

> He talked on the "theology of despair": the attempt to start with despair as a "limit-situation." It disappointed me a little, as I'd read enough Kierkegaard to figure it out myself. Even the feeling it gave me of being on top of Tillich was hollow: I didn't want to feel on top of Tillich: I wanted to feel a contact with something fresh. (CW 8: 248)

The next night Tillich lectured on "principle & substance," and although this was the lecture Frye really wanted to hear, he was worn out by already having heard four lectures within the week, and so he curled up instead with Jung's *Psychological Types* to reenergize himself (CW 8: 249). At this time Tillich had not yet moved from New York's Union Seminary to Harvard Divinity School and had not yet published the first volume of his *Systematic Theology*, but he had nevertheless already begun to make a name for himself in theological circles, and Frye was clearly aware of this.

Frye owned five of Tillich's books and he annotated all but the last: *Biblical Religion and the Search for Ultimate Reality*, *Christianity and the Encounter of the World Religions*, *Systematic Theology* (3 vols.), *Theology of Culture*, and *The Courage To Be*. From his references to the "Protestant principle," it appears he was also familiar with *The Protestant Era*, and he wrote a review (not published at the time) of the third volume of *Systematic Theology*, now available in volume 25 of the Collected Works.[221] In that review, written in 1964, Frye remarks that "Tillich is widely regarded as a seminal thinker of our time and as one of the few theologians who not only has a message for his age but can speak the language that his age understands. I think his reputation is deserved" (CW 25: 365). Given that there are more than thirty references to Tillich scattered throughout Frye's Collected

Works, what might we discover from examining them about the Frye–Tillich relationship?

Primary Concerns and Ultimate Concern

"Concern" is a word that Frye picked up from existentialist currents of thought that began to circulate after World War II. As we have seen, it seems likely that he first encountered the word in Kierkegaard, who in his *Edifying Discourses* speaks of concerned truths as over against objective truths (87), but Frye was no doubt familiar with Heidegger's use of *das Besorgen* (concern).[222] In "The Social Importance of Literature," Frye says that the arts and humanities deal with concern, which is to say "with man's fundamental questions about his whence and his whither, his nature and his destiny, and above all, the kind of society that he wants to live in" (CW 7: 333). His use of the word "concern" comes to the fore in his 1965 essay "Speculation and Concern" (CW 7: 242–58), as we have noted in the essay on Kierkegaard, and in his examination of the myth of concern in *The Critical Path*, which is set in a dialectical relationship with the myth of freedom. "Concern and Myth" is the title of chapter 2 of *Words with Power*, and in that book, as well as in *The Double Vision* and a number of essays from the 1980s, Frye distinguished between primary and secondary concerns. Primary concerns are the universal, individual, and physical needs and desires of human beings. In his *Late Notebooks*, Frye engages in uninhibited speculation about the primary concerns, letting his mind play freely with the basic things essential for our survival and noting a number of analogues and links with other categories in his thinking about his second book on the Bible. He eventually settles on four primary concerns: (1) food and drink and related bodily needs; (2) sex; (3) property: money, possessions, shelter; clothing, and everything that constitutes property in the sense of what is "proper" to one's life; or property in the Aristotelian sense of the material extension of the personality; and (4) freedom of movement; play.

Secondary concerns are social values or ideologies that often do battle with each other. They arise, Frye says, "from the social contract, and include patriotic and other attachments of loyalty, religious beliefs, and class-conditioned attitudes and behaviour. They develop from the ideological aspect of myth, and consequently tend to be directly expressed in ideological prose language" (CW 26: 51).

Tillich was also fond of using the word "concern," which often appears in the context of his definition of religion or faith as "ultimate concern."[223] As we saw in the essay on Kierkegaard, Frye sometimes wonders whether or not religion should be seen as a primary concern. He writes in the *Late Notebooks*, for example, "I should start thinking in terms of primary anxieties: they help to show how Tillich's 'ultimate concern' is also a primary one" (CW 5: 165). Or again: "I'm wrong about religion as an ultimate but not a primary concern. Where did I come from and where am I going are primary concerns, even if we don't believe there are any answers. But if only the social institution answers, the answer is ideological only. Maybe that *is* something we learn about only from literature, but God, the digging & burrowing to get at it!" (CW 5: 121–2). In the context of existential *Angst*, Frye speculates that primary concerns are united with ultimate concern:

> Thorkild Jacobsen's book *The Treasures of Darkness*, a sensitive and imaginative book about Sumerian and Akkadian culture, if somewhat over-bemused by Otto's book on the holy, says that two themes seem to assimilate the whole pantheon of gods, the wedding song and the underworld descent. That's my Eros-Adonis axis, of course, and it unites the primary concerns of life, food and sex, with its primary anxiety and ultimate concern, death, and the passage through death. I should start thinking in terms of primary anxieties: they help to show how Tillich's "ultimate concern" is also a primary one.[224] (CW 5: 165)

But then Frye has second thoughts. In a passage from Notebook 44, which dates from about 1986, he writes, "Religion may be an 'ultimate' concern, as Tillich says: it can't be a primary one. We can't live a day without being concerned about food, but we can live all our lives without being concerned about God, impoverished as such a life would be" (CW 5: 103). In a set of typed notes a few years later, Frye repeats the observation: "One can't live a day without being concerned about food, but one can live all one's life without being concerned about God: hence the religious concern, even if 'ultimate,' as Tillich says, isn't primary" (CW 6: 543).

What Tillich calls "preliminary concerns" arise from the experience of daily life and, as distinguished from ultimate concerns, are finite. While there is a marked difference between Tillich's ultimate concern, which is spiritual, and Frye's primary concerns, which are physical or material, there is a similarity between Tillich's preliminary concerns and Frye's secondary concerns. Preliminary concerns have to do with aesthetic and scientific value, historical conjecture, methods of social reconstruction, and solutions to political conflicts, among other things (*Systematic* 1:12). One commentator thinks that the distinction between preliminary and ultimate concern is ambiguous (Pullman), but however that may be, it seems possible that Tillich's preliminary concerns, which Frye encountered in the 1960s, were a source of the secondary concerns that Frye began writing about in the 1980s.

System and Fragmentation

It is understandable that Frye, as a systematic critic, would be interested in such comprehensive and methodical achievements in theology as Barth's *Church Dogmatics* and Tillich's *Systematic Theology*. Frye calls such extensive treatises, which can be traced back to Augustine and Aquinas and which continue up through his own *Anatomy of Criticism*, "the monumental style." The analogous literary genre is the epic—encyclopaedic, expansive, detailed, and continuous. At the beginning of his review of volume 3 of Tillich's *Systematic Theology*, Frye describes the systematic treatise and its opposite, the discontinuous and fragmented form, like this:

> Fashions come and go in literary genres, both inside and outside literature. There is, in particular, a constant pendulum-swing between the continuous and the discontinuous. In one age the major poetic genres are epic and narrative; in another these forms are out and fragmentation and anthological epigrams are in. It is the same in non-literary fields. In nineteenth-century philosophy and theology, especially in Germany, the three-decker synthesis was not merely an impressive monument to its author but a reassuring object in a scholar's study or a library stack: it gave dignity to the subject and prestige to the reader. Today philosophy has become more analytical, and the monumental style has accordingly suffered: now it is U[225] to be bitty and piecy, like Austin or Wittgenstein, imitating the scientists who work so much with abstracts and offprints. Theology, always more conservative as well as more German-based, has more of a functional place for the systematic treatment which is expressed by a continuous genre. In Protestantism, there is a strong discontinuous tradition descending from Luther, and passing through Kierkegaard; but there is an equally strong continuous one descending from Calvin and passing through Schleiermacher and Ritschl. This latter tradition is powerfully effective today in, particularly, Barth and Tillich. Tillich has been working for many years on a systematic theology, of which the third and final volume has just appeared. (CW 25: 363–4)

Frye makes the point a bit differently in "The Renaissance of Books":

> I have always been very touched by the preface to the third and last volume of Paul Tillich's *Systematic Theology*. This was a work on which Tillich had spent many years, because, he says, he had always wanted to write a systematic theology. I can think of no better reason for writing anything, but the ambition itself was typical of a certain period of culture. By the time he reached his last volume the fashion in theology had changed, the younger intellectuals had turned to much more simplistic versions of existentialism than the one that he held, and he was being told on all sides that the phrase "systematic theology" no longer made any sense, in fact was a contradiction in terms. (CW 11: 145)

In this review of volume 3 of *Systematic Theology*, Frye goes on the say that our own age has moved away from the Thomistic *summa* because our age is one of fragmentation. What he is establishing is one of his familiar dialectics: the monumental, the continuous, the synthetic, and the epic, on the one hand, and the discontinuous, the fragmented, the analytic, and the epigrammatic, on the other. "[F]ragmentation represents better the real genius of our age," Frye writes. "We do not really believe in the arguments for synthesis" (CW 25: 364). These words come from one who only seven years before had produced *Anatomy of Criticism*, a widely expansive study of literary conventions that were synthesized into a comprehensive order, an example *par excellence* of the systematic treatise.

Still, for all his systematizing and synthesizing, Frye devotes a great deal of attention to fragmentation, which he frequently refers to as "comminution," literally "a pulverizing" ("comminution" and its cognates appear more than fifty times in his work, beginning with *Fearful Symmetry*). Frye frequently calls the comminuted forms kernels—parable, aphorism, commandment, oracle, prophecy, proverb, and emblem. Comminution is also associated with *sparagmos*, and Frye even speaks at one point of the comminuted forms eventually becoming an anatomy (CW 23: 178)—the dissection or analysis of the total form. But in spite of what he says about not believing in "the arguments for synthesis," his drive is most often toward unifying the disparate, toward making a whole from the parts. That is the function of the notebooks, a discontinuous set of *aperçus*. Frye's books are an effort to give continuity and order to the speculative fragments of the notebooks.

If comminution describes the temper of the age—Eliot's fragments shored up against his ruins—Frye's goal is in fact synthesis. In the notebooks he is quite deliberate and self-conscious about what lies before him, and, as with his other writing projects, he ceaselessly turns over one organizing idea after another so as to develop the parts and get them in their proper order. Frye has learned a great deal from the epiphanic insights of the discontinuous thinkers, but when he is writing about fragmentation while working on the *Anatomy*, comminution is always a part of the larger synthetic whole.

So where does Frye stand with regard to the opposition between monumental systematizers like Tillich and discontinuous fragmenters like Kierkegaard? Michael Dolzani is likewise puzzled by the apparent contradiction between Frye's affirming of an order of words in the *Anatomy* and then, having rejected a theological order of words in *Systematic Theology*, affirming the comminuted vision. Dolzani writes:

> Not only does Frye seem to reverse himself, but his views about the systematic study of any subject seem contradictory to say the least, coming from the man who had published *Anatomy of Criticism*, one of whose key words is "systematic," a mere seven years before.... If we keep reading, though, we come only a few lines later to a sentence that, almost twenty years before *The Great Code*, provides a crucial insight into Frye's way of understanding the Bible: "The sense of religious experience as an interruption of continuity is expressed in one of the central theological conceptions of our time, 'kerygma' or proclamation, again an epiphanic and anti-systematic conception" (par. 2) [CW 25: 364–5]. Frye is not denying the unity of the Bible, which he worked so hard to demonstrate in *The Great Code*; nor, by implication, the unity of literature that he worked so systematically to outline in *Anatomy of Criticism*. Both the conception of the Word in the Protestant tradition and the conception of an "order of words" in literary criticism are based on a sense of a total pattern and coherence. However, as Frye states in the notes for "The Dialectic of Belief and Vision," "The GC, vulnerable as it was, did make the point that two aspects of the Bible were of primary importance: its unity and its disunity" (par. 5) [CW 25: 384]. What *kergyma*, the sudden and unpredictable epiphany of the Word, can do for us is to subvert, or deconstruct, our present understanding of that Word, confined as it inevitably is to the narrow dimensions of our intellectual limitations, our social conditioning, our individual neuroses. (CW 25: liv–lv)

As with practically all oppositions in Frye, the systematic versus the fragmented perspective is not an *either/or* matter. Another way of putting it is to say that during the first phase of his career the interest in the order of words and the system of literary conventions dominates, whereas in the latter, when moments of expanded consciousness become a dominant theme, the discontinuous, kerygmatic insight receives greater emphasis. In "Frye and Longinus" (chapter 2, above,) I characterize these differing emphases as Frye's Aristotelian and Longinian phases. Frye's reading of Tillich helped to focus the latter.

The Protestant Principle

Frye was always forthright in acknowledging the significance of the "mythological framework" he inherited. He was inescapably conditioned, he says, by the "cultural envelope" of the Classical and Christian traditions of Western culture, the Methodist heritage of his upbringing, and his white, male, middle-class identity. The Protestantism of this cultural envelope was not simply Methodism with its piety, which Frye rejected, and its emphasis on experience, which he did not; it was also the radical, dissenting, nonconformist Protestantism of William Blake. As a critic of English literature, Frye took some comfort in its overwhelmingly Protestant foundation, and on several occasions he referred to the resigned tone in Newman's remark, "We cannot undo the past. English literature will ever *have been* Protestant" (*Idea of a University* 300).[226] In his early twenties Frye wrote, "A Presbyterian is a sectarian armed with a solidified Calvinist creed which transforms the Protestant spirit which gave it birth into a Catholic one. The latter is thoroughly democratic and the community forms the criterion of heresy" (1932 Notebook, *Uncollected* 31–2). Later he developed a less charitable view of Catholicism both in its Anglican and Roman varieties, a view that has been examined in some detail by J. Russell Perkin.

Frye apparently picked up somewhere a reference to what Tillich called "the Protestant principle," and on four occasions he says that he must find out what Tillich meant by the phrase (CW 5:199; CW 13: 212, 232, 323). He eventually discovered in *The Protestant Era* and in *Systematic Theology* that the Protestant principle is the principle that critiques all historical and institutional representations of the divine, the principle that was at work in the challenge to the authority of the Roman Church during the Reformation. "The Protestant principle," writes Tillich, "is the restatement of the prophetic principle as an attack against a self-absolutizing and, consequently, demonically distorted church" (*Systematic* 1: 227).[227] In Tillich's lecture that Frye missed at Toronto, Tillich set the Protestant principle in opposition to what he called Catholic substance, by which he meant the traditions of dogma, liturgy, and ecclesiastical polity that had developed chiefly from the early church. Frye was aware of Tillich's understanding of Catholic substance,[228] and he embraced the criticism and recreation of this substance by the Reformation theologians and the latter-day adherents of the Protestant principle.

Frye's Protestant sympathies ran deep and they developed early. A student paper entitled "Gains and Losses of the Reformation" (CW 3: 265–71), written when he was in his early twenties, reveal that he was already developing his own understanding of the dialectic between Protestant principle and Catholic substance:

> ... Protestantism was, far more than Catholicism, on the side of liberalism and tolerance, imbued more than its adversary with the spirit of free enquiry and the use of critical intelligence in religious matters. Its record, particularly that of the Calvinist branches, is not snow white in this respect, but any rational comparison between Protestant rule in England under Elizabeth or even Edward and Catholic rule under Mary, or between the treatment of Catholic minorities in Scotland and Protestant minorities in Spain, should establish the point. There is probably no more inherent cruelty in one tradition than in the other, nor more sadism in Latins than in Nordics, but Protestant emphasis on the direct responsibility of the soul to God made heresy far less an outrage on society, and its punishment, consequently, less a venting of popular fury on its victims. The Catholic tradition of apostolic infallibility once denied, the enormity of the crime took on far less cosmic proportions. Another reason for the somewhat cleaner Protestant record is without doubt the influence of its intellectual and sensitive progenitors among the mystics and humanists. Protestantism contains, at its finest, the refusal of a fine mind to be bullied by inferior interpreters of tradition. Erasmus is a great Protestant in this sense; so more obviously is Zwingli; and so is Luther when we admire him most. (CW 3: 265–6)

The Protestant Church is not of course immune to the critique of the Protestant principle. In volume 3 of *Systematic Theology*, Tillich writes, "One can deal with the churches polemically or apologetically. If the intention is polemical (often born of undiscerning expectations and the disappointments which inevitably ensue), the rather miserable reality of concrete churches is emphasized and this reality is compared with their claim to embody the Spiritual Community. The church at the street corner hides the church Spiritual from view" (166). The phrase "miserable reality of concrete churches" resonated with Frye. In one of his *Late Notebooks* he writes, "Tillich on the miserable reality of the concrete churches: when I went to church in Montreal with Lorna[229] that jackass disrupted the whole feeling of the service by braying about homosexuals. Before the service, I met a woman I'd never seen before who pecked out of me in two minutes the fact that I had no earned doctorate. Malice, like other pacts with the devil, certainly gives one preternatural perceptions, up to a point" (CW 6: 698). And in his review of *Systematic Theology* he notes, "Tillich has a sad little phrase in his book: 'the rather miserable reality of the concrete churches.' What one wants from religion, at the very least, is social insight, or what Tillich calls prophetic criticism of the negativities of life. The social influence of this kind of thing is not pernicious, which would at least be a serious influence: it is merely frivolous. If the concrete reality actualized by the Christian vision is so miserable, what price a vision that insists on being known by its fruits?" (CW 25: 366–7). Tillich, in short, helped Frye to see that the contemporary church was in need of the Protestant principle, if not Catholic substance.

When Frye was a student at Emmanuel College, he wrote a spirited defence of Calvin, which he called "The Importance of Calvin for Philosophy." But in Frye's own low church, dissenting Protestant views derive less from Calvin and Luther than from other Renaissance reformers. "In the Blake book," he writes, "I speak of people in the sixteenth century who envisioned a greater and more radical reform of the church than either Reformation or Counter-Reformation achieved, thinking of such people as Erasmus, Ficino, Pico, Bruno, Rabelais and Reuchlin—perhaps Melanchthon too. I like to think of myself as descended from that tradition" (*Selected Letters* 206).

Jacob Boehme

Another point of contact between Tillich and Frye is the work of the seventeenth-century shoemaker, mystic, and theologian Jacob Boehme. According to Nels Ferré's account of Tillich's intellectual genealogy, Tillich claimed that "his spiritual father was Schleiermacher, his intellectual father was Schelling, and his grandfather on both sides was Jacob Boehme" (11). In one of Frye's projections of what he will include in the fourth part of his ogdoad, Rencontre, he proposes to examine "Protestant ideas in Barth & Berdyaev & Tillich that go back to Boehme" (CW 15: 139).[230] Frye encountered in the medieval mystical tradition, especially in Meister Eckhart and Boehme and in the fourteenth-century mystical treatise *The Cloud of Unknowing*, what he calls the "deification of the void," the apophatic disposition to discover God through the *via negativa*. In Boehme this is the abyss or nothingness of the *Ungrund* (Unground). Boehme, especially, is a Hermes or psychopomp figure for Frye and so represents a descent into the dark night of the soul that the *Ungrund* symbolizes. "I used to call this Unground mysticism the deification of the void," Frye writes in a marginal annotation to Boehme's *Six Theosophic Points*, "which apparently is just what it is."[231] Frye did not react approvingly to the "deification of the void" early in his career, calling it a form of false occultism (CW 15:137). What he found objectionable was the absence of a personal Creator. While Boehme does have the idea of a Father-God, this Nobodaddy God can be rescued, for Frye, only after it is humanized by the idea of the Son, which overcomes all of the wrath associated with the God of the deified void.[232] Frye finds Boehme unsatisfactory because *katabasis* involves more than deifying the void and finds him difficult because of the prolixity of his style: "I've also been trying to read Boehme because of his fire imagery and the way he talks about Urgrund and nothingness, but I've never got much out of Boehme" (CW 6: 480). Still, he continues "to struggle with Boehme and his abyss-fire-wrath world" (CW 6: 55), a struggle that had begun in the writing of *Fearful Symmetry*, where he calls Boehme's often impenetrable works, arising from the Anabaptist and alchemical traditions, "visionary poetry" (CW 14: 157). Frye appears gradually to have altered his opinion. In one of his notebooks from the 1980s he writes, "Boehme is making more sense as I move closer to light and signature symbolism," adding that "it's not that I 'believe' him but that this is the kind of link between the Bible and the creative imagination that I'm looking for" (CW 5: 35). This is a reference the *Signatura Rerum*, where Boehme advances the theory, not unlike that of Paracelsus, that the inner qualities and properties of all things are displayed in their outer forms, just as the character of a person shows itself in his or her facial expression.[233] He advised everyone to study Nature with this in mind, assuring them that "the greatest understanding lies in the signatures, wherein man (*viz*. the image of greatest virtue) may not only learn to know himself, but also the essence of all essences" (*Signature* 12). Then, in *Words with Power* we discover that Boehme takes his place alongside the Neoplatonists, Dionysius the Areopagite, Eckhart, and Ruysbroeck as one who approaches revelation by way of ecstatic metaphor (CW 26: 86). When Frye comes to his katabatic chapter on the furnace, which was the end of his own quest, he calls on Boehme to help illuminate the imagery of the radical creative descent and its Heideggerean distinction between nothing and Nothing:

> Of those in the Christian theological tradition, perhaps Boehme is the most thoroughgoing, in showing that the conception of God is essentially connected with nothingness, that the presence of God appears in an *Urgrund* from which all conditions and attributes of being have been withdrawn. Boehme's vision of the creation anticipates Hegel in speaking of a negating of negation, a transforming of God from nothingness to an infinite something, which left the nothingness behind as a kind of vacuum suction, drawing everything within its reach into non-being. The

> abandoned nothingness is the principle of evil, the Lucifer or light-bearer which turns into the adversary of light, or Satan, after the light or Word has freed itself. This may sound difficult, but Boehme is difficult. The essential point is the association of nothingness and divine creation, an association that fascinated Yeats, who refers to Boehme in his play *The Unicorn from the Stars*, in which the climactic phrase is "Where there is nothing, there is God." (CW 26: 246–7)

In the last chapter of *Words with Power*, Boehme's Nothing, as opposed to nothing, becomes a central theme. By Frye's own account Tillich was one of the writers who caused him to look back to Boehme. John Dourley has carefully traced the influence of Boehme on Tillich, but as it turns out, Boehme was the spiritual ancestor of Frye as well. The oppositions on the vertical axis of Frye's cosmology—divine vs. demonic, Logos vs. Thanatos, anabasis vs. katabasis, Eden vs. Ulro—are a version of what Tillich calls the ground-of-being and the abyss. Tillich puts it this way in *Systematic Theology*:

> The genuine mystery appears when reason is driven beyond itself to its "ground and abyss," to that which "precedes" reason, to the fact that "being is and nonbeing is not" (Parmenides), to the fact that there is something and not nothing.... The positive side of the mystery—which includes the negative side—becomes manifest in actual revelation. Here the mystery appears as ground and not only as abyss. It appears as the power of being, conquering nonbeing. It appears as our ultimate concern. And it expresses itself in symbols and myths which point to the depth of reason and its mystery. (*Systematic* 1: 110)

Karl Barth and Tillich

In 1962 Tillich left Harvard Divinity School and joined the faculty of the Divinity School at the University of Chicago, where, as a student at the time, I attended his lectures on the history of Christian thought. During April of that year Karl Barth, the other great Protestant theologian of the twentieth century, came to lecture at Chicago. Barth's trip to the U.S. was something of an event: that very month he was featured on the cover of *Time* magazine. I heard one of the lectures he gave at Chicago. It was held in the cavernous Rockefeller chapel, where I could understand very little, what with Barth's heavy German accent ricocheting off the Gothic stone walls. After the lecture, the students repaired to the Common Room in Swift Hall at the Divinity School, where Tillich and Barth had assembled themselves to answer questions. The room was filled to overflowing; the atmosphere, electric in anticipation. I expected the neo-orthodox Barth to be somewhat austere and distant and Tillich to be engaged and inviting. But Barth turned out to be the engaged one, sitting forward alertly on the edge of his chair, as if his life depended on his making genuine contact with the student questioner. Tillich, on the other hand, was withdrawn and somewhat aloof. He seemed to feel obliged, in a slightly defensive way, to translate the questions into the terms of his own abstract vocabulary ("ground of being," etc.) before formulating an answer. It was as if he were delivering an apologetic for his own theological position. Barth, on the other hand, appeared to be interested not in advancing an agenda but in responding to the students' questions. I don't remember a single thing that either of these two theological giants said, but I have a very clear sense of the persona that each of them projected—one warm and inviting, the other cool and detached.

This makes me wonder, years later, whether or not Frye's mostly positive reaction to Barth (there are almost twice as many references to Barth in Frye's writing as there are to Tillich) is not a function of Barth's commitment to the Word and the experiential reality of the Biblical text, something Frye doesn't find in Tillich. In his review of volume 3 of Tillich's *Systematic Theology*, Frye writes, "There are almost no specific allusions to contemporary literature and art, and not many to contemporary thought, apart from theology itself. In contrast to Barth, there is little sense even of the existential concreteness of the Bible. Paul is used a good deal, naturally, but for the most part the passion and power of the book specifically called the Word of God is replaced by an interlocking design of estrangement, being itself, ultimate concern, the demonic, the spiritual presence, and the like" (CW 25: 365). Later, Frye would say, "I suppose only the Swedenborgians really went all out for the identification of Word and Presence (written word, that is), but otherwise I'm close to Barth" (CW 6: 432).

On the matter of natural religion, Frye agrees with Blake's contention that there is none, and so he endorses Barth's attack on the *analogia entis*, the belief that there is an analogy between God and creation. The *analogia entis* is the basic premise behind natural theology and is therefore opposed to practically everything Barth took to be theologically viable. As he says, "I regard the *analogia entis* as the invention of the Antichrist" (*Doctrine* x). Frye's opposition is not stated so strongly, but it is present nevertheless (CW 6: 623; CW 19: 44; CW 13: 17, 359), and puts him in opposition to Tillich's understanding of *analogia entis*, which is more problematical, especially his identifying the name God with being-itself. "I speak of symbolic knowledge," he says, "and mean by it exactly what St. Thomas meant by *analogia entis*" ("Reply" 201). The debate about what both St. Thomas and Tillich meant has created a small library,[234] but we can be sure that Frye's views remained the same as those outlined in "A Note on Blake's Mysticism" at the end of *Fearful Symmetry*, where he contrasts Blake's *analogia visionis* with the "more orthodox" *analogia fides* and *analogia entis* (CW 14: 415)

Finally, Frye, like Tillich, stands in opposition to Bultmann's effort to "demythologize" the New Testament narrative as an initial stage in interpretation: the assumptions of the old mythologies, such as demonic possession and the three-storied universe, had to be purged before the genuine kerygma could be "saved," to use Bultmann's word (9). Frye, of course, has exactly the opposite view of myth: "[M]yth is the linguistic vehicle of *kerygma*" (CW 19: 48). Tillich also rejects the effort to demythologize scripture. Such an effort, he says, can "deprive religion of its language and silence the experience of the holy. Symbols and myths must be criticized on the basis of their power to express what they are supposed to express, namely, the New Being in Jesus as the Christ" (*Systematic* 2:152). Frye says that Tillich is "much shrewder" than the demythologizers because he "sees that the semantic problem is really one of deliteralizing. Such things as creation and the fall of man are not literally events: they are realities symbolically expressed. They are thus neither subjective ideas nor objective facts, but finite modes of perception correlated with something infinite" (CW 25: 367–8).

12

Frye and Frances A. Yates

Frances A. Yates was a British historian whose studies focused on the development of Western esotericism, particularly hermeticism, during the Renaissance. She taught at the Warburg Institute of the University of London. In 1977 she became Dame Frances Yates, having been made a Daughter of the British Empire. Yates's *Giordano Bruno and the Hermetic Tradition* (1964), published when she was sixty-four, assured her place as an important, though often controversial, early modern historian.[235] In that book Yates argued that the ancient Greek discourses of Hermes Trismegistus, which were translated into Latin by Marsilio Ficino in the fifteenth century, were crucial documents for understanding Renaissance thought. She also argued that the younger contemporary of Ficino, Pico della Mirandola, had discovered another source of ancient wisdom in the kabbalah. Yates's contention, controversial at the time, that there was a "Hermetic tradition" in early modern Europe has generated a large body of commentary. Jacob and Gosselin note that after the publication of the Bruno book

> [o]ne could no longer interpret Bruno as a prophet of modern science; he was a prophetic magician who had seized upon Copernicanism because he sought an alternative to the rigid orthodoxies of both the Reformation and the Counter Reformation. Suddenly the hermetic tradition—its naturalism, its magical and gnostic tendencies—had to be seen as a source of inspiration for scientific curiosity, and possibly for scientific creativity. The effect of Dame Frances's account of Bruno, combined with her next book, *The Art of Memory* (1966), was to make understandable an early modern world where Copernicans could be magicians, Baconians could be millenarians, Newton could be an alchemist, Leibnitz could dabble in astrology, Renaissance natural philosophies could nurture the Enlightenment, and Freemasons could be empiricists. (424)

This meant that it became difficult to make arguments in Renaissance studies based on such oppositions as science versus magic or rational versus irrational thinking. Such oppositions also held little appeal for Frye, who found Yates's books congenial to his own way of thinking. According to John Krois, what sets the Renaissance memory treatises that Yates examines apart from other hermetic studies "is that they are concerned with a matter of enduring significance: memory in a cultural sense" (149–50).

Frye owned and annotated four of the most important of Yates's fourteen books: *The Art of Memory*, *The Rosicrucian Enlightenment*, *Giordano Bruno and the Hermetic Tradition*, and *The Occult Philosophy in the Elizabethan Age*.[236] His notebooks indicate that he was also familiar with Yates's *Shakespeare's Last Plays* (1975) and *A Study of "Love's Labour's Lost"* (1936). The thesis of each of these books, broadly considered, is that Renaissance historians have tended to overlook the maverick, the esoteric, the eccentric, the arcane, the hermetic, and the imaginative. In this respect, she and Frye are intellectual comrades. They both believed that the study of Renaissance thinking as a rationally coherent structure overlooked a substantial amount of contrary evidence. Frye's personal library reveals that he read widely in the various esoteric traditions, and with the publication of his notebooks we know a great deal about the depth and breadth of his interest in alchemy, astrology, Gnosticism, gnosis, magic, mysticism, Rosicrucianism, secret societies, and other forms of arcane and mysterious thought such as theosophy, channelling, numerology, and the Tarot.[237] A person with these interests would naturally be drawn to Yates.

In one of his *Late Notebooks* Frye declares, "Frances Yates is wonderful: the combination of sober documentation and the wildest guesswork is very exhilarating" (CW 5: 51–2). He goes on to say that her book on *The Occult Philosophy in the Elizabethan Age* gives him another step on the great chain of being:

> the descent to a world below hell, from which the creative ascent comes, is linked to the theme of creative melancholy, Durer's Saturn,—melancholy link—not so much the planetary as the mythological Saturn, thrown down to "hell" (Sandys' rendering of Ovid's *Met.* 1.) at the end of the Golden Age. Lead, Saturn's metal, then rises to gold. Chapman's *Hymnus in Nocturn*, Burton's & Milton's pensive or creative melancholy, go on to Keats' melancholy Hyperion themes & the *poète maudit* theme in France. (CW 5: 52)

The references here are to Dürer's well-known engraving *Melencholia I*, George Sandys's translation of Ovid's *Metamorphosis*, part 1 of George Chapman's *The Shadow of Night*, Robert Burton's *Anatomy of Melancholy*, John Milton's *Il Penseroso*, John Keats's *Ode on Melancholy* and *Hyperion*, and Paul Verlaine's *Les Poètes maudits*. In *The Occult Philosophy in the Elizabethan Age* Yates devotes separate chapters to Dürer and Chapman, showing how both descend from *De occulta philosophia* of Henry Cornelius Agrippa, the sixteenth-century German astrologer, alchemist, theologian, and magician.[238] Both Frye and Yates see melancholy as a positive psychological force. He refers to it as "creative"; she as "inspired" (*Occult Philosophy* 164, 165, 177). How does this play out in Frye's understanding of the archetypal journey of the human spirit?

When Frye says that creative ascent comes from "the descent to a world below hell," he is referring to what he calls elsewhere the movement from oracle to wit, which stems from an epiphany he had in 1951 in Seattle, and which we examined in the essay on Mallarmé (no. 9, above). The movement from descent to ascent is a movement along the *axis mundi*, the familiar levels of reality that are part of the structure of Frye's cosmology and that we find everywhere in his work but most fully elaborated in the chapter on the mountain archetype in *Words with Power* (CW 26: 132–66). Yates examines the ladder of ascent and descent in the work of Ramon Lull, and she reproduces (1) a woodcut from Lull's *Liber de ascensu et descensu intellectus*, showing the steps that move up the chain of being toward God, and (2) a fourteenth-century miniature that illustrates several of Lull's ladders (*Art of Memory*, fig. 4, p. 180, and pl. 10, following p. 192). Frye's creative descent is quite similar to what Yates calls "inspired melancholy," which in someone like Chapman is "a refusal to accept the prohibition ... against deep studies as leading inevitably to Hell and damnation" (*Occult Philosophy* 164). Comedy and romance, we might say, triumph over irony and tragedy.

The Ramon Lull Connection

When Yates was doing her research for *Giordano Bruno and the Hermetic Tradition*, she kept running across the name of Ramon Lull in Bruno's Latin texts. She therefore interrupted her Bruno research to concentrate on cracking the code of Lull's "logic" system, which was based on geometry, the alphabet, and elemental astrology. The result was a series of essays, the first one published in 1954, eventually brought together as volume 1 of Yates's *Collected Essays*—on Lull and Bruno. Two decades earlier, Frye had written his own essay on Lull for a course in Christian Missions he took during his final year at Emmanuel College. He relied almost exclusively on one primary text, Lull's *The Book of the Lover and the Beloved*, edited by Allison Peers, and on one secondary text, Peers's biography of Lull. Frye's bibliographical note includes a reference to A.E. Waite's book on Lull, saying that "Mr. Waite, perhaps the greatest living authority on occultism, makes out a good case for a pseudo-Lull who was one of the greatest alchemists between Geber and Cornelius Agrippa and lived in the fourteenth century somewhat later than the genuine Lull, spending much of his life in England" (CW 3: 234).

Frye's earliest references to Bruno are in his Emmanuel College essays—once in "Gains and Losses of the Reformation," where he refers to the Inquisition's "bitter opposition" to Bruno's scientific thought (CW 3: 270). Bruno also appears in Frye's essay on Lull, where he notes that Bruno had been haunted by Lull's dialectic (CW 3: 230) and that Lull's belief, following the Pythagoreans and the occultist tradition,

> [was] that the world was basically mathematical rather than organic, complicated rather than complex. This feeling in Lull's case arose from his conviction of the absolute intelligibility, and, therefore, simplicity, of the nature of God, for as mathematics supplies the most irrefutable demonstrations in life, it has frequently appeared to thinkers, such as Bruno, "the best approach to the understanding of the divine nature". (CW 3: 229)

During the ten years between the early articles on Lull and her book on Bruno, Yates had discovered the hermetic tradition of magic in Renaissance philosophy. There are many parallels between hermeticsm and Lull's philosophy. The dialectic of Lull's elements of thought is, as Yates's painstaking research shows, quite complicated, but Frye gives a cogent summary of these principles as they are explicated in Lull's *Ars Magna*:

> The gist of the scheme of the *Ars Magna* is as follows. All possible objects of knowledge are reduced to nine categories: God, angel, heaven, man, the imaginative, the sensitive, the negative, the elementary, the instrumental. All relations in which these objects exist are reduced to nine predicates: goodness, magnitude, duration, power, wisdom, will, virtue, truth, glory. All possible questions concerning them are reduced to nine: Whether? What? Whence? Why? How large? Of what kind? When? Where? How? Probably nine was chosen because it is the number of the universe, which is a ninefold sphere, and the complete twenty-sevenfold scheme is the cube of three, the divine nature being threefold. These are placed in concentric circles, one is fixed, the other two revolve, and so by permutation and combination we get a series first of all possible questions, then of all possible answers. This is a genuine dialectic, and if it does not work, it has yet to be proved that any dialectic will; we have not yet stopped evolving dialectic, and we probably never shall. (CW 3: 229–30)

Frye annotated *The Art of Memory* as he read it, so it is likely he would have been familiar with the chapter on "Lullism as an Art of Memory" in that book, where Yates outlines the differences between the classical art of memory in the rhetorical tradition and Lull's art of memory, which derives from Augustinian Platonism and the neoplatonic system of Scotus Erigena. Given Frye's interest in schematic representation, he no doubt was attracted to the several geometric, alphabetic, and chain-of-being diagrams that Yates reproduces from Lull's *Ars brevis* and other works (*Art of Memory* 180, 182, 183, 186).

The point is that in Lull both Yates and Frye discovered a congenial forebear. Lull appealed to Frye not only as a visionary but also as a schematic thinker. Certainly this last was part of the attraction of Spengler's *Decline of the West*, the first volume of which had three fold-out tabular diagrams, each more than a foot long. Frye calls Lull's inveterate categorizing a "genuine dialectic," and he was drawn to Lull's numerological schemes as well. With his penchant for systems, taxonomies, and various diagrammatic frameworks, Frye himself, as it turned out, could hardly organize his thoughts without some underlying schematic structure. This is, of course, obvious in his published work. It is even more obvious in his notebooks, where he is forever toying with paradigms—colours, mythological characters, musical keys, the zodiac, various ogdoadic formulae—as a way to give shape to and organize his ideas. Frye's student essays reveal that what became a typical way of thinking began quite early, and over the years he developed all kinds of diagrammatic schema that were the foundation of his own art of memory. There are scores and scores of them in the notebooks. Imre Salusinszky, who has studied the memory-theatre connection between Yates and Frye and who is aware of the proliferation of diagrams in Frye's notebooks, concludes that the most important feature of Frye's art of memory is its "architectonic and pictorial" nature (42).

Memory Theatres: The Spatializing of Knowledge

Yates's *The Art of Memory* is devoted to the various devices used to enhance memory from Greek and Roman times through the Middle Ages up through the late Renaissance.[239] The foundation for all of the arts of memory, Yates discovered, was the creative organization of space and the placement of imagery into that space. Memory theatres had to do with *topoi*, not in the sense of rhetorical "topics," but in the literal sense of "places." The typical procedure was to select a structure, say a building containing a number of rooms or a theatre with its many sections and seats, and then to place into the rooms of the building or the seats of the theatre a list of mythological characters or the kings of France or the gods or whatever one wants to retain in memory. The sections of the building or theatre were often accompanied by symbolic figures, such as the signs of the zodiac, to help trigger the recall. The process was one of association: one could remember items by associating them with a particular space in a large structure. Bruno, for example, would use places in London—"the Strand, Charing Cross, the Thames, the French embassy, a house in Whitehall, on which to remember the themes of a debate about the Sun at Supper" (*Art of Memory* 311). The memory theatres studied by Yates include, in addition to Bruno's, those of Giulio Camillo, Ramon Lull, and Robert Fludd,[240] and she includes a fold-out hemispheric diagram of Camillo's memory theatre, astonishing in its complexity. Walter Ong says that some exemplars of the memory theatres "carried tens of thousands of these places (several whole buildings full) in their heads as a regular part of their thinking equipment" (255). In Camillo we get the beginnings of memory as an occult enterprise, so that the art of memory became a system for containing spiritual secrets. Yates calls this a "radical change" (*Art of Memory* 145), and much of the material from chapters 6 through 17 has to do with this change of "artificial" or "rational" memory into a hermetic or magical art. In *Bruno and the Hermetic Tradition* this transformation is present from the beginning.

In thinking about the direction for his so-called but never realized "third book," Frye speculates that Vico will have a central role. "I know of no other thinker," Frye writes, "who is as close to thinking of the entire structure of concern as a poetic myth. A much vaguer synthesis, also suggested by Vico, takes shape in the background, of an encyclopaedic spatializing of knowledge. The bases for this are Curtius' study of topoi, particularly their literal sense as 'places,' the book of Frances Yates on the arts of memory and the idea of a cave-theatre holding all the ghosts of imagination like the one in PU [*Prometheus Unbound*],[241] and the two books of Gertrude Levy on the early developments of meander & descent symbolism.[242] Compare Vico's 'mental dictionary,' apparently a table of the mythical constructs underlying language"[243] (CW 9: 78–9). Memory theatres, then, are one example of the "encyclopaedic spatializing of knowledge."

Did Frye, who had a prodigious memory, rely on memory theatres when writing *Anatomy of Criticism*, one of the great examples of the spatializing of knowledge? In an interview with David Cayley, he says that at the time, "I'd heard of memory theatres but not enough to know anything at all about them.... I just unconsciously acquired my own and had no idea about how you operated with memory theatres until Frances Yates's book came out, which was some time in the mid-'60s." (CW 24: 932). At the end of the second chapter of *The Art of Memory*, Yates writes, "Augustine conferred on memory the supreme honour of being one of the three powers of the soul, Memory, Understanding, and Will"

(49). In his own copy of the book Frye wrote below this, "the real 'memory' is an archetypal framework of myth / I don't have this kind of visual memory, but I think I could use musical phrases in similar ways." Then in the right margin Frye adds, opposite Yates's reference to Augustine, "here memory would be the HS [Holy Spirit]."

It appears that Frye did use musical keys in a similar way. The best and most complicated example is his remark in the *Anatomy* that there is an analogy between the twenty-four phases of the *mythoi* and the circle of fifths. Frye didn't diagram this but he provided the basis for constructing such a diagram in Notebook 18 (CW 23: 273–4, 276, 278). Here is a diagram reconstructed from these passages:

CIRCLE OF FIFTHS

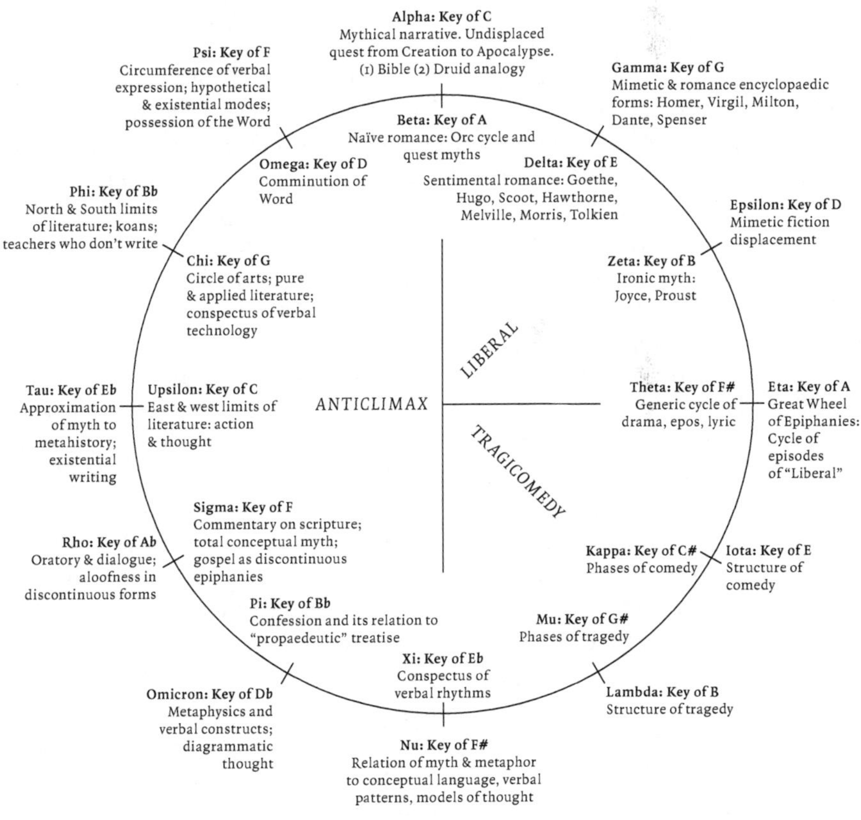

What Frye seems to be suggesting is that the analogy depends on whether there is a "harmony" or a "discord" between the phases. He says that the first three phases of a *mythos* are related to (in harmony with) the first three of an adjacent *mythos* (e.g., comedy and irony). But this relation does not obtain between the phases of opposite or discordant *mythoi* (e.g., irony and romance). What we end up with is an analogy between the overlapping keys in the circle of fifths and the overlapping phases in the circle of *mythoi*. And just as there are twenty-four keys, so there are twenty-four phases. It appears then, as suggested by Frye's marginalia to *The Art of Memory*, that the musical keys did serve as a kind of memory theatre for Frye, providing a means for him to keep straight the twenty-four separate phases.

What did Frye mean by saying that he unconsciously acquired his own memory theatres? My guess is that he is referring to the diagrammatic ways of organizing the categories of his criticism, which we glanced at above, and which we consider now in more detail. The most complicated and the most mysterious of Frye's schematic diagrams is the Great Doodle, the diagram of diagrams that Michael Dolzani has illuminated in his introduction to *The "Third Book" Notebooks* (CW 9). To his exposition I can only add a few footnotes, while observing the obvious difference between Frye's memory theatres, which are words arranged in geometrical space, as opposed to those memory theatres that arrange images in architectural space.

Frye writes at one point that he's not revealing what the Great Doodle is, because he does not really know (CW 23: 76–7), but his frequent references to it reveal that it is primarily his symbolic shorthand for the monomyth. Originally Frye conceived of the Great Doodle as "the cyclical quest of the hero" or "the underlying form of all epics" (CW 9: 214). But as he began to move away from strictly literary terms toward both religious language and the language of Greek myth and philosophy, another pattern developed, one with an east-west axis of Nous-Nomos and a north-south axis of Logos-Thanatos. At this point the Great Doodle took on an added significance, becoming a symbolic shorthand for what he called the narrative form of the Logos vision: "the circular journey of the Logos from Father to Spirit" (CW 9: 260) or "the total cyclical journey of the incarnate Logos" (CW 9: 201). But the Great Doodle is never merely a cycle. Its shape requires also the vertical *axis mundi* and the horizontal axis separating the world of innocence and experience. These, with their numerous variations, produce the four quadrants that are omnipresent in Frye's diagrammatic way of thinking. In Notebook 7 he refers to the quadrants as part of the Lesser Doodle (CW 23: 76), meaning only that the quadrants themselves are insufficient to establish the larger geometric design of the Great Doodle.

But the Great Doodle has still further elaborations. In the extensive notes he made for his Norton Lectures at Harvard (*The Secular Scripture*), Frye remarks self-referentially that in book 14 of Longfellow's *Hiawatha* the heroine "invents picture-writing, including the Great Doodle of Frye's celebrated masterpieces" (as yet unpublished). The reference is to Hiawatha's painting on birch-bark a series of symbolic and mystic images: the egg of the Great Spirit, the serpent of the Spirit of Evil, the circle of life and death, the straight line of the earth, and other ancestral totems in the great chain of being.[244] Frye elaborates his Great Doodle in a similar way, the Hiawathan "shapes and figures" becoming for him points of epiphany at the circumference of the circle—what he twice refers to as beads on a string (CW 9: 241, 245). The beads are various *topoi* and *loci* along the circumferential string. They can be seen as stations where the questing hero stops in his journey (CW 5: 416) or as the cardinal points of a circle.[245] Frye even overlays one form of the Logos diagram with the eight trigrams of the *I Ching*, saying that they "can be connected with my Great Doodle" (CW 9: 209), and one version of the Great Doodle recapitulates what he refers to throughout his notebooks as "the Revelation diagram," the intricately designed chart that Frye passed out in his course on "Symbolism in the Bible."[246]

The Great Doodle, then, is a representation, though a hypothetical one, that contains the large schematic patterns in Frye's "memory theatre": the cyclical quest with its quadrants, cardinal points, and epiphanic sites; and the vertical ascent and descent movements along the chain of being or the *axis mundi*. It contains as well all of the lesser doodles that Frye creates to represent the diagrammatic structure of myth and metaphor and that he frames in the geometric language of gyre and vortex, centre and circumference.

There are other large frameworks that structure Frye's imaginative universe, such as the eight-book fantasy —the ogdoad—that he invokes repeatedly throughout his career, or the Hermes-Eros-Adonis-Prometheus (HEAP) scheme, explored below, that begins in Notebook 7 (late 1940s) and dominates the notebook landscape of Frye's last decade. The ogdoad, which Michael Dolzani has definitively explained,[247] is fundamentally a conceptual key to Frye's *own* work, though it is related in a slippery and often vague way to the Great Doodle. The HEAP scheme in its half-dozen variations is clearly used to define the quadrants of the Great Doodle, and there are countless other organizing devices, serving as Lesser Doodles, that Frye draws from alchemy, the zodiac, the circle of fifths in music, colours, the chess board, the omnipresent "four kernels" (commandment, aphorism, oracle, and epiphany), the shape of the human body, Blake's Zoas, Jung's personality types, Bacon's idols, the boxing of the compass by Plato and the Romantic poets, the greater arcana of the Tarot cards, the seven days of

Creation, the three stages of religious awareness, numerological schemes, and so on. All of these, I think, are examples of the "encyclopaedic spatializing of knowledge" — mnemonic devices that serve as the memory theatres that Frye said he unconsciously acquired.

Imaginative Illumination

Practically all of Dame Frances Yates's readers agree that she is a compelling writer, one who uses her rhetorical skills to draw them into the excitement of her research into Renaissance hermeticism, and no one doubts that she is extraordinarily learned. Frye calls her one of the wise women.[248] Practically all of her readers also agree that she often pushes her arguments beyond what the evidence warrants. That is what Frye means by referring to her "wildest guesswork." One of her most outspoken critics has been Brian Vickers, who, after quoting the plaudits heaped upon Yates's *The Rosicrucian Enlightenment* by ten British historians, offers a thorough analysis of Yates's claims and concludes that she is given to distortion and exaggeration, that she engages in deceptive practices, that her arguments are based on groundless suppositions ("Frances Yates" 287).[249] This, at least, is the critique from a kind of empiricist view of historical explanation. Lisa Jardine has another perspective on Yates's achievement:

> Yates's intellectual interventions successfully, and permanently, cut us all loose from deeply ingrained and intellectually paralyzing habits of historical explanation. To put it bluntly: it was no longer possible to claim as adequate an account of "influences" which cobbled together isolated texts and their authors, into a specious chain of "cause" and "effect" (Roger Bacon caused Francis Bacon, caused John Locke, caused empiricism); instead, culture and ideology were foregrounded in all Yeats's [Yates's] work as essential components in intellectual historical explanation (180).

Another way of putting this is to say that the basis of the art of memory is, as John Michael Krois maintains, not logic but imagination (153). Frank Kermode, who had a long correspondence with Yates, also sang her praises (Jones 167, 169), as did Hugh Trevor-Roper, the Regius Professor of Modern History at Oxford (Jones *passim*).

In his *Late Notebooks*, Frye, engaging in one of his innumerable speculations on what he calls the "HEAP scheme," says "I've got stuck in my noddle the two names Prometheus and Hermes, and am beginning to feel that, apparently just for reasons of symmetry, there must be a second cycle incorporating the bulk of the imagery of modern poetry that doesn't get into the Eros-Adonis cycle (CW 6: 422). HEAP is, as already said, the acronym for Hermes, Eros, Adonis, and Prometheus. Frye is devoted almost to the point of obsession to exploring the metaphorical and thematic implications of these four gods. They are, he says following Blake, "the spectres of the dead" because they have no concentring vision, and Frye sets out like a questing knight to discover such a vision for them, the four quadrants of which will be, when the code is finally deciphered, Hermes Unsealed, Eros Regained, Adonis Revived, and Prometheus Unbound. Each of the four gods represents a cluster of numerous thematic associations: the number of entries dedicated to the HEAP cycle in all of the notebooks exceeds eight hundred, and in the *Late Notebooks* Frye devotes almost three hundred separate paragraphs to one or more of these "spectres of the dead," or what he calls, borrowing Emily Dickinson's phrase, "our confiscated gods." The four gods are also called "emblems" and "informing presences," and they eventually become, in the second part of *Words with Power*, "variations on a theme."

In the *Late Notebook* speculation just mentioned, Frye goes on to say, "I'm putting it in the strongest terms a hostile critic would apply: because I've got a pretty pattern to apply, the facts have simply got to conform to it, and naturally with that attitude I'll succeed sooner or later." And then he adds, "You can't be original unless you work with hunches and treat them exactly as a paranoiac would do. Of course I find what I want to find in the texts themselves: what else does the double meaning of 'invention' mean?" (CW 6: 422). Originality, madness, hunches, invention (in its two senses: the act of inventing something or something that has been invented)—these are all concepts that move away from rationality toward imagination, and it is the imaginative element in Frances Yates that draws Frye toward her: "There is, in fact, nothing in past literature that cannot become a source of imaginative illumination. One would say that few subjects could be duller or less rewarding than the handbooks studied by Miss Frances Yates in *The Art of Memory*, yet her study has all the mental exhilaration of the discovery of a fine new poet" (CW 27: 262).

Hermes and Hermeticism

Frye uses the word "hermetic" in a variety of contexts. Some relate to the archetype of Hermes—variously the psychopomp, the thief, the cunning one, and the inventor. Others are associated with his reading of G.R.S. Mead's *Thrice-Greatest Hermes*, a collection of the hermetic literature that was available at the beginning of the twentieth century, along with Mead's commentaries. Frye takes *Thrice-Greatest Hermes* to be not, as is ordinarily assumed, "a deservedly forgotten effort of pseudo-scholarship," but "the spiritual vision" of the *Corpus Hermeticum* (CW 6: 618).[250] His views on hermeticism were of course substantially influenced by Frances Yates, the other person who was centrally important in the revival of interest in the *Corpus Hermeticum*. For Yates hermeticism was generally a synonym for the various occult "sciences"—alchemy, magic, astrology, and Rosicrucianism.[251] Frye clearly means to include these Renaissance traditions in his own view of hermeticism, but the term often ranges freely beyond them, as in this catalogue of hermetic Romanticism:

> The suggestion of supernatural activity produces the tale form, where there's a series of events suggesting a superpersonal march of action which overmasters the characters or else identifies itself with the heroic will. In here come the myths of hermetic romanticism, as we get them in, for instance, Bulwer Lytton's *Zanoni* & *The Coming Race*. The essential romantic myths are founded, of course, on the mysterious Kantian unknowable noumenon which in rcsm. [romanticism] takes the form of the world as will. From this we get the Akasa-myth: Vril, Od, élan vital, creative evolution (when rescued from the mother-goddess cult of Darwin & Huxley), ether, electricity, magnetism & galvanism (for one *must* be scientific) & other adaptations of anima mundi & astral light theories. (These first turn up in Neo-Platonism: how the hell did they, & the elementals business, ever get stuck on Plato's name?). These of course account for mesmerism & the feats of Indian jugglers, who develop an extensive mythology in the 19th c. Another pattern is the (apparently always allied) theory of elementals or non-physical forms of existence. These merge with spiritualism & Bardo-theories. The neo-Pythagorean heroes, development of Simon Magus & Apollonius of Tyana, appear in Cagliostro, the Wandering Jew, Edmund Dantès (withdrawal & return) & Frankenstein as the portents of a nomadic & anarchic civn. [civilization].[252] (CW 15: 143)

There is not much in the noumenal world, then, that cannot be taken as hermetic. For Frye almost anything associated with Hermes can be hermetic: the Virgin Birth of the Word, themes of ascent and descent, fire symbolism, Boehme's "bitterness" or wrath, the secretly sealed message, recovery and transformation.[253]

Why, finally, did Frye devote so much energy to exploring the various esoteric and occult "sciences" that fall under the umbrella of hermeticism? First, the hermetic tradition comes to us largely in third-phase language, which means that its background is imaginative and symbolic and thus, like any other imaginative creation, it has a grammar, the rules of which operate in the same way as, say, the grammar of symbolism in Shakespeare or Dante. In his well-known essay "On Value-Judgements," which develops certain ideas from the "Polemical Introduction" to *Anatomy of Criticism*, Frye argues that the critic is not a judge, or at least should not be; the critic, rather, should display an attitude of total acceptance, whatever the textual data in front of her or him (CW 27: 258–65). "The dialectic axis of criticism ... has as one pole the total acceptance of the data of literature, and as the other the total acceptance of the potential values of those data" (CW 22: 26). This principle applies to discursive texts as well, such as works of philosophy or history. A corollary is that genres have a way of changing over time: Frazer may have little standing in the scholarly circles of anthropology or psychology, but he provides us a grammar of the imagination nonetheless. Moreover, there is the important Frygian epigram, "yesterday's kook book is tomorrow's standard text" (CW 5: 17). This grammar of the imagination has many common syntactic forms—religious, psychological, literary, philosophical, musical. The circle of fifths in classical music is a "symmetrical grammar" (CW 27: 406). And just as Dante's *Commedia* is an educational treatise that teaches "a grammar of the imagination" (CW 13: 396), so Jung's studies of alchemy provide a grammar of literary symbols (CW 21: 213). And as we have seen, Yates's *The Art of Memory* provided for Frye the same kind of exhilaration as the discovery of a new poet (CW 27: 262), meaning that the materials she studies, hermetic texts, yield that elation. In his early essay on "Yeats and the Language of Symbolism," Frye indicates that that he is a complete skeptic about the objective existence of Yeats's spiritual instructors. But the subjective aspect of *A Vision* is an altogether different matter, because it provides the symbolic structure of his poetry from 1917 onward and so it stands as "one of the grammars of romantic symbolism" (CW 29: 67).

Second, hermetic texts for Frye are removed altogether from considerations of belief. This means that they can provide the content for vision. In *Fearful Symmetry*, Frye writes that the

> doctrine of the Word of God explains the interest of so many of the humanists, not only in Biblical scholarship and translation, but in occult sciences. Cabbalism, for instance, was a source of new imaginative interpretations of the Bible. Other branches of occultism, including alchemy, also provided complex and synthetic conceptions which could be employed to understand the central form of Christianity as a vision rather than as a doctrine or ritual, preserving a *tertium quid* which, without detracting from the reality of the religion, would also avoid both the iconic and the iconoclastic pitfalls. (CW 14: 155)

Frye read widely in a number of fields, and the fact that he read something obviously does not mean that, using a theory of truth as correspondence, he accepted what he read. He could say, for example, that Lawrence's *Plumed Serpent* provided a good illustration of the recovery of projected gods, even though he thought the novel was "superficially the silliest and most wrong-headed book ever written" (CW 13: 368). To see Lawrence's story as an example of the recovery of projection is to put it in the context of an imaginative construct. To call Lawrence's ideas silly and wrong-headed —an existential rather than a mythological projection—is to remove it from that context. Frye was naturally willing to grant the powers of pure reason, Cartesian thinking, and the entire Enlightenment agenda, but the fundamental emphasis in all his work is that the imagination provides a critique of reason. He wrote an essay to that effect—"Literature as a Critique of Pure Reason" (CW 18: 230–44). In fact, it is to the credit of the Enlightenment that we can even speak of a shift in focus from the rational or scientific to the poetic, where the principle of identity means something more than an algebraic equation. Frye says that a remark by A. E. Waite in *The Pictorial Key to the Tarot* suggests something like this: "Christ is the buried {male} individuality in each of us; the rest of our individuality ought to become a unified symbolic female; these two unite, as in the conjunctio symbol of alchemy, and the child they produce is the eternal youth of the resurrection" (CW 6: 461). Here alchemical conjunction is no more or less than an example of metaphorical identity. It is no more or less mysterious than such an exoteric metaphor as the Incarnation.

Third, certain forms of the hermetic—alchemy, astrology, the kabbalah, the *I Ching*, the Tarot pack, numerology—help to confirm Frye's contention that imaginative or poetic thought is schematic. He sometimes calls this the "alphabet of forms," meaning that "they are expressions of the schematic ('all imagination') shape of the mythical apprehension of reality" (CW 9: 110–11). Mental systems, whatever else they are, are symbolic forms, and once they are conceived symbolically, Frye accepts them with a detachment that supercedes all skepticism as to their truth claims (CW 15: 149). "All my critical career," he writes, "has been haunted by the possibility of working out a schematology, i.e., a grammar of poetic language ... the kind of diagrammatic basis of poetry that haunts the occultists & others" (CW 9: 212). Frye's skeptical sense naturally manifests itself from time to time: Madame Blavatsky is a charlatan, some books are "kook books," Yeats's "spiritual instructors" produce a flood of nonsense, and so on. But for Frye the Cartesian mode of thinking cannot gainsay what is revealing in, say, Yeats's *A Vision*, when imagination rather than reason is taken as the primary perceptive and creative faculty. And what is revealing are the mental diagrams that seem always to arise from our subconscious, or whatever the source, when we begin to think poetically.

Finally, the esoteric tradition for Frye was a visionary tradition, analogous to other creative traditions, and analogies were the architectural blueprint for Frye's spiritual world.

> People think they're being iconoclastic & realistic when they ask me if there aren't differences as well as similarities in the patterns I put together. Of course there are, but that again is confusing imaginative & conceptual processes. In imaginative thought there is no real knowledge of anything but similarities (ultimately identities): knowledge of differences is merely a transition to a new knowledge of similarities. In conceptual thought analogy is tricky & misleading beyond the heuristic stage: in imaginative thought it's the *telos* of knowledge. The great ocean into which all analogy empties is the *via negativa* approach to God, which the Incarnation reverses into spring rain, the identity of God & Man. (CW 13: 215)

The note sounded here about identity and the Incarnation is an appropriate one on which to end, as it returns us to one of the core principles upon which Frye has constructed his large critical edifice: the priority of similarity (or analogy) and identity to difference. Such a principle is precritical, meaning that it is an assumption with which he begins but about which he is under no obligation to demonstrate. Aristotle does not try to demonstrate that art is mimetic. He simply begins with the assumption that some works of art happen to be imitations. Frye does not try to argue that identity is more important than difference, but he believes that it is, and the Incarnation for Frye turns out to be the most telling and extraordinary embodiment of the principle of identity. The principle of identity is, of course, what lies behind metaphor, which reminds us that the next book on Frye might well be devoted to his radically unique theory of that trope.

Notes

1 A start on a second volume has already been made. See my "Frye and Hegel" and "Frye and Nicolò Machiavelli." Essays on "Frye and Jacob Boehme," "Frye and Rabelais," and "Frye and Jane Ellen Harrison" have been written but are not published.

2 What follows is drawn largely from *Northrop Frye: Religious Visionary* and my introduction to *A Northrop Frye Chrestomathy*.

3 It took me and Michael Dolzani five years of fairly steady work to transcribe Frye's hieroglyphic scrawl and another ten years to edit the notebooks and other unpublished texts for the Collected Works.

4 Marginalia in Samuel Taylor Coleridge, *The Inquiring Spirit: A New Presentation of Coleridge from His Published and Unpublished Prose Writings*, ed. Kathleen Coburn (London: Routledge & Kegan Paul, 1951), 41. The book is in the Northrop Frye Library in the Victoria University Library, Toronto. Frye's annotation comes at the end of a selection of Coleridge's notes for "An Essay on Passions."

5 The most extraordinary example of Frye's paring down his note-taking for a particular writing project is his treatment of sentimental romance in *The Secular Scripture: A Study of the Structure of Romance*, which was distilled from more than 107,000 words, a text that is twice as long as his entire book on romance.

6 "Link" is one of Frye's favourite words. In the Collected Works, I count 1,576 instances of his use of the word or its inflected congeners ("links," "linked," "linking").

7 Twenty-five years after his review of the *Anatomy*, Abrams responded to a question about Frye by saying, "Let me affirm now my overall judgment that in that book, and in the many writings that have followed it, Frye has proved himself to be the most innovative, learned, and important literary theorist of my generation" (*Doing* 343).

8 The phrase in question is translated by Golden as "all happen to be, in general, imitations" and by Telford as "all happen to be imitations." Butcher renders it as "are all in their general conception modes of imitation." Else's version: "are in point of fact forms of imitation, by and large." Grube's translation: "are, in principle, imitations." In his literary criticism lectures, Frye said that Aristotle begins with "general remarks on imitation as basis of all art," which is, again, open to debate because of the qualifier "most" and the verb "happen to be." Frye is nevertheless aware of Aristotle's suggestion that there can be non-mimetic forms of art.

9 In her letter of 11 April 1939, Helen Frye writes to her husband: "Mary Louise Clarke told me the other day that she had been thinking fondly of you lately: she'd just finished an essay on Aristotle on the strength of lectures you gave in English to first year" (CW 2: 887).

10 See my "Frye and the Chicago Neo-Aristotelians" in the Introduction to CW 22, xlii–xliv.

11 In 1994 Virany sent me her class notes for this and six other courses she had with Frye. She was assisted in her note-taking, written neatly and thoroughly, by her training in Pitman shorthand, the keys to which she was kind enough to provide me.

12 The minor critics do not figure importantly in Frye's subsequent writings. He mentions Theophrastus's character book in "Charms and Riddles" (CW 27: 387); in one of his notebooks Theophrastus is referred to in connection with F.M. Cornford's account of the *alazon* (CW 20: 185); and in his history of English literature (*Rencontre*) Frye refers to Robert Burton's attraction to Theophrastus's *The Characters* (CW 10: 54–5). Isocrates appears in Frye's work only once, a passing reference to Milton's having taken his title *Areopagitica* from the Greek orator's address to the law court of Athens (CW 10: 54). Similarly, Aristarchus of Samothrace is mentioned only once in passing (CW 27: 332). Diogenes Laertius makes a cameo appearance in *Fearful Symmetry* in connection with his reference to the Druids (CW 14: 177). Dionysius of Halicarnassus gets mentioned in an endnote in *Anatomy of Criticism* (CW 22: 403). Otherwise, Frye does not refer anywhere else to Lucilius, Neoptolemus of Parium, or Philodemus of Gadara. As for Aristophanes, Frye's lecture focused on his critique of Euripides and Aeschylus in *The Frogs*. The standard for judgment in Aristophanes, Frye says, is twofold—whether the playwright had "skill in art" and whether his plays gave "good advice for citizenship." As we might expect from his interest in Old Comedy, Aristophanes makes repeated appearances in Frye criticism, and there are some two-dozen references to *The Frogs*. All but one of these, however, relate to Aristophanes as a playwright, not to the critical judgments he makes about other playwrights in his comedies.

13 Two studies devoted to the Aristotle–Frye connection should be mentioned: Deborah Lyons's "The Politics of Poetics: Northrop Frye's Rewriting of Aristotle" and Leon Golden's "Aristotle, Frye, and the Theory of Tragedy." Lyons maintains, on the one hand, that the *Poetics* cannot be understood except in a political context and, on the other, following the opinions of Fredric Jameson and Terry Eagleton, that Frye's criticism is too far removed "from the contested spaces of politics" (149). Neither claim, in my judgment, can be sustained. Golden suggests a method by which the theoretical statements about tragedy by Aristotle and Frye "can be harmonized to lead us to a fuller understanding of the potentialities and boundaries of the genre" (47).

14 Frye tells his students that the "chapters after 19 [are] of no particular use to us," but he goes on to say that chapter 25 is "very important from the point of view of ordinary criticism." This is the chapter on errors that may appear in poetry, and Frye gives a summary of it in his lecture of October 22.

15 Unless otherwise indicated, I follow Butcher's translation of the *Poetics*.

16 Else translates the participle here as "picking out"; Golden, as "bringing together"; Butcher, as "resulting from."

17 During Frye's Guggenheim year (1950–51) Edwin Honig, who was an instructor in the English department at Harvard, told Frye that there was that an explicit parallel recog-

nized in the Middle Ages between Aristotle's four causes and the well-known theory of levels of literary meaning: the literal level corresponded to the material cause, the allegorical to the formal, the moral to the efficient, and the anagogic to the final. In one of his notebooks for *Anatomy of Criticism*, Frye speculates that Honig's source may have been Helen Flanders *Dunbar's Symbolism in Medieval Thought* (CW 23: 217). But there is nothing in Dunbar's book that points to a parallel between Aristotle's four causes and the medieval theory of four levels of meaning. Later, Angus Fletcher notes the parallel (14–15). In his account of the levels of meaning in the second essay of the *Anatomy*, Frye says nothing about the parallel, nor does he ever refer to it elsewhere.

18 On precept and example, see CW 16: 338–9; CW 21: 94, 186, 218; CW 22: 77, 83, 84, 96–7, 225.

19 On this issue, see Lear 336 n. 10.

20 The assumption here that Aristotle thought the final cause for every fictional form was *catharsis* seems not to be correct. We do not know what he would have said about comedy (or did say, if in fact there was a part 2 of the *Poetics*, now lost, devoted to comedy), but the implication of chapters 1–6 is that each poetic species has its own particular end. Pity and fear, in any event, are not the emotions we associate with comedy. Perhaps, as Elder Olson argues, the final cause of comedy is a "*katastasis* [relaxation] of concern through the absurd" (*Theory* 47).

21 On *proairesis*, see Vernant 40–2.

22 Cf. "I think what Aristotle means partly by *hamartia* is being in a certain place which is especially dangerous or exposed; and very often the qualities that put you in such a place are the qualities of exceptional heroism" (CW 13: 569).

23 Even though Cave notes a great deal of "semantic slippage" in Frye's various accounts of *anagnorisis*, he nevertheless believes that Frye "gives the lover of recognition scenes better value for money than almost anything else in the history of poetics" (199). See also David Gay's study of recognition as a central focus in Frye's late work.

24 That the focus of Frye's view of *anagnorisis* slides back and forth between plot and reader (194–5) is noticed by Cave as well. For Frye's additional comments on the two meanings of *anagnorisis*, see CW 13: 354; CW 16: 320; CW 28: 364–5; and CW 4: 200–1.

25 In both Plato and Aristotle, *anagnosis* means reading, as it does in Acts 13:15, 2 Corinthians 3:14, and 1 Timothy 4:13. There appears to be no warrant for Frye's thinking that *anagnorisis* can also mean "reading." The only form of *anagnorisis* in the New Testament is *anagnorizomai* (Acts 7:13), which derives from *ana-* (in the midst) and *anagnorzio* (to know, to make known, to recognize), and translated as "made known" in the AV. The Liddell-Scott-Jones Lexicon of Classical Greek records only "recognition" for *anagnorisis*.

26 The word *anagnorisis* appears in the notebooks some sixty times; "recognition," as a literary category, hundreds and hundreds of times.

27 Frye records this response after hearing the performance by the Toronto Symphony Orchestra and the Mendelssohn Choir at the annual Bach Festival, 19 April 1950. Cf. the judgment in an earlier notebook: "I think Bach is the great Protestant poet of

the Pathos: not only two Passions, but even the B minor centres on the Kyrie and the Crucifixion. Milton and Bunyan are the Protestant poets of the Agon: Blake of the Anagnorisis. I wonder, if the Mass were analyzed from this point of view, what would happen" (CW 25: 166).

28 Cf. "You can't have humanism without the idea of Renaissance or rebirth: a gigantic anagnorisis or Kierkegaardian repetition of past culture" (CW 23: 232).

29 Cf. "Epiphany is not a new experience: it is the knowledge that one has the experience: it's recognition or anagnorisis" (CW 9: 34).

30 The foregoing commentary on *anagnorisis* draws on my study of the word in *Northrop Frye: Religious Visionary*.

31 Internal evidence suggests that Frye began writing in this notebook in 1949, put it aside, and then picked it up again in the mid-1950s.

32 *Autobiography* 262. Coleridge had written, "Schools of real philosophy there are but two,—best named by the arch-philosopher of each, namely, Plato and Aristotle. Every man capable of philosophy at all (and there are not many such) is a born Platonist or a born Aristotelian" (*Literary Remains* 33).

33 See n. 11 above.

34 Olson's essay is an analytically powerful examination of the argument of *On the Sublime*. On the Longinian influence on Frye, see Cotrupi and Veggian.

35 References to *On the Sublime* are to chapter and paragraph number. I am using the W. Rhys Roberts translation, rpt. in Richter 80–106.

36 Longinus uses the lightning and thunder metaphor on two other occasions: 12.4 and 34.4.

37 On this distinction, see CW 17: 110–11.

38 The passage from Genesis is quoted by Longinus in 9.9.

39 For these expansions of kerygma, see CW 26: 105–8. For a more detailed discussion of Frye's use of "kerygma," see Denham, *Northrop Frye: Religious Visionary* 65–9.

40 On the three awarenesses, see Denham, *ibid.* 76–9, 276–81.

41 On *participation mystique* see CW 22: 276; CW 5: 16; CW 6: 503; and CW 18: 347. There is no evidence that Frye had read Lévy-Bruhl. His source for *participation mystique* was doubtless Jung, a considerable portion of whose work Frye knew well.

42 Joachim's three major works are still only available, for the most part, in the Venice editions of the sixteenth-century. As I do not read Latin, I have had to rely chiefly on portions of the *Book of Concordance* or *Harmony of the Old and New Testaments* translated by E. Randolph Daniel in McGinn, 120–34, and on secondary sources, including the translation of portions of his works in those sources.

43 Frye twice makes note of Joachim's presence in the *Paradiso*: CW 5: 223 and CW 6: 720.

44 For the recurrence of Joachim's vision in the work of artists and thinkers from the eighteenth to the twentieth centuries, see Reeves, *Joachim of Fiore and the Prophetic Future*, 166–75. Frye was aware of Kandinsky's interest in Joachim: "Kandinsky says in his *Reminiscences* (1912) that this is the third age of the Spirit prophesied by Joachim of Floris. Of course he was a theosophist. I'm interested in statements like that, of

course, but one can't restrict such things to historical periods: at most they're new emphases only on something already there" (CW 5: 47). In *Reminiscences* Wassily Kandinsky refers to "the great period of the spiritual, the revelation of the spirit. Father—Son—Spirit," and he speaks of the "third revelation" as "the revelation of the spirit" (377, 379). Joachim's extensive influence has been traced by Reeves in *Prophecy* and *Joachim of Fiore*, and by West and Zimdars-Swartz in their chapter on "The Sustaining Influence of Joachim of Fiore" (99–112).

45 Frye had gone to Edmonton to dispose of the possessions of his mother's second youngest sister, Mary Howard, who had died on 28 July 1932.

46 On the radical difference between Augustine's view of history and that of Joachim, see Manuel's "Ascending Jacob's Ladder: The Way of St. Augustine or of the Abbot Joachim" 24–45.

47 The modern scholarly study of Joachim descends from Grundman, Töpfer, Reeves (*Influence of Prophecy*), and Mottu.

48 "Turning New Leaves," *Canadian Forum* 29 (September 1949): 138–9; rpt. as "The Rhythm of Growth and Decay" in *Northrop Frye on Culture and Literature*, 141–6; and as "Two Books on Christianity and History" in CW 11: 226–31. Frye says only that Joachim, "the great medieval prophet of historical progress," is one of the philosophical historians studied by Karl Löwith.

49 The opening phrase of the *Book of Concord*: "Non habentibus in hoc mundo manentem hereditatem sed futuram inquirentibus" ["Whereas they had not abiding inheritance in this world but seek the one to be"—Vulgate]. The passage from Hebrews: "Non enim habemus hic manentem civitatem sed futuram inquirimus" ["For here have we no continuing city, but we seek one to come"—AV].

50 For an account of these epiphanies, see Denham, *Northrop Frye: Religious Visionary* 20–1, 90–6.

51 Frye takes this tag from Milton's *Christian Doctrine*: "Under the gospel we possess, as it were, a two-fold Scripture: one external, which is the written word, and the other internal, which is the Holy Spirit, written in the hearts of believers" (*Prose Works* 447).

52 On Frye and typology, see Munk and Alter.

53 On the "scandal," see West and Zimdars-Swartz 101–3 and Reeves, *Prophecy* 59–70.

54 The clause ("and the Son") added to the Nicene Creed by the Latin Church in the late sixth century, reflecting the doctrine that the Holy Spirit descends from the Father and the Son (ex *Patre Filioque*), a position maintained by the Latin Church as against Eastern Christendom, which held that the Spirit descended from the Father only. The addition has been traditionally seen as having brought about the schism between Eastern and Western Christendom.

55 On the earlier influence of Joachim on the radical Franciscans (the Franciscan Spirituals) and others, see Reeves, *Prophecy*; Reeves, *Joachim of Fiore* 83–165; West and Zimdars-Swartz 99–112; and McGinn, *Apocalyptic* 149–81.

56 For Joachim's role in the revolutionary movement that worked in opposition to medieval structures of religious authority, see Dolzani, "Introduction," xli.

57 *fay ce que vouldras* = "do what you will," the motto of the Abbey of Thélème in Rabelais's *Gargantua*. Bodhisattva = literally in Sanskrit, the "enlightenment being"—the one who seeks Buddhahood but refrains from entering nirvana until all beings are saved.

58 1 Corinthians 1:22–3: "For the Jews require a sign, and the Greeks seek after wisdom: But we preach Christ crucified, unto the Jews a stumbling block, and unto the Greeks foolishness."

59 For a comprehensive study of Frye's attitudes toward the church, see O'Grady, who notes that Frye was much attracted to Joachim's speculations.

60 On Joachim's illustrations, see the definitive study by Reeves and Hirsch-Reich, *The Figurae of Joachim of Fiore*. They reproduce forty-seven of Joachim's figurae (351 ff.)

61 For an elaboration of some of these patterns see Denham, *Northrop Frye: Religious Visionary* 22–5.

62 In *Infinity and the Mind*, Rudy Rucker remarks, in an account of the special significance of the number 10, that the "Pythagorean would feel quite at home in a bowling alley, ritually building and destroying the *tetradactys* with a sphere punctuated by a triad of holes, and recording his progress with a series of numbers inscribed in squares" (59). The *tetradactys* was for the Pythagoreans a triangular symbol composed of ten dots moving upward from a base of four, like the arrangement of pins in a bowling alley. Frye's marginalia beside Rucker's comparison—"quite a flash of insight"—seems to refer only to the clever image Rucker used to describe what for the Pythagoreans was the sacred pattern of the fourth triangular number.

63 "Number Schemes, Numerology, and Synchronicity," in *Northrop Frye: Religious Visionary* 224–32.

64 Manuel, however, thinks that "Joachim's cumbersome numerological apparatus was historically far less significant than the attributes with which he clothed his three states" (40).

65 In his *Late Notebooks*, Frye writes: "What I seem to have is a revised Joachimism. The first age was prehistoric mythology. In the second age history became history, science science, separating from legend & cosmology. Hence myth became literary or hypothetical. Society's culture became pluralistic, following the Word that divided like a sword. The second age is the actualizing of prophetic authority. The third age is a reintegration of culture around post-mythological metaphor, a new kind of identification. This grows out of my three stages of metaphor [imaginative, erotic, and existential or ecstatic]. (CW 5: 63)

66 After I had completed this essay I came across Brian Graham's *The Necessary Unity of Opposites: The Dialectical Thinking of Northrop Frye*, a book that considers the various ways that Frye attempts to transcend oppositional thinking in the spheres of literature, politics, education, and religion. He does not discuss Bruno.

67 Frye never refers to the chapter on Bruno, but he twice mentions that he had read Yates's book: CW 24: 932 and CW 27: 262.

68 A similar form of this essay, entitled "Vico, Bruno, and the Wake," was published in Italian in *Mito Metafora Simbolo* 163–81.

69 "If the sun is one of the stars, it is at least conceivable that the stars are suns, centres of other systems with no relation to man. The espousal of this doctrine by Giordano Bruno was one of the reasons why he seemed so horrifying a figure to the jittery church of 1600" (CW 27: 339–40).

70 Frye refers to Cusa in his student essay on "The Augustinian Interpretation of History" (CW 3: 215).

71 See Hopkins's Introduction to *On Learned Ignorance*.

72 Frye writes that Bruno's "leaps are so vast and various that even specialists on him find him hard to keep up with" (CW 26: 48).

73 In *Two Essays on Analytical Psychology*, Jung writes: "it is necessary to give special attention to the images of the collective unconscious, because they are the source from which hints may be drawn for the solution to the problem of opposites. From the conscious elaboration of this material the transcendent function reveals itself as a mode of apprehension mediated by the archetypes and capable of uniting the opposites" (120).

74 Frye quotes the phrase, which also appears in *Paradise Lost* 3.341, in CW 6: 657; CW 18: 413; CW 13: 93; and CW 16: 44

75 See the "General Note: Blake's Mysticism," CW 14: 415–16, where Frye contrasts Blake's *analogia visionis* with "the more orthodox analogies of faith and being." On the *analogia entis*, see also CW 6: 623, 680; CW 9: 70, 84; CW 13: 17, 258, 350, 351, 359; and CW 19: 44.

76 Here is another example of the opposition: "Two Irish geniuses, Yeats & Joyce, sum up the cloven fiction of today. Yeats's traditions are Platonic, Protestant & concerned with an *analogia fides* antithetical to nature. Joyce's are Aristotelian, Catholic & concerned with an *analogia entis*" (CW 15: 96).

77 In "Cycle and Apocalypse in *Finnegans Wake*," Frye does not connect the rivalry of brothers to Bruno's principle of polarity, noting instead only the biblical parallels.

78 See chap. 2 of my *Northrop Frye: Religious Visionary*.

79 See especially, chap. 3, "Two Forces of One Power." Barfield's interest in interpenetration is recorded in another of Frye's notebooks as well: CW 6: 435.

80 Coleridge also speaks in one of his letters of the interpenetration of "opposite energies," and he uses the word as well in *The Friend* (qtd. by Barfield 34, 220). For other senses of interpenetration in Coleridge, see Barfield 93, 97, 145, 155, and 220. "Intussusception," the reception of one part within another, is a medical and a physiological term.

81 This collection never came to fruition.

82 The list is from the class notes provided me by the late James Reaney. Some of the mythographers in the bibliography are familiar: Sir James Frazer, Jane Ellen Harrison, F.M. Cornford, Carl Jung, and Robert Graves. Others are less so. Two are mentioned in only a single place in Frye's writing: Edward B. Hungerford's *Shores of Darkness* (1940) (CW 16: 282) and Edward Davies's *Celtic Researches on the Origin, Tradition, and Languages of the Ancient Britons* (CW 14: 76–7).

83 For the little information about Reynolds that has been dredged up, see Hobbs.

84 Douglas Bush quotes Spingarn on Reynolds's "tropical forest of strange fancies" but then chooses not to plunge into the forest, settling for a brief abstract of *Mythomystes*: Reynolds "expounds the geographical, physical, moral, and divine senses of the allegory in the medieval manner of a seventeenth-century Platonist and Cabbalist" (255, 335). Isabel Rivers says only that Reynolds seems to have wholeheartedly accepted the neoplatonist numerological tradition of Pico (182). For a brief treatment of Reynolds, see Arthur F. Kinney's entry on him in the *Spenser Encyclopedia*. Murrin has scattered references to Reynolds. The most substantial critical essay on *Mythomystes* is by Cinquemani, who focuses on the different levels of allegory in Reynolds—physical, moral, and psychological.

85 This is repeated in Frye's "New Directions from Old" (CW 21: 315) and in his *Diaries*, where, in reference to Blake, he writes about "Beulah, or the Gardens of Adonis, with its two gates, the upper one leading to Eden & the lower one to ηδονη [pleasure], the Bower of Bliss. The jingle is from Henry Reynolds" (CW 8: 329). The passage Frye is referring to is considered below. The etymological connection between Eden and Adonis had been made by others. See, e.g., Kavanagh 228–33.

86 "Essential form" is a phrase that Frye takes from Reynolds' prefatory address to his readers (142). The quotation about Proserpine is from *Mythomystes* 170.

87 Although "mystes" is also someone in the first stages of initiation into a mystery cult, Reynolds seems not to intend this meaning: the OED does not report such usage before 1676.

88 2 Esdras 12:37–8. Reynolds quotes from the King James Version.

89 Reynolds is paraphrasing Romans 1:20: "For the invisible things of him from the creation of the world are clearly seen, being understood by the things that are made, even his eternal power and Godhead; so that they are without excuse."

90 *Freistimmige*, a term Frye borrows from music, refers to the pseudocontrapuntal style where strict adherence to a given number of parts is abandoned, voices being free to enter and drop out at will.

91 See n. 85, above.

92 For biblical studies, for example, see Marks. For Classical studies, see Tsitsibakou-Vasalos.

93 "*nach Kunst, nicht nach Gunst*" = depend on merit rather than influence; "*Der Mensch ist, was er isst*" = man is what he eats. The Italian phrase is "*traduttore, traditore*."

94 See chaps. 6 and 7 of my *Northrop Frye: Religious Visionary*. For a catalogue of the various strands of the esoteric tradition, see Hanegraaff.

95 For a similar account of the same four features, see Faivre, "Preface: Esotericism and Academic Research."

96 Although Frye read and annotated Loomis's *The Grail: from Celtic Myth to Christian Symbol*, his critique of Loomis is taken directly from John C. Wilson's introduction to Waite's *The Holy Grail*, x–xii. Frye's annotated copies of both books are in the Northrop Frye Library.

97 Eight years earlier Frye said something quite similar to the editors of *Acta Victoriana*: "Well, 'anatomy' in the seventeenth century meant a kind of dissection and it also

extended itself to becoming the name of a literary form. Burton's *Anatomy of Melancholy* is one of my favourite books. It is ostensibly a medical treatise on the disease of melancholy, but actually it's an artistic reaction to the human experience. Similarly with Lyly's *The Anatomy of Wit*, which has a slightly deprecating quality, meaning that it's closer to satire. It's the use of a scientific term by literature to summon up the idea of something analytic yet at the same time comprehensive that I had in mind when writing the *Anatomy of Criticism*" (CW 24: 531–2).

98 The correspondence with Houston is in the Northrop Frye Fonds, Victoria University Library, 1988 accession, box 61, file 1. Neither Frye nor Princeton University Press was apparently aware that Henry Hazlitt had already used an almost identical title, *The Anatomy of Criticism* (New York: Simon and Schuster, 1933). Hazlitt (1894–1993), a well-known public intellectual, wrote his own *Anatomy* when he was literary editor of *The Nation*. In spite of the differences between the sensibilities and approaches of the two critics, some passages from Hazlitt sound almost Frygean.

99 Ayre reports that it was in this course that Frye "launched into" Burton's book (107). Frye probably read the two-volume edition published by J. M. Dent in 1932 (Everyman's Library). This, in any event, is the edition with Frye's annotations now in the Northrop Frye Library at Victoria University.

100 Johnson's remark is recorded in Boswell 1:389.

101 Frye was 19 at the beginning of the summer of 1932; he turned 20 on 14 July.

102 The record of the essays that Frye wrote for Blunden is incomplete, and most of those essays are not extant, but during the first year he wrote papers on Chaucer, Wyatt, and Fulke Greville, and he appears to have written essays on Sidney and Lyly as well. For his second-year tutorials (1938–39), he read papers on Crashaw and Herbert, Vaughan, Traherne, Herrick, Marvell, and Cowley, on the Dark Ages, on the character book, on *King Lear*, and on the history of the language. After his first year at Merton, Frye wrote to Roy Daniells that "Blunden is so much like God—very inspiring to talk to as long as you do the talking" (*Selected Letters* 19). And Frye did a great deal of talking. If his estimate of producing 5,000 to 6,000 words per week is accurate, his steady output resulted in about 100,000 words altogether. Frye sent the papers he had written during his first year to Pelham Edgar, who in turn passed them along to Roy Daniells. Neither the first- nor the second-year papers have ever turned up.

103 Anatomies that were published during Burton's lifetime:
Andrews, John. *Anatomie of Baseness* (1615)
Almond, Oliver. *The Uncasing of Heresie, or the Anatomie of Protestancie* (1624)
Anon. *The Anatomy of a Hande in the Manner of a Dyall, Necessary for All People* (1544)
______. *The Anatomie of Sinne* (1603)
Donne, John. *An Anatomy of the World* (1611)
du Moulin, Pierre. *Anatomy of Arminianism* (Eng. ed., 1620)
Grahame, Simeon. *The Anatomie of Humours* (1609)
Greene, Robert. *The Anatomie of Love's Flatteries* (1584)
______. *Arbasto, the Anatomie of Fortune* (1584)
Harington, Sir John. *Anatomy of a Metamorphosed Ajax* (1596)

Lyly, John. *Euphues: The Anatomy of Wit* (1578)
Nashe, Thomas. *The Anatomie of Absurdity* (1589)
Sidney, Sir Philip. *Valour Anatomized in a Fancy* (1581)
Stubbes, Philip. *The Anatomy of Abuses* (1583)

104 In both "Rencontre" and The *Well-Tempered Critic*, Frye discusses Burton's book, not as an anatomy, but as a form of rhetorical prose (CW 10: 54; CW 21: 424–7).

105 For Frye on Burton's sense of humour, see CW 27: 333.

106 In "Of Giving the Lie" Montaigne wrote, "I have no more made my book than my book has made me; 'tis a book consubstantial with its author" (*Essays*, bk. 2, chap. 18, par. 5). On Montaigne's "consubstantiality"—the identity of one with one's work—see CW 5: 88, 193, 196, 204; and CW 6: 555.

107 Frye also quotes this passage in "The Nature of Satire" (CW 21: 47–8).

108 Frye also quotes this passage in "Literature as Therapy" (CW 18: 466–7).

109 By "recreation" Frye means that while Burton's book contains little genuine information about the subjects of his various digressions, what it does is "recreate for us the entire seventeenth century" (CW 18: 467).

110 Abrams: Although the *Anatomy* "is not science, it is a thing no less valid or rare—it is wit, 'a combination of dissimilar things, or discovery of occult resemblances in things apparently unlike' [Aristotle].... Such criticism is animating; though only so, it should be added, when conducted with Frye's special *brio*, and when it manifests a mind that, like his, is deft, resourceful, and richly stored. An intuitive perception of similarity in dissimilars, Aristotle notes, is a sign of genius and cannot be learned from others. Wit criticism, like poetic wit, is dangerous, because to fall short of the highest is to fail dismally, and to succeed, it must be managed by a Truewit and not by a Witwoud" (196). Kermode: "I should call *Anatomy of Criticism* a work of sixth-phase Symbolism placed on the frontier of a purer Aristotelianism. Certainly it would be reasonable to treat this as a work of criticism which has turned into literature, for it is centripetal, autonomous, and ethical without, I think, being useful. As literature it has, if I may be permitted to say so, great value" (323). The most extensive cases for the *Anatomy* as an anatomy are argued by Louis Mackey, Hazard Adams, Minna Castrén, Eleanor Cook, Bert O. States, Harry Levin, and George Woodcock.

111 There seem to have been other stories. In the Northrop Frye Fonds, 1993, box 3, file 11 is a three-page typescript entitled "Two Preludes," followed by Roman numeral I. The typescript includes all but the last few lines of the story that was published as "Prelude." What happened to the remainder of the typescript, which presumably included a second 'Prelude," is unknown. And we know from Frye's correspondence with his wife Helen that in 1938 he submitted at least two stories to the *Atlantic Monthly* (CW 2: 800), the disposition of which is unknown.

112 The cover sheet preceding four of the stories in the Northrop Frye Fonds, 1991, box 37, file 5, is entitled "Four Dialogues."

113 On the various meaning of the word "anatomy" as applied to Frye's work and that of others, see my introduction to CW 22.

114 "Kierkegaard was half a nut, after all" (CW 5: 210). "[T]he great prophetic figures of modern literature, Rousseau or Swift or Kierkegaard or Dostoevsky, may often not have been much more than wrongheaded neurotics in their historical and biographical context" (CW 18: 168).

115 In his *Notebooks for "Anatomy of Criticism,"* Frye says about a lecture he gave in Vancouver: the "talk started with my usual stuff on nursery rhyme, then established that ordinary speech is associative & not prose, then said that associative babble was the voice of the ego, which is always sub-literary, that this ego-voice is projected in the dead-language, ation-ation, rhythmless impersonal jargon of the lonely crowd. That the impersonal babble is the voice of the collective or aggregate ego, & according to Kierkegaard 'essentially demoralizing.' It consists in prodding reflexes of [the] inattentive, & is seen in advertising, then propaganda, then exhortatory jargon of the collective tantrum kind" (CW 23: 285). The Kierkegaardian phrase he quotes is from this passage in *Concluding Unscientific Postscript*: "In this age, and indeed for many ages past, people have quite lost sight of the fact that authorship is and ought to be a serious calling implying an appropriate mode of personal existence. They do not realize that the press in general, as an expression of the abstract and impersonal communication of ideas, and the daily press in particular, because of its formal indifference to the question whether what it reports is true or false, contributes enormously to the general demoralization, for the reason that it is impersonal, which for the most part is irresponsible and incapable of repentance, is essentially demoralizing" (28).

116 In a 1952 diary entry, Frye writes: "At tea we got into a discussion of existentialism, prompted by the fact that Jessie [Macpherson] had just seen the Sartre play that Don Harron is in—they call it *Crime Passionel* here, although I think its original title was *Mains Sales*. I seemed to be the only one present who had much notion of existentialism, & of course I know very little, but we kept quite an animated discussion going" (CW 8: 583). For the other references to "existential" and "existentialism," see, in addition to those in the index of the *Diaries*, CW 8: 167, 243, 257, 376, 488, 591 and 592.

117 On Kierkegaard's use of *Bekymring* as a term of philosophical import, see Stokes.

118 "I cleared out & went to Tillich's lecture—a huge crowd in Wycliffe. He talked on the 'theology of despair': the attempt to start with despair as a 'limit-situation.' It disappointed me a little, as I'd read enough Kierkegaard to figure it out myself. Even the feeling it gave me of being on top of Tillich was hollow: I didn't want to feel on top of Tillich: I wanted to feel a contact with something fresh" (CW 8: 247–8).

119 *Biblical Religion and the Search for Ultimate Reality* (1964), *Christianity and the Encounter of World Religions* (1964), *Systematic Theology* (3 vols., 1951–63), and *Theology of Culture* (1964).

120 On the Kierkegaard–Auden connection see CW 6: 487; CW 8: 306; CW 10: 127; CW 12: 108; CW 13: 229–30; CW 16: 328; CW 17: 89; and CW 23: 234–5.

121 The fact that Frye separates freedom from concern and that freedom is a characteristic of Kierkegaard's concerned or ethical state should not be a stumbling block: they are using the word "freedom" in two different senses. Frye does say that the person

of "ethical freedom" is the one "who has passed beyond speculation" (CW 7: 256). For him there is a double opposition in Kierkegaard's notion of ethical freedom. It is opposed, on the one hand, to the aesthetic point of view, and on the other to the synthetic rationalism of Hegel (CW 19: 44).

122 *Quid agas* is the moral level of medieval allegorical interpretation, having to do with right action. In *Fools of Time*, Frye speaks of the "aesthetic in the perverted Kierkegaardian sense of externalizing man's ethical freedom" (CW 28: 323).

123 "Primary concerns a quincunx: breathing in the middle surrounded by (a) food & drink (b) sex (c) property (money, possessions, shelter, clothing) (d) freedom of movement" (CW 6: 701–2). "The most primary concern of all, breathing, is transformed into spirit, & the spiritual meaning of food & drink, of love, of security & shelter & the sense of home, all follow it (CW 5: 166). "Air, the primest of primary concerns" (CW 5: 125). "Spirit gets its name from the most primary of all primary concerns: breathing. And air is the medium for seeing and hearing" (CW 5: 175). "Spirit means breath, the most primary of all primary concerns, the great sign of the appearance of birth, the thing we can't live twenty minutes without. Spirit is the antitype then of air, the invisibility that makes the real world visible" (CW 5: 183).

124 "Is ultimate concern a primary concern? I think not. No one can live a day without being concerned with food: anybody can live all his life without being concerned about God (CW 5: 78). "I'm wrong about religion as an ultimate but not a primary concern. Where did I come from and where am I going are primary concerns, even if we don't believe there are any answers" (CW 5: 121). "That's my Eros-Adonis axis, of course, and it unites the primary concerns of life, food and sex, with its primary anxiety and ultimate concern, death, and the passage through death. I should start thinking in terms of primary anxieties: they help to show how Tillich's 'ultimate concern' is also a primary one" (CW 5: 165). In *The Critical Path*, Frye writes, "In origin, a myth of concern is largely undifferentiated: it has its roots in religion, but religion has also at that stage the function of *religio*, the binding together of the community in common acts and assumptions. Later, a myth of concern develops different social, political, legal, and literary branches, and at this stage religion becomes more exclusively the myth of what Tillich calls ultimate concern, the myth of man's relation to other worlds, other beings, other lives, other dimensions of time and space" (CW 27: 23). And in "Framework and Assumption" Frye writes, "Paul Tillich distinguishes the religious concern as 'ultimate': it may be that, but it can hardly be primary. One cannot live a day without being concerned about food, but one may live all one's life without being concerned about God. At the same time one hesitates to rule out the conscious and creative concerns from the primary ones" (CW 18: 432). See also CW 27: 247.

125 Cf. the almost identical formulations in CW 6: 434; CW 18: 266, 353; CW 26: 51–2.

126 Lest this account of primary concerns become too poker-faced and sober, we can remind ourselves of Frye's shorthand and somewhat indelicate notebook entry itemizing the primary concerns (food, sex, property, and freedom of movement): "history

moves toward the progressively clearer discovery of the utterly obvious: we want to eat, fuck, own, and wiggle" (CW 6: 640).

127 CW 4: 354; CW 6: 545; CW 18: 354, 434; CW 26: 52.

128 On Kierkegaard's ideas about time see the articles by Taylor and Bedell.

129 Cf. "We experience time in a way that is continually elusive and frustrating and exasperating, because we're dragged through time facing the past with our backs to the future. We know nothing about the future except by the analogy of the past. That means that all our hopes, when they're projected into the future, have this extraordinary limitation about them. If somebody starts out on a career, let's say as a doctor or a social worker, he or she must have some kind of vision of a world of better health or of better social organization in his or her mind in order to carry on the career with any kind of consistent energy. It's that sense of the vision in the present which is the real dynamic. You can die without seeing that come. In other words, you can give up the future as far as your own life is concerned and still carry on with the same vision" (CW 24: 1016). "We try to cope with time facing the past, with our backs to the future, and in relation to time human life seems to be a kind of untied Andromeda, constantly stepping back from a devouring monster whose mouth is the mouth of hell, in the sense that each moment passes from the possible into the eternally unchangeable being of the past. At death we back into a solid wall, and the monster then devours us too" (CW 27: 358). "[T]here is no such thing as a forward-looking person. That is a metaphor from car-driving, and it applies to space but not to time. In time we all face the past, and are dragged backwards into the future. Nobody knows the future: it isn't there to be known. The past is what we know, and it is all that we know" (CW 11: 285–6). "Man has doubtless always experienced time in the same way, dragged backwards from a receding past into an unknown future" (CW 11: 16). The notion of backing into the future is consistent with what Kierkegaard says in one of his journals: "It is quite true what philosophy says; that life must be understood backwards. But then one forgets the other principle: that it must be lived forwards" (*Papers* 161). The idea is ancient. According to Jay Griffiths, "To the Maori, the past is in front of them so they 'walk backwards into the future, facing the past,' as Maori writer Witi Ihimaera says" (*Sideways* 235–6).

130 Cf. "[T]he Kierkegaardian antithesis of ethical freedom & aesthetic idolatry is as unsatisfactory as ever" (CW 23: 253–4).

131 "The archetypal view of literature shows us literature as a total form and literary experience as a part of the continuum of life, in which one of the poet's functions is to visualize the goals of human work. As soon as we add this approach to the other three, literature becomes an ethical instrument, and we pass beyond Kierkegaard's *Either/Or* dilemma between aesthetic idolatry and ethical freedom, without any temptation to dispose of the arts in the process. Hence the importance, after accepting the validity of this view of literature, of rejecting the external goals of morality, beauty, and truth. The fact that they are external makes them ultimately idolatrous, and so demonic. But if no social, moral, or aesthetic standard is in the long run externally determinative of the value of art, it follows that the archetypal phase, in which art is

part of civilization, cannot be the ultimate one. We need still another phase where we can pass from civilization, where poetry is still useful and functional, to culture, where it is liberal, and stands on its own feet" (CW 22: 107).

132 On the "paranoia principle," see also CW 13: 93.

133 For the Kierkegaard–Hegel connection, see Westphal, Perkins, and Stewart.

134 For a fuller treatment of Hegel's influence on Frye, particularly Frye's appropriation of the Hegelian *Aufhebung*, see my *Northrop Frye: Religious Visionary*.

135 "Confession and anatomy are united in *Sartor Resartus* and in some of Kierkegaard's strikingly original experiments in prose fiction form, including *Either/Or*" (CW 22: 293).

136 Frye refers to the "sacramental repetition" elsewhere as the "sacramental analogy," by which he means the Neo-Thomist emphasis on belief as an imitation of Christ. That is, one sets up a construct or model, such as a saint's life or laws prescribed by Scripture, and then makes one's life a sacramental analogy to that, with the result of ritual or institutional continuity. See, e.g., CW 13: 81, 83, 234, 236, 247.

137 "It sounds as though 'recollection' is the word that translates as anamnesis, and refers to an accumulation or structuring of the past" (CW 5: 364).

138 In one of his notebooks, Frye equates repetition and *anagnorisis* (recognition, discovery). See CW 23: 232.

139 On the verse from Revelation, see also CW 13: 151. In one of his notebooks Frye says that "Kierkegaard's repetition doesn't have to replace Plato's anamnesis: they're two halves of the same myth, the visual certainty of past & future internalized in the present" (CW 13: 215).

140 Elsewhere, Frye says that Kierkegaard "recreates hieratic in the post-Hegel era" (CW 13: 277) and that he leans toward the poetic (CW 5: 261).

141 The passage Frye had in mind was written by Kierkegaard in 1846: "I wanted particularly to represent the various stages or spheres of life [aesthetic, ethical, religious], if possible in one work, and that is how I consider all my pseudonymous writings. With that in mind it was important to keep an unvarying balance so that, for instance, the Religious should not appear at a later time when I had become so much older that my style would have lost some of the lofty, imaginative expansiveness proper to the Esthetic. The idea is not that the Religious should have this exuberance, but that the writer should be capable of producing it and making it clear that if the Religious lacked this style the reason certainly was not that the writer lacked the necessary youthfulness" (*The Diary of Søren Kierkegaard* 60).

142 "The Spectre of Urthona is the isolated subjective aspect of existence in this world, the energy with which a man or any other living thing copes with nature. It is neither the Selfhood, which is Satan, nor the 'vegetable' existence, which is Luvah; it is that aspect of existence in time which is linear rather than organic or imaginative. If one had to pin the conception down to a single word, one might call Blake's Spectre of Urthona the will" (CW 14: 288).

143 The tiger limerick: "There was a young lady of Niger / Who smiled as she rode on a tiger; / They returned from the ride / With the lady inside, / And the smile on the face of the tiger."

144 On Kierkegaard's role in the elaborate scheme of the "three awarenesses" or revolutions in human consciousness, see my *Northrop Frye: Religious Visionary* 76–9, and charts 5–7 in the appendix.

145 On the Auden–Kierkegaard connection, see Auden's "Presenting Kierkegaard" in *The Living Thoughts of Kierkegaard* 3–22, and Mendelson *passim*. Auden was also significantly influenced by his reading of Tillich.

146 Expanding on infinity and eternity in a letter to a friend, Frye writes, "Revelation encourages us to think in terms of infinity and eternity, not in the mathematical sense, but in the religious sense. As we experience time, the present, the only part of it we do experience, never quite exists. As we experience space, the centre or the 'here,' never quite exists either--everything we experience in space is 'there.' Under the impact of revelation the whole fallen world turns inside out, into an eternal now and an infinite here. In terms of the Kantian distinction between the thing perceived and the thing in itself, we never see the thing in itself because we are the thing in itself. Reality is the immediate data of ordinary experience universalized--that it why it is revealed to the childlike rather than the sophisticated in us. The beginning of the vision of eternity is the child's realization that his own home is the circumference of the universe as far as he is concerned. The end of it is the regenerate Christian's realization that the universe is a city of God, the home of the soul, and the body of Jesus" (*Selected Letters* 31–2).

147 For the notebook entries having to do with the vortex, see CW 20: 100, 120, 148, 162, 164, 169, 171; CW 13: 47, 96, 217, 227, 332, 474; CW 5: 46; CW 6: 436, 437, 462, 690; CW 15: 33, 49, 55, 73, 101, 108; CW 9: 72, 77, 107, 179, 191, 197, 260; CW 23: 6, 19, 25, 26, 27, 33, 34, 37, 38, 39, 40, 59, 62, 263.

148 So far as I know, the only critic who has commented on the significant role that Carroll played in Frye's writings is Cristina Bertea in her essay on Frye and fairy tales (232–4).

149 In chap. 5 of *Alice's Adventures in Wonderland* the young heroine eats a mushroom that causes her neck to grow so long and serpentine that a pigeon nervously accuses her of being a serpent (*Annotated Alice* 73–6).

150 The reference is to the concrete poem about the mouse's tale (tail) in chap. 2 of *Alice in Wonderland* (*Annotated Alice* 51).

151 Marvell compares the soul to a drop of dew that descends to an alien world and longs to return from it "Because so long divided from the Sphere, / Restless it rolls and unsecure, / Trembling lest it grow impure: / Till the warm Sun pity its Pain, / And to the Skies exhale it back again, / So the Soul, that Drop, that Ray... / Does, in its pure and circling thoughts, express / The greater heaven in an Heaven less" (*On a Drop of Dew*, ll. 14–9, 25–6).

152 "[O]ne feels that Alice could hardly have held her Wonderland together if she had even reached the menarche, much less become an adult" (CW 26: 172). The point is

repeated in the *Late Notebooks*: "Alice could hardly have held her Wonderland together when she reached menarchy, much less marriage" (CW 5: 274).

153 "This is the third main characteristic of play: its secludedness, its limitedness. It is 'played out' within certain limits of time and place. It contains its own course and meaning.... Play begins, and then at a certain moment it is 'over.' It plays itself to an end" (*Homo Ludens* 9).

154 Frye annotated this edition, which is in his library at Victoria University. He also owned a copy of *The Annotated Alice*, but like Bill the Lizard's slate, he left no marks on it.

155 The words of the White Queen to the Red King at the trial of the Knave of Hearts (*Annotated Alice* 161). Cf. "There is a traditional metaphor which makes the critic the 'judge' of literature. Such a metaphor may imply that Shakespeare and Milton and other impressive people are, relatively to the critic, in the role of prisoners or petitioners, a prospect so exhilarating that many critics wish to leap into a judicial role at once, on the Alice-in-Wonderland principle of sentence first, verdict afterward. (CW 27: 120).

156 "It's my own invention": the White Knight's words to Alice when he sees her admiring his little wooden box (*Annotated Alice* 297).

157 In chap. 11 of *Alice's Adventures in Wonderland*, the guinea-pigs, who had applauded at the Mad Hatter's testimony, were thrust into bags and then sat upon by the officers of the court. Alice says that she now understands what it means when the newspapers note at the end of trials, "There was some attempt at applause, which was immediately suppressed by the officers of the court" (*Annotated Alice* 150).

158 "If you knew time as well as I do," said the Hatter [to Alice], "you wouldn't talk about wasting it. It's him" (*Annotated Alice* 97).

159 "Alice laughed. 'There's no use trying,' she said: 'one CAN'T believe impossible things.' 'I daresay you haven't had much practice,' said the Queen. 'When I was your age, I always did it for half-an-hour a day. Why, sometimes I've believed as many as six impossible things before breakfast'" (*Annotated Alice* 251).

160 The remark is from the prefatory poem to *Alice's Adventures in Wonderland*: "Imperious Prima flashes forth / Her edict to 'begin it': / In gentler tones Secunda hopes / 'There will be nonsense in it!' / While Tertia interrupts the tale / Not more than once a minute" (*Annotated Alice* 21).

161 Towards the end of chapter 2 of *Through the Looking Glass* the Red Queen says to Alice, "Now, here, you see, it takes all the running you can do, to keep in the same place. If you want to get somewhere else, you must run at least twice as fast as that" (*Annotated Alice* 210).

162 Or "the Antipathies," as Alice thinks to herself, realizing that "it didn't sound at all the right word" (*Annotated Alice* 28).

163 In the Looking-Glass House, Alice discovers she can read the backwards-written poem if she holds it up to a mirror.

164 This line is repeated in Frye's "Mythos and Logos." See CW 27: 280–1.

165 Cf. Joyce "seems to have avoided works that would come too close to what he was doing. I still have to look into the extent of his reliance on Dante, but he says he hadn't read Rabelais, and he doesn't make the use of Blake that one might have expected. Other sources, such as Alice Through the Looking-Glass, got in almost by accident" (CW 25: 292).

166 "Now, Kitty, let's consider who it was that dreamed it all. This is a serious question, my dear, and you should not go on licking your paw like that—as if Dinah hadn't washed you this morning! You see, Kitty, it must have been either me or the Red King. He was part of my dream, of course—but then I was part of his dream, too! was it the Red King, Kitty? You were his wife, my dear, so you ought to know—Oh, Kitty, do help to settle it!" (*Annotated Alice* 344).

167 *The Walrus and the Carpenter* appears in *Through the Looking-Glass*, chap. 4. In the first two stanzas of the poem, the sun shone mightily even though "it was / The middle of the night"; and the moon sulked "Because she thought the sun / Had got no business to be there / After the day was done." (*Annotated Alice* 233–6).

168 The reference is to the three brothers in John Ruskin's *King of the Golden River.*

169 Prima, Secunda, and Tertia are the names given to the Liddell sisters in the prefatory poem to *Alice's Adventures in Wonderland*.

170 About his daughter Mandane, Astyages, king of the Medes, dreamed that a stream of water flowed from her, so large that it covered all Asia. See Herodotus, *History* 1:48.

171 The reference is to Maureen Duffy's *The Erotic World of Faery*. An annotated copy is in the Northrop Frye Library at Victoria University.

172 Huizinga, *Homo Ludens* 9: "This is the third main characteristic of play: its secludedness, its limitedness. It is 'played out' within certain limits of time and place. It contains its own course and meaning.... Play begins, and then at a certain moment it is 'over.' It plays itself to an end."

173 Carroll, *Sylvie and Bruno*, in *The Complete Works of Lewis Carroll*: "And meanwhile, Baron, I'll just show you a most interesting map we have—of Outland, and Fairyland, and that sort of thing" (337).

174 Rabbit's watch (*Annotated Alice* 26); March Hare's watch (96); time as "him" (97); "lessoning" (130); old man (307–13).

175 The title of chap. 12 of *Through the Looking Glass*.

176 Frye owned and annotated the following editions of Mallarmé's work: *Mallarmé*, ed. Anthony Hartley (Harmondsworth: Penguin, 1965); *Poems*. With commentaries by Charles Mauron, trans. Roger Fry (New York: New Directions, 1951); *Selected Poems*, trans. C.F. MacIntyre (Berkeley: U of California P, 1957); and *Selected Poetry and Prose*, ed. Mary Ann Caws (New York: New Directions, 1982). His library also contained the standard French edition, *Oeuvres completes*, ed. Henri Mondor and G. Jean-Aubry (Paris: Gallimard, 1945). Mallarmé's poems referred to by Frye are *Toast Funèbre, Cantique de Saint Jean, Un Coup de Dés, Une Dentelle S'Abolit, La vierge, le vivace et le bel aujourd'hui, Ses purs ongles très haut dédiant leur onyx (Sonnet en x), Hérodiade, Le tombeau d'Edgar Poe, L'Après Midi d'un Faune, Prose (pour des Esseintes), Tombeau (de Verlaine), L'Azur,*

Quand l'Ombre menaça de la fatale loi. The prose works Frye refers to are *Igitur*, *Crise de vers*, letters (especially those to Henri Cazalis), and *Le livre, instrument spiritual*.

177 While Baudelaire and Rimbaud make appearances in *Fearful Symmetry*, Mallarmé does not.

178 Mallarmé makes a cameo appearance in another of Frye's 1952 essays, "Towards a Theory of Cultural History" (CW 21: 167)

179 The swan reference is to the sonnet *La vierge, le vivace et le bel aujourd'hui*.

180 CW 27: 19, 389; CW 18: 360, 376; CW 5: 399; CW 6: 426; CW 15: 353; and CW 25: 292.

181 Cf. "The conception of a verbal universe comes of course from Mallarmé" (CW 29: 126).

182 One version of the Logos diagram is reproduced in CW 24: 127. In a notebook entry Frye locates "The Fire Sermon" from Eliot's *Waste Land* at the top of the cycle and *Igitur* at the bottom (CW 5: 4).

183 Vera was Frye's older sister. *The Sleeping King* is a fairy tale in which a blacksmith descends into a deep cavern to shoe the horses of a sleeping king and is rewarded by having the horseshoes he replaced and carried out of the cave turn into gold.

184 The translation in square brackets is by Henry Weinfield in Mallarmé's *Collected Poems* 69. Patricia Parker, in the only sustained treatment of the Frye–Mallarmé connection I am aware of, gives a close reading of the so-called "Sonnet en x" (*Ses pur ongles . . .*) as a gambit for comparing Frye's conception of metaphorical identity ("A is B") with de Man's post-Nietzschean wariness about such identifications. She examines their common debt to Mallarmé, but also notes the diverging directions in the formalist tradition the two critics have taken regarding Mallarmé's poetry. She argues that Frye's view of metaphorical identity as "hypothetical" retains a temporal, dynamic, and revolutionary element that extends the vision of the function of metacriticism and the role of the critic in society.

185 "Chance and Choice have become interchangeable without losing their identity" (W.B. Yeats, *A Vision*, 136). Cf. "Chance being at one with Choice at last" (W.B. Yeats, "Solomon and the Witch," *Collected Poems* 175).

186 Rolland de Renéville proposed the link between *Igitur* and the Vulgate translation of Genesis 2:1, *Igitur perfecti sunt coeli et terra et omnis ornatus eorum*, "Thus the heavens and the earth were finished and all the host of them" (*L'Expérience Poétique* 90). For other references to the Genesis 2:1 link see CW 5: 70, 2: 754 n. 303.

187 The commentator Frye has in mind is apparently A.R. Chisholm. See his *Mallarmé's Grand Oeuvre* 130. On the matter of the Vulgate passage, see also CW 5: 70, 113, 207; CW 18: 115.

188 "Aboli" or some form of the word appears in seven of Mallarmé's poems: *A la nue accablante tu*, *Toute l'âme résumée*, *Ses purs ongles très haut dédiant leur onyx*, *Toast Funèbre*, *Une dentelle s'abolit*, *Un Coup de Dés*, and *Hérodiade*.

189 Frye is referring to the oft-quoted passage in Mallarmé's letter to Henri Cazalis, 14 May 1867: "I struggled with that creature of ancient and evil plumage [vieux et

méchant plumage]—God—whom I fortunately defeated and threw to earth" (*Selected Poetry and Prose* 87).

190 The passage is from Mallarmé's "The Book: A Spiritual Instrument" (*Selected Poetry and Prose* 80).

191 Letter to Henri Cazalis, 14 May 1867 (*Selected Poetry and Prose* 87). In one of his early plans for *Words with Power*, Frye proposed organizing the first three chapters on a Trinitarian scheme—the Book of the Father, the Book of the Son, and the Book of the Spirit—based on Joachim of Floris's theory of the three epochs. Only in the Age of the Spirit, according to Joachim, would humankind be able fully to understand spiritual truth. Mallarmé was to be a part of the Book of the Spirit (CW 5: 171).

192 For these associations, see CW 9: 162, 178, 231, 254; CW 15: 279; and CW 23: 333.

193 In the interview with Ian Alexander, Frye proposed the playing of five compositions during the course of the interview—Schubert's *Impromptu*, opus 90, no. 1, in C minor; "I am a courtier brave and serious" from Gilbert and Sullivan's *The Gondoliers*; "O Isis and Osiris" from act 2 of Mozart's *The Magic Flute*; Sir Hubert Parry's arrangement of Blake's *Jerusalem*; Clementi's sonata *Didone Abbandonata*, opus 50, no. 3, in G minor; and the fugue at the end of Verdi's *Falstaff*. When Alexander asked Frye whether he agreed with the sentiments of the Verdi finale—that the world is all jest—Frye replied, "[I]t was a very profound devotional, religious poet, George Herbert, who said, 'All things are big with jest; nothing's that plain / But may be witty, if thou has the vein.' I've always had a strong interest in the nature of comedy and the way in which even tragedy seems to fit inside as a kind of episode in a total story which is comic. While I'm not sure that everything in the world is simply a jest, there is a point at which the witty and the oracular come together" (CW 24: 742).

194 The material on oracle and wit that follows here draws on my *Northrop Frye: Religious Visionary*.

195 "After his ascent from Trophonius the inquirer is again taken in hand by the priests, who set him upon a chair called the chair of Memory, which stands not far from the shrine, and they ask of him, when seated there, all he has seen or learned. After gaining this information they then entrust him to his relatives. These lift him, paralyzed with terror and unconscious both of himself and of his surroundings, and carry him to the building where he lodged before with Good Fortune and the Good Spirit. Afterwards, however, he will recover all his faculties, and the power to laugh will return to him" (*Description of Greece*, bk. 9, chap. 39, par. 13). Frye makes this point in *Secular Scripture*, where he cites both Plutarch and Pausanias (CW 18: 85, 449 n. 144). In Plutarch's account, which is in his *A Discourse Concerning Socrates's Daemon* (par. 21), Timarchus, a friend of Socrates, is said to have emerged with a radiant countenance after two nights and one day in the cave. See also Robert Graves 180. Sára Tóth suggests that there is perhaps a Christian analogue of all this in the *risus paschalis*, the loud laughter that rang out in medieval churches from funny stories provided by medieval priests at the end of their sober Lenten sermons (personal correspondence).

196 Frye's copy of *The Lankavatara Sutra* is in the Northrop Frye Library at Victoria University.

197 In one of his many "doodles" where Frye outlines sets of opposing pairs (e.g., metaphorical / metonymic, centripetal / centrifugal), he includes this pair: "oracular magic / witty recognition" (CW 5: 400).

198 Frye's annotated copy of Walker's book is in the Northrop Frye Library.

199 For the displacement-condensation distinction, see CW 26: 136–7; CW 5: 308, 399–400; CW 18: 329, 480.

200 Frye writes that "the image of shaking dice in Mallarmé goes back to the juec d'amor in William of Poitiers, except that the sexual innuendo (allegory) is more explicit in the earlier writer" (CW 5: 405). Poitiers writes in "Song 6" that in the game of love he might bet the wrong way and miss his chance. See Bond 27.

201 One of his outlines for *The Secular Scripture* reveals that Frye planned to entitle chapter 10 of his book "From the Dice Throw to the Recovery of Laughter" (CW 15: 268).

202 Cf. "[O]ne does not write luminously on a dark field; the alphabet of stars alone, is thus indicated, sketched out or interrupted; man pursues black on white" (*L'Action restreinte* in *Selected Poetry and Prose* 77).

203 The Troy dance was a kind of game or parade associated with the Cretan labyrinth. See Levy 248–9, an annotated copy of which is in the Northrop Frye Library. Levy in turn is drawing upon W.F. Jackson Knight's *Cumaean Gates* (1936).

204 On Mallarmé and the *via negativa* see CW 5: 45, 184.

205 See Lacan, "The Mirror Stage," in *Écrits* 3–9.

206 Robert Greer Cohn in his book on Mallarmé's *Igitur*, which Frye owned and annotated, also applies the mirror stage to Igitur's descent (*Mallarmé: Igitur* 3). On the "prison of Narcissus," see also CW 26: 232; CW 4: 186–7, 194–5; CW 5: 211, 300, 394; CW 6: 421, 424, 428, 430, 525, 527, 542, 660–1.

207 Cf. "Keats speaks of the poet's 'negative capability'; Blake calls himself the 'secretary' of his poems; Eliot uses his well-known figure of the catalyzer, indicating, like all the poets who have invoked Muses and similar figures, that he is not the maker of the poem but simply the place where it comes to being; Mallarmé speaks of his vision as developing 'through what used to be me'" (CW 26: 82).

208 CW 5: 42, 206, 321, 329, 389; CW 6: 551; CW 25: 348.

209 In a letter to Henri Cazalis, 14 May 1867, Mallarmé writes, "my entrance into the last Abyss would be a truly crushing blow—if I were not able to finish my work; I mean the *Work*, the "Great Work," as our ancestors the alchemists called it" (*Selected Poetry and Prose* 88).

210 "'We make to ourselves pictures of facts,' says Wittgenstein, but by pictures he means representative illustrations, which are not pictures. Pictures as pictures are themselves facts, and exist only in a pictorial universe. 'Tout, au monde,' says Mallarmé 'existe pour aboutir à un livre'" ["All earthly existence must ultimately be contained in a book"] (CW 22: 114). "Sterne prefigures the cosmos of Mallarmé where the function of everything that exists is to border on (*aboutir*) a book" (CW 17: 38). "[E]very work of literature imitates, or finds its identity in, the entire 'world of words,' in Wallace Stevens's phrase [*Description without Place*, pt. 7, l. 5], the sense of the whole of reality as potentially literary, as finding its end in a book, as Mallarmé says" (CW

18: 378). Mallarmé's aphorism is from "The Book: A Spiritual Instrument" (*Selected Poetry and Prose* 80).

211 E.g., the Masonic overtones of *The Magic Flute* (CW 20: 101), the Masonic links with the trade unions in the nineteenth century (CW 15: 61), the affinity between the Freemasons and the Royal Society (CW 15: 71), and the Freemason scapegoat myths (CW 5: 96).

212 "An inquiry into Æneas' adventure to the shades, will have this farther advantage, the instructing us in the shows and representations of the MYSTERIES; a part of their history, which the form of this discourse upon them hath not yet enabled us to give. So that nothing will be now wanting to a perfect knowledge of this most extraordinary and important institution. For, the descent of Virgil's hero into the infernal regions, I presume was no other than a figurative description of an INITIATION; and particularly, a very exact picture of the SPECTACLES in the ELEUSINIAN MYSTERIES; where every thing was done in show and machinery; and where a representation of the history of Ceres afforded opportunity of bringing in the scenes of heaven, hell, elysium, purgatory, and what ever related to the future state of men and heroes" (Warburton 251). Still points to this passage in *Shakespeare's Mystery Play* 10; Frye notes it in CW 28: 341.

213 On the Frye–Knight connection in the 1930s, see Ayre, 111–13.

214 "Without pursuing that curious and obscure problem of the meaning of interpretation farther, it occurs to me as possible that there may be an essential part of error in all interpretation, without which it would not be interpretation at all: but this line of thought may be persevered in by students of *Appearance and Reality*. Another point, more immediately relevant, is that in a work of art, as truly as anywhere, reality only exists in and through appearances. I do not think that Mr. Wilson Knight himself, or Mr. Colin Still in his interesting book on *The Tempest* called *Shakespeare's Mystery Play*, has fallen into the error of presenting the work of Shakespeare as a series of mystical treatises in cryptogram, to be filed away once the cipher is read; poetry is poetry, and the surface is as marvellous as the core" (Eliot, xxii).

215 Cf. "Mr. Colin Still's remarkable analysis of *The Tempest* first drew my attention to the extreme importance of the 'Banquet' there, which he relates, with other themes, to ancient myth and ritual" (Knight, *Imperial* 136).

216 Frye has a similar statement in "Autobiographical Notes II" where Spengler is inserted into the summer between his third and fourth years as part of the "logical development" of his ideas: "Meanwhile, of course, my real critical interests were inexorably developing. Bernard Shaw had knocked the wind out of me at fifteen, and I started my sophomore year fascinated by dramatic patterns (a repertory company was doing comedies in Toronto at the time) and with an interest in Blake that got going my third year. My next summer (even at the time I was using my summers academically) saw an embryonic anatomy theory begin to shape itself in my notes, and of course it was that summer that I found myself reading Spengler in the Edmonton YMCA—one of the great nights of my life, & one that unknown to me had converted me into a critic of my own distinctive kind. My fourth year brought me to a fascinated study

of Romanticism, and theology, besides shaking up an interest in Biblical typology that had been in my mind as long as I can remember, brought Frazer, & with Frazer the key to drama. At that point the logical evolution of my ideas was interrupted by having to flounder through two years at Oxford, get myself established as a lecturer, and try to pound my Blake ideas into a thesis shape" (CW 25: 2).

217 Annotated copies of both books are in the Northrop Frye Library at the Victoria University Library.

218 "A mystic works, not only with a psyche, or subjectively idealistic soul, but with a *pneuma*, or universal spirit in which individuality is completely absorbed" (CW 3: 44).

219 Kind thanks to Nicholas Graham for providing me a scanned image of Frye's pencil diagram.

220 "Introduction to Shakespeare's *Tempest*" (CW 28: 44–52); "Shakespeare's *The Tempest*" (CW 28: 333–45); "*The Tempest*" (CW 28: 608–22).

221 In 1964 the *Hudson Review* sent Frye volume 3 of Tillich's *Systematic Theology*, giving him a deadline for submitting his review. Whether Frye ever submitted the review is uncertain. It was never published, and its rather abrupt ending suggests it may have been unfinished.

222 See *Being and Time* 83–4. Frye owned and annotated a copy of Heidegger's book.

223 This definition appears at a number of places in Tillich's work. See, for example, *Dynamics of Faith* 1–4, 52, and *Systematic Theology* 1:211–15.

224 The idea gets repeated still again in "Framework and Assumption": "Paul Tillich distinguishes the religious concern as 'ultimate': it may be that, but it can hardly be primary. One cannot live a day without being concerned about food, but one may live all one's life without being concerned about God. At the same time one hesitates to rule out the conscious and creative concerns from the primary ones" (CW 18: 432).

225 That is, appropriate or legitimate. "U" and Non-U," in which "U" stands for upper-class, were terms coined by the British linguist Alan Ross and popularized by Nancy Mitford in a 1954 article in *Encounter*.

226 For the references to Newman's remark, see CW 5: 217, 222, 223.

227 For Tillich's understanding of the Protestant principle, see especially *The Protestant Era*, xi–xxix.

228 See CW 5: 199; CW 13: 212, 231–2, 276, 323.

229 Lorna Brown, daughter-in-law of Frye's second wife, Elizabeth.

230 Frye uses the same language in CW 15: 52: "I think what I do is break open the symbolism of modern psychoanalysis, centring on Jung. This leads straight back to Renaissance occultism, via Jung & Silberer on alchemy. From there I can move into the Protestant field, going back similarly from Barth, Berdyaev, & Tillich to Boehme."

231 *Six Theosophic Points and Other Writings*, bottom margin of p. xxiii of Nicholas Berdyaev's introductory essay, "Unground and Freedom." It is not clear that Frye always keeps in mind the distinction between *Ungrund* (the unconditional being of God) and *Urgrund* (the abyss).

232 For the "deification of the void" see also CW 13: 103, 129, 248; CW 9: 214; and CW 15: 102, 292.

233 Boehme was influenced not only by Paracelsus but by the esoteric traditions of the kabbalah, alchemy, astrology, and hermeticism.

234 See, for example, Thomas, "Catholic Criticism of Tillich" 187–8 n. 5, and Palmer 171 n. 125.

235 On Yates's life and work see Jacob and Gosselin, and Jones.

236 For example, Frye made 41 marginal markings and two marginal annotations in his copy of *The Rosicrucian Enlightenment.*

237 See Denham, *Northrop Frye: Religious Visionary*, chaps. 5 and 6.

238 For Yates on Milton, see also *Giordano Bruno* 280; on Dürer, *ibid.*, 146; and on Burton, *Occult Philosophy* 159.

239 Yates concludes *The Art of Memory* by considering the survival of the art of memory into the seventeenth century with Leibnitz. Krois sees it continuing on into the nineteenth century with Hegel's *Phenomenology of Spirit* (153–6).

240 Frye comments on Yates's having been convinced that the design of the Globe Theatre was influenced by one of the memory theatres of Robert Fludd (CW 28: 448). One critic thinks that scholars will continue to quarrel over the validity of this claim (Pring-Mill 332). Another is less certain that there are two sides to the debate: "Not many scholars have professed themselves convinced of the Fludd–Globe argument" (Colie 159).

241 According to Rossetti's description of this cave: "In the third Act of the drama we find Prometheus unbound, and about to retire with Asia and their company into a cavern, which, as Prometheus avers, has a peculiar virtue of bringing to itself the echoes of the human world, and the lovely apparitions 'Of painting, sculpture, and rapt poesy, / And arts, though unimagined, yet to be.' This cavern (we may not be far wrong in thinking) is the cavern of the human mind—the recesses of creative and contemplative thought, vocal with human sympathy, fertile of human enlightenment and elevation" (19).

242 The books referred to here in addition to Yates's: Ernst Robert Curtius, *European Literature in the Latin Middle Ages* (1953). Gertrude Rachel Levy, *The Gate of Horn* and *The Sword from the Rock* (1953).

243 On the "mental dictionary," see Vico 22.

244 See Longfellow 228–30.

245 See CW 9: 147–8, 159, 177, 198, 200, 204, 249, and 254.

246 The chart is reproduced in CW 13: 591–4.

247 "The Book of the Dead: A Skeleton Key to Northrop Frye's Notebooks" 19–38. See also Dolzani's introductions to CW 9 and CW 15.

248 Frye includes Yates among a group of women he calls wise: Maud Bodkin, Jessie Weston, Gertrude Levy, Helen Flanders Dunbar, Madame Blavatsky, Enid Welsford, Jane Harrison, Bertha Phillpotts, and Ruth Benedict (CW 9: 71).

249 "I find the Yates thesis almost wholly unfounded" (Vickers, *Occult* 6). The Yates thesis is examined throughout this collection of essays, *Occult & Scientific Mentalities in the Renaissance*. Vickers's attack on Yates might well have been occasioned by Yates's sharply critical review of his *Francis Bacon and Renaissance Prose* ("Bacon and the

Menace"). That speculation is also advanced by Marjorie G. Jones, who notes that Yates's review faulted Vickers's book for its lack of a historical context (195–8).

250 Frye does think that Yates is overly concerned with the dating of the *Corpus Hermeticum*: "I've read Frances Yates on Bruno, and she's obsessed by the pseudepigrapha side of it; the hermetic literature wasn't written by an ancient Egyptian god or whatever, but, etc. That affects psychikon history, not spiritual history" (CW 6: 618). The psychikon/spiritual distinction comes from Paul's differentiating in Corinthians 2:14–15 between the *soma psychikos* ("natural man" in the AV) and the *soma pneumatikos* ("spiritual man"). In speaking of Yates's obsession, Frye is apparently referring only to the first chapter of *Giordano Bruno and the Hermetic Tradition*, "Hermes Trismegistus," for what really obsesses Yates is "spiritual history."

251 Although Frye read and occasionally refers in his notebooks to hermetic writers of late antiquity (Porphyry, Iamblichus, Proclus) and of the early Christian periods (Clement of Alexandria and Pseudo–Dionysius), his comments are too negligible to infer anything substantial about his attitude toward them.

252 "The *akasa* is a Sanscrit word which means sky, but it also designates the imponderable and intangible life-principle—the astral and celestial lights combined together, and which two form the *anima mundi*, and constitute the soul and spirit of man; the celestial light forming his *nous*, *pneuma*, or divine spirit, and the other his soul or *astral* spirit. The grosser particles of the latter enter into the fabrication of his outward form—the body. *Akasa* is the mysterious fluid termed by scholastic science, 'the all-pervading ether'; it enters into all the magical operations of nature, and produces mesmeric, magnetic, and spiritual phenomena" (footnote in Helena Petrovna Blavatsky, *Isis Unveiled* 1:139–40). "Vril," from Edward Bulwer Lytton's *The Coming Race*, is a "beneficent and all-purpose force," a "unity in natural energetic agencies." "Od force" or "odyle" is the name Baron Von Reichenbach gave to the force or emanations emitted by objects in his various experiments with clairvoyants and mediums. "Élan vital" is the life force that Henri Bergson says differentiates human beings from other forms of life. Philostratus's biography of Apollonius of Tyana, which Frye read, shows this neo-Pythagorean to be a miracle-worker and magician. Count Alessandro Cagliostro (1743–95) was an Italian adventurer and magician who performed his various occult arts (psychic healing, alchemy) throughout the courts of Europe). Edmund Dantès is the hero of Alexandre Dumas's *The Count of Monte Cristo*.

253 For these associations, see CW 9: 188, 231, 241, 283, 285; CW 5: 57; CW 6: 571–2, 618, 622; CW 13: 371; and CW 23: 272.

Works Cited

Abrams, M.H. "Anatomy of Criticism." *University of Toronto Quarterly* 28 (January 1959): 190–6.

______. *Doing Things with Texts: Essays in Criticism and Critical Theory*. Ed. Michael Fischer. New York: Norton, 1989.

Adams, Hazard. "Essay on Frye." In *Visionary Poetics: Essays on Northrop Frye's Criticism*. Ed. Robert D. Denham and Thomas Willard. New York: Peter Lang, 1991. 41–6.

Alter, Robert. "Northrop Frye between Archetype and Typology." In Donaldson 137–50.

Ayre, John. *Northrop Frye: A Biography*. Toronto: Random House, 1989.

Barth, Karl. *The Doctrine of the Word of God* (Prolegomena to *Church Dogmatics*, being vol. 1, pt. 1). Trans. G.T. Thomson. Edinburgh: T and T Clark, 1936.

Bauckham, Richard. "The *Figurae* of John of Patmos." In Williams 109–25.

Bedell, George C. "Kierkegaard's Conception of Time." *Journal of the American Academy of Religion* 37, no. 3 (1969): 266–9.

Bertea, Cristina. "Frye e la fiaba." In *Ritratto di Northrop Frye*. Ed. Agostino Lombardo. Rome: Bulzoni Editore, 1989. 225–35.

Blake, William. *The Complete Poetry and Prose*. Ed. David Erdman. Rev. ed. Berkeley: U of California P, 1982.

Barfield, Owen. *What Coleridge Thought*. Middletown, CT: Wesleyan UP, 1971.

Blavatsky, Helena Petrovna. *Isis Unveiled*. New York: J. W. Bouton, 1877.

Boehme, Jacob. *The Signature of All Things, with Other Writings*. London: J. M. Dent, 1912.

______. *Six Theosophic Points and Other Writings*. Trans. John Rolleston Earle. Ann Arbor: U of Michigan P, 1958.

Bond, Gerald A., ed. *The Poetry of William VII, Count of Poitiers, IX Duke of Aquitaine*. New York: Garland, 1982.

Bonnefoy, Yves. "Igitur and the Photographer." PMLA 114, no. 3 (May 1999): 329–45.

Boswell, James. *The Life of Samuel Johnson*. London: J.M. Dent, 1906.

Boyd, David, and Imre Salusinsky, ed. *Rereading Frye: The Published and Unpublished Works*. Toronto: U of Toronto P, 1999.

Bruno, Giordano. *The Ash Wednesday Supper*. Ed. Edward A. Gosselin and Lawrence S. Lerner. Hamden, CT: Archon Books, 1977.

______. *The Expulsion of the Triumphant Beast*. Ed. and trans. Arthur D. Imerti. New Brunswick, NJ: Rutgers UP, 1964.

______. *On the Infinite Universe and Worlds*. See Singer.

Bultmann, Rudolf. "New Testament and Mythology." In Bultmann, et al. *Kerygma and Myth: A Theological Debate*. Ed. Hans Werner Bartsch. New York: Harper & Row, 1961; orig. pub. 1953.

Burton, Robert. *The Anatomy of Melancholy*. Ed. Floyd Dell and Paul Jordan-Smith. New York: Tudor Pub. Co., 1955.

Bush, Douglas. *Mythology and the Renaissance Tradition in English Poetry*. Rev. ed. New York: Norton, 1963.

Butcher, S. H., trans. *Aristotle's Theory of Poetry and Fine Art*. 4th ed. New York: Dover, 1951.

Bywater, Ingram, trans. *On the Art of Poetry by Aristotle*. Oxford: Clarendon P, 1920.

Carroll, Lewis. *The Annotated Alice: Alice's Adventures in Wonderland* and *Through the Looking Glass*. See Gardner.

Castrén, Minna. "Northrop Fryen *Anatomy of Criticism* anatomiana" ["Northrop Frye's *Anatomy of Criticism* as an Anatomy"]; *Heteroglossia — Kirjallisuustieteellisiä tutkielmia. Helsingin yliopiston yleisen kirjallisuustieteen, teatteritieteen ja estetiikan laitoksen monistesarja*, ed. Pekka Tammi. No. 22 (1993): 16–31.

Cave, Terence. "Northrop Frye: Recognition at the Center." *Recognitions: A Study in Poetics*. Oxford: Clarendon P, 1988. 190–9.

Chisholm, A. R. *Mallarmé's Grand Oeuvre*. Manchester: Manchester UP, 1962.

Cinquemani, A. M. "Henry Reynolds' *Mythomystes* and the Continuity of Ancient Modes of Allegoresis in Seventeenth-Century England." *PMLA* 85, no. 5 (October 1970): 1041–49.

Clark, Donald Lemen. *Rhetoric and Poetry in the Renaissance: A Study of Rhetorical Terms in English Renaissance Literary Criticism*. Columbia University Studies in English and Comparative Literature. New York: Columbia UP, 1922.

Cohn, Robert Greer. *Mallarmé: Igitur*. Berkeley: U of California P, 1981.

Coleridge, Samuel Taylor. *The Friend: A Series of Essays*. London: George Bell and Son, 1890. Section I, Essay 13.

______. *The Literary Remains of Samuel Taylor Coleridge*. Ed. Henry Nelson Coleridge. Vol. 3. London: William Pickering, 1838.

Colie, Rosalie. Untitled review of Frances A. Yates, *The Art of Memory*. *Comparative Literature* 21, no. 2 (Spring 1969): 155–9.

Cook, Eleanor. "Anatomies and Confessions: Northrop Frye and Contemporary Theory." *Recherches sémiotics/Semiotic Inquiry* 13, no. 3 (1993): 13–22.

Cosh, Colby. "Frye-ing in Hell?" ColbyCosh.com. 30 November 2002. http://www.colbycosh.com/old/november02.html. Accessed 5 August 2012. No longer active.

Cosser, Michael. "Shakespeare's Mystery Drama." *Sunrise: Theosophic Perspectives* 49 (December 1999–January 2000). http://www.theosociety.org/pasadena/sunrise/49-99-0/ar-mcos2.htm. Accessed 6 December 2013.

Cotrupi, Nella Caterina. *Northrop Frye and the Poetics of Process*. Toronto: U of Toronto P, 2000.

Crane, R. S. *The Languages of Criticism and the Structure of Poetry*. Toronto: U of Toronto P, 1953.

Cusa. See Nicholas of Cusa.

Damon, S. Foster. *A Blake Dictionary*. Rev. ed. Hanover and London: UP of New England, 1988.

Daniel, E. Randolph, trans. and ed. *Abbot Joachim of Fiore: Liber de Concordia Noui ac Veteris Testamenti. Transactions of the American Philosophical Society* 73 (1983), part 8.

Dawkins, Peter. *The Wisdom of Shakespeare in "The Tempest."* Warwickshire: I.C. Media Productions, 2000.

Denham, Robert D. "Frye and Hegel." *University of Toronto Quarterly* 83, no. 4 (Fall 2014): 780–802.

______. "Frye and Niccolò Machiavelli." *Quaderni d'italianistica*, forthcoming.

______. *Northrop Frye: Religious Visionary and Architect of the Spiritual World*. Charlottesville: U of Virginia P, 2004.

______. ed. *A Northrop Frye Chrestomathy*. Newcastle upon Tyne: Cambridge Scholars Publishing, 2015.

Dolzani, Michael. "The Book of the Dead: A Skeleton Key to Northrop Frye's Notebooks." In *Rereading Frye: The Published and Unpublished Works*. Ed. David Boyd and Imre Salusinszky. Toronto: U of Toronto P, 1999. 19–38.

______. "Introduction." *Words with Power* (CW 26).

Donaldson, Jeffery, and Alan Mendelson, ed. *Frye and the Word: Religious Contexts in the Writings of Northrop Frye*. Toronto: U of Toronto P, 2004.

Dourley, John P. "Tillich on Boehme: A Restrained Embrace." *Paul Tillich, Carl Jung and the Recovery of Religion*. New York: Routledge, 2008. 58–74.

Drayton, Michael. *Epistle to Henry Reynolds, Esquire, of Poets and Poesie*. In Spingarn 134–40.

Drob, Stanford L. *The Doctrine of Coincidentia Oppositorum in Jewish Mysticism*. 2000. http://www.newkabbalah.com/Coincshort.pdf. Accessed 6 December 2013.

Dryden, John. "An Essay of Dramatic Poesy." In Richter 163–96.

Duffy, Maureen. *The Erotic World of Faery*. St. Albans, UK: Panther, 1974.

Eliade, Mircea. *Myths, Rites, Symbols: A Mircea Eliade Reader*. Vol. 2. Ed. Wendell C. Beane and William G. Doty. New York: Harper, 1976.

Eliot, T.S. "Introduction" to *The Wheel of Fire*. See Knight, G. Wilson.

Else, Gerald. *Aristotle's Poetics: The Argument*. Cambridge, MA: Harvard UP, 1967.

Erdmann, Johann. *A History of Philosophy*. 2d ed. 3 vols. New York: Macmillan, 1892.

Faivre, Antoine. "Introduction." *Modern Esoteric Spirituality*. Ed. Antoine Faivre and Jacob Needleman. New York: Crossroad, 1992. xi–xix.

______. "Preface: Esotericism and Academic Research." In *Theosophy, Imagination, Tradition: Studies in Western Esotericism*. Trans. Christine Rhone. Albany: State U of New York P, 2000. xxi–xxiv.

Ferré, Nels S. F. "Tillich and the Nature of Transcendence." *Paul Tillich: Retrospect and Future*. Nashville and New York: Abingdon P, 1966.

Fletcher, Angus. "Allegory without Ideas." In *Thinking Allegory Otherwise*. Ed. Brenda Machosky. Stanford, CA: Stanford UP, 2010. 9–36.

Fowlie, Wallace. *Mallarmé*. Chicago: U of Chicago P, 1952.

Frye, Northrop. *The Double Vision: Language and Meaning in Religion*. Toronto: U of Toronto P, 1991.

______. *Mito metafora simbolo*. Trans. Carla Pezzini Plevano and Francesca Valente Gorjup. Roma: Editori Riuniti, 1989.

______. *Myth and Metaphor: Selected Essays, 1974–1988*. Ed. Robert D. Denham. Charlottesville: UP of Virginia, 1990.

______. "Mythos and Logos." *The School of Letters, Indiana University: Twentieth Anniversary, 1968* (Bloomington, IN: N.p., 1968), 27–40. Rpt. in *Yearbook of Comparative Literature* 18 (1969): 5–18, and summarized in CW 27: 280–1,

______. "Towards Defining an Age of Sensibility." *ELH, A Journal of Literary History* 23 (June 1956): 144–52. Rpt. in *Fables of Identity*, 130–7; and in CW 17: 7–15.

Galván, Luis, ed. *Visiones para una poetica: en el cincuentenario de "Anatomy of Criticism" de Northrop Frye*. Pamplona, Spain: RILCE (*Revista del Instituto de Lengua y Cultura Españolas*) 25, no. 1 (2009).

Gardner, Martin. *The Annotated Alice: Alice's Adventures in Wonderland & Through the Looking Glass by Lewis Carroll, Illustrated by John Tenniel*. New York: Bramhall House, 1960.

Gay, David. "'The Humanized God': Biblical Paradigms of Recognition in Frye's Final Three Books." *Semeia* 89 (2002): 39–57.

Gilby, Emma. "Longinus." Chap. 1 of *Sublime Worlds: Early Modern French Literature*. London: Modern Humanities Research Association and W.S. Money and Son, 2006.

Gill, Glen Robert. *Northrop Frye and the Phenomenology of Myth*. Toronto: U of Toronto P, 2006.

Golden, Leon. "Aristotle, Frye, and the Theory of Tragedy." *Comparative Literature* 27, no. 1 (Winter 1975): 47–58.

______. *Aristotle's Poetics: A Translation and Commentary* [by O. B. Hardison] *for Students of Literature*. Englewood Cliffs, NJ: Prentice-Hall, 1968.

Graham, Brian Russell. *The Necessary Unity of Opposites: The Dialectical Thinking of Northrop Frye*. Toronto: U of Toronto P, 2011.

Graves, Robert. *The Greek Myths*. New York: George Braziller, 1959.

Griffiths, Jay. *A Sideways Look at Time*. New York: Jeremy P. Tarcher/Penguin, 2004.

Grube, G. M. A., trans. *Aristotle: On Poetry and Style*. Indianapolis, IN: Bobbs-Merrill, 1958.

______. "Notes on the *Peri Hupsous*." *American Journal of Philology* 78 (1957): 355–74.

Grundmann, Herbert. *Neue Forschungen über Joachim von Fiore*. Marburg: Simons Verlag, 1950.

Hanegraaff, Wouter J. "Some Remarks on the Study of Western Esotericism." *Esoterica* 1 (1999): 3–19.

Hardison, O. B., Jr., ed. *English Literary Criticism: The Renaissance*. New York: Appleton-Century-Crofts, 1963.

Heidegger, Martin. *Being and Time*. Trans. John Macquarrie and Edward Robinson. New York: Harper and Row, 1962.

Hobbs, Mary. "Drayton's 'Most Dearely-Loved Friend Henery Reynolds Esq.'" *Review of English Studies*, New Series. 24, no. 96 (November 1973): 414–28.

Hobsbawm, Eric J. *Primitive Rebels: Studies in Archaic Forms of Social Movement in the 19th and 20th Centuries*. New York: Norton, 1965.

Hopkins, Jasper. *Nicholas of Cusa on Learned Ignorance: A Translation and an Appraisal of "De Docta Ignorantia."* 2nd ed. Minneapolis: Arthur J. Banning Press, 1990. http://jasper-hopkins.info/DI-Intro12-2000.pdf

Huizinga, Johan, *Homo Ludens: A Study of the Play-Element in Culture*. Boston: Beacon Press, 1955.

Irenaeus. *Against Heresies*. Trans. Alexander Roberts and William Rambaut. From *Ante-Nicene Fathers*, vol. 1. Ed. Alexander Roberts, James Donaldson, and A. Cleveland Coxe. Buffalo, NY: Christian Literature Publishing Co., 1885. http://www.newadvent.org/fathers/0103520.htm. Accessed 6 December 2013.

Jacob, Margaret, and Edward Gosselin. "Éloge: Dame Frances Amelia Yates, 28 November 1899–9 September 1981." *Isis* 73, no. 3 (September 1982): 424–6.

Jardine, Lisa. Untitled review of Frances Yates, *Ideas and Ideals in the North European Renaissance*. *History Workshop Journal* 21 (Spring 1986): 179–81.

Joachim of Floris. See McGinn, *Apocalyptic Spirituality*.

Jones, Marjorie G. *Frances Yates & the Hermetic Tradition*. Lake Worth, FL: Ibis Press, 2008.

Jung, Carl. *Psychology and Alchemy*. Trans. R.F.C. Hull. 2nd ed. Princeton, NJ: Princeton UP, 1968.

______. *Two Essays on Analytical Psychology*. Trans. R.F.C. Hull. Cleveland, OH: World Pub. Co., 1953.

Kandinsky, Wassily. *Complete Writings on Art: 1901–1921*. Boston: G.K. Hall, 1982.

Kavanagh, Morgan P. *Myths Traced to Their Primary Source through Language*. London: T.C. Newby, 1856.

Kierkegaard, Søren. *Concluding Unscientific Postscript to "Philosophical Fragments."* Trans. Howard V. Hong & Edna H. Hong. Princeton, NJ: Princeton UP, 1992.

______. *The Diary of Søren Kierkegaard*. Trans. Gerda M. Anderson. Ed. Peter P. Rohde. New York: Philosophical Library, 1960.

______. *Edifying Discourses: A Selection*. Trans. David F. Swenson and Lillian Marvin Swenson. Ed. Paul L. Holmer. New York: Harper, 1959.

______. *Eighteen Upbuilding Discourses*. Trans. Howard V. Hong and Edna H. Hong. Princeton, NJ: Princeton UP, 1990.

______. *Fear and Trembling / Repetition*. Trans. Howard V. Hong and Edna H. Hong. Princeton, NJ: Princeton UP, 1983.

______. *The Living Thoughts of Kierkegaard*. Presented by W.H. Auden. New York: David McKay, 1952.

______. *Papers and Journals: A Selection*. Trans. Alastair Hannay. London: Penguin, 1996.

Kermode, Frank. Review of *Anatomy of Criticism*. *Review of English Studies* 10 (August 1959): 317–23.

Kinney, Arthur F. "Reynolds, Henry." In *The Spenser Encyclopedia*. Ed. A. C. Hamilton. Toronto: U of Toronto P, 1990. 598.

Knapp, Bettina. "'Igitur or Elbehon's Folly': The Depersonalization Process and the Creative Encounter." *Yale French Studies* 54 (1977): 188–213.

Knight, G. Wilson. *The Imperial Theme*. London: Routledge, 2002; orig. pub. 1931.

______. "Mystic Symbolism." In Knight's *Shakespeare and Religion*. New York: Simon and Schuster, 1967; first published in *The Aryan Path* 2 (1931): 4.

______. *Shakespeare and Religion: Essays from Forty Years*. New York: Simon and Schuster, 1968.

______. *The Wheel of Fire: Interpretations of Shakespearean Tragedy*. Fifth rev. ed. Cleveland: World Pub. Co., 1957; orig. pub. 1930.

Knight, W.F. Jackson. *Cumaean Gates*. Oxford: Blackwell, 1936.

Krois, John Michael. "*Ars Memoriae*, Philosophy and Culture: Frances Yates and After." In *Philosophy and Culture: Essays in Honor of Donald Phillip Verene*. Ed. Glenn Alexander Magee. Charlottesville, VA: Philosophy Documentation Center, 2002. 149–162.

Lacan, Jacques. "The Mirror Stage." *Écrits*. Trans. Bruce Fink. New York: Norton, 2002. 3–9.

The Lankavatara Sutra: A Mahayana Text. Trans. Daisetz Teitaro Suzuki. London: George Routledge and Sons, 1932.

Lear, Jonathan. "Katharsis." In Rorty 315–40.

Levin, Harry. *Why Literary Criticism Is Not an Exact Science*. Cambridge, MA: Harvard UP, 1967.

Levy, Gertrude Rachel. *The Gate of Horn: A Study of the Religious Conceptions of the Stone Age, and Their Influence upon European Thought*. London: Faber and Faber, 1948.

______. *The Sword from the Rock: An Investigation into the Origins of Epic Literature and the Development of the Hero*. New York: Grove P, 1953.

Lezard, Nicholas. "The Book to End All Books." *The Guardian* 18 August 2001. http://www.guardian.co.uk/books/2001/aug/18/history.philosophy/print. Accessed 6 December 2013.

Longfellow, Henry Wadsworth. *Poems and Other Writings*. New York: Library of America, 2000.

Longinus. *On the Sublime*. Trans. W. Rhys Roberts. In Richter, 86–106.

Loomis, Roger Sherman. *The Grail: from Celtic Myth to Christian Symbol*. Cardiff: U of Wales P, 1963.

Lull, Ramon. *The Book of the Lover and the Beloved*. London: Macmillan, 1923.

Lyons, Deborah. "The Politics of Poetics: Northrop Frye's Rewriting of Aristotle." *Helios* 24, no. 2 (Fall 1997): 136–50.

McGinn, Bernard, ed. and trans. *Apocalyptic Spirituality: Treatises and Letters of Lactantius, Adso of Montier-en-Der, Joachim of Fiore, the Franciscan Spirituals, Savonarola*. New York: Paulist P, 1979.

______. "Symbolism in the Thought of Joachim of Fiore." In Williams 143–64.

Mackey, Louis. "Anatomical Curiosities: Northrop Frye's Theory of Criticism." *Texas Studies in Language and Literature* 23 (Fall 1981): 442–69.

Macnichol, Nicol, ed. *Hindu Scriptures: Hymns from the Rigveda, Five Upanishads, the Bhagavadgita*. London: J. M. Dent, 1938. An annotated copy is in the Northrop Frye Library.

Mallarmé, Stéphane. *Collected Poems*. Trans. Henry Weinfield. Berkeley: U of California P, 1994.

______. *Divagations*. Trans. Barbara Johnson. Cambridge, MA: Harvard UP, 2007.

______. *Selected Letters of Stéphane Mallarmé*. Ed. and trans. Rosemary Todd. Chicago: U of Chicago P, 1988.

______. *Selected Poetry and Prose*. Ed. Mary Ann Caws. New York: New Directions, 1982.

Manuel, Frank E. *Shapes of Philosophical History*. Stanford, CA: Stanford UP, 1965.

Marchand, Philip. "Frye's Diaries Confirm McLuhan's Suspicion." *Toronto Star*, 30 November 2002.

______. *Marshall McLuhan: The Medium and the Messenger*. Toronto: Random House, 1989.

Marks, Herbert. "Biblical Naming and Poetic Etymology." *Journal of Biblical Literature* 114, no. 11 (1995): 21–42.

Mendelson, Edward. *The Later Auden*. New York: Farrar Straus Giroux, 1999.

Mill, John Stuart. "Coleridge." In *Autobiography and Other Writings*. Ed. Jack Stillinger. Boston: Houghton-Mifflin, 1969.

Milton, John. *The Prose Works*. Vol. 4. Ed. Charles Sumner. London: George Bell and Sons, 1891.

Montaigne, Michel de. *The Essays of Montaigne*. Trans. Charles Cotton; ed. William Carew Hazlitt. London: Reeves and Turner, 1877.

Mottu, Henry. *La manifestation de l'Esprit selon Joachim de Fiore*. Neuchâtel: Delachaux et Niestlé, 1977.

Munk, Linda. "Northrop Frye: Typology and Gnosticism." In Donaldson 151–63.

Murrin, Michael. *The Veil of Allegory: Some Notes toward a Theory of Allegorical Rhetoric in the English Renaissance*. Chicago: U of Chicago P, 1969.

Nemerov, Howard. "The Gift of the Whole." *Sewanee Review* 80, no. 3 (Summer 1972): 468–70.

Newman, John Henry Cardinal. *The Idea of a University*. In *A Newman Reader*. Ed. Francis X. Connolly. New York: Image Books, 1964.

Nicholas of Cusa. *On Learned Ignorance*. See Hopkins.

______. *The Vision of God*. Trans. Emma Gurney Salter. New York: Frederick Ungar, 1978.

Nussbaum, Martha. "Tragedy and Self-Sufficiency: Plato and Aristotle on Fear and Pity." In Rorty 261–90.

O'Grady, Jean. "Frye and the Church." In Donaldson 175–86.

Olson, Elder. "The Argument of Longinus *On the Sublime*." In *Critics and Criticism*. Ed. R.S. Crane. Chicago: U of Chicago P, 1952. 232–59.

______.*The Theory of Comedy*. Bloomington: Indiana UP, 1968.

Ong, Walter, SJ. Untitled review of Frances Yates, *The Art of Memory*. *Renaissance Quarterly* 20, no. 2 (Summer 1967): 253–9.

Palmer, Michael F. *Paul Tillich's Philosophy of Art*. Berlin and New York: de Gruyter, 1983.

Parker, Patricia. "What's a Meta Phor?" In *Visionary Poetics: Essays on Northrop Frye's Criticism*. Eds. Robert D. Denham and Thomas Willard. New York: Peter Lang, 1991. 113–35.

Pausanius. *Description of Greece*. Trans. W. H. S. Jones and H.A. Ormerod. Loeb Classical Library. Cambridge, MA: Harvard UP, 1918.

Peers, Allison. *Ramon Lull: A Biography*. London: Macmillan, 1929.

Perkin, J. Russell. "Northrop Frye and Catholicism." In Donaldson 187–202.

Perkins, Robert L. "Hegel and Kierkegaard: Two Critics of Romantic Irony." *Review of National Literatures* 1, no. 2 (Fall 1970): 232–54.

Plutarch. *A Discourse Concerning Socrates's Daemon*. In *Plutarch's Morals*. Vol. 2. Trans. from the Greek by Several Hands. Corrected and revised by William W. Goodwin. Boston: Little, Brown, and Co., 1878.

Pring-Mill, Robert D. F. Untitled review of Yates, *The Art of Memory*. *Review of English Studies*. New Series. 20, no. 79 (August 1969): 331–3.

Pullman, Daryl. "Ultimate and Preliminary Concern: A Puzzle in Tillich's Moral Theology." *Journal of Speculative Philosophy* 3, no. 1 (1989): 39–51.

Rabelais, François. *The Histories of Gargantua and Pantagruel*. Trans. J. M. Cohen. Harmondsworth, Eng.: Penguin, 1955.

Rampton, David, ed. *Northrop Frye: New Directions from Old*. Ottawa: U of Ottawa P, 2009.

Reeves, Marjorie E. *The Influence of Prophecy in the Later Middle Ages: A Study of Joachimism*. Oxford: Clarendon P, 1969.

______. "Joachim of Fiore." Britannica On–line. http://www.britannica.com/EBchecked/topic/304176/Joachim-Of-Fiore.

Accessed 6 December 2013.

______. *Joachim of Fiore and the Prophetic Future*. New York: Harper, 1977.

______. "The *Liber Figurarum* of Joachim of Fiore." *Medieval and Renaissance Studies* 2 (1950): 57–81.

Reeves, Marjorie E., and Beatrice Hirsch-Reich. *The "Figurae" of Joachim of Fiore*. Oxford: Clarendon P, 1972.

Reid, Robert Lanier. "Sacerdotal Vestiges in The Tempest." *Comparative Drama* 41, no. 4 (Winter 2007–8): 493–513.

Reynolds, Henry. *Mythomystes*. In Spingarn 141–78.

Richter, David, ed. *The Critical Tradition: Classic Texts and Contemporary Trends*. New York: St. Martin's Press, 1989.

Rivers, Isabel. *Classical and Christian Ideas in English Renaissance Poetry*. London: George Allen & Unwin, 1979.

Rolland de Renéville, Andre. *L'Expérience Poétique*. Paris: Gallimard, 1938.

Rorty, Amélie Oksenberg, ed. *Essays on Aristotle's "Poetics."* Princeton, NJ: Princeton UP, 1992.

Rossetti, William Michael. *"Prometheus Unbound": A Study of Its Meanings and Personages*. London: Printed for Private Circulation, 1886.

Russell, Ford. *Northrop Frye on Myth: An Introduction*. New York: Garland, 1998.

Salusinszky, Imre. "Frye and the Art of Memory." In *Rereading Frye: The Published and Unpublished Works*. Ed. David Boyd and Imre Salusinszky. Toronto: U of Toronto P, 1999. 39–54.

Shapiro, Herman, and Arturo B. Fallico, eds. *Renaissance Philosophy: Volume II: The Transalpine Thinkers: Selected Readings from Cusanus to Suarez*. New York: Modern Library, 1969.

Shelley, Percy Bysshe. *A Defence of Poetry*. In *Shelley's Critical Prose*. Ed. Bruce R. McElderry. Lincoln: U of Nebraska P, 1967.

Sidney, Sir Philip. "An Apology for Poetry." In Richter 134–59.

Simpson, George G. "The Principles of Classification and a Classification of Mammals." *Bulletin of the American Museum of Natural History* 85 (1945): 1–350.

Singer, Dorothy Waley. *Giordano Bruno: His Life and Thought, With Annotated Translation of His Work "On the Infinite Universe and Worlds."* New York: Henry Schuman, 1950. http://www.positiveatheism.org/hist/bruno00.htm#TOC. Accessed 6 December 2013.

Spengler, Oswald. *The Decline of the West*. Trans. Charles Francis Atkinson. 2 vols. New York: Knopf, 1929.

Spingarn, J.E., ed. *Critical Essays of the Seventeenth Century*. Vol. 1. Bloomington: Indiana UP, 1957.

Srigley, Michael. *Images of Regeneration: A Study of Shakespeare's "The Tempest" in Its Cultural Background*. Uppsala: Studia Anglistica Upsaliensis, no. 58, 1985.

States, Bert O. "Northrop Frye: The Anatomy of Wit." *Hudson Review* 40 (l988): 457–79.

Stewart, Jon. *Kierkegaard's Relations to Hegel Reconsidered*. Cambridge: Cambridge UP, 2003.

Still, Colin. *Shakespeare's Mystery Play: A Study of "The Tempest."* London: Cecil Palmer, 1921.

______. *The Timeless Theme: A Critical Theory Formulated and Applied*. London: Ivor Nicholson & Watson, 1936.

Stokes, Patrick. *Kierkegaard's Mirrors: Interest, Self, and Moral Vision*. New York: Palgrave Macmillan, 2009.

Tamplin, Ronald. "*The Tempest* and *The Waste Land*." *American Literature* 39 (1967): 352–72.

Taylor, Mark C. "Time's Struggle with Space: Kierkegaard's Understanding of Temporality." *Harvard Theological Review* 66, no. 3 (July 1973): 311–29.

Telford, Kenneth A. *Aristotle's Poetics: Translation and Analysis*. Chicago: Henry Regnery, 1961.

Thomas, J. Heywood. *Paul Tillich: An Appraisal*. Philadelphia: Westminster P, 1963.

Tillich, Paul. *Biblical Religion and the Search for Ultimate Reality*. Chicago: U of Chicago P, 1964.

______. *Christianity and the Encounter of World Religions*. New York: Columbia UP, 1963.

______. *Dynamics of Faith*. New York: Harper, 1957.

______. *The Courage To Be*. New Haven, CT: Yale UP, 1964; copyright 1952.

______. *A History of Christian Thought: From Its Judaic and Hellenistic Origins to Existentialism*. Ed. Carl E. Braaten. New York: Simon and Schuster, 1968.

______. *The Protestant Era*. Chicago: U of Chicago P, 1948.

______. "Reply" to Gustave Weigel. "Contemporaneous Protestantism and Paul Tillich." *Theological Studies* 9, no. 2 (June 1950): 177–201; "reply," 201–2.

______. *Systematic Theology*. Three vols. in one. Chicago: U of Chicago P, 1967.

______. *Theology of Culture*. Ed. Robert C. Kimball. New York: Oxford UP, 1964.

Töpfer, Bernhard. *Das kommende Reich des Friedens; zur Entwicklung chiliastischer Zukunftshoffnungen im Hochmittelalter*. Berlin: Akademie-Verlag, 1964.

Tóth, Sára. "Recovery of the Spiritual Other: Martin Buber's 'Thou' in Northrop Frye's Late Work." In *Northrop Frye: New Directions from Old*. Ed. David Rampton. Ottawa: U of Ottawa P, 2009. 125–42.

Tóth, Sára, Tibor Fabiny, János Kenyeres, and Péter Pásztor, ed. *Northrop Frye 100: A Danubian Perspective*. Budapest: L'Harmattan Kiado, 2014.

Tsitsibakou-Vasalos, Evanthia. *Ancient Poetic Etymology: The Pelopids: Fathers and Sons*. Stuttgart: Franz Steiner Verlag, 2007.

Ueberweg, Friedrich. *A History of Philosophy from Thales to the Present*. 2nd ed. London: Hodder and Stoughton, 1875.

Veggian, Henry. *Mercury of the Waves: Modern Cryptology and United States Literature*. Ph.D. dissertation, University of Pittsburgh, 2005. 143, 149, 160–2, 193.

Vernant, Jean-Pierre. "Myth and Tragedy." In Rorty 33–50.

Vickers, Brian. "Frances Yates and the Writing of History." *Journal of Modern History* 51 (June 1979): 287–316.

______. *Francis Bacon and Renaissance Prose*. London: Cambridge UP, 1968.

______. ed. *Occult & Scientific Mentalities in the Renaissance*. Cambridge: Cambridge UP, 1984.

Vico, Giambattista. *The New Science of Giambattista Vico*. Trans. Thomas Goddard Bergin and Max Harold Fisch. Rev. and abridged. Ithaca, NY: Cornell UP, 1968.

Waite, A. E. *The Holy Grail: The Galahad Quest in the Arthurian Literature*. New Hyde Park, NY: University Books, 1961.

Walker, Benjamin. *Beyond the Body: The Human Double and the Astral Planes*. London: Routledge & Kegan Paul, 1977.

Warburton, Bishop William. *The Divine Legation of Moses Demonstrated*. London: Thomas Tegg and Son, 1837.

West, Delno C., and Sandra Zimdars-Swartz. *Joachim of Fiore: A Study in Spiritual Perception and History*. Bloomington: Indiana UP, 1983.

Westphal, Merold. "Kierkegaard and Hegel." In *The Cambridge Companion to Kierkegaard*. Cambridge: Cambridge UP, 1997. 101–24.

Williams, Ann, ed. *Prophecy and Millenarianism: Essays in Honour of Marjorie Reeves*. London: Longman, 1980.

Wimsatt, William K., Jr., and Cleanth Brooks. *Literary Criticism: A Short History*. New York: Knopf, 1959.

Windelband, Wilhelm. *A History of Philosophy*. 2nd ed. New York: Macmillan, 1921.

Woodcock, George. "Diana's Priest in the Bush Garden." *boundary 2*, 3 (Fall 1974): 185–96.

Wright, Thomas. "Top Five 'Cult' Writers." *The Telegraph*, 10 August 2002. http://www.telegraph.co.uk/culture/books/3581278/Top-five-cult-writers.html. Accessed 6 December 2013.

Yates, Frances A. *The Art of Memory*. Chicago: U of Chicago P, 1966.

______. "Bacon and the Menace of English Lit." *New York Review of Books* 12, no. 6 (27 March 1969): 37.

______. *Giordano Bruno and the Hermetic Tradition*. Chicago: U of Chicago P, 1964.

______. *Lull and Bruno: Collected Essays, Volume I*. London: Routledge & Kegan Paul, 1982.

______. *The Occult Philosophy in the Elizabethan Age*. London: Routledge & Kegan Paul, 1979.

______. *The Rosicrucian Enlightenment*. London: Routledge & Kegan Paul, 1972.

Yeats, W.B. *Collected Poems*. Rev. ed. New York: Macmillan, 1959.

______. *A Vision*. New York: Collier Books, 1966.

Index

CANADIAN LITERATURE COLLECTION /
COLLECTION DE LITTÉRATURE CANADIENNE

Series Editor: Dean Irvine

The Canadian Literature Collection / Collection de littérature canadienne (CLC) is a series of nineteenth- to mid-twentieth-century literary texts produced in critical editions. All texts selected for the series were either out of print or previously unpublished. Each text appears in a print edition with a basic apparatus (critical introduction, explanatory notes, textual notes, and statement of editorial principles) together with an expanded web-based apparatus (which may include alternate versions, expanded textual notes, previous editions, correspondence, photographs, source materials, and other related texts by the author).

The Literary Studies sub-series of the CLC features monographs and edited collections that complement the historical focus of these critical editions.

Previous titles in this collection

Emily Robins Sharpe (editor), *Hugh Garner's Best Stories*, 2015

Bart Vautour (editor), *This Time a Better Earth* by Ted Allan, 2015

Patrick A. McCarthy (editor), Chris Ackerley (notes), and Vik Doyen (foreword), *In Ballast to the White Sea* by Malcolm Lowry, 2014

Ruth Panofsky (editor), *The Collected Poems of Miriam Waddington*, 2014

Michael A. Peterman (editor), *Flora Lyndsay: or, Passages in an Eventful Life* by Susanna Moodie, 2014

Vik Doyen (editor), Miguel Mota (introduction), and Chris Ackerley (notes), *Swinging the Maelstrom* by Malcolm Lowry, 2013

Alan Filewod (editor), *Eight Men Speak* by Oscar Ryan et al., 2013

For a complete list of our titles in this collection, see:
http://www.press.uottawa.ca/collection/canadian-literature-collection